From Subjects *to* Citizens

THE CENTRE ON GOVERNANCE SERIES

Governance is about guiding: it is the process whereby an organization steers itself. Studying governance means probing the distribution of rights, obligations, and power that underpins organizations and social systems; understanding how they co-ordinate their parallel activities and maintain their coherence; exploring the sources of dysfunction and lackluster performance; and suggesting ways to redesign organizations whose governance is in need of repair. Governance also has to do with the complex ways in which the private, public, and civic sectors co-ordinate their activities, with the manner in which citizens produce governance through their active participation in a democratic society, and with the instruments and processes required to ensure good and effective stewardship.

This series welcomes a range of contributions – from conceptual and theoretical reflection, ethnographic and case studies, and proceedings of conferences and symposia to works of a very practical nature – that deal with particular problems or nexus of issues on the governance front.

Director   Gilles Paquet
Editorial Committee   Caroline Andrew
                          Daniel Lane
                          Donna Winslow

Centre on Governance   http://www.governance.uottawa.ca

Governance
Series

From Subjects
to Citizens

A Hundred Years of Citizenship in Australia and Canada

Pierre Boyer, Linda Cardinal, *and* David Headon

UNIVERSITY OF OTTAWA PRESS

National Library of Canada Cataloguing in Publication

From subjects to citizens : a hundred years of citizenship in Australia and Canada / edited by Pierre Boyer, Linda Cardinal and David Headon.

(Governance series)
Includes bibliographical references.
ISBN 0-7766-0553-4

1. Citizenship – Canada – History. 2. Citizenship – Australia – History.
I. Boyer, Pierre, 1963– II. Cardinal, Linda, 1959– III. Headon, David John,
1950– IV. Series: Governance series (Ottawa, Ont.)

JQ4083.F76 2004   323.6'0971   C2003-905702-X

University of Ottawa Press gratefully acknowledges the support extended to its publishing programme by the Canada Council and the University of Ottawa.

We acknowledge the financial support of the Government of Canada through the Book Publishing Industry Development Program (BPIDP) for our publishing activities.

 UNIVERSITY OF OTTAWA
UNIVERSITÉ D'OTTAWA

Cover design: John Beadle

ISBN 0-7766-0553-4   ISSN 1497-2972

© University of Ottawa Press, 2004
   542 King Edward, Ottawa, Ontario Canada K1N 6N5
   press@uottawa.ca   http://www.uopress.uottawa.ca

Printed and bound in Canada

Contents

PART IV: The Future of Citizenship

Acknowledgements

International conferences are not always the easiest activities to organise. Despite the wonders of the electronic age, the tyrannies of distance can still have an impact. However, after the wonderful success of the conference "Shaping Nations: Constitutionalism and Society in Australia and Canada," held in Ottawa in December 1999 (the papers of which were recently published by University of Ottawa Press), the editors of this volume confidently pursued a second conference in a semi-regular series of Canadian/Australian scholarly collaborations.

"A Century of Citizenship in Australia and in Canada" was, if anything, even more enjoyable than the "Shaping Nations" experience. Teething problems were eradicated. For this, we thank the Institute of Canadian Studies at the University of Ottawa, the Australian High Commission in Ottawa, the Forum of Federations (Ottawa) and the Centre for Australian Cultural Studies (Canberra). Without their efforts, we simply would not have had the quality gathering that took place.

You also need sponsorship. The creative approach of the Canada team resulted in an enthusiastic and generous set of sponsors: from the University of Ottawa, the Department of Political Science and the Faculties of Arts and Social Sciences; the Integration Branch, Citizenship and Immigration Canada; the Department of Foreign Affairs and International Trade Canada; and the International Council for Canadian Studies. Qantas Airways and Australia's National Council for the Centenary of Federation also helped out when asked.

Special mention, however, must be made of the contribution of the Australian High Commission in Ottawa. High Commissioner Greg Wood and his wife, Marie Wood, were towers of strength. The Commission's contribution to Winterlude 2001 attracted the highest praise in Ottawa, and throughout Canada, for very good reasons. It was both imaginative and inclusive. Unfortunately, the outstanding Australian events for Winterlude were not widely reported down under. We acknowledge the triumph here, including, of course, the conference which was the catalyst for this book.

It is to be hoped that University of Ottawa Press, a great supporter of cross-cultural publications, will continue its vital involvement in this productive bi-nation endeavour.

Pierre Boyer, Linda Cardinal and David Headon – Editors.

Contributors

(in alphabetical order)

Caroline Andrew is a Professor of Political Science at the University of Ottawa. Her fields of research are women and politics, municipal politics, urban development and intergovernmental relations. She serves on the editorial boards of *Studies in Political Economy* and the *Canadian Journal of Development Studies* and is a past member of the Editorial Board of the *International Journal of Canadian Studies*. Caroline Andrew is presently Dean of the Faculty of Social Sciences at the University of Ottawa.

Constance Backhouse is a Professor of Law at the University of Ottawa. She is the author of *Colour-Coded: A Legal History of Racism in Canada, 1900–1950* (1999), which was awarded the 2002 Joseph Brant Award by the Ontario Historical Society, and *Petticoats and Prejudice: Women and the Law in Nineteenth-Century Canada* (1991), which was awarded the 1992 Willard Hurst Prize in American Legal History by the (U.S.) Law and Society Association. In 1999, she received the Bora Laskin Human Rights Fellowship.

Pierre Boyer is Institutional Affairs Attaché at the Québec Government Office in London. He is also a fellow of the Centre on Governance at the University of Ottawa. With Linda Cardinal he recently co-edited a special issue of *Politique et Sociétés* on republicanism (2001).

Jeff Brownrigg is Director of "The People's Voice" project of the National Council for Centenary of Federation. He holds a position as Head of Academic Outreach and Research at Screen Sound Australia, formerly the National Film and Sound Archive. With David Headon he edited *The People's Conventions: Corowa and Bathurst* (1997), recently published by the Australian Senate. His account of the life and career of Amy Castles was published in 2001. He is currently preparing a biography of Roger Garran which has the working title *Federation's Prodigy*.

Linda Cardinal is a Professor of Political Science at the University of Ottawa. She has published widely on linguistic minorities as well as on identity and citizenship issues in Canada. She also has a special interest in Canadian and Quebec political theory. She is author of *L'engagement de la pensée* (1997), *Chroniques d'une vie politique mouvementée. L'Ontario francophone de 1986 à 1996* (2001), and has co-edited *Shaping Nations: Constitutionalism and Society in Australia and Canada* with David Headon (2002). She is the Editor of *Politique et Sociétés*, the journal of the Québec association of political science. She currently holds the Craig Dobbin Chair of Canadian Studies at University College Dublin in Ireland.

Sara Dowse was born in the US and migrated to Australia in 1958. In 1974 she joined the federal Department of Prime Minister and Cabinet to head its newly created women's affairs section, which under her leadership became the Office of Women's Affairs, later the Office of the Status of Women. After resigning from the public service she became a journalist and a writer and is the author of five novels. She has only recently recovered her US citizenship which she lost when she became a naturalised Australian in 1972. She is currently living in Canada.

René Dussault, Justice of the Québec Court of Appeal, received his law degree from Laval University and a Ph.D. from the London School of Economics and Political Science. A former Québec Deputy Minister of Justice, he taught at the National School of Public Administration in Montréal and was the first incumbent of the Bora Laskin Chair in Public Law at Osgoode Hall Law School in Toronto. A fellow of the Royal Society of Canada, he was awarded an honorary Doctor of Laws degree from York University and from Dalhousie University. From

1991 to 1996 he co-chaired the Royal Commission on Aboriginal Peoples.

David Headon is Cultural Adviser to the National Capital Authority and Director of the Centre for Australian Cultural Studies (Canberra). He teaches in the School of English, University of New South Wales (Australian Defence Force Academy). His publications include: *Crown or Country – The Traditions of Australian Republicanism* (1994), *The Abundant Culture – Meaning and Significance in Everyday Australia* (1995), *Our First Republicans: Selected Writings of John Dunmore Lang, Charles Harpur and Daniel Henry Deniehy 1840–60* (1998) and *Makers of Miracles, the Cast of the Federation Story* (2000).

François Houle is a Professor of Political Science at the University of Ottawa. His main areas of research are political thought and Canadian politics. He recently published a chapter in *Dislocation et permanence. L'invention du Canada au quotidien* (1999) and articles in *Carrefour* (1997), *Sociologie et sociétés* (1999) and *Politique et Sociétés* (2001).

Helen Irving is a Senior Lecturer in the Faculty of Law at the University of Sydney. She is the author and editor of a number of works in Australian constitutional history, and most recently of *Unity and Diversity: A National Conversation* (2001).

Micheline Labelle is a Professor of Sociology at the Université du Québec à Montréal. She is also the director of the *Centre de recherche sur l'immigration, l'ethnicité et la citoyenneté* and was holder and founder of the *Chaire Concordia – UQAM en études ethniques* (1993–1996). She has published widely on immigration, citizenship, the nation, and ethnocultural diversity. She is the author of *Idéologie de couleur et classes socials en Haïti* (1987). She co-edited *Histoires d'immigrées. Itinéraires d'ouvrières colombiennes, haïtiennes, grecques, portugaises de Montréal* (1987) as well as *Ethnicité et enjeux sociaux. Le Québec vu par les leaders de groups ethnoculturels* (1995). She serves on the editorial boards of *Canadian Ethnic Studies* and the *Cahiers de recherche sociologique*. She is a member of the Conseil des relations interculturelles du Québec (2002–2003). In 1990, she was awarded the Thérèse Casgrain Scholarship by the Canadian Social Sciences and Humanities Research Council.

Marcia Langton holds the Foundation Chair of Indigenous Studies at Melbourne University. Previously she held the Ranger Chair of Aboriginal Studies at Northern Territory University where she co-founded the Centre for Indigenous, Natural and Cultural Resource Management. One of Australia's leading authorities on contemporary social issues in Aboriginal affairs, she has many years' experience as an anthropologist working in indigenous affairs with land councils, the Queensland government, commissions and universities. She has published extensively on Aboriginal affairs issues including land, resource and social impact issues, indigenous dispute processing, policing and substance abuse, gender, identity processing, art, film and cultural studies. She is currently teaching on media and cultural difference, native title, managing heritage and cultural environments and field studies in Arnhem Land. Professor Langton was awarded an AM in 1993 for services to anthropology and advocacy of Aboriginal rights.

Alasdair McGregor has visited the Antarctic region six times since the early 1980's as an artist, writer and photographer, most notably as a member of the 1983 Heard Island Expedition and more recently with two AAP Mawson's Huts Foundation work parties at Cape Denison. He has designed Antarctic stamps for Australia Post and is the author of *Mawson's Huts: An Antarctic Expedition Journal* (1988). In 2000 McGregor curated the exhibition *"that sweep of savage splendour". A Century of Australians in Antarctica* for the Australian High Commission to Canada. A graduate in architecture, McGregor's interests also centre around natural history. He is the co-author of two books in this field: *The Kimberley: Horizons of Stone* (1997) and *Australia's Wild Islands* (1999). Alasdair McGregor has participated in twenty group exhibitions and has held fourteen solo exhibitions over the past twenty-five years. He has completed corporate and public commissions both in Australia and Asia and his paintings are represented in many public and private collections. He is currently writing a biography of the pre-eminent polar photographer, Frank Hurley.

James R. Mitchell is a partner in Sussex Circle, an Ottawa policy consulting firm. He began his career as a lecturer in philosophy and later served in the Policy Planning Secretariat in Canada's Department of External Affairs. From 1991-94 he was Assistant Secretary to the Cabinet (Machinery of Government) in the Privy Council Office.

Gilles Paquet is Professor Emeritus in the Faculty of Administration at the University of Ottawa. He is also founder and former Director of the

Centre on Governance at the University of Ottawa. He studied philosophy, social sciences and economics at Laval, Queen's (Canada) and at the University of California where he was a Postdoctoral Fellow in Economics. He was Dean of the Faculty of Graduate Studies and Research at Carleton in the 1970s and Dean of the Faculty of Administration at the University of Ottawa in the 1980s. He is a Fellow of the Royal Society of Canada and of the Royal Society of Arts of London and was named a Member of the Order of Canada in 1992. He has been active in broadcasting and has written a number of books and many papers in various journals on Canadian economic history, public policy and governance issues.

François Rocher is a Professor of Political Science at Carleton University in Ottawa where he is also director of the School of Canadian Studies. His research interests are Canadian federalism, citizenship, and interethnic relations in Canada. He is a member of the Centre de recherche sur l'ethnicité et le citoyenneté at the Université du Québec à Montréal and of the Groupe de recherche sur sociétés plurinationales at McGill University. He has published *New Trends in Canadian Federalism* (1995 – a second edition is forthcoming) and *Bilan québécois du fédéralisme canadien* (1992). He was President of the Quebec Society of Political Science from 2001-2002 and co-editor of the *Canadian Journal of Political Science* from 1996-1999.

David E. Smith is a Professor of Political Studies at the University of Saskatchewan. He is the author of *Prairie Liberalism: The Liberal Party in Saskatchewan, 1905-71* (1975); *Regional Decline of a National Party: Liberals on the Prairies* (1981); *Jimmy Gardiner: Relentless Liberal* with Norman Ward (1990); *The Invisible Crown: The First Principle of Canadian Government* (1995); and *The Republican Option in Canada, Past and Present* (1999). He edited *Building a Province: A History of Saskatchewan in Documents* (1992), and co-edited *After Meech Lake: Lessons for the Future* (1991); *Drawing Boundaries: Courts, Legislatures and Electoral Values* (1992), and *Citizenship, Diversity and Pluralism* (1999). He was elected Fellow of the Royal Society of Canada in 1981. In 1994-95 he was President of the Canadian Political Science Association. His current research interest is bicameralism in Canada and abroad.

Peter J. Smith is a Professor of Political Science at Athabasca University. He has published on Canadian political thought, public policy, political economy, new communications technologies, and citizenship. He is the co-editor (with Janet Ajzenstat) of *Canada's Origins: Liberal, Tory, or Republican?* (1995). His current research interests include the role of civil society and its use of new technologies in shaping trade and investment negotiations.

Gerry Turcotte is currently Head of the School of English Literatures, Philosophy and Languages at the University of Wollongong. He is Past President of the Association for Canadian Studies in Australia and New Zealand (ACSANZ), Past Secretary of the International Council for Canadian Studies (ICCS) and Founding Director of the Centre for Canadian–Australian Studies (CCAS). He is the author and editor of numerous publications including *Jack Davis: The Maker of History* (1994), *Neighbourhood of Memory* (1990), *Writers in Action* (1990), *Masks, Tapestries, Journeys* (1996) and *Canada-Australia: Towards a Second Century of Partnership* with Kate Burridge and Lois Foster (1997). His most recent publications are a co-edited text entitled *Compr(om)ising Post/colonialisms: Challenging Narratives & Practices*, with Greg Ratcliffe (2001) and *Winterlude* (2002). His novel, *Flying in Silence* (2001), was published in Canada and in Australia and was shortlisted for *The Age* Book of the Year in 2001. He is the winner of the 2000 OCTAL/Vice-Chancellor's Award for Outstanding Contribution to Teaching and Learning and an inaugural winner of the 2001 New South Wales Government/ACE Teaching Excellence Award.

John M. Williams is a Senior Lecturer in Law at the University of Adelaide (Australia). He has degrees from the University of New South Wales, the University of Tasmania and the Australian National University. His main areas of research are constitutional law, human rights and Australian legal history. He is co-editor of two journals: *The New Federalist* and *The Australian Journal of Legal History*. His most recent publications include *Makers of Miracles: The Cast of the Federal Story* (2000) and *Manning Clark's Ideal of de Tocqueville* (with Dymphna Clark and David Headon, 2000).

Introduction

Citizenship, in essence, concerns the individual's political and legal interaction with the nation state. But unlike the nation state, "citizenship is not a subject with definite boundaries."

For most Australians, and no doubt for most Canadians, citizenship is a practicality. Most commonly it determines the right to vote, to be employed by the public service or the armed forces, to hold a passport and to leave and re-enter the country without a visa. For those who so aspire it is a precondition to becoming a Member of Parliament.

For most Australians and Canadians citizenship is also a birthright. It is decided by the serendipity of where we were born, an accidental but automatic entitlement that requires no separate action or decision by us. Arguably it is taken for granted, and not thought about, for that very reason. More recent arrivals in Australia or Canada attain citizenship by conscious decision, by choosing to self identify as Australian or Canadian. Those who take that decision, and go through the formalities and the ceremony conferring citizenship, commonly speak of both in emotional terms. It means a great deal to them. We others want that to be their reaction.

This suggests that citizenship has a deeper connotation even in every day parlance. It immediately connotes identity, commitment and belonging.

When we start delving into this interaction between the individual and the society, we are immediately led to ask what precisely it is we are identifying with: what is it we see ourselves as belonging to? This is where the boundaries become unclear, the ideas harder to define and hence more interesting. Clearly, our concept of citizenship evolves as our sense of ourselves and our society changes. We are constantly redefining our values, attitudes, aspirations and hence revisiting our history. Both as individuals and nations we have to adjust constantly to the ongoing tide of events. In the process we are inevitably revisiting the essence of citizenship, the nature of the two-way commitment between the individual and the society, the nature of our identity. Australians and Canadians are more ready than most to do this, accepting that our countries are societal experiments, a work in progress.

By referring to a "century of citizenship" the conference title sends a message in itself. One hundred years ago Canadian and Australian citizenship, defined specifically as national citizenship, did not exist in legal construct. The concept is not mentioned in the Australian Constitution, though the ultimate authority derived from the "people" is there in the opening preambular words: "Whereas the People ..".

Formally, it was just over fifty years ago, Canada in 1946 and Australia two years later, that the two countries adopted national citizenship. In the aftermath of World War II both countries chose to part company with the pre-existing concepts of nationality that applied more generally to those in the British Empire. Both wished to use national citizenship to define the distinct character of our respective societies and to emphasise to the rest of the world that they were independent, vibrant nations. Even more importantly, the proponents saw national citizenship as a means of promoting national identity and influencing each country's own sense of self. Paul Martin Sr., introducing the Canadian legislation, spoke of the

> [o]ne thing from which we in Canada have suffered to the detriment of this magnificent country, it is from a feeling of divisiveness. .Sectional differences and sectional interests must be overcome if we are to do our best for Canada. .Citizenship means more than the right to vote; more than the right to hold and transfer property; more than the right to move freely under the protection of the state; citizenship is

the right to full partnership in the fortunes and the future of the nation.

His Australian counterpart, Arthur Calwell, two years later concluded his Second Reading Speech by saying:

My aim, and that of the Government, is to make the word "Austra-lian" mean all that it truly stands for to every member of our commu-nity. We shall try to teach the children that they are fortunate to be British and even more fortunate to be Australian. We want to empha-sise the brief but glorious Australian history, in which so much has been accomplished so quickly, and to foster and encourage our young but vigorous traditions of mateship, cooperation and a fair deal for everybody.

Therefore, I commend this legislation to the House, deeply con-scious that it marks yet another historic advance towards national greatness. .We owe that much to our forebears who pioneered this country .with stout hearts and limited courage. They opened its fertile plains, explored its rivers and won the bounty of its soil and the min-eral treasures below. We owe it to those who will come after us to develop the splendid heritage that is ours. We must hand it on to them untarnished.

This Bill is more than a cold legalistic formula. It is a warm pulsat-ing document that enshrines the love of country of every genuine Australian.

Even fifty years later the two speeches seem preordained to press most of the "hot buttons" that trigger political and societal debate in either country today. If nothing else, they point to the brittleness of social engineering. But they do provide a starting point to consider identity and citizenship as our societies tackle those issues today.

Canadian observers of Australia sometimes feel that we debate issues of identity with a vigour they deny themselves. Australians tend to see themselves as tongue-tied around these self-same issues. The referendum process for amending the constitution is perhaps the one context that forces Australians to consider the deeper governmental and societal issues: the recent referendum on a Republic was an exam-ple.

Citizenship per se is not an issue caught by that referendum process. Since Arthur Calwell's time, Australians have definitely become more circumspect about defining "Australianness." There has been next to no public discussion of the nature of citizenship in the broader sense, of belonging, identity, loyalty, of the individual's rights and responsibilities both moral and legal vis-à-vis the society. Nor is there real consideration of the legal mechanics of citizenship. The issues are not simply neglected; they are ones Australians prefer to avoid. To the extent that public discussion does take place, it tends to associate citizenship with immigration and multiculturalism, rather than more broadly with the national sense of self.

That hesitancy is apparent in the report of a distinguished group of Australians who were commissioned by the Australian Government to report on issues related to citizenship. The Council on Citizenship report, published in 2000, set about providing a modern definition of the core civic values relevant to Australian citizenship. The Council crafted "an Australian compact." The values include a commitment to the land, to the rule of law and to equality under the law, to the basics of Australia's representative liberal democracy, to the principles of tolerance and fairness, to cultural diversity, to the well-being of all Australians, and to the unique status of the Aboriginal and Torres Strait Islander peoples. Few Australians would have much difficulty with any aspect of them, but many would feel that the society was discounted rather than defined by their very generality.

Consequent to the Council's report, Australia joined Canada in accepting universal dual citizenship. In Australia's case, this passed into law with bipartisan political support. While the Government created a context for discussion there was next to no public debate. Public and parliamentary discussion focussed on practicalities. The development shows how far the philosophy that Australians attach to citizenship has shifted over fifty years.

The issues raised in these papers are, therefore, all the more important. Between them, they open up a wide range of topics for reflection. They examine such things as the health of civic debate and deliberative democracy; the historical development of different ideas of citizenship in Australia and Canada; the relationship between culture and the citizen's sense of identity; multiculturalism; the implications of multiple and overlapping commitments and identities; the meaning of "nation"; women and citizenship; aboriginal citizenship and governance; and influence on decision-making in a globalising world.

All these papers were presented at the conference entitled "A Century of Citizenship in Australia and Canada", held at the University of

Ottawa in February 2001. Pierre Boyer, Professor Linda Cardinal, and Dr David Headon were the conference coordinators. The conference was one facet of a major celebration marking Australia's Centenary of Federation, organized by the Australian High Commission to Canada. The Ottawa Centenary celebration coincided with the Winterlude Festival, which is held in Canada's national capital each year at that time.

The conference showed yet again how much Australia and Canada have to share with each other and how much they gain by doing so. The historical development of the two countries has much in common. We also share similar constitutional and governmental designs. Similarities in national character and temperament make the knowledge and experience of one uniquely worthwhile to the other. If either country is wrestling with a particular issue, it is almost certain that the other will be similarly engaged.

In fact, each country makes an ongoing contribution to the other, of itself an unconscious but generous act of recurrent citizenship.

Greg Wood
Former Australian High Commissioner to Canada

PART I

Defining Citizenship

1

Citizenship and Subject-Hood in Twentieth-Century Australia

HELEN IRVING

Australians were "subjects" before they were citizens. For almost the first fifty years after the Federation of the Australian colonies in 1901, they were – at least in law – exclusively British subjects. Following the passage of the Nationality and Citizenship Act which took effect on Australia Day, 26 January 1949, there existed for the first time a legal category of Australian citizen, although not an exclusive one. For over three more decades Australians were to remain, simultaneously, both citizens and subjects. Following amendments to the Citizenship Act in 1984, the status of "subject" no longer exists in Australia's citizenship law, but Australia's Constitution still refers to "subjects" (most significantly in section 117), rather than citizens. The scope and application of this constitutional reference is yet to be clearly determined.

What did it mean to be a subject? Other members of the former British Empire, and then of the British Commonwealth, were also subjects. At the beginning, to be a subject arose simply through birth, as a matter of common law. Any child born in Britain or within British territory, or on board a British ship – regardless of parentage, regardless of colour or race – was a British subject. A person was a subject because he or she owed allegiance to the King or Queen. Subject-hood was not alienable: it could not be renounced, abandoned or confiscated.

As it evolved in the nineteenth century, the status of subject also carried with it in theory – and theory has often generated practice – the right to protection and enjoyment of the common law, and increasingly the right to participate in government. In addition, to be a British subject gave the bearer entitlement to an imaginary international fellowship. It even suggested a type of superior character or "breed" of manhood. In the words of Lawrence James, the ideal of the British subject was "an abstraction compounded in equal parts of patriotism, physical toughness, skill at team games, a sense of fair play (sometimes called "sportsmanship"), self-discipline, selflessness, bravery and daring." Intelligence mattered less than "character."[1]

The notion of "fellowship" or common heritage among British subjects was very thin in the "coloured" Crown colonies, and in respect of subjects of non-British origin. But it was widely understood and embraced until well into the 1950s. In 1973, amendments were made to the Act, among other things reducing the residency requirement for naturalization and standardizing the classes of naturalized citizens. British subjects were now to be treated under Australian law as no more than the holders of the citizenship of a Commonwealth country. But there was an anomaly which, one journal commented, lay in the fact that the Act retained what it called "the vague concept of British subject." This was, according to *The Bulletin*, a "uniquely Australian idea that no one anywhere else (including Britain) understands."[2] Being either a British subject by birth or a naturalized Australian citizen (and thereby subject) would remain for some years the alternative bases for permanency in the Commonwealth public service as well as for the entitlement to vote in Australian elections. But British subject status, it was claimed in 1973, had nothing to do with Britain.

This claim stood in striking contrast to the rhetoric surrounding the introduction of the Nationality and Citizenship Act in 1949, which emphasized membership of the British "race." Following similar Acts in Britain and the Dominions (of which Canada was the pioneer and, in large measure, the catalyst), the Australian Act was passed by the Labor government under Prime Minister Ben Chifley. There were now different laws and concepts of "citizenship" within the former Empire, each exclusive to specific national requirements.

Importantly, these Dominion Acts were not the first initiatives to depart from the old, common law notion of uniform subject-hood by simple birth and allegiance. The writing was already on the wall by the time of the First World War, perhaps even earlier. As early as 1870, Britain's first Naturalization Act permitted individual colonies to provide for naturalization of British subjects on effectively their own terms. Naturalization as a British subject was, however, recognized only in the colony in which it was granted, and was not a passport to membership in the great fellowship of subjects by birth. The Australian colonies were to find this aspect of the Act very convenient.

In 1914 the British passed their first Nationality Act. To be a British subject was now a matter of legislation, and the definition was narrowing. It was no longer a matter of simple birth, and subject status could now be lost or renounced. Dominion laws quickly mirrored the British Act. A so-called "common code" system henceforth existed in the Empire. But the common code was under strain right from the beginning. It was increasingly recognized, for example in the Report of the Conference on the Operation of Dominion Legislation in 1929, that there were populations within Dominion countries who did not regard themselves as British subjects. As early as 1929 it was suggested that member states might need to consider introducing legislation defining their nationals. Again, at the Imperial Conferences 1930, and in 1937, it was acknowledged that Commonwealth members distinguished for practical purposes "between British subjects in general and those British subjects they regard as being members of their own respective communities."[3] In 1931 the Statute of Westminster repealed the Colonial Laws Validity Act of 1865 and made the Dominions (once they had ratified it) independent of British law. Separate citizenship was, in the eyes of many, an inevitable product, or correlate of the Statute.

Difficulties with the "common code" only multiplied. In Australia's case, there had already been a departure, in the introduction of special legislation which allowed Australian women who married aliens to remain subjects in Australia, and in special provisions for residents of New Guinea. By 1945, Australia was already considering separate citizenship law. One year later, they were beaten by Canada in its passage of a Citizenship Act.

At a Conference of Nationality Experts called by the UK government in 1947, discussion focussed on a draft scheme prepared by the British authorities, which provided for the combination of local citizenship with the wider status of British subject. This scheme formed the basis of the British Act of 1948, as well as the various Dominion Acts around this time.

It should have come, thus, as a surprise to no one in Australia, let alone in political life, that a Citizenship Act would be on the government's agenda around this time. But, surprise, alarm and dismay there was. In 1948, when the Act was introduced as a Bill into the Australian Parliament, it was met with a storm of opposition from the non-Labor parties, including the Liberal Party (who, in government in 1999 and forgetful of history, would lead Australia's celebration of fifty years of "citizenship").

Introducing the second reading of the Bill on 30 September 1948, the Minister for Information and Immigration, Arthur Calwell, spoke of maintaining the "common bond of British nationality," at the same time as taking "another step in the development of Australian nationhood." The Bill, Calwell said, "is not designed to make an Australian any less a British subject, but to help him to express his pride in citizenship of this great country." "To say that one is an Australian is," he continued, "of course, to indicate beyond all doubt that one is British."[4]

But, Calwell acknowledged, the common code system had effectively broken down, and "the only means of maintaining the existing common status of British subjects throughout the British Commonwealth is in the concept that citizenship of an individual member of the Commonwealth shall carry with it the common status," that is, British subject. Membership in a community, the Minister continued, involved a decision about "belonging," about who had a "definite connexion" for the purposes of civil and political rights. The government's aim, he said,

> is to make the word "Australian" mean all that it truly stands for to every member of our community. We shall try to teach our children that they are fortunate to be British, and even more fortunate to be Australian. We want to emphasize the brief but glorious Australian history, in which so much has been accomplished so quickly, and to foster and encourage our young but vigorous traditions of mateship, co-operation and a fair deal for everybody [in] ... this vast and virile country. [This Bill] ... is more than a cold, legalistic formula. It is a warm, pulsating document that enshrines the love of country of every genuine Australian.[5]

But the Opposition were not persuaded. Eric Harrison, Acting Leader of the Opposition, began by raising the spectre of an Australia increasingly isolated, drifting apart from allegiance to the Crown, becoming estranged from the Mother Country and losing crucial support on defence and trade. The Bill, he said, was designed to bring about the liquidation of the Empire. Canada was to blame. It had forced the hands of the other Dominions because of its "racial" problems, whereas "[w]e in Australia have no such problem":

> We are essentially British. We take pride in the fact that 96 percent of our people are of British stock. Why should we be forced, as an essentially British community, to tail along with Canada? ... Australians will resent this attempt to deprive them of British subject-hood ... The Government has not obtained a mandate to ... sever the crimson thread of kinship which formerly bound Australia to other parts of the British Empire.[6]

This speech was not improvised. As most would have realized, Harrison's words evoked the glorious memory of the "Father of Federation," New South Wales Premier Sir Henry Parkes, who told the representatives of the Australasian colonies at the first Federation Conference in 1890 that the things that united them were greater than those that divided them, and that the "crimson thread of kinship" ran through them all. At the time, Parkes's strategy was to prove a success. But those who remembered the history of Federation would also have known that the "crimson thread" did not run through all British subjects, even in the nineteenth century.

A Labor member who remembered this history well responded with the inevitable observation. Mr. Harrison, he said, was wrong that Australian citizenship had automatically been conferred on all British subjects. It had never been freely conferred on subjects from Hong Kong, or Malaya, or India, or any other "coloured" members of the Empire. There is, he concluded, "no racial discrimination in the concept of British nationality or citizenship of the United Kingdom as far as the British Government is concerned, but I doubt whether any honourable member would say that Australia should follow suit."

Here was the rub. While British subject status was intended to be a wide and generous embrace, an attribute of birth, a common fellowship of allegiance, a matter of good character and sportsmanship, it had always been a matter of race for Australians. Australians had early-on departed from British ideals of subject-hood. From the 1840s, there were local initiatives designed to limit the number of Chinese immigrants coming to the colonies. The "loophole" in the British Naturalization Act of 1870 which meant that naturalized subjects were only recognized as subjects in their own colony was used in the Australian colonies to restrict naturalized Chinese subjects crossing colonial borders, as a means of reinforcing the colonies' race-based immigration policies. By the 1880s, almost all colonies had adopted harsh restrictive immigration laws which they applied to British subjects of Asian origin as well as non-subjects, and which they standardized at the end of the 1890s in preparation for the first Australian Immigration Act. This Act, passed in December 1901, notoriously, created the "White Australia" policy, virtually ruling out "coloured" immigration for the better part of seven decades. Significantly, it was passed against the wishes of the British colonial authorities and, as a means of meeting the British half-way, it was based on the "Natal" test – a test of European language skills – rather than colour. But, as the Australians intended, it was to have the same effect as a race-based Act.

As far as the Australian Aborigines were concerned, subject status still applied formally, although on more than one occasion the British authorities reminded white Australians that they were required in practice to protect their fellow subjects and to extend the protection of the law to them, and on several occasions, Aborigines appealed directly to the Queen for her protection. By 1902 their common status as subjects did not prevent the first Commonwealth Franchise Act from prohibiting Australia's Aborigines from enrolling to vote in Commonwealth elections, along with what the Act called the "Aboriginal Natives" of Asia, Africa and the South Pacific (except for New Zealand). (We should, however, recognize here that the majority of Australian states did not prohibit Aborigines from voting, even if in practice many were discouraged from doing so, and also that an Aboriginal native was defined by the Commonwealth as having a "preponderance" of Aboriginal "blood," that is, more than "half." Therefore, very many who identify as Aboriginal today would not have been excluded from the vote. But the point is, being a British subject in Australia did not automatically confer equality under the law.) The first Australian Naturalization Act, in 1903, was similarly designed to rule out individuals becoming "subjects" if they were coloured. The Labor response to the Acting Leader of the Opposition in 1948 was a reminder, not a rebuke. Restricting citizenship on grounds of colour was a goal they all had in common.

The Opposition, however, were determined simply to overlook this departure from the British heritage to which they otherwise clung. For Jack McEwen from the Country Party, the extension of the principle of individual nationhood carried "within it the germs of the dismemberment of the British Empire, and of ultimate disaster for the British peoples." McEwen predicted that "in years to come many looking back on the present occasion will say that when the British peoples took steps to separate themselves into different nationalities, it was a black day in their history ... a day which led to disaster."[7] Another conservative Member declared the Act to be the work of Marxist traitors, "allegedly British people," who wanted to destroy Britain in the interests of foreign elements: "There is something warm and homely about the term British," he said, "which has proved to be sanctuary and security for the politically oppressed and the homeless of all countries. What will the term 'British' mean in the future?"[8]

What indeed? In some paradoxical respects, despite their hysteria, the critics of the Act were right. The Empire was at an end. The common code had failed, and it would mean less and less to be "British" as the years went by. The mass immigration program put in place in Australia in the late 1940s and throughout the 1950s was accompanied by a program designed to assimilate "new Australians" of non-British background, to educate them in the ethos of openness and fairness, the easy-going, emotionally-restrained masculine culture that Australians had embraced as their own. The Act was, as its author Mr. Calwell had told the Parliament, a charter of "mateship."

In 1999, following a commitment given at the conclusion to the 1998 Constitutional Convention, Australia's Prime Minister, John Howard, attempted to insert the term "mateship" into the new draft Preamble which the government proposed to put to the voters for their approval at a referendum that year. Howard's attachment to the "uniquely Australian" concept of mateship, as he termed it, remained undimmed, but under a barrage of media criticism, and much to his disappointment, the Prime Minister was forced to abandon the word. In the event, it made little difference. The alternative Preamble adopted by his government expressed very similar sentiments, but was roundly defeated in the referendum, along with the question of whether Australia should become a republic. The ethos we still find in Australia, where "sportsmanship", the "fair go," "mateship" and the "Anzac spirit" stand as national ideals and where "intellectual" is a term of derision, in fact closely resembles the British imperialist "muscular Christianity" of the nineteenth century. Paradoxically, it has been turned into a core part of Australian nationalism, all the while remaining detached from its nineteenth-century imperial context as well as from its colonial counterpart of republicanism.

Australia's Citizenship Act has undergone numerous amendments since 1949, including reductions in the residency period which an applicant for naturalisation must satisfy. To become an Australian citizen by naturalisation is relatively simple compared to many other countries. Each time, however, the entitlements of (non-citizen) subjects and then the entitlements of residents who are not legally Australian citizens have narrowed. In addition, in 1992 the High Court decided that people with dual nationality were constitutionally ineligible to stand for the Commonwealth Parliament,[9] and in 1999, it applied this principle to a candidate with dual Australia-British nationality. Britain was, it concluded, now a "foreign power" for the purposes of the Constitution.[10]

Today, many in the Australian community would want to disenfranchise British subjects who are not legal citizens but who, having exercised the right to vote prior to 1984 (after which voting became exclusive to legal citizens), still retain it. And yet, our Constitution still refers to "subjects of the Queen," not citizens. In the eyes of the Court, it appears likely that these will be regarded as the same thing. One of the changes that would have been made to the Constitution had the republican referendum been successful in 1999 was to alter the word, so that "subject" would be replaced by "citizen." Citizen was to be defined as someone with legal Australian citizenship. And yet, a "subject" was never intended to be someone who met restrictive national legislative criteria. A subject included members of the wider community of British peoples; a subject was a special kind of person, a member of an international fraternity. Citizenship was intended to sit alongside, but not displace, subject-status.

Australians now pride themselves – quite rightly – on having an independent citizenship. But they confuse independence with exclusiveness. They have, in fact, always had a separate, exclusive "citizenship" policy, built around race. Now, many Australians are adamant that, although the racial element has gone, only Australian-born citizens (or those who renounce all other national allegiances) are really entitled to enjoy the full rights of citizenship. Permanent residents or those with dual nationality are not real "citizens." Although most agree that naturalization should be easy for those who come to live here, many at the same time believe that immigrant numbers should be kept low and eligibility criteria should be narrow. The "British" immigrant still remains, if only tacitly, the cultural ideal, even though many who embrace an exclusionist nationalism are also republican, and believe that full Australian nationhood can only be attained when Australians cease to be "subjects."

At the same time, Australia is experiencing the challenges of globalization, being forced as elsewhere to consider its "citizenry" in international terms. The paradox is that the type of "global citizen-ship" envisaged by many who support Australian independence resembles the old notion of the British subject, and forces a reconsider-ation of Australia's exclusionary history. The song sung by all Austra-lian school children, in which Australia's commitment to multi-culturalism is meant to be captured – "We are one, but we are many" – might well have been the theme song of the British Empire. The para-doxical commitment to Australian "mateship," in contrast – a commit-ment shared by many, even those who did not wish to see the word included in the Constitution – is to a concept that appears to be inclu-sive, but is in fact an exclusive one, in which assistance and comfort and support are generously given, but only to one's "mates."

The type of global or "cosmopolitan citizenship" advocated by theorists like Jurgen Habermas might serve as an alternative model for the Australian approach. This envisages the enlargement of the moral, rather than political boundaries of community. It is compatible with the multiculturalism officially adopted in Australia in the 1980s. It "uncouples" citizenship from an exclusive attachment to the nation-state. It permits the recognition of sub-national groups, and encour-ages a sense of international community membership.

How could it work in practice? With the retained control of citizen-ship law by the nation-state, but mutual recognition (as in the Euro-pean Community) of the citizenship entitlements of non-Australian nationals, a sense of obligation and responsibility for those seeking to become members of the Australian community when they are either stateless or driven from their country, and with a recognition that resi-dence and community participation are a form of citizenship, even in the absence of legal indicia. The baby of international "subject-hood" should not be thrown out with the bath water of British dominion.

Notes

1. Lawrence James, *The Rise and Fall of the British Empire* (London: Abacus, 1995), 206.
2. *The Bulletin*, Sydney, (28 April, 1973), leading article.
3. *Commonwealth Parliamentary Debates*, House of Representatives, vol. 200 (17 November to 10 December 1948), 1061.
4. *Commonwealth Parliamentary Debates*, House of Representatives, vol. 200 (17 November to 10 December 1948), 1060.
5. Ibid., 1066.

6. Ibid.
7. Ibid., 3251.
8. Ibid., 3569.
9. *Sykes v. Cleary* (1992), 176 CLR 77.
10. *Sue v. Hill* (1999), 199 CLR 462.

2

Indices of Citizenship

DAVID E. SMITH

One of the easiest demands of academic life to meet is to accept an invitation to present a paper at some distant conference. Almost as easy is to compose a one-paragraph synopsis of that future paper. Here is a setting that offers a wide range of possibilities. The inexorable passage of time will, as Dr. Johnson said of another, less happy event, concentrate the mind wonderfully well. Or, at least, that is the perennial hope of authors. When, at last, the program appears, and you find yourself listed as the first presenter, a shadow of self-doubt darkens this expectation.

The struggle between potential and reality mounts when the theme of the conference turns out to be "a century of citizenship," and not only a whole century but in two countries. Where to drop anchor in this sea of uncertainty? For citizenship is still an area of exploration; its terminological boundaries expand and, on occasion, contract. Sometimes debate focuses on uniformity, with the words most often heard being assimilation and integration. Sometimes (increasingly so today), there is a disposition to emphasize difference, and to talk about diversity. In short, there is a tension in citizenship discourse and, more to the point in daily public debate, conflict over the very meaning of the term.

Is citizenship about one or many? Is it about both? This paper will argue that citizenship is a layered concept. This is not to say that there are gradations of citizenship, although that may have once been the case, but that the topic is encircled by rings of time, if you will. Most of the references below are to Canadian experience, although there may well be strong Australian parallels. The discussion over the next two days will confirm or contradict that supposition. Three Canadian examples of how time intrudes and moulds perceptions of citizenship follow.

First, there is the story of the relocation within Canada of Japanese-Canadians after 1941, and the government's attempt to deport these native-born Canadians to Japan at the end of the Second World War. While the Canadian Citizenship Act was passed only in 1946, there was no doubt in the minds of the courts that the persons to whom the policy applied were Canadian citizens, nor that the government could deprive those persons of their Canadian citizenship, as well as their status as British subjects as far as Canada was concerned.[1] Whether or not the policy was defensible is not the issue here. The notable aspect of this sorry story is that the policy was public not secret and, except for a minority of critics, accepted without protest for approximately three decades. Then, in the 1970s and 1980s, the treatment of the Japanese-Canadians became a matter of intense debate. Repeatedly, this treatment of Canadian citizens was described as shocking. Why then? What had happened to alter opinion?[2] The Japanese-Canadians were not alone in being interned by their government during the War, although others, such as Italian-Canadians, were not singled out for later deportation.

The second example extends back still further to the First World War and the internment of Ukrainian-Canadians. Several thousands of these persons, who were residents of Canada, were placed in camps across the country, including Banff National Park where they built many of the facilities for which the Park is widely known. Three-quarters of a century later the internment of Ukrainian-Canadians as enemy aliens has led to calls for acknowledgement and redress.[3] Again, debate on the rightness of that wartime policy is for another time. Instead, the question that requires an answer here is why the event has been resurrected now and why its terms of discussion have been reconstituted in the language of citizenship. Again, there is no shortage of examples of deprivation of rights in Canada during the Great War: provisions of the Wartime Elections Act that disenfranchised categories of male persons in the election of 1917 but enfranchised other categories of hitherto excluded female persons constitute the most egregious instance.

A final illustration not associated with war – which itself is an important but understudied dimension of citizenship debate – is the Persons Case. In 1929, the Judicial Committee of the Privy Council overturned a Supreme Court of Canada decision and found women eligible to be called to the Senate of Canada under Section 24 of the now Constitution Act, 1867, which specified that "qualified Persons" could be so summoned. There is no question that *Edwards v. the Attorney-General of Canada*, [1930] A.C. 124, the official and for many years thereafter the general citation of this case, marked an important advance in citizenship for women. Nonetheless, the meaning of the Persons Case and the "Famous Five" women who instituted the judicial challenge has over the decades assumed far wider significance than at the time the opinion was handed down. As recently as in the 1980s, the Historic Sites and Monuments Board of Canada declined to recognize the litigants as of national historical significance. This past year, however, a monument (the only non-royal, non-party political statue on Parliament Hill) was erected to commemorate the achievement of the five women and to signify the singular importance of the Persons Case. A recent issue of *The National*, a publication of the Canadian Bar Association, ranked the Persons Case as the fourth of twenty "significant legal events of the last 100 years."[4]

Public and professional understanding of history and historical events is fluid, agreement on their significance contentious. For this reason citizenship should be viewed less as a concept to be described than as a subject for interpretation. To do otherwise, to see citizenship as a constant, immutable rather than malleable, is a recipe for disillusionment and a reproachful reminder of failure.

With those thoughts as prologue, I turn to the subject advertised in your program, "Indices of Citizenship." In my remarks, I will discuss chronologically six indices – imperial, legislative, social, cultural, legal and global – each of which surrounds the concept and thus reforms public understanding of citizenship.

Canada and Australia are two of a handful of countries of settlement whose origins lie in the age of empire. Their experience is not the experience of former imperial possessions in Asia, Africa or even South America. In them, as in the United States and New Zealand, new British societies based on mass immigration were replicated with little regard for the social, economic or political practices of existing people.

In each, settlers inexorably took possession of territory – whole continents even – and just as inexorably dispossessed indigenous populations. In Canada, the conquest of one European people by another
constituted a second act of dispossession, although not as total as the
first. For both the indigenous peoples and conquered Europeans, the
consequence has been the same – subordination within demarcated
boundaries. With settlement came hegemony and, with hegemony,
hierarchy and gradations of status originating in a narrow interpretation of citizenship.

Like a matruschka doll, which within conceals yet another identical representation of itself, Canada and Australia, as imperial crea-
tures, experienced a hierarchy of their own. Canadian school children
might sing "God Save the King" each morning; they might gaze at the
Neilsen Chocolate Company's Mercator projection maps that adorned
hundreds of the country's school rooms and whose most prominent
feature was the swath of red that illuminated the Empire around the
globe; their government (as in the case of loyal Ontario) might anticipate the mother country and introduce Empire Day celebrations in
1899; everyone might agree that it was best to be British – and at the
same time know that they fell short. English Canadians belonged,
more than the French, more than the Indians, but not totally – and the
sense of difference was mutual. The word "colony" we do not like, and
we usually speak of ourselves as a "nation." So said *Canadian Civics*, a
popular primer that first appeared in 1910.[5] A nation, perhaps, citizens
maybe, but subjects too. For those who belonged almost, there was a
wholeness, a completeness to the Empire – one flag, one fleet, one
throne, one family – that would disappear with the First World War,
and never return.

Here, tortuously and with a disregard for detail, is the first indice
of citizenship – the securing of independence, or in the language of the
Empire-Commonwealth, autonomy. The empire on which the sun
never set eventually cast a long shadow after 1918, as the unity of
empire dissolved into declarations of common allegiance and statutory
equality. Professions of common status slowed but did not stop the
emergence of a second indice, the concept of national, legislative citizenship, which took form in the Canadian Citizenship Act of 1946. The
sense of a received citizenship was replaced by a self-conscious act of
citizenship on the part of both the bestower and the applicant. In his
first public address after the Act's passage, the prime minister, Louis
St. Laurent, asserted that "a constructive national consciousness has to
be built," and the crucial emphasis in that important pronouncement

lay in its verb.[6] In future, citizenship by design was to be the Canadian way. The calculation implied by that phrase is not intended either to disparage the policy or suggest that calculation had been absent from citizenship-related activities at an earlier date. The manipulation of the franchise to exclude as voters categories of persons on the grounds of race or national origin was well established even before the First World War.[7] Nevertheless, a policy and a branch of a government department now undertook to make citizenship both a "constructive" and a priority activity.

Paul Martin Sr., the acknowledged father of the Act, believed that citizenship would provide "an underlying community of status for all our people in this country that binds them together as Canadians."[8] "Community," "status," "bind," "together," "Canadians" – here at last were the lineaments of the citizenship toward which Canada had been moving: Canadian not English, national not imperial, "underlying" not overt.

The third indice of citizenship takes the form of social rights. That phrase is permanently associated with the British sociologist, T.H. Marshall. Marshall argued that the rights of citizenship fall into three broad categories – civil, political and social – and had accumulated over the last three centuries. Social rights, identified with the expansion of social programs following the Second World War, included "the whole range from the right to a modicum of economic welfare and security to the right to share to the full in the social heritage and to live the life of a civilized being according to the standards prevailing in the society."[9] It is common to identify social citizenship with the welfare state, and there is no reason here to dissent from that proposition. Family allowances, introduced in 1944, constitute one demonstration of that claim. More central to the discussion, however, is the emergence of a concept of national standards: that is to say, standards of living, care and treatment integral to citizenship. In Canada, the earliest complete statement of support for national standards appears in the recommendations of the Royal Commission on Dominion-Provincial Relations (the Rowell-Sirois Commission) in 1940. There the commissioners develop a scheme for what they call national adjustment grants that will, if accepted, equalize services across Canada. The Commission also recommended a transfer of jurisdictional responsibility for unemployment insurance, since it was clear from evidence taken at the hearings and from research studies that the fiscal capacity of the provinces and municipalities to deal with unemployment hardship varied greatly across the country.[10]

Unemployment insurance became a responsibility of the federal government in 1940 following an amendment to the Constitution Act, 1867. National adjustment grants took another two decades to make their appearance, and then under a different name, equalization payments. First paid in 1957, the payments have used different formulae over the intervening decades but, always, they have been based on the principle of promoting the capacity of the provinces to provide minimum services to residents at comparable cost. In 1982, that principle received constitutional recognition in Part III of the Charter. Social citizenship in Canada is not solely the product of redistribution schemes fostered by government agreement. Medicare, which has been described as a twentieth-century equivalent of the Canadian Pacific Railway in its contribution to a sense of national unity, embodies such principles as portability, universality and access. To promote provincial compliance with the objectives of Medicare, the federal government passed the Canada Health Act, 1984. That Act establishes penalties to be applied against defaulting provinces.

It is widely assumed that social citizenship, in the form of the preceding and other similar programs, defines Canadians to themselves, since it helps bind a country that experiences pronounced regionalism, and to others, especially the United States, in the era of global economic conformity.

If, as argued earlier, the meaning of citizenship is subject to transformation, so too are its indices, none more so than social citizenship. The subject (or object) of social citizenship in the post-war years was the citizen-worker – usually male, probably a retired serviceman, in need of stable employment and affordable housing. Post-war economic policy was planned, even before hostilities ended, to serve male citizens on the assumption that benefits accruing to the head of the household would be distributed to the family. Half a century later, the focus of social citizenship has shifted to the disadvantaged – to the homeless, women and children, and the marginalized. If social integration is a function, at least in part, of social citizenship, then the "community of status" that Paul Martin Sr. thought underlay citizenship is far more complex than the post-war world knew.

Nor was it unique, for as the diversity of social citizenship proliferated so, too, did another, unimagined world, cultural citizenship. This is the fourth indice of citizenship. To the extent that there was an earlier cultural dimension to citizenship, it comprised what would now be seen as high English-Canadian nationalism propagated, before 1939, by the founders of *Canadian Forum*, the CBC and the adult education movement, and afterwards, by the authors of the report of the Royal Commission on National Development in the Arts, Letters and Sciences (the Massey Commission). The Massey Commission spoke of the role a strong federal government must play in this enterprise, but several of its major recommendations – university grants and grants to artists for example – strengthened regional activity.[11] For English-speaking Canadians, it was no longer necessary to go to Toronto to pursue a career in most arts. If culture is an essential part of community and, therefore, essential to an understanding of ourselves, Massey was not the centralizing endeavour its critics believed.

But culture is about something deeper than mere expression; it is about the core of identity – language. The Quiet Revolution introduced language to the centre not only of Quebec life but, through yet another royal commission, the Royal Commission on Bilingualism and Biculturalism (Dunton-Laurendeau), to the centre of Canadian life. The story of language in Canada is oft-told, long, complex, controversial and unfinished. There is no need or time to enter upon it here, except to emphasize that the contribution of bilingualism, in the form of the Official Languages Act, 1969, and the federal government's response to the opposition that followed in the form of the Multiculturalism Act in 1971, recast Canadian politics and broadened still further Canadian ideas of citizenship. Not immediately and not intentionally, perhaps, but multiculturalism within a bilingual framework promoted more than pluralism and tolerance: "Its secondary objective was the fostering of a new and inclusive national, Canadian identity appropriate for all Canadian citizens regardless of ethnic heritage."[12]

Citizenship based on language and symbolized in parallel language regimes within federal (and some provincial) jurisdiction, along with promotion of second-language education and training, increasingly asserted new claims to recognition. Throughout the twentieth century, the goal of equality of status and equality of treatment drove all citizenship debate. Bilingualism constituted a lone deviation from those norms. Developments outside of Canada, in the fields of international human rights, civil rights in the United States, feminist and, later, gay activism introduced diversity of claims and theory into an area which, in retrospect, appeared narrow and constrained. Diversity in Canada was becoming more complex.

A major contributing factor to this broadening of citizenship was the Canadian Charter of Rights and Freedoms. The Charter specifically protects individuals from discrimination based on grounds of race, national or ethnic origin, color, religion, sex, age or mental or physical disability. It also acknowledges (section 27) Canada's multicultural heritage. As an indice of citizenship, number five in the list being discussed, the Charter must stand alone in importance. First, because it underlines the federal government's primacy in the field of citizenship: that is, rights were deemed to inhere in the government as a consequence of its citizenship responsibilities. Second, the Charter granted special constitutional status to various racial, ethnic, religious, gender, age and ability groups. According to Alan Cairns, in Canada "the written constitution is a powerful symbolic statement of inclusion or exclusion."[13] Third, the measure of citizenship advanced through the Charter lies not in access to participation but in recognition of particularistic group identity: corporate not universal in extent, diverse not uniform in appearance. John Diefenbaker's call for an unhyphenated Canadianism no longer resonates, and not only because Quebec's ethnic nationalism has grown stronger. Not just in Canada but throughout the developed world, what James Tully labels "the empire of modern constitutionalism" is under attack.[14] Its sin is to ignore difference and impose uniformity; as a result, modern constitutionalism stands against the politics of the age – the politics of cultural recognition.

Nowhere is the subject of cultural recognition more evident than in the status sought by Canada's Aboriginal peoples. Past experience of exclusion – the First Nations were given the right to vote (what James White describes is "the full mark of citizenship") only in 1960 – and of pressure to assimilate, as set out in the Trudeau Government's *Statement of the Government of Canada on Indian Policy* (the so-called White Paper) 1969, have made Aboriginal peoples deeply suspicious of the topic.[15] And like the Quebecois, that suspicion extended to proposals that did no more than recognize cultural difference. In their eyes this was the threat posed by the Charter.

Something more was required to fuse (but not integrate) distinctiveness and citizenship. The concept of global citizenship, the last of the indices to be discussed in this paper, offered one possible resolution. If the end of empire opened the door to a domesticated citizenship in Canada and Australia, it also exerted a unique influence on people subjected to imperial-like rule within those countries. The independence of former colonies abroad, the international attention given to human rights after 1945, and the dispersal of these events and ideas by modern technology and communications eroded old ideas of subjection and promoted new ambitions for self-determination. Within Canada, court decisions, government policy leading, for example, to the creation of Nunavut, the negotiation of treaty land entitlement (Nisga'a) and the recommendations by yet another royal commission (Royal Commission on Aboriginal Peoples) have produced a new vocabulary that speaks of an autonomous citizenship for the First Nations. Arguably, this most recent metamorphosis in the language of citizenship moves the subject beyond intelligible boundaries of meaning. That is one conclusion to draw from Alan Cairns' book *Citizens Plus: Aboriginal Peoples and the Canadian State*. Cairns marshalls a strong countervision to refute "the closed citizenship nature of Aboriginal nations." He believes that the resulting boundaries between Aboriginal and non-Aboriginal peoples "will inhibit feelings of fraternity between citizens and non-citizens within the [Aboriginal] nation territory, as well as between nation citizens and Canadians outside the nation territory."[16] He argues, instead, that the Canadian constitution has demonstrated the capacity to sustain multiple identities and that interdependence and interconnectedness are the real basis of a common citizenship. As with the Quebecois, the future of the Aboriginal peoples in Canada lies in their acceptance that they are part of Canada. To that end, mutual citizenship is an essential first principle.

This paper began with the claim that Canada and Australia are two of a very small number of countries of settlement. Except for the minority of their population that is Aboriginal, all Canadians and Australians are immigrants or descendents of immigrants. This demography sets them apart from European nations, even those that have experienced the influx of large numbers of immigrants since 1945; it also sets them apart from Latin-American nations, whose indigenous populations are large and have, to a degree not found in Canada and Australia, intermarried with European settlers. More than that, these two countries were creations of an imperial monarchy, and themselves remain surrogate monarchies. The influence of that form of constitution on interpretations of citizenship is a subject neglected in this paper but it remains important, if only for its dilution of a sense of national citizenship.

For the last half-century in Canada, citizenship has been used as a device for interpreting order and reinterpreting history. Bilingualism and multiculturalism have moulded the sense Canadians have of themselves. They, and the Charter, constitute what might be called

Canada's representative world. The discordant elements in this happy picture are those Quebecois and First Nations persons who seek a new autonomous order for themselves.

Citizenship, once a primary source of identity and mobilization conferring political rights and entitlements associated with one's adherence to the single national system, has fragmented as a unifying concept. In its place are multiple indices that reflect cross-cutting loyalties, personalized interests and even consumer preferences which find global currency across national and institutional boundaries.

Notes

1. Robert R. Wilson and Robert B. Clute, "Commonwealth Citizenship and Common Status," *American Journal of International Law*, LVII (no. 3, July 1963): 566–87.
2. Compare Forrest E. La Violette, *The Canadian Japanese and World War II* (Toronto: University of Toronto Press, 1948) and Ann Gomer Sunahara, *The Politics of Racism: The Uprooting of Japanese Canadians During the Second World War* (Toronto: J. Lorimar, 1981).
3. See Bohdan S. Kordan, *Canada's First National Internment Operations: Acknowledgement and Redress*, a submission from the Ukrainian Canadian Congress to the Government of Canada, 31 May 2000 ; Bill Waiser, *Park Prisoners: The Untold Story of Western Canada's National Parks, 1915–1946* (Calgary: Fifth House, 1995).
4. A panel of forty judges, academics and lawyers made the selection from a list of fifty-five events submitted to them by *The National*. Ranked ahead of the Persons Case were patriation of the Constitution and, with it, the Canadian Charter of Rights and Freedoms (1982), the Statute of Westminster, 1931, and the female franchise (1918). Trailing the Persons Case were abolition of appeals to the Judicial Committee of the Privy Council (1949), the end of capital punishment (1976), Aboriginal voting rights (1960), and the Bill of Rights, 1960. Jordan Furlong, "Our Legal Century." *National*, 9, (no. 8, December 2000): 11–18.
5. R. S. Jenkins, *Canadian Civics* (Toronto: Copp, Clark Co., B.C. ed. 1910; Ontario ed. 1918), 8–9.
6. National Archives of Canada, MG26, L, Papers of Louis St Laurent, vol. 253, Speeches, Canadian Citizenship, Canadian Club Address, (Montreal, 6 January 1947).
7. See, for instance, the case of Tommey Homma (*Cunningham and Attorney-*

General for British Columbia v. Tommey Homma and Attorney-General for the Dominion of Canada, [1903]A.C. 151, 152). Here the JCPC "sustained a British Columbia Act prohibiting the placing of Chinese, Japanese and Indians upon the voting register, despite the fact that Tommey Homma was a native-born British subject." Wilson and Clute, "Commonwealth Citizenship and Common Status," 578.

8. House of Commons *Debates*, 20 March 1946, 131, cited in Jennifer Stewart-Toth, "Constructing Citizenship: A Study of the Institutional Development of Citizenship in Canada" (MA thesis, University of Saskatchewan, 1995), 54. The debate on the bill is analysed by Mildred A. Schwartz, "Citizenship in Canada and the United States" *Transactions of the Royal Society of Canada*, (1976), 83–96.

9. T. H. Marshall, "Citizenship and Social Class", in *Citizenship and Social Class*, eds. T. H. Marshall and T. Bottomore (London: Pluto Press, 1950), 8, cited in Keith G. Banting, "Social Citizenship and the Multicultural Welfare State" in *Citizenship, Diversity, and Pluralism: Canadian and Comparative Perspectives*, eds. Alan C. Cairns, John C. Courtney, Peter MacKinnon, Hans J. Michelmann and David E. Smith (Montreal: McGill-Queen's University Press, 1999), 111.

10. Canada, Royal Commission on Dominion-Provincial Relations, *Report* Book II, "Recommendations" (Ottawa: King's Printer, 1940), 83f. For further on the federal government's assumption of responsibility for western farm incomes, see discussion on introduction and passage of the first income support program, Prairie Farm Assistance Act, 1939 in Norman Ward and David Smith, *Jimmy Gardiner: Relentless Liberal* (Toronto: University of Toronto Press, 1990), 256f.

11. Canada, Royal Commission on National Development in Arts, Letters and Sciences, *Report* (Ottawa: King's Printer, 1951). The authors warn against the federal government "renounc[ing] its right to associate itself in the general education of Canadian citizenry", 8.

12. Richard Sigurdson, "First Peoples, New Peoples, and Citizenship" (paper presented at annual meeting of the Canadian Political Science Association, St. Catharines, Ontario, June 1996), 19.

13. Alan C. Cairns, "The Fragmentation of Canadian Citizenship", in *Belonging: The Meaning and Future of Canadian Citizenship*, ed. William Kaplan (Montreal: McGill-Queen's University Press, 1993), 205–06.

14. James Tully, *Strange Multiplicity: Constitutionalism in an Age of Diversity* (Cambridge: Cambridge University Press, 1995), 136.

15. James Boyd White, *When Words Lose Their Meaning: Constitutions and Reconstitutions of Language, Character and Community* (Chicago: University

of Chicago Press, 1984), 225. See, too, Judith Shklar, *American Citizenship: The Quest for Inclusion* (Cambridge: Harvard University Press, 1991).

16. Alan C. Cairns, *Citizens Plus: Aboriginal Peoples and the Canadian State* (Vancouver: University of British Columbia Press, 2000), 141. In this comment, Cairns excludes "the public government model favoured by the Inuit, which would include all residents of the territory." n. 138, 243.

PART II

The Early Politics of Citizenship

3

Sycophants, Citizens and the Majesty of Nature: Some Thoughts on the History of Australian Civic Debate

DAVID HEADON

In August 1995, the Centre for Australian Cultural Studies, which I direct, collaborated with the fledgling Independent Scholars Association of Australia to host a conference at the National Library of Australia entitled "Against the Grain."[1] I delivered a paper which addressed the sharp increase, during the previous six or eight years, in the amount of commentary on Australian intellectual life and, broadly, in the levels of civic debate throughout the country. Published works cited to reinforce the point included a 400 page scholarly work, edited by Brian Head and James Walter, on the history of Australian intellectual movements in the Bicentenary Year, 1988; special issues by the *Age Monthly Review* and *Meanjin* magazine, at the start of the 1990s, on the role of the "Public Intellectual"; a series of pamphlets, inspired by Australia's most respected social commentator Donald Horne, pursuing his "Ideas for Australia" and handsomely fortified with Hawke Labor Government money; and a controversial *Bulletin* article written by then Labor Minister for Science, the indefatigable Barry Jones, which cited his controversial list of the Australian "Minds That Matter." Seventeen "Minds That Matter," in fact – the "Jones seventeen."[2] The Jones list really got people talking.

Between that busy period of activity at the beginning of the 1990s and my "Against the Grain" paper a few years later, Paul Keating orchestrated his palace coup to depose Bob Hawke as Australian Prime Minister. When Prime Minister Keating launched his cultural policy, in October 1993, he talked up the "clever country," the "creative nation" as he termed it. With characteristic bravado, he declared that the years leading up to 2001 and the Federation Centenary would be a "watershed" time in our history. Confident and aggressive, with the Mabo Native Title legislation confirmed and the new millennium beckoning, Keating expressed his sense of certainty that Australians had witnessed "a sea change – the tide of our national consciousness has turned."[3]

Was this to be the onset of the Age of Aquarius of civic debate in Australia? Certainly there appeared to be grounds for optimism. But no. History records that in 1996 John Howard's Liberal/National Party Coalition was elected to power in what constituted a near landslide victory. The quality and quantity of national discussion stopped as if shot. Yes, individuals such as Sir William Deane, Michael Kirby, Pat Dodson, Noel Pearson, Judith Wright, Henry Reynolds, the Rev. Tim Costello, Phillip Adams, Humphrey McQueen, Hugh Stretton, Donald Horne, Peter Singer and Lowitja O'Donohue, and university-based scholars such as my colleagues here in Canada, Marian Sawer, Marcia Langton and Helen Irving – while these individuals and others struggled hard to maintain a credible level of social discourse, over these last few years it has not been easy. It has been, as the Australian vernacular phrase would have it, "a big ask."

There are numerous reasons for this, but one stands out as unavoidable – as a cultural road-block – the Rt. Hon. John Howard, MP and Prime Minister. As the *Australian* feature writer, Nicolas Rothwell, wrote in October 2000 in an article instructively entitled "The Road to Nowhere":

> After five years of populist conservative government, at the high point of an extraordinary growth cycle ... faring well in the polls, in the wake of the greatest public festival in Australian history and with another national celebration close at hand, the Prime Minister has no significant visions or dreams to share. Existing problems are downplayed. Great episodes of change galvanize no bold designs. Howard's vision of the future is not some ideal-strewn super-highway so much as a quiet, grey road, graced only by occasional vistas of a far-off, fondly imagined past.[4]

This is a Prime Minister, the sub-heading to the Rothwell articles suggests, who is ambling along the same old trail with one eye on the rear-view mirror.

Where now the optimism and possibility of only a few years earlier? The "sea change"? What "watershed"? Australia in the first months of 2001 has its Council for Reconciliation disbanded, universities gasping for the next drip-feed of government dollars, *Australian* columnist and social commentator Phillip Adams reduced to writing about cocky well-fed conservatives and brooding, emaciated "lefties," the ABC constantly pressured to "balance" its reporting, and community debate often appearing to be nothing so much as a cowering whinge. From watershed to near despair in a flash. From a Prime Minister focused arrogantly and, in the end, a little naively, on the Big Picture in the mid-1990s to one who, in his Australia Day address in the Centenary Federation year, when asked whether the republic would be an issue at the next election (given that 65–70 percent of Australians routinely poll as republicans) replied categorically "no." "I mean it, mate," he said, "it will not ... I am personally against any mucking around and change. You can't keep changing national symbols like this." And he went on. "I know girt might be out of place" (Howard was talking about the use of the archaic word "girt" in the national anthem "Advance Australia Fair"), "but I think we're stuck with it for a while yet."[5]

In just a few short years, from a leader seriously ego-driven but having an honest crack at the "vision" thing, and encouraging Australians to join in, to a Prime Minister girt by a galling conservatism. The tone, temper and actual amount of community debate has, for the time being at least, gone into freefall.

The central argument of my paper addresses this volatility. Over a period of some 150 years of mostly Europe-shaped history in Australia, where the level and frequency of civic debate is concerned, the only certainty has been uncertainty. Engaged civic debate in Australia has always gone in cycles of boom and bust. In order to prove the point, this paper will concentrate on some of the vigour, passion and civic commitment exhibited during four significant historical periods: first, the 1840s and early 1850s, as the colonies agitated for self-government and first-generation Australian republicanism had a short but striking first flowering through the visionary output of a handful of committed adherents; secondly, the late 1880s and 1890s, as the tone of cultural and political debate in the colonies shifted from a fleeting second-wave republicanism to the middle-class, lawyered contemplation of Federation of the colonies into states of the Commonwealth; third, the 1960s, a period of cultural re-appraisal in Australia, one crucial catalyst of which was Donald Horne's seminal work *The Lucky Country* (1964); and fourth and finally, some concluding thoughts on the last two decades, the 1980s and 90s – replete with anti-nuclear protests, the Bicentenary year 1988, Mabo, Wik, reconciliation marches and the commentary accompanying the commencement of the Centenary of Federation year.

Throughout the last 150 years of at times active, at times utterly uninspired civic debate, Australia has produced its fair share of sycophants determined to possess the baubles of Empire. Fortunately, such individuals have always had to contend with citizens equally determined to articulate an Australian consciousness, a distinctive set of national characteristics and styles which collectively have formed the lasting images Australia now conveys to the world. My eye will fall largely on this latter group.

For the first thirty years or so in the history of European Australia after 1788, as historian Ken Inglis has observed, public speech was "the voice of authority"[6] – amongst others, the futile orthodoxy of first Botany Bay chaplain, the Rev. Richard Johnson; Governor Lachlan Macquarie's energetic expositions to his "Fellow Citizens and Fellow Soldiers"; and Governor Ralph Darling's hopelessly misguided attacks on those who would undermine his edicts. These instances typify the pattern of an infant Botany Bay civics shaped by penology and the weight of the Gulag. However, when the numbers of free-born immigrants to the colonies and the numbers of emancipated convicts substantially increase, in the 1830s and early 1840s, abrupt changes to this authoritarian social climate occur. We begin to hear "voices of dissent, protest, reform."[7] In order to hear these voices, the disparate colonial communities in Australia witnessed the emergence of a forum peculiarly suited for civic debate and agitation – the public meeting. It was, says Ken Inglis, "a new cultural form" which Australian colonists took to with great enthusiasm, especially in Sydney, Melbourne and Hobart. When still young, hot-headed and even idealistic, William Charles Wentworth uses the public meeting, of mostly disenchanted emancipists, effectively to foreclose on Governor Darling's unpopular governorship of the late 1820s and 1830s. Robert Lowe, destined for eminence in Britain's House of Commons, exploits the vehicle of the public meeting with immense skill in the late 1840s as he denounces the attempted re-introduction of convict transportation to New South

Wales and argues passionately for direct election. And Henry Parkes, youthful and still reasonably principled mid-century, publicly admonishes "Her Majesty's Government [for] ... alienating the affections of the people of this colony from the mother country."[8]

Yet, in 1850, with the anti-transportation protests in the Australian colonies dominating the public sphere, it is none of these three charismatic men whom colonists in New South Wales and the further colonies really take to their hearts. Rather, it is two individuals of a different type, with sharply different social and cultural backgrounds: the Rev. John Dunmore Lang, born near Glasgow in 1799, who came to New South Wales as a Presbyterian minister in 1823 and whose politics steadily radicalized as his years spent in the colonies increased; and Daniel Henry Deniehy, son of Irish convict parents who, when they made good in the retail fruit industry as emancipists, were able to see their only child, young Dan, given as good an education in the 1830s and 40s as their situation would allow.

Through the pen and public performances of Lang and Deniehy, for a brief but dazzling few years – from 1850 until self-government in 1856 – the standard of civic debate throughout the colonies, principally in New South Wales, reached an impressive level. This was no accident. Both men were well-educated, with vast personal libraries, and both became students of the American revolutionary writers and of the birth and progress of American democracy. Thomas Jefferson, Benjamin Franklin, James Otis, Thomas Paine, Alexander Hamilton, James Madison, Patrick Henry, John Dickinson, William Ellery Channing and, for Deniehy, the New England transcendentalists Ralph Waldo Emerson, Theodore Parker and Margaret Fuller – New World democratic writers, at the heart of the burgeoning American intellectual tradition – assumed elevated status for the two Australians.

Lang took some years negotiating the journey of political and cultural self-discovery but finally, after enduring for too long what he characterized as the appalling arrogance of the British Colonial Office, and after a trip to America in 1840 where he was everywhere fêted (and met American President Martin Van Buren) he began publicly to assert his republican sympathies. Well familiar with the rhetorical tactics and devices of his radical American cousins, in a speech in the Legislative Council in October 1843 Lang first used the "No Taxation without Representation" slogan:

> But if, as a community of British origin, with British feelings and British affections, glorying in the name of Britons and justly proud of the

high distinction it implies – if we are notwithstanding to be treated by the Home Government, as we evidently are, with cold suspicion and distrust, and if all the precautions of a jealous despotism are to be had recourse to [to] ensure our obedience – then what can we expect but that a feeling of alienation toward the Home Government will take deep root and become universal among the people of this colony; what can we expect but that that feeling will gradually ripen into disaffection, and that disaffection will at length display her insurgent flag and rally around it a hundred thousand free-born Australians, to repeat the same scenes in these uttermost parts of the earth as have been exhibited already in the misgoverned colonies of Britain in other and far distant lands.[9]

After an unhappy time in England, 1846–9, during which his immigration schemes for the Australian colonies were ignored by the Colonial Office, Lang returned to New South Wales "cherishing," as he put it, "precisely the same feeling as the celebrated Dr. Benjamin Franklin did, when he left England as a British subject, for the last time."[10] Armed with his now extensive knowledge of republican philosophy and precedents, Lang began educating his fellow colonists, first in a brilliant series of lectures gathered in print in 1850 as *The Coming Event* and next, in 1852, in his monumental yet now sadly forgotten republican work, *Freedom and Independence for the Golden Lands of Australia*.[11]

During this period, Lang dramatically enlarged the terms of civic debate in his community and, in the process, inspired a generation of young-currency lads and lasses. Dan Deniehy acknowledged this in what is certainly Australian republicanism's most precious letter, written to Lang in June 1854:

A Dr Lang is solitary ... and towers above neighbouring altitudes like a cathedral dome above a city's roofs and spires ... Go on in your great labour! The approval of every *thinking* son of the soil, ever is surely an antepast of what shall be yours in the coming ages.[12]

Lang's example proved crucial when Deniehy produced his best-known and probably finest speech, delivered at a public meeting in the Victorian Theatre, Sydney, to an overflowing crowd gathered to denounce the conservative (in later years) William Charles Wentworth's self-government blueprint, in which he [Wentworth] carefully and mischievously proposed a New South Wales House of Lords. Deniehy destroyed the scheme's credibility, labelling it nothing but a "bunyip aristocracy," but it was the substance with which he followed this satirical masterstroke that caught the imagination of his audience. Deniehy outlined his own social vision, directed at those who would yearn to make Australia their home:

> Bring them not here with delusive hopes – let them not find a new-fangled aristocracy haunting these free shores (*Cheers*). But it is to yours to offer them a land, where man is rewarded for his labour, and where the law no more recognizes the supremacy of a class, than it recognizes the predominance of a religion (*Great cheering*). But there is an aristocracy worthy of our ambition. Wherever man's skill is eminent, wherever glorious manhood asserts its elevation, there is an aristocracy that confers honour on the land that posses it. That is God's aristocracy (*Great cheering*). That is an aristocracy that will grow and expand under free institutions, and bless the land where it flourishes.[13]

If the Australian colonies were to get an aristocracy, Deniehy concluded in his speech, he trusted that it would "not resemble that of William the Bastard [he was referring to the pervasive speculation about William Charles Wentworth's birth] but of Jack the Strapper."[14]

Less than a year after this speech, Deniehy had re-located his solicitor's practice to the thriving southern New South Wales town of Goulburn, situated between Sydney and Canberra. With what he described as "a regular Reign of Terror" over the editorial pages of the town's principal newspaper, the *Goulburn Herald*, he proceeded to detail over the next three years his elaborate plan for a republican, federated Australia.[15] The imaginative and scholarly range of these editorials is astonishing. Arguably the finest of them, one entitled "Our Country's Opportunity," of 10 June 1854, begins with an epigraph taken from Ralph Waldo Emerson: "We cannot look on the freedom of the country in connection with its youth, without a presentiment that here shall laws and institutions exist on some scale of proportion to the majesty of nature."[16] The eloquence of Deniehy's discussion of community established a civic benchmark for excellence that political and cultural leaders in the Australian colonies would take generations to match.

The confirmation of self-government for most of the colonies in the late 1850s effectively halted a period of intense and, at times, courageous social and cultural speculation. The passion of the free-for-all public meeting gradually succumbs to the stylized discourse of the parliamentary debate, a pattern which continues up to and well beyond Federation in 1901.

However, important as the parliamentary and convention discussions were to informed debate in the 1880s and 90s, it is really the sudden, dramatic influx of working class argument and analysis that energizes society in the Australian colonies in the pre-Federation years. Henry Parkes' much-touted Tenterfield oration, while a useful but by no means inspiring statement of the Federation case circa 1889, pales alongside the youthful writings of Australia's best known creative writer of this era, Henry Lawson. Lawson understood what the thrust of nationhood had to be, and wrote accordingly. This is obvious in a little-known, short essay that Lawson placed in the *Republican* newspaper in April 1888. Remember that this is white Australia's one hundredth year. Subtitled "A Neglected History," the essay begins: "We must admit that the Centennial celebrations in Sydney were not wholly useless."[17] He goes on to praise the fact that all the daily, weekly and monthly periodicals made it their business to provide a compendium of a century of white history. For Lawson, this represented the first exposure of the youth of the colonies to such seminal local material. For the first time, many were provided with the detail of the first settlements, the Vinegar Hill uprising, the Rev. John Dunmore Lang and the Eureka Stockade. Lawson could see that information of this kind, at last in the hands of the country's youth, might sow the seeds of a sentiment likely to provide the perfect antidote to Australia's "loyal and sceptre loving" aristocracy, the squattocracy – the forces, as he memorably described it, of "Australian Groveldom."[18] In 1888 he might even have had Sir Enery Parkes in mind.

Symbols were not important to Lawson; he held no particular brief for federating the colonies. He wanted concerted political action that improved local conditions of life:

> When the school children of Australia are told more truths about their own country, and fewer lies about the virtues of Royalty, the day will be near when we can place our own national flag in one of the proudest places among the ensigns of the world.[19]

Four years later, with his poetry now praised in all the Australian colonies, Lawson briefly assumed his most determined political stance in the poem "Freedom on the Wallaby":

> We'll make the tyrant feel the sting
> Of those that they would throttle;
> They needn't say the fault is ours
> If blood should stain the wattle![20]

At precisely the time this poem was written, the forces of labour were continuing to absorb a battering in the maritime and shearers strikes and their aftermath. But the poets, publicists and pamphleteers determined to survive, learn lessons and write about them. The *Hammer* newspaper, published in Wagga Wagga (New South Wales) in the heart of sheep and shearing country, advised its readers utterly to reject political federation until the country had instituted a "Federation of Labor."[21] Other labour papers, like the Brisbane *Worker*, the Sydney *Worker* and Melbourne's *Tocsin*, pleaded with their readers to do likewise. They did so, not only through editorial policy and propagandizing, but also through the strong advocacy of ideologically sympathetic works such as Henry George's *Progress and Poverty*, Edward Bellamy's utopian novel *Looking Backwards*, Laurence Gronlund's *Co-Operative Commonwealth and Wealth of Nations*, as well as Dickens and Carlyle.[22] William Lane's *Boomerang* newspaper in Brisbane, in the early 1890s, ran a very successful lending library, while Melbourne's *Tocsin* magazine, strongly opposed to the Federation Constitution Bill, assumed a high level of understanding and engagement from its readers. It took them through the Bill clause by clause. A poem published in *Tocsin* in June 1898 sought to generate active opposition to what was considered an undemocratic Constitution:

> And do they think we sleep, boys,
> Lulled by their Siren Song;
> And do they think to creep, boys,
> And bind with parchment thong.
> But, no, we're wide awake, boys;
> We'll make them fear and quake, boys,
> All for Australia's sake, boys,
> Australia[23]

The activists of the women's movement at this time generated a similarly impressive standard of political debate, in part at least motivated by the social conscience and example of the Grand Old Lady of South Australia, Catherine Helen Spence. From the time Spence wrote under her own by-line in a newspaper, in the late 1870s, the first woman in the country to do so, she adopted an uncompromising position. Spence scorned "the weaklings and crawlers" in Australian electorates, and took a particular dislike to Australia's "bastard aristocracy."[24] A tireless advocate of proportional representation, Spence was far ahead of her time. It was no good women getting the vote, she argued, if they used it unwisely: "If we elect bad men to Parliament we will have a bad Government."[25] Spence's younger contemporaries, such as Rose Scott, Maybanke Wolstenholme and Vida Goldstein, built on the Spence example in the 1880s and 90s in a range of independent directions. Organizations such as the WCTU (the Women's Christian Temperance Union), the separate suffrage Leagues, the Karrakatta Club, the National Council of Women, the Women's Literary Society and the Women's Federal League, all added to the civic ferment of an extraordinary period of Australian social history.[26] The achievement of Federation, however, measurably slowed this momentum in the first years of the new century, as the Boer War continued and colonial xenophobia deteriorated into a national obsession. Middle-class Australians strove to protect what they had.

When Donald Horne published *The Lucky Country* in 1964, the catalyst for his work was definitely not social engagement; quite the opposite. Horne deconstructed Australia in the early 1960s, towards the end of an era of deeply conservative national politics under Prime Minister Robert Menzies. It was an Australia, Horne accused, unhurried and self-satisfied to the point of torpidity. Australians were not "lucky." Tough but fair observations mount rapidly in the book's opening pages: Australians are too easy going, too preoccupied with sport, inimical to ideas. In short, they live in a society of "triumphant mediocrity."[27] If one book might be said to have dragged cultural and political debate in Australia beyond a sort of stunned self-absorption and systemic parochialism, it was *The Lucky Country*. Eight years after its publication, Australia decided it was at last "time," and elected a Prime Minister from an alternative political party to Menzies for the first time in twenty-three years.

Many thought the era of Menzies, the social malaise of the 1950s, was over forever in 1973. They were wrong. If one frequents the present-day corridors of Kirribilli House, the Sydney residence of Australia's Prime Minister Howard, Menzies ideology continues to prevail. The majority of Australians in recent years have, willingly or unwillingly, had to engage in an active debate on the prospect of an Australian republic. Such discussion has gone on everywhere – everywhere, it seems, except in Kirribilli House. According to Prime Minister Howard: "[Republicanism] is never raised with Australians I mix with, and I mix with a very wide cross-section of the community."[28] Cynics might say that the closest this Prime Minister gets to a wide cross section of Australians is when he is two grandstands away at the

Sydney Cricket Ground, watching the summer game from the salubrious confines of the Members Lounge.

In his Centenary of Federation message, syndicated around Australia on 8 January 2001, Canadian Prime Minister Jean Chretien spoke eloquently:

> I am certain the prosperous and cheerful interchange between our citizens will flourish throughout the second century of your Federation. As Canadians seek to bring to other parts of the world the peace and good fortune we enjoy, we very much appreciate having as our allies the vigorous, confident and imaginative people of Australia.[29]

Each of these qualities – vigour, confidence, imagination – was on show at the Sydney Olympics. Australia's finest living author, David Malouf, summed it up when he described the Games as "the apotheosis of Australia's national achievement and a revelation, to ourselves as much as to others, of an achieved national style."[30]

But one deeply satisfying summer Games, as the old Sydney prophet might have said, does not a country make. History shows that engaged civic debate in Australia demands that we be on guard. A charged and vital civic debate can be silenced virtually overnight. In a few short years in Australia, Centenary of Federation activity notwithstanding, it has. The challenge for the citizenry, as always, is to regain the initiative. Australians need once again to rediscover the majesty that Dan Deniehy so creatively pursued.

Notes

1. Papers collected in *"Against the Grain" – The Independent Scholar* (Canberra: Independent Scholars' Association of Australia, 1996).
2. Barry Jones, "Minds that Matter," *Bulletin*, 17 September 1991.
3. "Farewell all to the cringe and hello to diversity," Paul Keating, quoted in *Canberra Times*, 19 October 1994.
4. Nicholas Rothwell, "The Road to Nowhere," *Weekend Australian*, 14–15 November 2000.
5. John Howard, quoted in Ross Peake, "Howard says no changes needed to anthem or flag," *Canberra Times*, 26 January 2001.
6. Ken Inglis, *"Men and Women of Australia": Speech Making as History* [Barry

Andrews Memorial Lecture] (Canberra: Department of English, ADFA, 1993), 17.

7. Ibid., 20.

8. Ibid., 24. See also 17–24.

9. David Headon and Elizabeth Perkins, eds., *Our First Republicans* (Sydney: The Federation Press, 1998), 8–10.

10. Headon and Perkins, *Our First Republicans*, 12.

11. John Dunmore Lang, *The Coming Event; or, The United Provinces of Australia* (Sydney: D. L. Welch, 1850); John Dunmore Lang, *Freedom and Independence for the Golden Lands of Australia* (London: Longman, Brown, Green and Longmans, 1852).

12. Headon and Perkins, *Our First Republicans*, 139.

13. Ibid., 129.

14. Ibid., 130.

15. Ibid., 138.

16. Ibid., 140.

17. Henry Lawson, *Henry Lawson – Stories, Poems, Sketches and Autobiography,* ed. Brian Kiernan (St Lucia: University of Queensland Press, 1976), 74.

18. Ibid., 76.

19. Ibid., 76.

20. Ibid., 85.

21. Quoted in C.M.H. Clark, ed., *Select Documents in Australian History 1851– 1900* (Sydney: Angus and Robertson, 1955), 495.

22. Ibid., 563.

23. Quoted in Raymond Evans et al, eds., *1901 – Our Future's Past* (Sydney: Pan Macmillan Australia, 1997), 123.

24. Quoted in Helen Irving, ed., *A Women's Constitution? Gender and History in the Australian Commonwealth* (Sydney: Hale & Iremonger, 1996), 50.

25. Ibid., 51.

26. Ibid., 2–3, 8–10.

27. Donald Horne, *The Lucky Country* (Ringwood, Victoria: Penguin Books, 1964), 22.

28. Quoted in Jon Marsh, "Sydney's Shakers for a Change a Cut Above Average," *Sydney Morning Herald*, January 19, 1999.

29. Jean Chretien, "Federation Message," *Daily Telegraph*, (Sydney) January 8, 2001.

30. David Malouf, "Here we are, against the plan and against the odds – Centenary of Federation Commemoration," *The Australian*, January 1 2001.

4

Deliberative Democracy and the People: The Australian Experience

JOHN M. WILLIAMS

The events of 6 November 1999 in Australia did much, and in the same stroke, did very little. Australians dithered in a manner that only we can do – we declared simultaneously that the Monarchy was a spent force, but at the same time endorsed its continuing existence. The Australian republic failed.

The Australian people have determined that the Monarch of the United Kingdom, the Queen of Australia and Canada, is no longer relevant to her people. However, not unlike an old heavy piece of furniture bequeathed by some dear departed relative the Monarchy sits in the corner of the front room. No one wants to keep it – but the effort of taking it to the dump seems beyond us.

The question left for Australians, and perhaps for Canadians, is what is the role of the people in a constitutional system where sovereignty is divided between the Crown and its people? What role for a force so important to the legitimacy of the modern democratic state that appears to be diffident to the very act of asserting its own sovereignty?

This paper will explore the notion of the people and their manifestations in the evolving deliberative democracy. While this topic can be explored from any number of avenues, the approach of this paper is limited to a constitutional focus. The constitution provides the underpinnings for acts done in the name of the people.

The People: a Constitutional Fact or Fiction?

The concept of "the people" is one that has a rhetorical value that is rolled gold. Recourse to the people, "the will of the people" or the "interest of the people" is essential to our political discourse. Indeed, the value of the people or, more correctly, the public interest, which is manifest in the exercise of political power on their behalf, has its own ramifications. As Cass Sunstein has noted, one of the republican virtues of deliberative democracy is that the will of the people forces debate in terms of the public interest. The "civilizing force of hypocrisy" means that

> public discussion requires people to speak in public-regarding terms. Policies must always be justified on the basis of reasons, or on the ground that they promote the public good. In a deliberative politics, even the most venal or self-interested participants in politics must invoke public justifications in their support.[1]

Despite the centrality of the people in setting the parameters of public discourse, there is often little or no discussion of what this fundamental body is or means.

The people as political and constitutional mainstay have been deployed to denote ownership, either of the form of governance or the outcomes of the process. For instance, the literature reflecting on the effect of the *Canadian Charter of Rights and Freedoms* and the *Australia Act* (Cth) 1986 notes the place of the people and their new role in relation to constitutional sovereignty.[2]

The people are generally a category of inclusion. The "people" unlike the "citizen" or "resident" is often less rigid in its status. These later categories have themselves changed over time, incorporating various legal and social requirements.[3] However, it should be noted that as a matter of historical record the category "people" has been subject to construction. Famously, in the *Dred Scott* decision the Supreme Court of the United States concluded that slaves were not people for the purposes of the Constitution:

> The words "people of the United States" and "citizens" are synonymous terms, and mean the same thing. They both describe the political body who, according to our republican institutions, form the sovereignty, and who hold the power and conduct the Government through

their representatives. They are what we familiarly call the "sovereign people," and every citizen is one of this people, and a constituent member of this sovereignty. The question before us is, whether the class of persons described in the plea in abatement compose a portion of this people, and are constituent members of this sovereignty? We think they are not, and that they are not included, and were not intended to be included, under the word "citizens" in the Constitution, and can therefore claim none of the rights and privileges which that instrument provides for and secures to citizens of the United States. On the contrary, they were at that time considered as a subordinate and inferior class of beings, who had been subjugated by the dominant race, and, whether emancipated or not, yet remained subject to their authority, and had no rights or privileges but such as those who held the power and the Government might choose to grant them.[4]

That being said, it should be noted that the political entitlements associated with "the people" and other categories such as citizenship are tightly regulated and the product of ongoing debate.

In this paper I will reflect on a particular manifestation of the people. That is in terms of the constitutional notions of sovereignty and the emerging literature of public trust. As will be argued, these two approaches provide an adequate understanding of the foundational role of the people. However, the deployment of this notion in anything but an aspiration form returns us to the well-worn questions of political representation and democracy.

The Sovereign People

The people, as suggested above, have had an ambiguous place in the Australian constitutional landscape. Unlike the great revolutionary flourish of the United States, it is not "We the people" of Australia who adorn the introductory words of the covering clauses to the Australian Constitution. In a manner consistent with its statutory heritage, and colonial past, the Preamble to the Australian Constitution speaks in terms of:

WHEREAS the people of New South Wales, Victoria, South Australia, Queensland, and Tasmania, humbly relying on the blessing of Almighty God, have agreed to unite in one indissoluble Federal Com-

monwealth under the Crown of the United Kingdom of Great Britain
and Ireland, and under the Constitution hereby established.

This opening is perfectly reasonable given the evolutionary manner in which the Federation of the colonies was achieved. It was not a
contest between "federation" or "revolution" as Manning Clark may
have suggested.[5] Notwithstanding the indications that sovereignty
and authority reside with the people in association with the States, it is
possible to reflect on the people in a more creative sense. If we have a
more distant perspective on the process of constitution-making then it
is possible to see the people as providing some greater authority.

The story of Federation is well known though in this context
deserves some retelling.[6] The "people" elected delegates to the various
constitutional conventions after 1897. Ultimately, the "people" passed
judgment on the final draft of the Constitution. The stalled attempts at
Federation gave rise to a "people's movement" to save the process
from the constitutional doldrums. Finally, the delegates to London
invoked the name of the "people" in 1900 to resist the Colonial Office's
attempts at amendment. John Quick and Robert Garran, those great
chroniclers of the Australian Constitution, dedicate their *Annotated
Constitution* to "The People of Australia" in recognition of their efforts.[7]
All these incidents appear to endorse the central role of the people in
the constitutional process.

As noted, such a broad prospective fails to acknowledge that the
"people" were a limited category with women (leaving aside the obvious situation of South Australia and Western Australia), unpropertied
males and Aboriginal and Torres Strait Islanders in most colonies
being generally excluded from the process.[8] Without entering into the
question of the "popularity" of the federation movement, it is enough
to note that it is a hotly debated subject.[9]

Leaving aside the fact that the Federation movement may not have
been that popular, the authority of the Australian Constitution was a
belt and braces effort. The authority of the people was supported, if not
supplanted, by the passage of the constitutional Bill through the Imperial Parliament[10] and adorned with the signature of the fading Queen
Victoria. As Sir Owen Dixon noted:

> It [the Constitution] is not a supreme law purporting to obtain its
> force from the direct expression of a people's inherent authority to
> constitute a government. It is a statute of the British Parliament

enacted in the exercise of its legal sovereignty over the law every-where in the King's Dominions. In the interpretation of our Constitu-tion this distinction has many important consequences. We treat our organs of government simply as institutions established by law, and we interpret their powers simply as authorities belonging to them by law. American doctrine treats them as agents for the people who are the source of power and their powers as authorities committed to them by a principal.[11]

This view of the Imperial Parliament as the ultimate authority for the Australian Constitution remains the orthodox theory in Australia. Geoffrey Lindell has correctly stated what in 1900 was the position of the Australian Constitution. "[I]n 1900, the Constitution was legally binding *because of the status accorded to British statutes as an original source of law in Australia and also because of the supremacy accorded to such statutes.*"[12]

This constitutional fact, the authority of the Imperial Parliament, creates a tension with the other political (and constitutional) reality of the sovereignty of the Australian community. Thus is it still correct to maintain that the Imperial Parliament is sovereign? Or that events since have changed the authority of the Constitution?

The Australian Constitution makes reference to "the people" in a number of places. As noted above, the covering clauses speak of the people of the States "unite[d] in one indissoluble Federal Common-wealth under the Crown of the United Kingdom." Australian constitu-tional lawyers, especially after the 1920s, would have seen this statement as an allusion to the intellectual inheritance of the British parliamentary system. In 1920 the High Court delivered the famous *Engineers'* case that radically altered the interpretative assumptions in relation to Australian federalism.[13] An outcome of this case was a realignment of constitutional thinking away from the American jurisprudence back to the more traditional British approach. Such an approach returned to the Diceyan notions of parliamentary sovereignty.

For Dicey the division of sovereignty into its political and legal con-stituencies provided simultaneously the role and passivity of the peo-ple. Legal sovereignty was said to reside with the parliament, while political sovereignty was said to be the province of the people. As was argued this view had almost universal currency in Australia until recently. As Paul Finn states, the creation of this "troubling distinction

... [has] ... produced the fissure which was to divorce the legal and political identities of the Australian people for much of this century."[14]

The Dicey thesis, despite its basic implausibility to a written federal constitution that divided and separated power, was of great doctrinal force in Australia. Partly this was achieved through two factors. First, the want of any challenge to the framers' view that the Australian Constitution was an atheoretical document. As I have argued elsewhere, the Australian constitutional heritage, with some notable exceptions, has been to rejoice in the pragmatic nature of the Constitution.[15] The contractual agreement approach of the Constitution misunderstands the deep theoretical foundations of such basic constitutional furniture as the separation of powers, federalism, and the role of the people. A second aspect to the authority of Dicey in Australia was the reluctance on the part of legal academics and the High Court itself to challenge it. Until recently Dicey had a major hold over "Australian legal consciousness."[16] As John Doyle notes, Dicey "has a firm grasp on lawyers' patterns of thought,"[17] he "has played a major role in the shaping of twentieth-century thought in public law."[18]

The result of the authority of Dicey was to reinforce the orthodox view that the people had only a political foothold in the constitutional edifice. As Brian Fitzgerald states:

> For too many years Dicey's theory of legal sovereignty residing in the parliament and political sovereignty existing in the people has been used by those in power to the disadvantage of the ultimate generators of power, the people.[19]

The challenge to Dicey, and the reconsideration of the people as sovereign, was addressed by the High Court in the late 1980s. Prompted, if not justified, by the passage of the *Australia Act* (Cth) in 1986, the High Court started to unpack an argument about the nature of Australian constitutionalism.

The *Australia Acts*[20] ended the authority of the United Kingdom Parliament with respect to the Commonwealth. The very passage by the United Kingdom Parliament, in constitutional terms, was the antithesis of Dicey's description of the omnipotent parliament. As the High Court noted in *Sue v. Hill*:

> The expression in s 1 of the 1986 [*Australia Act*] UK Act "[n]o Act of the Parliament of the United Kingdom passed ... shall extend, or be

deemed to extend" was used in s 4 of the *Statute of Westminster* 1931 (UK). Provisions such as s 1 may present doctrinal questions for the constitutional law of the United Kingdom, in particular for the dogma associated with Dicey's views as to the sovereignty of the Parliament at Westminster. Professor Sir William Wade pointed out more than 40 years ago that Dicey never explained how he reconciled his assertions that Westminster could destroy or transfer sovereignty and the proposition that it could not bind future Parliaments. The effect in the United Kingdom of any amendment or repeal by the United Kingdom Parliament of s 1 would be for those adjudicating upon the constitutional law of that country. But whatever effect the courts of the United Kingdom may give to an amendment or repeal of the 1986 UK Act, Australian courts would be obliged to give their obedience to s 1 of the statute passed by the Parliament of the Commonwealth.[21]

This political act of sovereignty coincided with a judicial one. Part of the challenge to the Diceyan notion of parliamentary sovereignty was an assertion that the Australian people are the ultimate source of *both* political and legal authority. In *R v. Duncan; Ex parte Australian Iron and Steel Pty Ltd*[22] Justice Deane stated that:

> The Constitution of Australia was established not pursuant to any compact between the Australian Colonies but, as the preamble of the Constitution emphatically declares, pursuant to the agreement of "the people" of those Colonies.[23]

In the next year in *University of Wollongong v. Metwally*[24] Justice Deane further declared that

> the Australian federation was and is a union of people and that ... the provisions of the Constitution should properly be viewed as ultimately concerned with the governance and protection of the people from whom the artificial entities called Commonwealth and States derive their authority.[25]

Thus for Justice Deane the authority of the Constitution was derived from the Australian people and its objectives were to protect and promote their interests. Justice Deane hinted in following cases that the rejection of the "traditional legal theory" that the Australian Constitution was wholly an enactment of the Imperial Parliament would require "at some future time to consider whether traditional legal theory can properly be regarded as providing an adequate explanation of the process which culminated in the acquisition by Australia of full 'independence and Sovereignty.'"[26] In 1988 Justice Deane answered his own speculation by suggesting that the better way of viewing the Australian Constitution was as a "compact between the Australian people, rather than the past authority of the United Kingdom Parliament under the common law as offering a more acceptable explanation of the authority of the basic law of the Constitution."[27]

In *Leeth v. Commonwealth*[28] Justices Deane and Toohey again restated the place of the people in the Australian polity. They said:

> The States themselves are, of course, artificial entities. The parties to the compact which is the Constitution were the people of the federating Colonies. It is the people who, in a basic sense, now constitute the individual State just as, in the aggregate and with the people of the Territories, they constitute the Commonwealth.[29]

The "fullest flowering"[30] of the doctrine of the people's sovereignty occurred in 1992 in *Nationwide News Pty Ltd v. Wills*[31] and *Australian Capital Television Pty Ltd v. Commonwealth* (No 2).[32] In *Nationwide* Justices Deane and Toohey state that

> the central thesis of the doctrine [representative government] is that the powers of government belong to, and are derived from, the governed, that is to say, the people of the Commonwealth.[33]

In his judgement in *ACTV* Chief Justice Mason also outlined his views on the sovereignty doctrine. He said that:

> The very concept of representative government and representative democracy signifies government by the people through their representatives. Translated into constitutional terms, it denotes that the sovereign power which resides in the people is exercised on their behalf by their representatives.[34]

Chief Justice Mason outlined the evolutionary process that advanced Australia to this point:

Despite its initial character as a statute of the Imperial Parliament, the Constitution brought into existence a system of representative government for Australia in which the elected representatives exercise sovereign power on behalf of the Australian people. Hence, the prescribed procedure for amendment of the Constitution hinges upon a referendum at which the proposed amendment is approved by a majority of electors and a majority of electors in a majority of the States (s.128). And, most recently, the *Australia Act* 1986 (U.K.) marked the end of the legal sovereignty of the Imperial Parliament and recognized that ultimate sovereignty resided in the Australian people.[35]

Only Justice Dawson has expressly rejected the notion that the Australian people are sovereign.[36] In *Theophanous v. Herald and Weekly Times Ltd*[37] Justice Deane, following Madison's thesis that the "people, not the government, possess the absolute sovereignty," draws the same conclusions as Chief Justice Mason as to the central place of the people in the fabric of Australian constitutional theory.[38]

After the articulation of the Madisonian notion of the authority and sovereignty of the people many were left to ponder what this all meant. Was this the establishment of a new constitutional *grundnorm*? Or was this merely the restatement of the symbolic position of the people in light of the change in historical circumstances?

Sovereignty and the Deliberative Democracy

The examination of the people and sovereignty has been explained in a number of ways. The evocation of the people in Madisonian terms immediately raises the question of the republicanisation of the Constitution. Many, including Brian Galligan, have noted that (with the exception of the monarchical irritant) Australia is already a republic. "Australia's system of government is in formal terms a constitutional monarchy but in efficient terms a federal republic."[39]

On this view of republicanism, Australia's Constitution heritage has been republican since 1901. Indeed, Patrick Glynn, a South Australian delegate to the Constitutional Convention made the same point in Adelaide in 1897. While ruminating on the Canadian and Australian federal systems he made the following observation:

The comparative weakness of the Canadian Federation is due to its being too much impregnated with the monarchical element. Edward Freeman says:

> On the whole, the general teaching of history is to show that, though a monarchical Federation is by no means theoretically impossible, yet a republican Federation is far more likely to exist as a permanent and flourishing system. We may, therefore, in the general course of comparison, practically assume that a Federal State will also be republican State.

Of course that would not tell against our Federation, because we really set up a *crowned republic*.[40]

The shift in the High Court's thinking with respect to the people and their constitutional authority underlined a move to a more robust view of democracy. It is argued that this move is consistent with the revivalist writing on civic republicanism,[41] in particular the emphasis these writers have placed upon the notion of deliberative democracy. That is, the democratic process should be more than merely representative. The character of a deliberative democracy, for writers such as Sunstein, is that the system covers means as well as ends. The task of the so-called "republican revivalists" was, in the words of its chief proponents, to "integrat[e] aspects of traditional republican thought" into contemporary political situations so as to "satisfy republican goals."[42] According to Sunstein, the "goals" of republicanism can be characterised by four inter-related features: deliberation in politics; equality of political actors; universalism; and citizenship.[43] For Sunstein these features have particular analytical importance for contemporary society. For instance, the concept of deliberation gives rise to more than just the requirement that decisions be made after consideration of certain relevant facts. According to Sunstein, the republican notion is predicated on a view that political outcomes will be supported by "reference to a consensus (or at least broad agreement) amongst political equals."[44] This last idea, that of agreements made by political equals, Sunstein sees as a strong justification for the "protection of freedom of speech" (the means by which opinions may be expressed and agreement reached) and "the prohibition of discrimination against blacks and women" (the distortion of the rights of political equals).[45]

Much of the thinking of the Court on the political process and the implication of political communication was outlined in the *ACTV* case.[46] In that case the High Court developed the implied notion of political communication that served to reinforce the system of representative and responsible government.[47]

Civic republicanism in its revivalist form often concentrates on the judicial process and the means by which it ensures the authority of the people through constitutional interpretation. But here is the rub for Australia and its constitutional methodology. The move to the new authority of the people as sovereign means what for constitutional interpretation? As Leslie Zines has argued:

> The idea that the sovereignty of the people requires a court to determine whether Parliament has satisfied its duty to its constitutional masters by ensuring that its laws are for the "protection and governance" of the people as a whole would constitute a rather breathtaking transfer of power. The criterion would permit the application of a wide range of political philosophies.
>
> It would also, ironically, in the name of popular sovereignty, transfer power from institutions over which the electors have some control to a body that cannot be so easily checked or removed.[48]

This leaves the recourse to the mystical notion of the people as an authority with some theoretical discomfort. The alternatives would appear to limit the reach of the people as an interpretative conduit. This appears to be the concession offered by Justice McHugh in *McGinty.*

> The Constitution is contained in a statute of the United Kingdom Parliament. In the late twentieth century, it may not be palatable to many persons to think that the powers, authorities, immunities and obligations of the federal and State parliaments of Australia derive their legal authority from a statute enacted by the Imperial Parliament, but the enactment of that statute containing the terms of the Constitution is the instrument by which the Australian people have consented to be governed. Since the passing of the *Australia Act* (UK) in 1986, notwithstanding some considerable theoretical difficulties, the political and legal sovereignty of Australia now resides in the people of Australia. But the only authority that the people have given to the parliaments of the nation is to enact laws in accordance with the terms of the Constitution.[49]

For Justice McHugh the people's authority is to command that Parliament act in accordance to the Constitution. Thus judicial review proceeds upon the proposition that the Constitution, that embodies the "political and legal sovereignty" of the people, is supreme. Such an approach appears to be consistent with a view of constitutionalism that grants supremacy to the Parliament within limits and maintains sovereignty with the people as expressed in the Constitution.[50] Of course it is important not to overextend the role of the judiciary in this process. There remains a distinction between the judiciary monitoring, and if necessary correcting, the democratic machinery established by the constitution and acting in the people's name to establish judicial values. The former is by way of Ely's "representation-reinforcing orientation"[51] to judicial review whereas the latter confirms many of the fears raised by Zines.

A second approach to the role of the people is captured in the language of "public trust." The concept is that government in its broadest configuration are trustees of the people and their interests and thus are accountable for them. This fiduciary relation gives rise to what Finn describes as the "core idea of trusteeship."

> [That] government exists to serve the interests of the people and that this has a limiting effect on what is lawfully allowable to government [...] has remained an undertone, if not more, in common law doctrine itself. The practical expression of this is often to be found in the link between the actions of government and the "public interest." The interests of government are not, as such, synonymous with the public interest.[52]

Finn declares there to be five "constitutional" imperatives that derived from the notion of a public trust. They are: "the democratic principle," "the public servant principle," "the integrity principle," "the open government principle" and "the accountability principle." The "democratic principle" requires the maintenance and extension of the system of representative government.[53] The public service principle reflects the view that public officers act in a manner on behalf of the public and not solely the government they serve.[54] The integrity principle, as the name suggests, requires that the people must be able to place their trust in their officials.[55] Thus codes of parliamentary and administrative conduct are essential to the exercise of power. The open government principle is essentially that "in a polity based on popular sovereignty and practicing representative government, openness must be accepted as the predominant constitutional value with secrecy only justified by clear and demonstrable need."[56] The last principle that Finn outlines is one of accountability. While the courts may have a marginal role in establishing the public accountability (the media and interest groups may be more influential) there remains a place for some oversight of the parliamentary processes.[57]

The notion of a fiduciary interest was considered by the High Court in the landmark *Mabo* decision. In that case it was argued, amongst other things, that the Crown held an obligation to native title holders in relation to the extinguishment of that title. Justice Toohey noted that:

> To say that, where traditional title exists, it can be dealt with and effectively alienated or extinguished only by the Crown, but that it can be enjoyed only by traditional owners, may be tantamount to saying that the legal interest in the traditional rights is in the Crown whereas the beneficial interest in the rights is in the indigenous owners. In that case the kind of fiduciary obligation imposed on the Crown is that of a constructive trustee. In any event, the Crown's obligation as a fiduciary is in the nature of, and should be performed by reference to, that of a trustee.[58]

As with the "people as sovereign" approach to constitutional authority, it is difficult to see, or rather to see the limits of, public trust as a constitutional tool. To say that the interests of the sovereign people are to be held in trust by the government is itself an attractive means of viewing the people and their role. However, what remains unclear is how that trust is to be giving meaning within a judicial setting. Should the High Court, for instance, invalidate a statute on the basis that it offends the trustee relationship but *not* the express Constitution? While the private law may be well accustomed to the language of trust, the same is not true of the area of public law where judicial deference and democratic oversight are well-established constraints.

Conclusion

The final republicanisation of the Australian Constitution will one day be achieved and the monarchical irritant will be removed from the Australian body politic. However, what is needed is an appreciation before that time of the authority and role of the sovereign people in our constitutional system. The language of sovereignty and trust are synonymous with the ongoing relationship between the governed and the governing and may yet prove to be the conduit through which we can make sense of the relationship. Less clear, however, are the imperatives this would place on the juridical process in a democratic state such as Australia.

Notes

1. Cass Sunstein, *Democracy and the Problem of Free Speech* (New York: Free Press, 1993), 243–4.
2. For a discussion of this and the broader influence on the Canadian understanding of citizenship see David E. Smith, *The Republican Option in Canada, Past and Present* (Toronto: University of Toronto Press, 1999), 193–6.
3. See generally, Alastair Davidson, *From Subject to Citizen* (Melbourne: Cambridge University Press, 1997).
4. *Dred Scott v. Sanford* 60 U.S. 393 (1856).
5. C. H. M. Clark, *A History of Australia* Vol. V (Melbourne: Melbourne University Press, 1981), chp. 5.
6. J. A. La Nauze, *The Making of the Australian Constitution* (Melbourne: Melbourne University Press, 1972) and Helen Irving, *To Constitute a Nation: A Cultural History of Australia's Constitution* (Melbourne: Cambridge University Press, 1987).
7. John Quick and Robert R. Garran, *The Annotated Constitution of the Australian Commonwealth* (Sydney: Angus & Robertson, 1901).
8. However, it is incorrect to suggest that the Constitution itself disenfranchised Aboriginal and Torres Strait Islanders. See Brian Galligan and John Chesterman, "Aborigines, Citizenship and the Australian Constitution: Did the Constitution Exclude Aboriginal People From Citizenship?" *Public Law Review* 8, 1, (1997): 45.
9. Stuart Macintyre, "Corowa and the Voice of the People," in *The People's Convention Corowa (1893) and Bathurst (1896)*, eds. David Headon and Jeff Brownrigg (Canberra: Papers in Parliament, 32 December 1998): 1; Stuart Macintyre, "The Idea of the People," Ibid., 76; and John Hirst, "Federation and the People: a Response to Stuart Macintyre," Ibid., 80.
10. *Commonwealth of Australia Constitution Act* 63 & 64 Vict. (1900)
11. Sir Owen Dixon, *Jesting Pilate* (Melbourne: Law Book Company, 1965), 44.
12. G. J. Lindell, "Why is Australia's Constitution Binding? – The Reasons in 1900 and Now, and The Effect of Independence," *Federal Law Review* 16, 1 (1986): 32 (emphasis in original).

13. *Amalgamated Society of Engineers v. Adelaide Steamship Co Ltd* (1920), 28 CLR 129.
14. P. D. Finn, "A Sovereign People, A Public Trust," in *Essays on Law and Government: Principles and Values* Vol. 1, ed. P.D. Finn (North Ryde: Law Book Co, 1995), 1 at 2–3.
15. John Williams, "The Australian Constitution and the Challenge of Theory," in *Beyond the Republic*, eds. Tom Round and Charles Samford (Leichhardt, NSW: Federation Press, 2001), 119–129.
16. P. D. Finn, "A Sovereign People, A Public Trust," 3.
17. J. J. Doyle, "Common Law Rights and Democratic Rights," in *Essays on Law and Government: Principles and Values* Vol. 1, ed. P.D. Finn (North Ryde: Law Book Co, 1995), 147.
18. M. Loughlin, *Public Law and Political Theory* (Oxford: Oxford University Press, 1992), 156.
19. B. F. Fitzgerald, "Proportionality and Australian Constitutionalism," *University of Tasmania Law Review* 12, (1993): 265.
20. There were two Acts in identical terms passed by the Commonwealth Parliament and the Imperial Parliament.
21. *Sue v. Hill* (1999), 119 CLR 462, 491–2 (McHugh J.).
22. (1983), 158 CLR 535.
23. Ibid., 589.
24. (1984), 158 CLR 447.
25. Ibid., 477.
26. *Kirmania v. Captain Cook Cruises Pty Ltd [No 1]* (1985), 159 CLR 351, 442.
27. *Breavington v. Godleman* (1988), 169 CLR 41, 123.
28. (1992), 174 CLR 455.
29. Ibid., 484.
30. K. Mason, "Citizenship," in *Courts of Final Jurisdiction: The Mason Court in Australia*, ed. C. Saunders (North Ryde: Federation Press, 1996), 38.
31. (1992), 177 CLR 1.
32. (1992), 177 CLR 106.
33. *Nationwide News Pty Ltd v. Wills* (1992), 177 CLR 1, 72.
34. *Australian Capital Television Pty Ltd v. Commonwealth* (No 2) (1992), 177 CLR 106, 137.
35. Ibid., 138.
36. Ibid., 180–1.
37. (1994), 182 CLR 104.
38. Ibid., 180.
39. Brian Galligan, *A Federal Republic* (Melbourne: Cambridge University Press, 1995), 21.

40. *Official Record of the Debates of the Australasian Federal Convention, Adelaide* (1897) (Sydney: Legal Books, 1986), 73 (my emphasis).

41. See F. Michelman, "The Supreme Court 1985 Term – Foreword: Traces of Self-Government," *Harvard Law Review* 100 (1986): 4 and generally the special edition of the *Yale Law Journal* 97 (1988).

42. Cass Sunstein, "Beyond the Republican Revival," *Yale Law Journal* 97 (1988): 1539.

43. Ibid., 1541.

44. Ibid., 1550.

45. Ibid., 1550.

46. *Australian Capital Television Pty Ltd v. Commonwealth (No 2)* (1992), 177 CLR 106.

47. G. Rosenberg and John M. Williams, "Do Not Go Gently into that Good Right: The Pernicious Effects of First Amendment Jurisprudence on the High Court of Australia," *Supreme Court Review* (1997): 439.

48. Leslie Zines, "The Sovereignty of the People" in *Power, Parliament and the People*, eds. M. Coper and C. Williams (Leichhardt, NSW: Federation Press, 1997), 104.

49. *McGinty v. Western Australia* (1996), 186 CLR 140, 230 (McHugh J.).

50. Keith Mason, "The Rule of Law," in *Essays on Law and Government: Principles and Values*, ed. P.D. Finn (Sydney: Law Book Company, 1995), 123.

51. John Hart Ely, *Democracy and Distrust: A Theory of Judicial Review* (Cambridge Mass: Harvard University Press, 1980), 101.

52. P. D. Finn, "A Sovereign People, A Public Trust," 13–14.

53. Ibid., 24.

54. Ibid., 35.

55. Ibid., 26.

56. Ibid., 29.

57. Ibid., 29–30.

58. *Mabo v. Queensland* (No. 2) (1992), 175 CLR 1, 203 (Toohey J.).

5

Inventing the Nation Through the Ballot Box

MARIAN SAWER

My Ancestress and the Secret Ballot,
1848 and 1851[1]

Put about, wee ship, on your Great Circle course,
don't carry Bella's Murray daughter and boys
to the British Crown's stolen Austral land!
In ten years the Secret Ballot will force its way
into law in those colonies...

Don't sail, don't sail, Great-grannie (cubed) dear:
wait just a century and there'll be welfare
in full, and you won't play the Settler role.
The polling booth will be a closet of prayer.
Les Murray 1996

Australia has been described as the first nation created through the ballot box. Much of Australia's early identity as a nation revolved around its democratic experiments. In this paper I look at how Australian elections became family festivals rather than the drunken riots of nineteenth-century Britain, focusing on the invention of the secret ballot. While the right to vote is frequently commemorated, the freedom to vote without intimidation or corruption and the abolition of open nomination and open voting is less often celebrated. Yet the elimination of violence and drunkenness prepared the way not only for fair elections but also for participation of what was called the "fair sex." It became possible for women not only to vote but to stand for parliament without any threat to their modesty.

The flip-side of Australia's early democratic identity was its racial identity – there was pride in the ballot box but it was by no account to be a "piebald ballot box" as one Senator described it when opposing the franchise for Aborigines or coloured aliens in 1902. Australia was proud of belonging to what was called the "British race," even while trying to teach the British a thing or two about democracy. Today we are no longer a "British" nation in the sense we were in 1901. Post-Second World War immigration from Europe, the dismantling of the White Australia policy and the assertion of Aboriginal identity from the 1960s has led to today's cultural diversity. There remain questions, however, about the extent to which democratic or civic identity has been successfully combined with pride in multiculturalism rather than the scarlet thread of kinship.

Elections Before the Ballot

In democracies we often take voting for granted, particularly in the "old" democracies such as Australia where democratic institutions have been in continuous existence for most of our history. Indeed, we hear complaints that we have too many elections and we may be in danger of that new democratic complaint – "voter fatigue." It is difficult to recall the intense struggles over the vote, and the belief in its power to make a difference. Both those struggling for the right to vote and those resisting thought important issues were at stake, such as the protection of property from the enfranchised working man or the defence of "manly pursuits," such as war and alcohol, from enfranchised women.

It is not only the right to vote, but the freedom to vote without intimidation or corruption, that is such a significant, though often forgotten, part of our political history. The violence, drunkenness and bribery associated with elections before the introduction of the ballot are vividly portrayed by the English painter William Hogarth in his series entitled "An Election" that hangs alongside "The Rake's Progress" at Sir John Soane's Museum in London. The series was inspired by the 1754 election in Oxfordshire and depicts in grotesque detail the abuses involved in all stages of the election, from "treating" and canvassing through to polling and the declaration of the poll.

Such abuses became the stuff of great literature in the nineteenth century, when George Eliot wrote her election book, *Felix Holt, the Radical*. Eliot describes the nature of electioneering in the English Midlands immediately after the Reform Bill. Her theme is the systematizing of bribery and intimidation as the pocket boroughs are abolished and elections become more competitive. Felix Holt is the maverick who takes a stand against the system of "treating" and the use of voteless men to cause mischief at nominations and elections.[2]

Charles Dickens' account of the Eatanswill election in *Pickwick Papers* is even more famous, reinforcing the picture of violence surrounding the hustings.[3] Some writers were directly affected – as when novelist Anthony Trollope stood as a Liberal candidate in Beverley in 1868. The Conservative agent was systematic in his approach to bribery, entering the names of voters and the amount paid to each. When the successful Conservative candidates arrived at the hustings, enraged Liberals tore down the barricades and threw rocks and beams of wood. Despite this, Trollope remained an opponent of the secret ballot on the grounds it was unmanly.

In Australia, we need only dip into Samuel Shumack's *Tales and Legends of Canberra Pioneers* for similar vignettes of nineteenth-century electioneering as observed in the NSW seat of Queanbeyan.[4] Squatters intimidated those, such as the local blacksmith, known to be supporters of free selection; they also put on free beer in the hotels, leading to riot. As in the UK, hotels played a central role in elections; election agents "treated" voters there and hotel balconies or verandahs were frequently used for electioneering purposes.

The 1869 Braidwood election, the so-called "pick-handle election," was another notorious example of intimidation. Polling in the goldrush settlement of Araluen was aborted when the supporters of one of the candidates "armed to the teeth with pick-handles, shovel-handles, and bludgeons of every description" blockaded all approaches to the polling place.[5] Nor was electoral mayhem unknown in South Australia, despite its more sedate reputation and lack of convict heritage. In the seat of West Adelaide in 1855, Douglas Pike tells us: "On election day there was a serious riot, some civilians and a constable were injured and it took mounted police to disperse the crowds. Several electors voted twice, others were prevented from voting at all by a returning officer who .locked a polling booth for part of the day."[6]

The South Australian Constitution Act and related Electoral Act, which introduced manhood suffrage and the secret ballot in 1856, also included a prohibition on locating polling booths within a hundred yards of a public house. To be on the safe side, however, the Electoral Act still covered the possibility of nomination or voting being interrupted by riot or open violence – in which case proceedings were to be adjourned. Other colonial Acts adopted similar provisions and there was an adjournment in case of riot in the Araluen case.

The Introduction of the Ballot and an End to the Hustings

In the 1850s, all of the self-governing colonies followed Victoria and South Australia in introducing the new system whereby voters had their names marked off on the electoral roll at the polling place, were presented with a printed ballot paper, and retired to separate compartments to mark their ballot paper in secrecy before depositing it in a locked box watched over by the presiding officer, poll clerks and scrutineers. It is the system now regarded as synonymous with voting in most countries, but it was only invented in 1856 by Henry Chapman, author of the pioneering ballot provisions in the Victorian Electoral Act of that year. Chapman was a philosophic radical and friend of John Stuart Mill, and had been influenced by his experience of elections in Canada during 1834. He had loudly protested while in Canada against the suggestion that employers use their power and the fact of open voting to compel their employees to vote against radical candidates.[7] Chapman believed that the secret ballot was essential for the protection of the "dependent classes" against intimidation.

The ideas of the philosophic radicals were, along with Chartism, an important influence on Australia's electoral history. A significant number of Chartists had emigrated to the goldfields of Victoria after the collapse of the Chartist movement in Britain. They were veterans of the new techniques of mass action and the ballot was one of the six points of the People's Charter, although their views on how it was to be operationalized were somewhat vague.

Chartist agitation provided the backdrop to the achievement of the ballot and manhood suffrage in the 1850s, while Chapman provided the practical detail. By the time of its passage, his friend John Stuart Mill no longer supported the secret ballot – believing intimidation was no longer a real problem. On the other hand, an Irish observer of the first Victorian election after its introduction claimed there could be no greater contrast: "An elector, exercising his franchise under the ballot, instead of running a desperate gauntlet through corruption, drunkenness, violence and uproar, walks, as it were, in an even frame of mind, through a smooth, private avenue to discharge the political duties of citizenship."[8]

Even Anthony Trollope, as we have seen an opponent of the secret ballot on the grounds that it was unmanly, was forced to admit when visiting Australia in 1872 that it was generally popular and led to more orderly elections. There was none of the violence customary with open polling when numbers were near each other as the poll drew to a close. He questioned, however, whether tranquility at elections was an unmixed blessing, feeling it might be akin to apathy and suggested that "broken heads are better than political indifference."[9] As part of its campaign for reform in Britain, the Ballot Society prepared a pictorial broadside comparing the mayhem associated with "English" open voting with the decorous mode of election in the Australian colonies.

The law and order issue helped secure the eventual passage of the Ballot Act in the United Kingdom in 1872, despite the lingering reservations over the un-Britishness of secret voting and other concerns. The House of Lords initially rejected the bill, on the grounds it would lead to the overthrow of the monarchy. Lord Shaftesbury had been warned: "Resist to the very last the introduction of the ballot; for, as a Republican, I tell you that the ballot can never co-exist with monarchical institutions."[10]

The new electoral acts in the Australian colonies provided that polling using the ballot was all to be conducted on the same day (except where adjourned on account of riot), eliminating some of the dubious practices occurring when polling was spread out over weeks as in the UK and Canada. In South Australia and Tasmania, the secret ballot was accompanied by the abolition of the public nomination of candidates – another practice associated with riotous behaviour. Up until this time in Australia (and until the 1870s in the UK and Canada), candidates were nominated and addressed electors from hustings – a temporary platform erected in a public place such as a market on nomination day. Then a show of hands took place for each candidate. After results were declared, a poll could be demanded by either a candidate or a specified number of electors (see, for example, the NSW Electoral Acts of 1858 and 1880). In *Felix Holt*, the nomination experience included "the hustling and the pelting, the roaring and the hissing, the hard hits with small missiles, and the soft hits with small jokes."[11]

In the period before the introduction of the secret ballot, the hustings could also be the place where voters had to stand and declare their

Table 1 Innovation in representational arrangements

Lower Houses

Parliament	Manhood Suffrage[1]	Adult Suffrage[2]	Abolition of Plural Voting	Secret Ballot	Abolition of open nomination	Payment of Members	Compulsory Registration of Voters	First Election with Compulsory Voting
United Kingdom	1918	1928	1948	1872	1872	1911	—	—
Canada	1920	1920	1920	1874	1874	1867	—	—
NSW	1858	1902	1894	1858	1893	1889	1921	1930
Victoria	1857	1909	1899	1856	1865	1870	1923	1927
Queensland	1859	1905	1905	1859	1872	1886	1914	1915
South Australia	1856	1894	Never Existed	1856	1856	1887	—	1944
Western Australia	1907	1907[3]	1907	1877[4]	1895	1900	1919	1939
Tasmania	1901	1903	1901	1858	1858	1890	1930	1931
Commonwealth	1901	1902[5]	Never Existed	1901	Never Existed	1901	1911	1925

Notes

1. Except for the final column, the legislative date is given, rather than date of coming into effect.
2. I.e. votes for women. But note some States did not enfranchise Aborigines or indigent inmates of State charitable institutions until later.
3. WA gave some women the vote in 1899 on the same restricted franchise then applying to men.
4. This was for the elective element of the old Legislative Council of the years before self-government.
5. In 1901, women generally in SA, and some women in WA, had a vote for the first Commonwealth parliament, which in turn legislated for complete adult suffrage for subsequent federal elections.

Source: Adapted from L. F. Crisp *Australian National Government* 1967 with the help of Tom Flanagan.

Beverley election. Part of a pictorial broadside, issued at the time by the Ballot Society advocating the secret ballot. This was one of the two issues to which Trollope in his autobiography professed himself hostile at the election.

preferred candidate on polling day. In Canada, as elsewhere, such declarations from the hustings were often associated with intimidation
and violence. In 1832, during a by-election in Montreal, the army was
called in and three people were shot dead. As a result, the House of
Assembly of Lower Canada adopted a bill depriving women of the
right to vote, believing that polling stations had become too dangerous
for the weaker sex. The bill was rejected by London on a legal techni-
cality and propertied women retained the vote in Lower Canada
between 1791 and 1849.[12]

In Victoria, the reform of nomination procedures came later than
the secret ballot. The Irish observer we have already encountered singing the praises of the secret ballot was also an eloquent advocate of
nomination reform:

> .all that is wanting to render such an election a really halcyon scene
> from beginning to end, where the proudest civil rights may be exer-
> cised with all the peace and security of a religious ceremony, is .the
> abolition of the barbarous parody of bull-baiting that candidates
> undergo on the hustings, without use or object, and which, after all, is
> nothing more or less than pantomime in a frenzy.[13]

One thing that is notable about Australia's electoral history is that
modern political parties were relatively slow to emerge – there were
factions and pressure groups but not parties in the period up until the
1890s. Then the Labor Party, with its new forms of party discipline
over MPs, quickly became a catalyst for the transformation of Australian politics, forming its first minority government in Queensland in
1899. By 1910 a two-party class-based political system had taken shape
and liberal reformers were no longer an independent force. Many of
Australia's electoral reforms dated from the earlier period, when liberals and radicals were able to garner support on the floor of the house
for democratic experiments.

Election Day – From Free Beer to Family Festival

South Australia not only led the way with manhood suffrage in 1856,
but also led the way with universal suffrage in 1894. Elimination of the
free beer and rioting associated with elections earlier in the century,
even in relatively sober South Australia, was reinforced by the advent
of women's political rights on the "watery tide of temperance." It was

not the case that women became "coarsened" by the "roaring, hustling and pushing at the polling booth" as had been anticipated by some,[14] but rather that women's suffrage, if anything, reinforced the trend towards more orderly elections. Certainly the curbing of the violence and drunkenness associated with nomination and voting helped prepare the way for women's political participation, as did the "unmanly" practice of the secret ballot.

James Vernon, on the other hand, argues that these reforms, and particularly the abolition of open nomination, removed the influence of the disenfranchised from the electoral process: "No longer could the disenfranchised vote at the nomination or hold a vigil beside the hustings to intimidate the voters ".[15] He is writing about the United Kingdom, where these reforms preceded both manhood and universal suffrage, rather than following the achievement of manhood suffrage, as in Australia. Nonetheless, the Australian evidence throws doubt on his interpretation of the British Ballot Act as "the closing down of the public political sphere by officials who sought to replace the public and collective experience with an increasingly private and individual male one." The intimidation of voters and the pelting of candidates with missiles were not gender-inclusive forms of political participation. As I argue here, the secret ballot paved the way for women's suffrage, rather than reinforcing male privilege, as only the most conservative could argue that the polling booth (as contrasted with the hustings) was an inappropriate place for a woman.

Another electoral innovation for which South Australia was responsible was legislation in 1896 to ensure that "No day other than Saturday shall be fixed as polling day."[16] South Australia was followed by Queensland and then by the Commonwealth in 1911. Already by the end of the nineteenth century most Australian workers had a half-holiday on Saturday, making this the most convenient day for electors to vote.

The establishment of Saturday elections was the beginning of the great Australian tradition of the festive nature of polling day. The local primary school becomes a political market-place on election day, with the umbrellas and tables of the rival political parties and groups, the line of booth workers handing out "how-to-vote" cards, and the Parents and Citizens Association running a sausage sizzle or a cake stall. Schools were already singled out as appropriate polling places in early electoral acts and helped make voting a family occasion.

The *Adelaide Observer* (2 May 1896) provided a comprehensive account of polling on the previous Saturday – the first election in which women voted for the State parliament. There were familiar features, such as the "candidate cards and leaflets" that strewed the path to the poll and the workers outside the booths who thrust flyers into the hands of electors as they walked into the polling booth. A slightly higher proportion of enrolled women than men voted (66 percent), including the Dominican nuns who voted at the North Adelaide Temperance Hall. The *Adelaide Observer* was quite carried away by the refining influence of women voters: "Never have we had a more decorous gathering together of the multitude than that which distinguished the first exercise of the female franchise." The journalist suggested that pre-poll verses were borne out on the day, although not the aspersions on women's competence to vote:

> Lovely woman, hesitating
> Round the booths in sweet dismay
> Her gentle bosom palpitating
> Lest she cast her vote away
> And when she glides in graceful, pretty,
> To vote in her most charming frock
> The poll clerks in suburb and city
> Will thrill with an electric shock.

Provisions for postal voting had become permanent in South Australia in 1894 and some conservative politicians, such as Sir John Downer, the grandfather of our present Foreign Minister, believed that this was necessary to protect women's sensitivities. He suggested that every member of parliament would sooner his lady relatives voted by post than "amid the bustle of the open polling booth."[17] In the event, women did not make as much use as expected of the right to cast a postal vote, preferring to attend the polling booth in person.

Ironically, the solidary character of the Saturday polling day has been threatened in the last decade by the deregulation of the labour market and the increasing prevalence of work on Saturdays. Pre-poll voting was largely introduced to cater for this phenomenon and represented about 6 percent of all votes cast in the 1998 federal election.

Payment for MPs and Professionalizing of Electoral Administration

Shumack's *Tales* also illuminate the problems involved in broadening the representation of the people before the achievement of the Chartist demand of payment for parliamentarians. Shumack's candidate eventually had to leave parliament because not enough of his electors honoured their promises to pay his salary (Shumack himself had pledged £2 a year). One of the Chartists who emigrated to Victoria, Charles Jardine Don, was elected to the Victorian parliament in 1859. He was said to be the "first working-class representative in any legislature in the British Empire" and was in constant financial strife. After his election he continued working by day as a stonemason while working at night as Member for Collingwood.[18] Parliamentary salaries were finally introduced in Victoria in 1870 – at the quite generous £300 a year.

Meanwhile, the Australian colonies were not only introducing payment for MPs, but also developing a professionalized approach to electoral administration characterized by a centralized electoral administration and paid electoral officials. The absence of entrenched local authority structures encouraged this development and provided a significant contrast with the United Kingdom. Electoral administration was at first conducted by public servants in a standard ministerial department, but was later given increased independence by the creation of statutory bodies. At the federal level, the establishment of the Australian Electoral Commission as an independent statutory body in 1984 was an important milestone, as was the establishment at the same time of the Joint Standing Committee on Electoral Matters. This parliamentary committee has proven an extremely important forum for obtaining bipartisan support for technical improvements in electoral administration. This had previously been difficult to achieve even on such apparently straightforward matters as the closing time for polling booths.

The early development of specialist electoral administrators enabled other innovations such as continuous roll maintenance – where there was proactive canvassing to ensure eligible voters were on the electoral rolls and at the right address. This contrasted strongly with systems in use in other countries where voters had to wait for rolls to open. Other developments included arrangements intended to maximize access to voting such as the introduction of provisions for absent and postal voting in the nineteenth century and of mobile polling booths in the twentieth. South Australia had introduced postal voting as early as 1890, initially to ensure the voting rights of those working away from their electorate, such as seamen and railwaymen. The introduction of "compulsory voting" (actually compulsory attendance) at both Commonwealth and State levels in the twentieth century, with financial penalties for non-compliance, meant that much more elaborate provision needed to be made for voters unable to attend a polling place.

The spirit of professional electoral administration was to maximize accessibility as well as integrity of the system. This spirit was often notably absent when it came to the administration of Aboriginal voting rights, as in the process whereby Aboriginal people "lost the vote" at the Commonwealth level after 1901. As recently as 1977, electoral administrators, together with intimidatory party scrutineers, were found to have effectively impeded Aboriginal voting rights in the Kimberley. Another problem before 1980 was reliance on postal voting in remote areas, where many Indigenous voters had low literacy skills. Third parties providing assistance to such voters might abuse their position as intermediaries.

Mobile polling was first used extensively at the State and Territory level in 1980 and at the federal level in 1984 to try to address this problem. Mobile polling booths with experienced officials would travel through sparsely settled remote areas collecting votes for a week or two leading up to polling day.

From the 1980s, Commonwealth electoral education targeted to Indigenous voters gradually became more effective in achieving a high level of formal votes, before being abruptly terminated by the newly elected Howard Government in 1996. Other recent encroachments on the principle of access have included requirements making enrolment more difficult and expensive for those who do not already possess the necessary documentary evidence.

The Right to Stand But Not to Sit

John Stuart Mill and his circle were of considerable importance in Australian electoral history, with supporters of women's suffrage or proportional representation clothing themselves in his intellectual authority. Mill famously wrote to Henry Chapman, after the latter had become Attorney-General in Victoria, to congratulate him on the recent extension of the suffrage: "The only thing which seems wanting to make the suffrage really universal is to get rid of the Toryism of sex, by admitting women to vote."[19] Mill urged his friend to quote him on the issue of women's suffrage and also on the subject of the representation of minorities. It is interesting that Mill was able to write such lengthy letters during his working hours at East India House.

Mill continued urging women's suffrage on the Australasian colonies, while failing in his own attempt to achieve women's suffrage during his brief term as a British MP. It was one of Mill's followers who introduced the first women's suffrage bills into the South Australian parliament and he also inspired suffrage leaders in the other colonies. The rise of the women's movement had political effects even before the achievement of suffrage, with male votes becoming conditional on behaviour towards wives under the NSW Elections Act of 1893. One disqualification for electors was having an outstanding maintenance order against them; another was a conviction for aggravated assault on their wife in the previous year.[20] These disqualifications remained in the Act until 1928.

Soon after achieving the vote, suffragists were travelling to London to help the cause in the mother country. Attractive "women voters" from Australia took the platform in the Albert Hall to demonstrate that political rights did not "unsex" women. Others took more militant action, such as Adelaide-born Muriel Matters, who became known as the first woman to give a speech in the House of Commons – while chained to the grille of the Ladies' Gallery in 1908. She and her colleague from the Women's Freedom League were removed still attached to the grille.[21] Subsequently, she floated over the House of Commons at the time of the State opening of parliament in 1909, in an airship inscribed "Votes for Women." Unfortunately at this stage she was up about 3,500 feet so she was unable to use her megaphone but she did scatter a large quantity of handbills. The airship photographed well and the *Daily Mail* even provided fashion notes: "Miss Matters wore a large green coat, motor cap and veil and woollen gloves. She also wore a rosette of the [Women's Freedom] League's colours – white, yellow and green – and took into the basket-car a large supply of handbills, flags and a megaphone"[22] (17 February 1909).

It was not only expatriates who enlisted in the cause; federal parliament also played its part. In 1909, a motion put forward by prime minister Alfred Deakin concerning the positive effects of women's suffrage in Australasia was unanimously passed in both houses. The following year, Senator Arthur Rae was responsible for another resolution being passed by both houses and cabled to the intransigent British prime minister, Asquith. The text of the resolution was drafted by Vida Goldstein and spoke of consequences in terms of "more orderly elections" as well as of greater prominence being given to legislation particularly affecting women and children.[23]

The Woman's Press in London rushed out the text of the Senate debate under the title *Australia's Advice* (1910). Such advice was presented pictorially during the great coronation year suffrage procession when women voters, including the wife of Australian prime minister Andrew Fisher, marched behind the banner that depicted the young Commonwealth of Australia pleading with Britannia to "Trust the women, mother, as I have done."

Pride in democratic credentials was particularly true of those representing the first majority Labor government, newly elected that year. They had signalled the new order in federal parliament by doing away with the ceremonial wigs and gowns of the presiding officers. The President of the Senate was a former wharf labourer who had become Home Secretary in the world's first Labor government in Queensland in 1899. While the Senators agreed Australia was a young country, they spoke of its seniority in democratic experience and expertise.

Other Democratic Experiments

Of course from the nineteenth century the Australian colonies were initiating many other democratic experiments such as the development of new voting systems. All the major forms of preferential voting – the alternative vote, the contingent vote and Hare-Clark, also known as the Single Transferable Vote (STV) were substantially developed here. Catherine Helen Spence played a major role in popularizing STV in the late nineteenth century and, interestingly, was also the author of Australia's first civics textbook, commissioned by the South Australian Minister for Education in 1880.

The extent of electoral experimentation in some States was truly remarkable and quite unlike the stolid reliance on first-past-the-post voting in the United Kingdom and other dominions. NSW, for example, tried the second ballot from 1910, the single transferable vote from 1918 to 1926, contingent voting from 1926 to 1928, compulsory preferential from 1929 to 1980 and optional preferential from 1981.

Another crucial aspect in ensuring that elections mirror the nation's mind is the institution of compulsory registration and voting. Compulsory registration was introduced at the federal level in 1911 by the Fisher Labor government, who argued it was as much a part of democracy as compulsory education or compulsory arbitration. Australia was the first English-speaking country to introduce compulsory voting, starting with Queensland in 1914 and followed at the federal level ten years later. Belgium had led the way with the introduction of compulsory voting in 1893 (Article 48 of its new constitution). In Australia compulsory voting was famously introduced at the federal level under a conservative government, without serious discussion either on the floor of the house or in committee, where only fifteen minutes were spent on it. Both major parties had an interest in increasing turnout.

If we ask the question "Whose vote does compulsion protect?" we find that compulsory voting plays a crucial role in reducing the social bias in turnout. In voluntary systems it is the poor and the marginalized who are the non-voters, something that decreases even further their capacity to influence government or achieve better welfare outcomes. Compulsory voting underpins all the other innovations in electoral administration found in Australia, designed to ensure the integrity of the rolls and accessibility of voting, whether voters are in prison or in the outback or overseas.[24] It contributes to social capital by ensuring solid participation in Australian elections, with door-knocking by electoral officials and birthday cards to seventeen-year-olds to ensure the rolls are as comprehensive as possible.

When so many other democratic experiments were taking place, it is perhaps not surprising that Australia's constitution-making process of the 1890s was also uniquely democratic in form. Whatever the flaws, no other country had created itself in this way. The process of federation was built around popular election of delegates to the Constitutional convention and popular ratification of the Constitution Bill. The delegates were also highly conscious of the advanced democratic nature of the provisions they were entrenching for the new federal parliament, such as the direct popular election of both houses and the ban on plural voting. The provision made for payment of members of the new federal parliament was regarded as another democratic advance – pioneered in the colonial parliaments but highlighted by its inclusion in the Constitution of the new Commonwealth.

Conclusion

Australia has long enjoyed stable democratic institutions, and at Federation took pride in being a young country but an old democracy. Australia is now quite a different type of country than it was in 1901 and "Britishness" no longer provides the other aspect of its identity.

Since 1989, when the *National Agenda for a Multicultural Australia* was released, there have been various attempts to articulate a civic identity as an alternative to an ethnically based national identity. Sets of core values or basic principles associated with Australian democracy have been identified, and, recently, the Australian Citizenship Council[25] has urged acts of public commitment to these shared civic values, including acceptance of cultural diversity and recognition of the unique status of Aboriginal and Torres Strait Islander peoples as well as the strengthening of parliamentary democracy.

Despite such affirmations, many believe that trust in representative institutions has been eroded rather than strengthened in recent times. Surveys find a gap between the policy preferences of voters and those of their elected representatives. This gap can be particularly large on issues such as immigration. There has been resentment in some parts of Australia that immigrants no longer have to be of British origin or at least to assimilate to Britishness to become full citizens. This resentment fuelled support for populist politicians such as Pauline Hanson who claimed to be a voice for the people rather than for the political elite. Hanson, however, is now in jail for election fraud.

Moreover, as Will Kymlicka has pointed out, a civic identity based on good democratic principles is not in itself sufficient to ensure national cohesion, particularly in multi-ethnic or multinational states.[26] There needs to be some emotional identification with the history of the nation. In the Australian context, knowledge of, and pride in, our democratic struggles and accomplishments might promote such emotional identity without the need for racial pride. There is evidence from the 1996 International Social Survey Program that pride in Australia's democracy is very high by international standards, exceeded only by Norway and well ahead of Britain, Canada and New Zealand. There is distrust of politicians, and Australia does not rank so highly on this indicator, but there is still less distrust than in most countries. While pride in democracy still plays such a large role in Australian national identity, there can be some optimism for the future, despite the economic and cultural insecurities of the present.

Notes

1. I am grateful to Mark McKenna for alerting me to the existence of this poem. A hundred years earlier William Kidston, later Premier of Queens-

land, also published a poem about the secret ballot, entitled "The Ballot's The Thing" (*The Worker* 4 April 1891).

2. George Eliot, *Felix Holt, the Radical* (1866) (Oxford: Oxford University Press, 1988), 110.

3. Charles Dickens, *The Pickwick Papers* (1837) (Ware: Wordsworth Editions, 1993).

4. Samuel Shumack, *An Autobiography or Tales and Legends of Canberra Pioneers*, eds. J. E. and Samuel Shumack (Canberra: Australian National University Press, 1967).

5. The *Yass Courier*'s description underlined the ethnicity of the rioters by describing them as "a mob of about 150 determined looking men, in shirt sleeves, carrying shillelahs about two and a half feet long" (*Yass Courier* 21 December 1869; *Goulburn Herald & Chronicle*, 22 December 1869).

6. Douglas Pike, *Paradise of Dissent: South Australia 1829–1857* (Melbourne: Melbourne University Press, 1957), 477.

7. R. S. Neale, "H. S. Chapman and the 'Victorian Ballot'," *Historical Studies*, 12 (1967), 509.

8. William Kelly, *Life in Victoria or Victoria in 1853 and Victoria in 1858*, 2 vols. (London: Chapman & Hall, 1859), 318.

9. Anthony Trollope, *Australia and New Zealand*, 2 vols. (London: Chapman and Hall, 1873), v.2: 245.

10. Hartley Kemball Cook, *The Free and Independent: The Trials, Temptations and Triumphs of the Parliamentary Elector* (London: Allen and Unwin, 1949), 121.

11. George Eliot, *Felix Holt, the Radical*, 1866, 242.

12. Elections Canada, *A History of the Vote in Canada* (Ottawa: Minister of Public Works and Government Services Canada, 1997), 22.

13. William Kelly, *Life in Victoria or Victoria in 1853 and Victoria in 1858*, 2 vols., 318.

14. *Country*, 14 April 1894.

15. James Vernon, *Politics and the People: A Study in English Political Culture, c. 1815–1867* (Cambridge: Cambridge University Press, 1993), 158.

16. *The Electoral Code Act, 1896*, no. 667 (South Australia), Clause 87.

17. South Australia Parliamentary Debates, 17 December 1894.

18. Raymond Wright, *A People's Counsel: A History of the Parliament of Victoria 1856–1990* (Melbourne: Oxford University Press, 1992), 35.

19. J. S. Mill, personal correspondence with Henry Chapman, 8 July 1858. Provided by Mrs. W. Rosenberg of Christchurch, New Zealand.

20. Colin Hughes and B. D. Graham, *A Handbook of Australian Government and Politics 1890–1964* (Canberra: Australian National University Press, 1968).

21. Marion Holmes, "Concerning Muriel Matters," *The Vote*, 19 February 1910.

22. "Suffragette in an Airship, Attempt to Reach the House of Commons, Handbills from the Clouds," *Daily Mail*, 17 February 1909

23. Commonwealth of Australia Parliamentary Debates LIX, 17 November 1910: 6300.

24. Similarly elaborate arrangements are made to ensure that Australians stationed at Antarctic bases are able to vote, although this is one category of elector for whom voting is not compulsory. The reason for this exception is that because of the uncertainty of communications, voting is not secret – the Antarctic Returning Officers have to telephone the votes back to Australia.

25. Australian Citizenship Council, *Australian Citizenship for a New Century* (Canberra: Commonwealth of Australia, 2000).

26. Will Kymlicka, *Politics in the Vernacular: Nationalism, Multiculturalism, and Citizenship* (Oxford: Oxford University Press, 2001).

6

" ... That Sweep of Savage Splendour ... "
A Century of Australians in Antarctica

ALASDAIR McGREGOR

As outposts of Empire, late nineteenth- and early twentieth-century Australia and New Zealand lay on the outer margins of civilized existence. Even at that time, to progress into the high latitudes of the Southern Hemisphere was to effectively sail over the edge of the then known world. Because of their location both were convenient staging posts for the last great phase of terrestrial exploration of our planet, so it is therefore not surprising that Australians and New Zealanders are well represented in the pantheon of early Antarctic exploration. Initially lured south perhaps as much by virtue of opportunistic geography as their undoubted ability, a number of remarkable individuals from that era would in time forge an enduring link between their new nations and the seventh continent. Of absolute prominence among the Australians were Douglas Mawson and Frank Hurley – one a leader, organizer, scientist and academic, the other a daring photographer and adventurer who would go to any extreme in pursuit of his craft. Their legacies, in science, geo-politics and artistic expression, would through dint of their exploits, quickly transcend the bounds of mere exploratory achievement or documentation.

Mawson, the son of immigrants from Yorkshire, arrived in Australia in 1884, aged two. James Francis Hurley – or Frank, as he is always known – was born in Sydney a year later. The lives of these two men would intersect at various times over the ensuing fifty years and despite youthful adventure that brought each to the face of death on numerous occasions, both were blessed with the luck of the bold, living to see the onset of old age in the 1950s and 60s.

In the short span of human activity on Earth, Antarctica is but a footnote. To set the scene on an early twentieth-century Antarctic stage where both men would make their reputations, a brief historical digression is useful. In geological times, Australia and Antarctica were part of the enormous southern supercontinent, Gondwana. Much of its extent supported vast forests of temperate verdure while warm shallow seas teemed with aquatic life. But some 140 million years later, all has changed utterly. Today, the two continents are the driest on Earth, with Antarctica also the highest, coldest, windiest, least populated and most recently explored landmass on the planet.

A great southern continent, *Terra Australis Incognita*, was speculated from the beginning of civilization but it was not until the eighteenth century that myth finally began to yield to reality. Successive expeditions probed the oceans of the Southern Hemisphere and with the exception of Australia and New Zealand found no significant new landmass. The widest of searches was made by James Cook and it is with Cook that the history of Antarctic exploration properly begins.

With his ships *Resolution* and *Adventure*, Cook had first crossed the Antarctic circle in 1773 during one of the greatest-ever voyages of exploration. In late January 1773, after a month imperiled by pack ice, and prevented from pushing further south, Cook noted that the "ice extends quite to the pole, or perhaps joins to some land to which it has been fixed since creation."[1] In the course of his three-year voyage Antarctica was circumnavigated but the elusive continent never sighted.

Cook's journals told of a Southern Ocean churning with spouting whales and sub-Antarctic islands whose beaches were crowded with squabbling fur seals. There also for easy taking were corpulent elephant seals heavy with oily blubber. Exploitation followed swiftly and the economic plunder of Antarctic resources reached astonishing heights before the continent had ever been sighted. With mainly American crews working the south Atlantic, some came tantalizingly close to the Antarctic Peninsula, but for decades the elusive southern land remained shrouded in mystery. A handful of French, British, Russian and American expeditions through the course of the nineteenth century did little to unlock Antarctica's secrets and in all likelihood by Hurley and Mawson's earliest years, no human had ever set foot on the Antarctic mainland.

The earliest definitive sighting of the continent had been made by Russian explorer Bellingshausen in 1820 but it was not until the end of the century, when Mawson was a 17 year old, that men first endured an Antarctic winter. Yet by the time of Mawson's death in 1958, a mere fifty years later, all but the most remote parts of the interior had been explored and mapped. For the last time in the geographic history of our planet – at least on a continental scale – the unknowable had become known.

Australians were there from the start. The first wintering party – the erroneously named British Antarctic Expedition of 1898–1900 – was led by Carsten Borchgrevink, a Norwegian immigrant to Australia of ten years standing. (All but three of the expedition were Norwegian – the financiers of the expedition did the talking and by implication held sway with the "naming rights.") The expedition included Louis Bernacchi, an Italian-born Tasmanian physicist. Bernacchi's initial assessment of the Cape Adare coast that was to be his home through the winter darkness was grim. He wrote that "one sight in bad weather of that sinister coast is enough to make a landsman dream for weeks of shipwrecks, perils and death."[2] However, the experience must not have been too harrowing for the young Bernacchi, as he immediately backed up as member of the National Antarctic Expedition of 1900–04 – Robert Falcon Scott's first venture south.

At the opening of the new century the north and south geographic poles were the two greatest prizes yet to adorn the trophy cabinet of European exploration. Four centuries of colonial expansion were drawing to an end and British hegemony over much of the planet was still in the ascendant. Conquest of the seventh continent was one means of prolonging the imperial twilight. With science a convenient foil for the more visceral pursuit of the South Pole, successive British expeditions under the leadership of Scott and Ernest Shackleton ground their way inland from bases on the edge of the Ross Sea, largely through the agonizing strain of human muscle. They are recognized as the quintessential journeys of the "heroic" age in Antarctica – a span of barely thirty years from the first footsteps on the ice to the advent of ship-based whaling in the 1920s.

As well as marking a decline in imperial fortunes, the heroic age in Antarctica presaged a shift to another great phase of human endeavour – that of our own contemporary world – the mechanical age. Bold new technological advancements – motor cars, aircraft and radio – were trialed from the beginning, often with poor results, while sail-assisted shipping, proven over centuries, still ruled the pack ice. Photographers such as Hurley were also there from the start. The Antarctic continent holds a unique place in human history, in that, from first contact to the present it has been observed and recorded through the lens of the camera.

In 1907, Shackleton invited the eminent Australian geologist and authority on glaciation T.W. Edgeworth David to accompany his British Antarctic Expedition on the round trip to the ice aboard the vessel *Nimrod*. Shackleton was in fact in David's debt, after the well-connected professor had persuaded his friend, Australian Prime Minister Alfred Deakin, to provide a grant from Treasury of £5,000 to the expedition.

David suggested that Shackleton also include his young protégé, Douglas Mawson, then a promising doctoral student with undergraduate degrees in geology and mining engineering. With an eye for talent, Shackleton went further, appointing Mawson as physicist for the entire expedition. David too would stay for the duration. The pair were in the party that first climbed the near-4,000-metre active volcano, Mt Erebus, and together with Scottish surgeon Alistair Forbes Mackay, sledged an incredible 2,000 kilometres in a quest for the South Magnetic Pole. Their death-defying feat represented the longest unsupported land journey yet made in Antarctica.

On their return to Australia in 1909, both Mawson and David were embraced as heroes, the pride of a young nation less than ten years a federation. Both Sydney and Adelaide greeted them with great enthusiasm and the *Sydney Morning Herald* gave extensive coverage of their exploits. For the 51-year-old-David, the privations of Antarctic sledging had almost been too much. He would never return South. Mawson, however, a fit, tall and impressive figure, still in his twenties, was smitten with the lure of the ice. In tribute to his young colleague David described him as an "Australian Nansen, of infinite resource."[3] His destiny as an explorer seemed assured. In later writings Mawson reminisced that:

> .once more in the world of men, lulled in the easy repose of routine, and performing the ordinary duties of a workaday world, old emotions awakened, the grand sweet days returned in irresistible glamour, far away voices called .[4].

Mawson, David and Bernacchi had all noted possible geological links between Australia and Antarctica. Mawson also foresaw as yet undefined commercial potential and therefore a national imperative in the South. His focus was inexorably drawn towards what he referred to as the "Australian quadrant." The idea of exploring his "Land of Hope and Glory" west of Cape Adare took hold during a visit to England in 1910.

Mawson's Antarctic credentials established, he felt confident that he could gain the backing of Scott and mount an expedition to explore the Antarctic coast and hinterland directly to the south of Australia as an adjunct to Scott's own plans for an assault on the pole. Mawson's ideas were rejected, but in deference to the Australian's undoubted strength and stamina, Scott offered Mawson a place in his polar party. Fortuitously, he declined. Had Mawson accepted, his place in history may well have been relegated to that of a footnote to British imperial folklore. Mawson's interests outshone pure geographical conquest and he persisted, this time putting the idea to the recently knighted Sir Ernest Shackleton, who embraced it with enthusiasm. Shackleton at first insisted on leading any expedition himself but then eased off, citing recently failed business speculations as requiring his immediate attention. Mawson became suspicious of Shackleton's ability to see the project through.

Confident and assertive, Mawson resolved to organize his own expedition. Furthermore, while within the bounds of Empire, it was to be a distinctly Antipodean endeavour. In *The Home of the Blizzard*, Mawson's account of what came to be known as the Australasian Antarctic Expedition (AAE), he confided:

> For many reasons, besides the fact that it was the country of my home and Alma Mater, I was desirous that the Expedition should be maintained by Australia. It seemed to me that here was an opportunity to prove that young men of a young country could rise to those traditions which have made the history of British Polar exploration one of triumphant endeavour as well as tragic sacrifice. And so I was privileged to rally the "sons of the younger son."[5]

Mawson was a gifted organizer and successfully petitioned governments and private backers in both Australia and Britain for financial support. It is interesting to note that the New South Wales, Victorian and South Australian governments gave a combined total of £18,000 to the expedition, whereas the Commonwealth's initial contribution came to only £5,000. Can this be seen as rivalry among former colonies or their assertiveness in wanting to share the expected kudos from a successful expedition? It may also indicate that the concept of a truly national initiative was still in its formative years. A ship was purchased – the 50 metre *Aurora* – a former member of the Newfoundland sealing fleet and a vessel with proven capabilities in sea ice. Amongst his personnel, Mawson gathered around him a group of young graduates from Australian and New Zealand universities. Youthful energy in the service of science and exploration was to be the flavour of the expedition.

Enter Frank Hurley. The son of a trade union official, Hurley had run away from school at the age of thirteen after an altercation with a teacher. He tried various jobs before turning an early found passion for photography into a profession by acquiring a half share in a postcard business. The business began to prosper but in 1911, learning of the impending expedition, Hurley bribed his way into Mawson's train compartment for the journey from Sydney to Adelaide. He used the captive setting to persuade Mawson to appoint him as photographer in preference to more seasoned contenders. Mawson reacted not so much to Hurley's photographic skills as his initiative. He was hired and so began the career of arguably the greatest-ever polar photographer.

The AAE left Australia on the grossly overloaded *Aurora* in late 1911. Her decks awash for much of the journey, she had effectively sailed out of reach of rescue and into the deep unknown. Every inch of space on the *Aurora* was crammed with supplies. Difficult, dangerous or unwieldy cargo was consigned to the decks – so the expedition's forty-nine Greenland sledge dogs shared their breezy quarters with timber radio masts, building materials and as Mawson put it "six thousand gallons of benzine, kerosene and spirit, in tins which were none too strong [that] we might well have been excused a lively anxiety."[6] Also stored on deck and out of reach of the dogs were several sheep, a couple of tonnes of butter and a few fowls.

No one had glimpsed that stretch of the Antarctic coast aspired to by the AAE since 1840 when the French explorer Dumont d'Urville and the American, Wilkes, each in close succession, skirted what had come to be known as Adélie Land. In a bold plan, Mawson hoped to establish three separate coastal bases on the continent and a fourth, primarily to act as a radio relay station, on sub-Antarctic Macquarie Island. After landing a party of five on Macquarie, the *Aurora* pushed south through heavy seas towards an alien coast. She reached pack ice at the end of December but land was not sighted for another week.

Forced well west of its intended landfall, the expedition finally located a broad bay on 8 January 1912, which Mawson named Commonwealth Bay in commemoration of Australia's nationhood.

Ice was everywhere. Mawson remarked that "here was an ice age in all earnestness; a picture of northern Europe during the Great Ice Age some 50,000 years ago ..."[7] Bare rock rather than glacial ice was what the men now craved – somewhere to build a hut ready for the rapidly approaching winter. Their wishes were soon realized when they happened on a small peninsula with its own miniature land-locked harbour. A suitable site for the hut lay only 50 metres from the shore. The momentousness of the occasion was not lost on Mawson who later stated that "the Sun shone gloriously in a blue sky as we stepped ashore on a charming ice-quay, the first to set foot on the Antarctic continent [within] a distance of about two thousand miles."[8]

With the brief summer almost over, plans for three bases were abandoned. Two parties were merged at what Mawson called Cape Denison (after a Sydney patron), while the *Aurora* was dispatched westward a further 2,500 kilometres. A month later, seven men landed on the ice off Queen Mary Land, under the command of Shackleton expedition veteran Frank Wild. It had been a close-run thing, with the party thwarted by near continuous ice cliffs. In desperation they established their base on the floating ice shelf. Any anxiety was unfounded and the hut they built – now long consigned to the sea – served them well as they came and went, exploring over 500 kilometres of difficult coastal terrain.

Back at Cape Denison, a prefabricated living hut and workshop were built and by January's end eighteen men had taken shelter from the atrocious gales that blew with mounting ferocity as the summer waned. All too quickly the party realized that the local geography conspired against them. They had inadvertently built their home in a raging river of wind. The already furious winds draining off the polar plateau accelerated at a terrifying pace as they funnelled uninterrupted down the broad gully behind the camp. During May 1912 the *average* wind speed for Cape Denison was recorded at just over 47 knots. Recent data has confirmed Cape Denison to be the windiest place on the entire planet close to sea level.

But the hut stood firm, providing a base from which much was achieved in the name of science and exploration by Mawson and his young party. It proved a haven for longer than first envisaged. After the deaths of two sledging companions and his own herculean lone

Fig. 1. Midwinter Dinner, Cape Dennison 1912. Photographer Frank Hurley

Fig. 2. Out in the blizzard, Cape Dennison 1912. Photographer Frank Hurley

struggle back to Cape Denison, Mawson just missed relief by the *Aurora* in February 1913. With six remaining expeditioners, he was forced to endure a second winter. In all, the AAE managed to explore more than 6,500 kilometres of Antarctic coast and ice cap before finally returning home, in early 1914. Shortly after, Mawson was knighted on a visit to London, but with the calamity of war just months away, the sweet taste of success was not destined to linger.

Two years earlier, as the Cape Denison quarters were being established, a shattered Scott and four companions struggled to their deaths after being usurped at the pole by Amundsen. The myth of spectacular ambition transfigured to glorious failure that now enshrouded Scott suited the psyche of an Empire spoiling for a fight. The AAE's achievements were largely eclipsed in the popular imagination, even in Australia. Mawson's success as a leader and organizer did not earn him fame through the epitaph of foolhardy misadventure that followed the deaths of the likes of Burke and Wills – perhaps Australia's equivalent of the Scott legend. He was in a sense too successful. Patrician, if not by birth but by achievement, Mawson is obviously as far removed from the folk hero and anti-establishment figure in the Ned Kelly mould as is possible. Such comparisons border on the absurd.

Yet in the history of Australian exploration, there are parallels. Ernest Giles and Augustus Gregory were arguably the two most successful nineteenth-century European explorers of the Australian continent, yet their fame is eclipsed in the modern imagination by the hapless Burke and Wills, or the ill-fated Ludwig Leichhardt. Perhaps also time and place play a part in the placement of Mawson in the pantheon of Australian exploration. The mythology that has grown around the vanquished explorer, swallowed up by a hostile and merciless desert located just over the geographic shoulder of a coastal dwelling populace has all the force of a searing north westerly wind on a summer's day in Adelaide, Melbourne or Sydney. The notion of hostility found at our continent's heart is perpetuated by deeds of long ago that linger in the national psyche. These were obviously more palpable than the heroic feats of Antarctic explorers separated from their countrymen by many thousands of kilometres of ocean .

Barely a year passed between the eventual return to Australia of the AAE in early 1914 and the landing at Gallipoli. The deeds of fit young men pitted against nature's worst in Antarctica were soon overwhelmed by the tragedies of war. The idea of nationhood forged through collective sacrifice was implicit in the Gallipoli campaign and provided the new Commonwealth with the exemplar of the citizen soldier, the hero giving all for king, country and Empire on a foreign field. Mawson's lone, dogged refusal to be swallowed up by defeat, whilst very much in the ANZAC mould, is but the story of one, puny man beside the patriotic force of many.

As could be expected of the nation's finest, the ranks of the AAE were readily transposed to those of the first AIF. Robert Bage, regular soldier on secondment to the AAE as astronomer and assistant magnetician, was among the fallen at Gallipoli, and Leslie Blake, cartographer, was killed in Flanders in the last week of the war. On the back of the door to one of the scientific observatories at Cape Denison, Bage left a tragically poignant note for future visitors that could almost be taken as an unwitting epitaph. It ended with the words "good luck and a speedy release. R.B. 18.12.13." In less than two years the young man was dead. One can only hope that his release came quickly.

Mawson himself was a keen supporter of the war effort, seeing the Germans as going beyond the bounds of decency and fair play in such actions as the sinking of the *Lusitania* and the deployment of poison gas. Through the second half of 1915 he organized the pro-conscription campaign in South Australia and then sailed for England seeking war work appropriate to his talents. Mawson ended the war with the honorary rank of major, involved in coordinating the supply of high explosives, petroleum and chemical weapons to the allies.

With the war over, Mawson returned to Australia and the laborious demands of completing the AAE scientific reports. In time, the reports would bear permanent witness to the AAE as ranking among those of the greatest of polar expeditions. The expedition gave Australia the authority to aspire to a prominent geo-political standing in matters Antarctic. Mawson argued publicly that Australia should make its own territorial bid for Antarctic territory as part of the Treaty of Versailles. Other nations were also stirring. In 1924 France made a claim to a slice of Antarctica directly to the south of Australia in recollection of the voyage of nineteenth-century explorer Dumont d'Urville. Around the same time, Norwegian whaling and scientific activity increased in the seas around Antarctica and a claim was made for land and waters between 20× W and 60× E. This in part overlapped British claims dating back nearly a century. Australia decided to take action and in 1928 Britain and New Zealand joined in promoting an expedition to assert territorial rights to large swathes of the Antarctic. Mawson was appointed leader and J.K. Davis (formerly in command of the *Aurora*) captain of the expedition's ship. Over the summers of 1929–30 and 1930–31, the British Australian and New Zealand Antarctic Research Expeditions (BANZARE) cruised southern waters. Flag waving and research did not ride easily among the pack ice and the two voyages were not entirely successful. However, as a result of BANZARE, an Order in Council of the British Parliament in 1933 asserted the King's sovereignty over an area south of 60×S and between 160×E and 45×E (excluding the French claim to Adélie Land). The British claim soon passed to Australia with the assent to the Commonwealth Acceptance Act in 1936.

Mawson went on from the AAE to a distinguished academic career. In 1921 he became professor of Geology and Mineralogy at the University of Adelaide, a post he held for the rest of his life. He maintained a strong interest in the Antarctic and was a prime mover in the establishment of a permanent Australian presence after the Second World War.

And of Hurley? Joining the AAE was definitely his big break. The restless, impulsive Hurley combined an almost foolhardy sense of adventure with a passion for his craft. Many of his images of the AAE exude a youthful sense of daring, as both photographer and subject pit themselves against the forces of nature. They display an ennoblement of the human spirit through stoic disregard for adversity – a theme that recurred in Hurley's work throughout his life. After accompanying the *Aurora* on its relief voyage of 1914, Hurley headed for another extreme – remote north-west Queensland. But his newly established reputation was never far behind and he soon earned a summons delivered by Aboriginal tracker – "be in Buenos Aires within five weeks." Sir Ernest Shackleton wanted Hurley to join his forthcoming Imperial Trans-Antarctic Expedition. When events went horribly awry and the expedition vessel *Endurance* was first imprisoned then crushed by the pack ice of the Weddell Sea, Hurley's skills as both seasoned adventurer and gifted photographer came to the fore. The resultant images of the demise of the *Endurance* and the ordeal that followed are Hurley's finest – a defiant record of triumph against overwhelming odds. In extracting the last ounce of drama from his subject, Hurley often made composite images – sunbursts heightening drama, contrasting with skies for powerful effect. Crude by modern standards, they show that the camera does in fact lie and did so a long time before computer enhancement. Hurley further refined the technique in 1917 as he witnessed the carnage of Flanders as an official war photographer.

In a life of innumerable adventures, all seemingly piled one after the other, Hurley went on to record the next war as an official photographer, journeying through Central Australia, Java and still mysterious New Guinea. Predictably, Hurley was there again with Mawson for the two BANZARE cruises, recording a claim to an area greater than Australia itself. His latter years were spent productively, if a little more sedately, producing travel books, calendars and returning to the roots of his craft, scenic postcards, which sold in abundance. Hurley died in Sydney in 1962, aged 76.

On the wall of the darkroom at Cape Denison, Hurley inscribed in pencil in neat capitals the words, NEAR ENOUGH IS NOT GOOD ENOUGH. Here was a man whose life exploits and photographic legacy bore close witness to that rather Victorian admonition. To us, they may seem quaint and old fashioned and indeed they echo much of the sentiment of Hurley's time, where personal morality, stoicism and a sense of duty were directed to the service of a greater good – that of one's country and ultimately that of the Empire. It was a time when the chivalric ideal fitted well with Hurley's own outlook. As a result of his energy and talent, Hurley was present at the great and calamitous events of the first half of the twentieth century. As well as witnessing the twilight of the imperial age through the heroic struggle for the seventh continent, he recorded the beginning of the end for undisturbed indigenous life in Australia and New Guinea and recorded a world again racked by war. Hurley's sense of the moment or its place in history may not have always matched the heights of his technique and artistry, but against a background of such events lies the dramatic story of an adventurous spirit adrift on an ocean of change.

Tapping a vein shared by Hurley's darkroom words, Mawson inscribed a copy of *The Home of the Blizzard* for his old friend Edgeworth David. His annotation acknowledges the Canadian poet Robert Service – a favourite of Mawson's judging by the frequency with which he is quoted. The words, say much about the romance of the heroic era and are very much in sympathy with Hurley's imagery and the ideals of sacrifice. For Service, one could almost substitute Kipling, laureate of Empire:

Perhaps when on my printed page you look,
Your fancies by the fireside may go homing
To that land where bravely you endured.

And if perchance you hear the silence calling,
The frozen music of star-yearning heights,
Or, dreaming, see the seines of silver trawling
Across the sky's abyss on vasty nights,
You may recall that sweep of savage splendour,
That land that measures each man at his worth,
And feel in memory, half fierce, half tender,
The brotherhood of men that know the South.
Apologies to Service. [9]

Mawson and Hurley lived to see a new generation of Australians pitted against the mighty forces of Antarctica, and today, Australia maintains a permanent national presence in the region of more than 50 years standing. Life in the South may no longer be the romantic "brotherhood" of the heroic age but after a century of meeting Antarctica's challenge, Australia enjoys an impressive reputation for its research effort, environmental stewardship and contribution to the Antarctic Treaty System. Geographic conquest and territorial ambition have given way to wider concerns that address the very future of life on the planet.

Through the quest for knowledge of Antarctica we still share a direct connection to the bold aspirations of those few men who knew the heroic age, first-hand. It is to be hoped that this link will see the "savage splendour" long endure. Today, we are the inheritors of a polar heritage of unrivalled breadth, one born in the very earliest years of our nation's united history. As part of a larger imperial endeavour, it is nonetheless a distinctly Australian heritage, imbued with intelligent enquiry, resourcefulness, tenacity, innovation and sheer courage. Before the calamitous events of war that are usually espoused as catalysts of the Australian ethos, a tradition of mateship and sacrifice was being hard won on the endless expanse of Antarctic ice. Exemplifying what we might like to regard as "Australian values," our Antarctic history surely deserves greater prominence in the national consciousness and identity.

This paper is based on a lecture delivered by the author at the Canadian Museum of Nature on 6 February 2001 in accompaniment to the photographic exhibition " *.that sweep of savage splendour ..". A Century of Australians in Antarctica.*

Notes

1. Reader's Digest, *Antarctica: Great Stories from the Frozen Continent* (Sydney: Reader's Digest, 1985), 77.
2. Ibid., 135.
3. Philip Ayers, *Mawson, A Life* (Melbourne: Melbourne University Press, 1999), 29.
4. Douglas Mawson, *The Home of the Blizzard*, Facsimile (Adelaide: Wakefield Press, 1996), xvii.
5. Ibid., xviii.
6. Ibid., 15.
7. Ibid., 40.
8. Ibid., 41.
9. Jonathan Chester, *Going to Extremes: Project Blizzard and Australia's Antarctic Heritage* (Sydney: Doubleday, 1986), 10.

7

Women as Citizens in Canada

CAROLINE ANDREW

It is impossible to understand the place of women as citizens in Canada without understanding the moment of women's inscription as citizens. This moment, and the terms of inscription, have marked and continue to mark the role of women in politics in Canada. The objective of this chapter is double: describe this moment of inscription and then attempt to indicate how this plays itself out in current public policy, in explaining why some areas of Canadian public policy have taken greater, and better, account of women than some others.

As Alan Cairns has written, "citizenship has both a vertical and a horizontal dimension."[1] It refers to the way both individuals and groups of individuals are linked to the state, the rights and responsibilities that are seen as defining membership and participation in that particular political unit. At the same time, citizenship also refers to the way all members of a civic community define their common belonging to that community. Another important lesson from the recent studies of citizenship is that "citizenship is a social construction."[2] This is why it is essential to understand the ways in which women were understood, and understood themselves, to be playing a public role and to be participants in Canadian society. The notion of citizenship evolves over time but the moment of initial definition is important; it marks the way that groups relate to the state and to each other. Public policies then institutionalize relationships and frame the context for on-going understandings. As Margaret Little says in her study of the mothers' allowance program in Ontario:

> By exploring the "maternal origins" of the Canadian welfare state we can examine the important roles women played as lobbyists for such policies, and the manner in which women were defined and incorporated into the state as citizens and as clients.[3]

Even in the modern understanding of citizenship as involving a complex network of social, political and civil dimensions, the obtaining of the right to vote is a significant moment in the move to full citizenship. In the case of Canada, women first get the vote in 1916 when Manitoba, Alberta and Saskatchewan extend the suffrage to women. By 1922, women can vote across Canada, except in Quebec and the then British colony of Newfoundland. The federal government extended its franchise to women in a peculiar way, according in 1917 the vote first to women nurses serving in the war, then to wives, widows, mothers, sisters and daughters of those serving in the armed forces. Only in 1918 were women as women, and not as potential supporters of conscription, given the vote in federal elections.

The Moment of Inscription

The crucial period for the definition of women's citizenship in Canada is the period from the 1880s to the 1920s. The vote comes at the end of this period, a period of considerable social change and social reform. It is in seeing the role women played in the public realm and the ways in which this role was constructed that it is possible to understand the inscription of women as citizens in Canada. To simplify greatly, one can think of two definitions by which women could get recognized as citizens: as "mothers" playing a role different from those of other social actors, or as "humans" playing an identical role to that of other citizens. In Canada, women were seen more as mothers than as humans. They were seen in this way by the major social and political actors of the period and this was also true for the majority of the organized and active women. Maternal or social feminism was stronger in Canada than was equality feminism.

This is not a new argument in Canada. Carol Bacchi, in *Liberation Deferred?* argued that Canadian suffragettes had been conservative, interested in protecting white middle-class values and imposing a middle-class family model. The early suffrage movement had been feminist but it was taken over by the social reformers.

> These people flooded into the suffrage societies and took over the leadership of the movement. The reasons they offered for giving women a vote were very different from those used by the feminists. Essentially woman suffrage suggested a simple means of strengthening the stable part of the population. Women were considered to be religious, pure, the "harbingers of civilisation" and the protectors of the home. Their help in controlling social deviants would be welcome. Moreover, the reformers wanted to strengthen the family, which they considered the foundation of their new social order, and believed that woman suffrage would double its representation. For these reasons women were invited into the "public sphere" but only in a very limited capacity. The vote meant simply a public voice for their domestic virtues.[4]

Joan Sangster also underlines the importance of maternal feminism in the suffrage movement, but her interpretation insists more on the variety of views as to why the vote was important.

> There is no doubt that the vote was an important emblem of women's initiation into the body politic, symbolizing women's emergence from reliance on a male family member to full rights of citizenship in the public sphere. The struggle for the right to vote was undertaken by different groups of women across Canada, groups that did not always share the same view of women's place in society or even a rationale for why women needed the vote. Some women, largely from middle-class backgrounds and often referred to as social or maternal feminists, argued that women's distinct role as homemakers and mothers and their commitment to family and moral issues – such as temperance – would provide an important antidote to male political perspectives. ... Others argued decisively that women were the intellectual and social equals of men and deserved the same rights. ... Still other women, generally of the working class and often socialists, supported suffrage and advocated women's "emancipation" but they saw the vote as a means of achieving social equality for working people, not just women. They were sceptical that the vote, without more fundamental economic change, would usher in equality for women.[5]

And, finally, this is the view of the first wave of the women's movement in *Canadian Women: A History*.

> As Canadian women organized to change society, they found it neces-
> sary to defend explicitly the goals they had always taken for granted
> ... The arguments they used in response were the basis of the "woman
> movement," incorporating the two perspectives that continue to be
> influential today. The first of these, and the most characteristic of
> Canadian feminism, was a "maternal" or "social" feminism, based on
> woman's role as guardian of the home. Arguing that women had spe-
> cial experience and values that would be crucial to society, if society
> would only allow them free rein, women activists insisted on their
> responsibility to establish order and well-being, not just for their fam-
> ilies, but for the country ... At the same time, a version of feminist
> beliefs often called "equal rights" or "equity" feminism focused more
> directly on arguments of simple justice. It was a viewpoint that
> stressed how much women resembled men, and how unjust it was
> that they should have fewer rights. As human beings, women were
> endowed with souls and abilities, but they were barred by custom
> and law from participating in public life. In such a context the vote
> became the symbol of citizenship.[6]

These long quotations serve to illustrate the differing interpretations as to the dominance of maternal feminism in Canada. They do
less to indicate the activity that generates this worldview. What exactly
were these women doing? To get a better idea of the ways in which
women's citizenship was constructed in this period from the 1880s to
the 1920s, it is important to look at some of the areas in which women
took the lead in social reform.

Women were the predominant workers in the settlement houses
that established themselves in the central city areas in the early years of
the twentieth century.[7] These settlement houses, introduced to Canada
from Britain via the United States, offered services to the urban immigrant poor, particularly to women and children, as part of a process of
Canadianization. They offered a variety of services, "including day-
care and employment referrals, medical and dental clinics, English-language instruction, high school upgrading and university preparatory
classes, lunch rooms for working women, Well Baby Clinics and pure
milk depots, and, prior to the expansion of public health departments
in the latter part of the 1910s, district nursing services."[8] This organiza-

tion of pilot projects, to be taken over by other public agencies if successful, was also a strategy used by the local councils of women.

These local councils sprung up across Canada, particularly after the founding of the National Council of Women of Canada, in 1894. By the end of 1894, local councils existed in Toronto, Montreal, London, Hamilton, Ottawa, Quebec City, Winnipeg and Kingston.[9] The Montreal Local Council organized pure milk depots, parks and playgrounds, published material on infant care and public health, and pressured the city to set up the first public bath and hire female factory inspectors.[10] Julia Drummond, first president of the Montreal Local Council, was then active in the establishment, in 1902, of the Parks and Playground Association with the double objective of protecting open space and developing playgrounds.[11] By 1919 the Parks and Playground Association was operating five playgrounds in the summer while putting pressure on the municipal government to set up a Department of Parks and Playgrounds. The city contributed financially to the playgrounds ($10,000 by 1913) but municipal responsibility for the service took place only after the Second World War.

Women were also active in setting up specialized hospitals for children. Both the Hospital for Sick Children in Toronto and St Justine in Montreal were created by women. In Toronto the women pushed for state financing almost from the very beginning whereas in Montreal this happened much later on and with more consciousness of the loss of women's power that would occur with state control.

The importance of the social role played by mothers is also clear in the campaign to introduce domestic science into the schools. With immigration, industrialization and urbanization, it was seen as crucial to formalize the training of working class girls to acquire the skills needed for successful motherhood. Adelaide Hoodless was the leader in Canada of the move to introduce domestic science in the schools. She was also one of the founders of the Women's Institutes, of the National Council of Women of Canada, of the YMCA and of the Victoria Order of Nurses.

The YWCA's offered services to urban working women. The first Canadian branch was set up in St John in 1870, followed by Toronto (1873), Montreal (1874), Quebec City (1875) and by 1893, a national association. Strong-Boag describes the maternalism of the Y's.

Like other women's organizations, the "Y" emphasized the importance of family life for the Dominion. The girl had to be protected

because she represented a future mother, the guardian of a household. Summer and holiday camps, recreation and study programmes
and urban housing for working women were all intended to guide
girls into a disciplined and moral womanhood.[12]

And, of course, the prohibition movement was one of the areas of
women's public activity. The Canadian leader of the Women's Christian Temperance Union (WCTU) was Letitia Youmans. The WCTU was
in favour of women's suffrage: "The liquor sellers are not afraid of our
conventions, but they are afraid of our ballots."[13] Abolishing the sale of
alcohol was seen as an essential step to the improvement of the living
conditions of the urban working class.

All of these areas illustrate the intersections of gender, class and
race interests of the women active in the reform movement.

> In coming together, these women were motivated by, among other
> factors, a sense of the restrictions placed on them by the ideology of
> "separate spheres," a sense of sisterhood in relation to the conditions
> endured by working class women as well as an essentially class-
> determined sense of social concern for the unsettled and potentially
> chaotic conditions of urban existence.[14]

Linda Kealey's description of maternal feminism illustrates this same
set of intersecting realities.

> Maternal feminism, then, was the result of the blending of several tra-
> ditions. As an ideology and rationale for women's participation in the
> public sphere it arose from a middle-class milieu in which women
> had come to question what they saw as the frivolity of upper-class
> social life and the viciousness and misery of working-class existence.
> Drawing initially on the support of the churches, women became
> involved in reform. Many were inspired by the social gospel attempt
> to make religion relevant to the mass of working people and immi-
> grants. Nevertheless neither the churches nor the reformers managed
> to shed racist attitudes toward non-Anglo-Saxons. The social and nat-
> ural sciences of the day supported the notions of British superiority as
> well as of the nurturing qualities of women. These nurturing qualities
> were an important aspect of the professions in which middle-class
> women were employed. The shaping of these new areas (like social
> work, nursing and librarianship) according to maternal feminist

norms reinforced the power of maternal feminism in the larger reform and suffrage movement.[15]

This predominance of maternal feminism can also be seen in the reaction of the state to the changing environment created by industrialization, urbanization and immigration. Jane Ursel describes the ways in which the early factory legislation dealt with women.

> The manifest concern of the early factory legislation was the improvement of the condition of labour. However, beneath this manifest goal, there was a more fundamental and determinative concern – the coordination of the productive-reproductive needs of society ... As architects of this legislation, reformers and commissioners clearly had a one-dimensional definition of womanhood – woman as mother ... The most significant omission, however, was the legislation's failure to address the most compelling problem for women workers – the wage disparity between men and women.[16]

Another indication from state policies of the strength of maternal feminism came in the 1920s, after the right to vote had been granted to women, with the wave of legislation introducing mother's allowances. Legislation was first introduced in Manitoba (1916), followed by Saskatchewan (1917), Alberta (1919), British Columbia and Ontario (both in 1920).[17] This legislation was the result of pressure from women's organizations but also a clear recognition that government felt this legislation would be popular with their new group of voters – women.

It is therefore this period of social activism that sets the stage for women acquiring the right to vote in Canada and, in 1929, the legal status as persons.[18] The 1880s to 1920s was a period marked by a whole variety of separate but interrelated movements that can be seen as reactions to the changes being brought about by industrialization, urbanization and immigration. As has been shown, women played very important roles in these movements, sometimes in public and sometimes behind the scenes, and it is this activity that defines the moment of inscription of women's citizenship in Canada.

It is a citizenship defined primarily in terms of women as mothers, bringing particular and different talents to the public realm and to the political system. Women's more social orientation came about because of the role they played as mother; they were more concerned about the difficulties faced by poor children and more willing to see the state as the instrument that should act for the collectivity. The organizations created by women argued in terms of the role of women as mothers and so did other major social groups – it was therefore the vision of the organized women's movement and, in addition, a vision shared largely by the rest of society. This is not to argue that there were no alternative voices but that it was the vision of maternal, or social, feminism that was dominant. For this reason the public role of women was seen as one based on difference – on the political values of women's particular role in society.

Current Public Policy

The importance of understanding the ways in which women in Canada became citizens is of more than historical interest; this initial inscription plays itself out in terms of current Canadian public policy. The argument here is that Canadian public policy has taken a gender perspective into consideration on some issues more than on others and that part of the explanation lies in that moment of inscription into citizenship – public policy questions that play upon visions of women as having particular characteristics that relate to their role as mothers get taken more seriously in Canada than do issues that are equality-based. The comparison that will be developed here is between policies in regard to violence against women, an area that Canada has, on an international comparison, taken seriously, and policies with regard to equal pay, an area where Canada does not fare so well.

The argument is not that everything post-1920 is unimportant and that nothing can change after the moment of inscription. It is rather that the initial moment is important because it defines the ways in which the state interacts with women and the ways in which public policy defines the problems, and therefore the solutions, it should be acting upon. It sets a framework that can, and does, evolve but the evolution tends to be incremental and therefore reflects the initial understanding.

In addition, in Canada, the currents that have marked the organized women's movement have both weakened and strengthened the dominance of maternal or social feminism. Second wave feminism in Canada has probably had a stronger strand of equal-rights feminism and, to this extent, acted to lessen the dominance of maternal feminism. However the recent debates about diversities within feminism, and particularly the emphasis on the inclusion of racialized women, has meant a diversification of the vision of women and, to some extent, the reintroduction of women as mothers as one of the positive visions of women in Canada.

It is also important to underline the political ambiguity, or polyvalence, of maternal feminism. There is a left, and a right, version of maternal feminism. The left version links to the egalitarian thread of Canadian society – that public policy should be primarily directed to reducing the inequalities in Canadian society – whereas the right version is that certain groups need to be protected, and also controlled, in order that the overall structure of society be maintained. These two visions are of course interrelated; concern for the poverty of poor women leads both to wanting to ensure that they have more money and to helping them behave more like the middle-class so as to get more money. Putting the needs of poor women above those of all women can be both egalitarian and a reflection of a class-based attitude of "noblesse oblige."

This ambiguity certainly plays itself out in relation to public policies on violence against women. They appeal to a vision of women as needing protection and as being vulnerable and of society's role as providing this protection. But, at the same time, these policies also reflect the organized strength of the women's movement and the understanding that violence against women is one of the important factors that contributes to the poverty of women and to their marginalization and that acting to eliminate violence both empowers women and improves their position of equality within Canadian society.

It is not the intention here to present a detailed analysis of Canadian policy in regards to violence against women. It is an area that has been actively addressed by federal, provincial and municipals levels of government. In general, the major policy thrusts have been to support women and their children who have been victims of violence, through the creation and the financing of a network of transition houses but also through counselling programs, special court facilities, and public education activities. There have been policies directed towards the male perpetrators of violence, including counselling, but also through the criminalization of domestic violence, but these have been less important than the policies aimed at putting women (and children) into protective environments. The funding of transition houses was stimulated by federal-provincial agreements and these transition houses were usually the result of the local activity of women's groups. Negotiations with the state in relation to financing take place between provincial government and transition houses and, as Masson[19] has shown, the results of these negotiations are not predetermined but reflect levels of organization and of mobilization.

Even the municipal level of government has been active on questions of women's safety and security[20] and, in some provinces, on issues of domestic violence as well. This activity has led to grants to women's groups for pilot projects in areas such as counselling and public education and, as well, to activity relating to safety audits and to planning for safer cities.

Compared on an international basis, Canada has taken the question of violence against women very seriously. It is certainly a policy area where women are seen as different rather than identical. It appeals to an egalitarian vision of Canadian society – as a fundamental right to live a life free from violence but also as an understanding of the links among violence against women, women's poverty and women's marginalization. At the same time it a conservative vision of Canadian society – that women need looking after and that their protection is a collective responsibility of the whole community.

On the other hand, Canada does not do so well in international comparisons when it comes to equal pay. Jackson gives some comparative material which indicates the relatively poor standing of Canada.

> The existence of wage floors and the wage compression which results from collective bargaining have been very significant in promoting greater equality between women and men in the labour market and in the wider society. In liberal labour markets (the U.S., Canada, the UK) employment rates for women are high, but beyond (limited) public services, women are disproportionately employed in low wage, non-union jobs in smaller firms in private services. In some European countries, employment rates in public services tend to be higher and, most importantly, the quality of jobs in the small firms, private services sector is directly raised by labour market regulation.[21]

The reasons for the relatively large gap between men's and women's incomes in Canada are obviously complex. They relate, as Jackson's quotation indicates, to the structure of the Canadian economy but also to the ways public policy has tried to influence this structure. This, is turn, relates to the state's political will to act in this area and also to the interrelated capacity of mobilization of civil society and public opinion. It would seem more difficult in Canada to create a strong and visible coalition around a policy that is to treat equals equally than a policy directed to favouring certain groups of unequals.

Conclusion

The comparison of women as citizens in Canada and Australia is a broad-ranging and complex question. It relates to the structures of state institutions, but also to the profile of the economy and of civil society. What this chapter has attempted to argue is that one of the fundamental dimensions to this comparison is an understanding of the ways in which women became citizens, of the terms of inscription of their citizenship. In Canada, women became citizens as mothers, as part of the vision of maternal feminism that their participation in public life was needed because they represented different values from men, values of caring, of nurturing and of a concern for the social conditions of poor women and poor children. Women's full citizenship would improve Canadian society. The chapter has further argued the contemporary relevance of this vision by comparing the serious nature of state intervention in the area of violence against women with the less successful public policy results in terms of women's income. Canadian society continues to favour interventions that see women as different, as in greater need of protection because of a vulnerability that relates to their maternal role. Women's citizenship in Canada is not only as mothers, but it is as mothers.

Notes

1. Alan Cairns, " Introduction," in *Citizenship, Diversity and Pluralism: Canadian and Comparative Perspectives*, eds. Alan Cairns et al. (Montreal: McGill-Queens University Press, 1999), 4.

2. Jane Jenson and Susan Phillips, "Regime shift: New Citizenship Practices in Canada," *International Journal of Canadian Studies* 14 (1996): 113.

3. Margaret Little, "The blurring of boundaries," *Studies in Political Economy* 47 (1995): 89–109.

4. Carol Lee Bacchi, *Liberation Deferred? The Ideas of the English-Canadian Suffragettes, 1877–1918* (Toronto: University of Toronto Press, 1983), 147.

5. Sharon Cook, Lorna McLean and Kate O'Rourke, *Framing our Past: Canadian Women's History in the Twentieth Century* (Montreal: McGill-Queens University Press, 2001), 201–203.

6. Alison Prentice et al., *Canadian Women: A History* (Toronto: Harcourt Brace Jovanovich, 1988), 169.

7. Cook, McLean and O'Rourke, *Framing our Past: Canadian Women's History in the Twentieth Century,* 222–227.

8. Ibid., 227.

9. Veronica Strong-Boag, " 'Setting the Stage': National Organization and the Women's Movement in the Late Nineteenth Century" in *The Neglected Majority,* eds. Susan Mann Trofimenkoff and Alison Prentice (Toronto: McClelland and Stewart, 1977), 99.

10. Yolande Pinard, " Les débuts du mouvement des femmes à Montréal, 1893–1902" in *Travailleuses et féministes,* eds. Marc Lavigne and Yolande Pinard (Montréal: Boréal Express, 1983), 189–193.

11. Jeanne M. Wolfe and G. Strachan, "Practical Idealism: Women in Urban Reform, Julia Drummond and the Montreal Parks and Playgrounds Association," in *Life Spaces,* eds. C. Andrew and B.M. Milroy (Vancouver: UBC Press, 1988), 73.

12. Strong-Boag, "'Setting the Stage': National Organization and the Women's Movement in the Late Nineteenth Century," 92.

13. Ibid., 90.

14. Caroline Andrew, "Women and the Welfare State," *Canadian Journal of Political Science* XVII; 4 (1984): 669–683.

15. Linda Kealey, ed., *A Not Unreasonable Claim: Women and Reform in Canada 1880s–1920s.* (Toronto: Women's Press, 1979), 13.

16. Jane Ursel, *Private Lives, Public Policy: 100 years of State Intervention in the Family* (Toronto: Womens' Press, 1992), 91–94.

17. Prentice, et al. *Canadian Women: A History,* 209.

18. Ibid., 282.

19. Dominique Masson, *With and Despite the State: Doing Women's Movement Politics in Local Service Groups in the 1980s in Quebec* (Ph.D. thesis, Ottawa: Carleton University, 1998).

20. Caroline Andrew, "Getting Women's issues on the Municipal Agenda: Violence against Women," in *Gender in Urban Research,* eds. Judith Garber and Robyne Turner (Thousand Oaks: Sage, 1995).

21. Andrew Jackson, *Why we don't have to choose between Social Justice and Economic Growth: the myth of the equity/efficiency trade off* (Ottawa: Canadian Council of Social Development, 2000), 21–22.

8

Citizens of the Fifth Continent: Unexpected Culture in the Late Nineteenth Century

JEFF BROWNRIGG

In a collection of essays entitled *Mistaken Identity, Multiculturalism and the Demise of Nationalism in Australia* Stephen Castles argues:

> Australia grew as part of the British Empire. Unlike the USA, India or Britain's other far-flung possessions, Australia never managed a decent independence movement let alone a liberation struggle. Australia was made a nation by an Act of the British Parliament in 1901. The creation of a nation in a struggle for independence is usually the pre-eminent moment for the definition of national character, language, culture and myths. Australia has missed out on this ... [1]

In expanding and justifying their position, the editors of *Mistaken Identity* also confidently claim that Australia:

> has been racist, justifying genocide and exclusionism, and denying the role of non-British migrants. It has been sexist, ignoring the role of women in national development and justifying their subordinate position. It has idealized the role of the "common man" in a situation of growing inequality and rigid class division. [2]

These traits are of very long standing in the Australian psyche and form a part of a more complex and often richer tapestry than Australian historians have routinely woven. That is not, of course, an indication that I personally approve of or believe in such things as racism or genocide.[3] But they are, inevitably, indelible facts about Australia's past that no amount of forelock-tugging to political correctness can expunge. We ignore them at our peril. The comfortable reality for most Australians from the first half of the nineteenth century has been an urban ethos increasingly far enough away from the daily trials of Australia's indigenous people for the progress of their actual plight to have been largely invisible. White Australia and exclusionism linger from the nineteenth century, transmuted into frightened ignorance which has sometimes found a voice in the substantial, opportunistic politics that thrives on fear. And it is an attitude buried just beneath the surface.

In this paper I will pursue one of the issues that Castles et al. raise concerning the role that women, in particular, have played both at home and abroad; especially that group of women who became internationally eminent and conspicuously representative of Australia on the world opera and concert stage after about 1870.

It was this group that first took Australia to the world, becoming the first internationally conspicuous Australians. At the time when national interest in these singing women was at its peak, the late 1890s, an effort by Australian Catholics to supplant a Protestant diva with a Catholic aspirant to her throne produced a battle royal. No blood was shed, but the social pages of newspapers whose journalists and editors were drawn up along sectarian lines generated one of the most vigorous exchanges short of actual violence yet seen in the Australian colonies.[4]

The most difficult, interesting and misunderstood person in this group was the diva Nellie Melba, daughter of a Scot who was committed to his Kirk. In pursuing nineteenth century women in general and Melba in particular, substantial detail of her time is revealed; the richness and complexity that we are prone to ignore in drawing pictures of another age. I will examine the idea that Australia missed out on those "pre-eminent moments" that might have made her a man.

Also, I will touch upon the idea of the British and non-British caste of Australian culture. One way or another, a few years at Eton or in the Guards or spirited meetings behinds closed doors in the damp cellars where revolutions are hatched and nations conceived might have created a unique set of "national feelings." And while such a direction might have been a serious option in the early 1850s when the New South Wales well-to-do called for the formation of a colonial clone of the House of Lords, a so called "bunyip aristocracy," it ceased to be an option after the colonial parliaments were formed in the mid to late 1850s.[5] But colonial mandarins continued to crave British Imperial honours, upheld the model of the Westminster system of government and called Britain home. Even the colonial Catholic Irish accepted knighthoods with alacrity and pleasure regardless of the fact that late in the century some were flummoxed that the Australian colonies had practiced home rule for half a century while Ireland remained closely tied by the Act of Union.

The situation for Australians, especially their own definition of who they were and what they wanted, was not black and white. And by the time that the Sydney *Bulletin* was indulging the easily digested generalities about the ascendancy of the bloke, creating as it did so an attractive, enduring but false stereotype, the chosen model Australian was already an anachronism based upon a myth.

What sort of Australianess, then, did Australians take to the world especially when they went "home" to Britain and were recognized as different." I need to explain and then set aside much that will need to remain in the background.

I accept as proven very little that has been written about Australian identity: the male-centred myths of the 1890s that grew through World War One into the taciturn heroics of the pioneering-bushman-volunteer-infantryman who wandered during the depression and who consolidated in all of his actions the distinctive "bloke-iness" of Australian history, especially in the early years of the twentieth century.

I have proposed elsewhere that by neglecting a broader and more inclusive cultural history we have neglected what actually happened as Australia grew, including the emergence of an independent spirit (or a spirit of independence from Britain) and the recognition that European, American and Asian settlers in the Antipodes had, by the late nineteenth century and in the words of the Melbourne poet of the era, Bernard O'Dowd, established, in the south either a "millennial Eden" or "a new demesne for Mammon to infest." (O'Dowd is finally unsure.[6]) It was inevitable that European Australia, owing more to Britain than to other places, would draw on the customs and traditions that had been transported with those who came immediately after the invasion of 1788 and that these would include many things that were current and popular elsewhere, for example, in mainland Europe.

While twentieth-century commentators concentrated our attention on the old simplistic, congenial paradigm of convicts, settlers, squatters, gold rushes and World War One, they almost always missed the richness and variety of detail. It is there if you look closely and it is often surprising. The *Bulletin*, sceptical about the reasons for the Catholic Church's promotion of a "young convent girl," took up arms against all sorts of "superstition" wherever it appeared. In doing so it left a discernable trail of accusation and elucidation in some of these areas of unexpected cultural history. Together with its broadly anticlerical stance, the *Bulletin*, and other papers such as the *Truth*,[7] stigmatized quacks and fraudulent professors, some of whom were treading a fine line between science and faith and gobbledygook.

Take, for example, instances of the emergent science of psychology and the growth of two of its bastard children, paranormal psychology and mystical revelation. The Sydney salon of Nicol Drysdale Stenhouse[8] in the 1840s attracted (with a letter of introduction to Stenhouse) the son of the celebrated Scottish phrenologist George Combe who had recently analyzed the bumps on the skull of Robert Burns.[9] (Novelist George Eliot had her head shaved three times in order to better know herself and her propensities.) In the 1870s Alfred Deakin explored the spirit world and dabbled with the fringes of theosophy as well as writing passionate sonnets for his wife.[10]

At about the same time Henry Havelock Ellis taught for a couple of years at Sparkes Creek public school in New South Wales, reading the mystical philosophy of James Hinton and discovering his own vocation in medicine – especially in the study of human sexuality.[11] Often described as the English Freud, Ellis was, rather, a Freudian contemporary pursuing the same ends into the first decades of the twentieth century. (I will return to Ellis later.) In the 1920s a special pavilion was constructed at Balmoral in Sydney in preparation for the impending arrival of Christ. At that time Australia had the largest and best-endowed theosophical group in the world and its messianic predictions encompassed the arrival of Jiddu Krishnamurti who was expected to sail through Sydney Heads,[12] disembark at sea and walk across the water to Balmoral. As it happened Krishnamurti reneged, and by 1929 had renounced organised mysticism.

Of all the places in the world that the Second Coming might have occurred, the *Bulletin*'s Australia seems to be one of the least likely. Education had been "free, *secular* and compulsory" since the 1870s (the Victorian Act, 1872) and anti-clerical journals such as the *Bulletin* thrived from the 1890s, its readers sceptical about that other world probably to come.

But all of these things are connected to a pervasive climate of interest in such things. They are manifestations of fashion and culture and belief, in this case, belief that the rational methodologies of science might usefully intersect with the long accepted understanding of the Christian order of thing. And most of all they are the rich detail of the complex society that existed even in the early years of European settlement.

We have been taught that in the 1890s as the cultural climate contracted to focus upon those elements of national interest that the *Bulletin* journalists encouraged. (Sylvia Lawson's classic study *The Archibald Paradox* explores some of these elements.[13]) In fact, mainstream religious differences blended with other cultural elements, especially after the arrival from Ireland and Rome in 1884 of the Catholic Archbishop Moran. Sectarianism had simmered, probably from the earliest days of settlement at Sydney Cove, appearing from time to time in, for example, attempted assassinations[14] as well as exchanges of opinion from clerics of different creeds in the letters columns of the daily papers.[15]

But the most significant element of Australia's cultural history in the 1890s was the recognition of the soprano Dame Nellie Melba as the principal agent of international Australian profile.

Robert Garran, in his autobiography, relates a story he heard in London in the early 1920s. He recalls that a question was asked: "Who were the great and memorable Australians." His British interlocutor suggested three names in a hierarchical list: Melba, Victor Trumper and Sam Griffith. It seems reasonable to argue that this view was shared in Europe and, perhaps, in North America.[16]

Curiously Melba's pre-eminence was confirmed twice by Australians. The first recognition of her international standing came after triumphant opera debuts at La Monnaie in Brussels in 1886, and in Paris, London and New York. It was an unprecedented success for an Australian although she was not the first Australian singer to win acclaim abroad.

The second confirmation came as a result of the discovery of a need to ensure that she had a successor. A curious urgency seemed to infect Australian thinking in the later 1890s. Melba, who had not yet returned home from her overseas triumphs, must be replaced. It was at once a recognition of Melba's international stature and also a measure of acceptance of the bona fides of Australian musical culture, as it was expressed in singing.

The urbane and scholarly Archbishop Moran, keen to avoid any replication of an Irish belligerence in his new constituency, became patron to one who appeared to be the most credible candidate, after looking to his flock for a singer who might dislodge and replace Melba. This would, he hoped, create a Catholic triumph of similar dimensions to Melba's success and with similar potential for kudos at home and abroad. He had watched the development of the centenary of the 1798 Irish rebellion and its potential to politicize otherwise pacific members of his Church. His response was to desire cultural successes without the taint of actual violence. A Catholic weapon was required, one equipped with Melba-like vocal capabilities but not the supposed moral shortcomings of lady theatricals.

In 1899 Catholic and Protestant differences were thrown into sharp contrast by the emergence of Amy Castles, a Bendigo "convent girl" with a big voice who, the Catholic presses confidently trumpeted, would become the "New Melba."

As soon as an opportunity arose to score points for an unambiguously Catholic cause, the aggressive Catholic weekly the *Freemans Journal* began by pointing out some differences between Melba and Amy. Amy had, for example, received seventy-five pounds at a single Melbourne concert in 1899, largely provided by what the *Bulletin* called "those of her Faith." At her Melbourne Farewell thirteen years earlier, the *Freeman* curtly noted, Melba "received one guinea: enough for a pair of gloves and a cab." What followed was the most succinct statement of the obligation set for Amy.

> A prophecy! Amy Castles will follow in Nellie Melba's footsteps ... musically, not morally ... overtake her, and outshine her in Grand Opera.[17]

Almost inadvertently the *Freeman* had initiated the "Melba bashing" that would consolidate into an elaborate Australian indignation, initially among Catholics; later, it firmed into a national preoccupation. Australians soon appeared to love or to hate Melba, to account for her success in stories both grotesque and absurd. Even her voice it was said owed its purity and smooth production to the ingestion of semen, provided at the drop of a hat during performances by any male, usually the stagehands. Many of the Melba "stories" moved accountability for the exceptional quality of her singing and her voice away from Melba's own steely determination to more arbitrary forces thereby reducing a reliance on her personal skill and her own responsibility for what she achieved.

By the time Amy appeared, Australia already had a venerable tradition of producing talented vocalists, particularly sopranos and contraltos. In the 1870s Amy Sherwin, the Tasmanian nightingale, was discovered by a peripatetic Italian opera company which just happened to pass her home paddock (with the intention of having a picnic in the Huon Valley) while she was feeding the chickens.[18] Hearing her serenading a feathered flock, they were astonished at the purity and character of her voice, and within weeks she was a principal soprano with the Pompi e Cagli Italian Opera Company, playing Norina in Donizetti's *Don Pasquale* at Hobart's Theatre Royal.

The evolution of opera as a reputable career for women had taken about 100 years. Australians read with relish recent publications such as the biography of Jenny Lind, the Swedish nightingale, which described successful women.[19] Such books demonstrated that illustrious careers might spring from humble beginnings, that the crowned heads of Europe and others were eager to hear great voices. The attention of royalty imbued vocal art with a degree of respectability, regardless of the reputations of those doing being imbued. Discovery might be sudden and unexpected. When Melba finally left for Europe it was argued that she was a good singer but unlikely to eclipse the great Amy Sherwin who, with her own opera company, toured Europe and North America achieving considerable notoriety, including being the leading soprano in the American premiere of Berlioz's *Damnation of Faust*.

Other women followed. Frances Saville sang "Fiodiligi" in Mahler's 1900 production of *Cosi fan tutti* at Vienna's Hofoper to great acclaim in a Mozart season that is still remembered in Austria.[20] The Miranda sisters, Lalla and Beatrice, as well as having substantial concert careers, helped to create the Scottish Opera. Ada Crossley, (in the UK she was styled Miss Southern-Crossley) became an immensely popular concert contralto in the last years of the nineteenth century.[21] Helen Porter Mitchell, later Nellie Melba, from Richmond in Victoria, proved to be greater than all of these.

Australians had, in fact, enjoyed an ambivalent relationship with Melba from the start. At first, in the 1870s and early 1880s, they failed to notice her. Once she was successful they noticed she was a woman; a woman with energy, determination and talent, well able to fend for herself, anywhere. As the first real ambassador of Australia's imported European culture to present herself to the world, she also became a source of considerable national pride. But stories of her personal resourcefulness were less attractive than stories about success achieved through the generous distribution of sexual favours. This ambivalence became concentrated in the squabbles about Amy Castles in the pages of the Catholic *Freeman's Journal* and the secularist *Bulletin* during 1899. What appeared in print might have been a distorted reflection of the world Melba inhabited with its aura of art and vulgarity, of intelligence and impulsiveness, of good humour and sour intolerance, which still shape our responses to her. The agenda for Melba studies was quickly fixed. Those who have followed have (unfortunately) taken their direction from it. Even supposed friends and supporters have taken up the cry that proposes jealousy of potential rivals as a first principle. Both those who had not met her and those who knew her well contributed, cementing new bricks into the edifice of Melba mythology.

The crucial thing to note here is that people cared enough not only to celebrate and to vilify the old Melba but to instigate a search for a new one.

Australian opinions of Melba's character that began to take root in discussions of Amy Castles as "the new Melba" flowered prodigiously after Melba's death in 1931 and Melba's reputation has not recovered. As late as 1983 Max Harris's lively prose cast in concrete the accepted, quintessential Melba. In *The Unknown Great Australians* he wrote:

> She was the all-Australian world champion bitch. She was a humdinger. There have been megalomaniac prima donnas before and after Richmond's own Nellie Melba, but history records none of them as quite in Melba's class. She made Callas look like a shy violet. She made La Pasta as bland as spaghetti ... She was about as lovable as the bubonic plague virus.[22]

It is not difficult to trace this perception of Melba back to 1899 and to the dynamics of the first stirrings of interest in Amy Castles. But all this was in the future in September 1899, as Amy Castles prepared to leave Australia. The Catholic presses had only recently initiated their assessment and their animosity towards Melba was not strong enough to stop Amy taking with her to Europe a letter of introduction to the diva she was touted to topple. Melba, as it turned out, demonstrated a generous interest.[23]

The Castles boom indicated, more than anything else, that finding a "New Melba" had become a priority for Australians. They clearly recognized that a singer with a unique voice provided an Australian presence on the international stage; that the fifth continent was not just a collection of skinny natives, Europeans who were the progeny of transported criminals, or residual Chinese, left over from the gold-rushes. Melba might have had anxious moments as potential New Melbas were discovered in Australia or in other places, but Amy Castles was the sole serious contender to have her cause was taken up by an influential section of the press at home. After 1890 almost any new soprano drew comparisons with Melba's vocal qualities, her personality or her potential for success abroad, but none was dubbed the New Melba like Amy Castles. Later, Melba would herself assist young women with their careers. One, Stella Power, was pointedly promoted by Melba (and others) as the "Little Melba." She was not anointed as the "New" one. Occasionally Melba's supposed jealousy and eagerness to destroy potential rivals excited Australian's imagination, stirred by a press that sneered at her success. Graphic stories that "exposed" her prodigious sexual appetite, many of them conceived as jokes at her expense, became accepted as the twentieth century progressed, the weight of their number seeming to lend them credence.

Early in 1899 many journalists had entered into the spirit, trying to account for the Catholic energy to promote Amy Castles and the success that Amy's publicists achieved in attracting attention to her. Even *Table Talk*, usually contented to be plodding and amiable, indulged in rather waspish humour when it documented the strange ethnic mixture in the Cathedral for one of the Masses-that-were-concerts arranged to show off the Catholic gem.

> Tens of thousands trooped into St Patrick's Cathedral on Sunday, at the 11 o'clock Mass to hear Miss Amy Castles sing the "Ave Maria." Long before the service commenced every seat in the vast Cathedral was occupied. The people pressed into the vast aisles and, failing that, crowded under the organ-loft. There were members of all denominations, some of whom did not appreciate the Catholic spirit on Dives and beggar, the perfumed beauty and the Mongolian sitting side by side in the sacred edifice. I saw a Society matron sandwiched between an Arabian woman of the hawker type and a masher Chinaman. Her young friend a well-known Toorak belle ... who was (Oh ye gallants!) standing in the aisle, near by, had a twinkle in her eye every time she glanced at her chaperone in the crowd.[24]

After 1899 Australia's relationship with Melba presented as a vex-
ing dichotomy. Her voice was glorious. This was uncontroversial. Her
manner and her reported behaviour were another matter. Few people
have claimed that Melba had no voice; was no singer. But from 1899
onwards and as a direct result of the Castles boom Melba's calculated
diva-ish mannerisms and her morals became the subject of close critical attention and carefully orchestrated dismay. In the early 1890s the
social gossip cables published in Australian papers had raised eye-
brows as reports of her affair with the Duc d'Orléans first appeared.
Louis Philippe, the pretender to the French throne, posed a number of
threats to Melba's status. He was French, Catholic and foreign in many
important senses; both in Britain and Australia journalists scoffed at
the relationship. Melba was not smitten, they argued, only social
climbing in a rarefied zone so far above her station that everybody was
amazed, and most were critical. A divorce suit followed quickly, after
an action brought by Melba's long-absent husband, Charlie Arm-
strong. But the negative press proselytizing those parts of the population that viewed a wife leaving her husband and child, and having an
affair as un-Christian and unacceptable commenced in earnest after
Amy was styled the "New Melba."

Ironically, Amy Castles' career depended, in its first steps, on the
reputation of Nellie Melba. Those who promoted Amy consciously
used Melba's name and, for the most part, its positive associations:
the quality of her voice, her stature as an international Australian,
her obvious success. There were occasional swipes at her morals,
especially in the Catholic press as Amy's boom gathered momentum. Comparisons arose innocently, almost inadvertently and then,
pragmatically, they became malicious. What people read in 1899
astounded them. Here was Amy, a very young, untrained singer with
an extraordinarily rich and powerful voice. There can be little doubt
that the reactions of those who heard her sing confirmed the rumours
and the newspaper reports that something unusual was happening in
Victoria. An opportunity to support a rising star had presented itself. A
high level of subliminal guilt prevailed among Australians after they
had all but ignored the initial performances of the most notable and
recognizable Australian in the world, and certainly the most successful
to that time. The *Bulletin* said as much as it tried to account for the
"paroxysm of credulousness" that sustained the Castles boom, particularly in Melbourne. On 1 June 1899, the Melbourne *Argus* suggested
that audiences were driven to attend Amy's concerts not for the music

but because they recalled the shabby treatment of Melba on the eve of her departure for Europe and harboured "regret" now that it was clear what Melba had become. Australians would not make the same mistake twice. If this was the "New Melba" she would go to Europe with ample financial support and general, favourable recognition. She would have more than a pair of gloves and a cab fare.

An article in the Catholic *Freeman's Journal* as early as 6 May 1899, reporting an auction of Castles concert tickets at Bendigo, took up an idea put about by Amy's concert promoters, the Tait Brothers, flourishing the heading "Amy Castles ... The New Melba." The headline was repeated in the same newspaper on 27 May, in even more conspicuous bold letters, but this time Amy's name was excluded. It was enough to mention the "New Melba."

It was the *Freeman* too which suggested that Melba had been moved to take an interest in Australia as a result of hearing that a "New Melba" had appeared in Bendigo. In June 1899 the *Freeman's* anonymous critic wrote:

> Madame Melba has heard of her new rival ... Amy Castles. All at once "the illustrious diva" has begun to take an interest in her native country about which she has never troubled her mind since she went to Europe.

The *Bulletin* that took up the critical challenge of addressing the notion that Amy might be the "New Melba" and that the old one might have been provoked by the needling of Australian Catholic journalists.

> Sydney's *Freeman's Journal* has got Castles fever very badly indeed. It straightly insinuates that the recent calling to account of Melba's successes are due to what she has heard of "her new rival." Whatever Miss Castles' pretensions may be worth such imbecile drivel as this can do her no good.[25]

After Amy's first huge concert at the Exhibition Building, the Melbourne *Argus*, on 1 June, also suggested a comparison with Melba, but offered it in a different spirit, also summoning pervasive retrospective guilt.

> It was no music loving mass, no wildly patriotic multitude; it was a vast gathering of people stirred by curiosity, excited by anticipation.

Australians did not rush to hear Melba when they might have done
so; and those who did not hear her regret it now the world is at her
feet.

It is likely that Melba's curiosity would have been stirred when she
read or heard reports of an unprecedented response to Amy Castles in
Australia. But, equally, she cannot have had any doubts about the
young singer's ability once she heard Amy in the flesh in London in
late October or early November 1899. As well as any of the critics, she
would have recognised that there was no imminent threat to her own
position from Amy's singing. This view would have been supported at
this time by the fact that Amy was clearly tired and still hoarse as a
result of her Australian promotional tour. And she remained largely
untrained.

Graciously, Melba listened to the young Bendigonian with critical
interest. The diva offered Amy the use of her box at Covent Garden on
the understanding that exposure to fine singing was an important part
of the younger woman's training. To date Amy would have heard very
little professional opera, perhaps none. And Melba continued to show
an interest in the younger woman's career at least as late in November
1901 when Amy made her London debut.

Among those who either attended or sent personal messages of
goodwill were the Marchioness of Bute, Earl Carrington, Madame
Melba ... [26]

Melba also counselled that Amy nurse her damaged voice back to
health, after the 1899 concert tour in Australia, with Mathilde
Marchesi. Marchesi recognized that Amy's voice was damaged and
commenced a regime of short lessons and an investigation of the
proper placement of Amy's voice. It was, she said, a small, decent
voice but unsuitable for opera. Under these circumstances and in the
view of Amy's supporters, at a jealous Melba's behest, Amy could not
hope to supplant Melba. Amy, Marchesi finally opined, might even be
a natural contralto.

It is not surprising, especially given the size of the national, financial and ideological stakes involved, that any attempt to divert Amy
from her mission would be seen as mischief. Mathilde Marchesi, as
Melba's agent, took on the role of principal villain almost at once by
suggesting that Amy might have been a contralto. If Amy was to

replace Melba, she needed to be able to sing the sorts of roles that Melba had made her own, particularly characters such as Mimi, Juliet and Violetta, all of them high soprano roles.

What Marchesi is reported as having said was flourished in the Australian press as evidence that confirmed the confidence expressed by those who had originally *paid* to hear Amy sing. Such was the need that the opinions of credible critics who thought that she had "everything to learn" were forgotten or ignored. So was the almost universal observation that by August 1899 any vocal quality, evident in the early months of that year, had all but disappeared.[27] But as well as justifying the time and money spent by thousands of Australians in 1899, preparations for a triumphant return are implicit in the drip-feeding of exaggerated or false "progress reports" evident in the cables columns. The wonder of it all is that people in Australia actually cared passionately.

Melba died in Sydney in 1931 and made her last long, regal progress south to her Melbourne home. By this time Amy's career was over and had been moribund since 1920. The train paused in towns along the way so that country folk might pay their last respects. They turned out in their thousands. Even in death Melba commanded a huge audience. Thousands more lined the way from Scots Church in Collin's Street to the cemetery at Coldstream. For many miles crowds stood shoulder to shoulder, more numerous than those who had regularly turned out for St Patrick's Day. It was a huge display of national feeling. There is no obvious record that Amy Castles was in the crowd, but she might have stood on Dandenong Road to see the undisputed Queen of Australian song pass that way. Less than twenty-four hours later, in Vienna, where Amy had faltered in an attempt to be a force in international opera, the *Neue Freie Presse* carried a substantial obituary on its front page. Newspapers in Paris, London and New York followed in the same spirit as the world mourned her passing. Such was her stature.

And what of other women? What happened to the dozens who went abroad to try their luck on the stage or with the pen? How many have we missed and what of those who stayed at home? Where, for example, is the bushwoman who is more than the hapless partner of absent drover or the mother of larrikins who drop an explosive charge in a billabong to stun the resident fish?

In 1922, nine years before Melba's funeral, Henry Havelock Ellis released an autobiographical novel, *Kanga Creek*, based on his experiences as a young school teacher in the Australian bush in 1879. The young hero of the novel, on his journey to a region away from Sydney, observes two young women at a bush pub.

> Two tall muscular girls came in for the evening meal. They said nothing, but began at once. The swift and silent way with which they ate and drank and struck their mugs down on the table fascinated the young Englishman. Directly they had finished they went out.[28]

It is a short but revealing observation. Are these the partners of the taciturn bushman, or some sort of female equivalent? Is there a national type, a bushwoman we have utterly forgotten? Perhaps. What is beyond doubt is that they are the antithesis of Melba, who, regardless of what she had to say, said it to the world. As Melba took to the concert platform in Melbourne these young women more or less simultaneously took their evening meal, watched by the young Henry Havelock Ellis.

Perhaps the sort of pre-eminent moments that Stephen Castles saw as being absent in Australia's development, but necessary for the definition of national character, were achieved another way that was entirely different. There has been no Antipodean Bodicaea, no southern Joan of Arc. Perhaps the idealization of the common man that Castles identifies ought to be accompanied by a recognition and acknowledgement of a good many exceptional women.

Notes

1. S. Castles, M. Kalantzis, B. Cope and M. Morrisey, eds., *Mistaken Identity, Multiculturalism and the Demise of Nationalism in Australia* (Sydney: Pluto Press, 1990).
2. Ibid., Introduction.
3. There is ample published evidence of these things. See, for example, writings of Henry Reynolds and Maurice French (below).
4. See, for example, Maurice French, *Conflict on the Condamine* (Toowoomba: Darling Downs Institute Press, 1989), especially Chap. 7.
5. See section about Daniel Deniehy, who coined the description "Bunyip aristocracy," in David Headon and Elizabeth Perkins, *Our First Republican* (Sydney: Federation Press, 2000), 58–194.
6. O'Dowd's sonnet, "Australia," is widely anthologized.
7. See, for example, Michael Cannon, *That Damned Democrat* (Melbourne: Melbourne University Press, 1981), 117–118, 163–165.

8. See Ann-Marie Jordens, *The Stenhouse Circle* (Melbourne: Melbourne University Press, 1979).

9. George Coombe's conclusions were published in Robert Chambers, ed., *Life and Works of Robert Burns*, Vol. IV (Edinburgh: Chambers, 1856), 309–314.

10. See Al Gabay, *The Mystic Life of Alfred Deakin* (Cambridge University Press, 1992), 109–120 (for example) and also John Rickard, *A Family Romance: The Deakins at Home* (Melbourne: Melbourne University Press, 1996), especially Chap. 2.

11. See Jeff Brownrigg, "Havelock Ellis in Australia," *Quadrant* Number 219, Vol. XXX, 1 and 2 (January / February double issue, 1986): 131–133.

12. See, for example, Evelyne Blau, *Krishnamurti: 100 Years* (New York: Stewart, Tabori and Chang, 1995), 29–42. There are passing references here to C W Leadbeater and the very large Theosophical Society membership in Australia.

13. Sylvia Lawson, *The Archibald Paradox* (Melbourne: Penguin Books, 1989).

14. These included an attempt on the life of the Editor of the Melbourne daily, the *Age*, in 1870 and of the Duke of Edinburgh in 1867, in Sydney. See Patrick O'Farrell, *The Irish in Australia*, rev. ed. (Sydney: University of New South Wales Press, 1993), 100, 209–211.

15. Exchanges between Catholic Archbishop Moran and Camidge, Anglican Bishop of Goulburn in 1896, were published in the *Sydney Morning Herald*.

16. Robert Garran, *Prosper the Commonwealth* (Sydney: Angus and Robertson, 1958), 94

17. *The Freeman's Journal*, 10 June 1899, 22.

18. See Judith Bowler, *Amy Sherwin, The Tasmanian Nightingale* (privately published, Hobart, 1982), 13–14.

19. H. S. Holland and W. S. Rockstro, *Memoir of Madame Jenny Lind-Goldschmidt* (London: John Murray, 1891).

20. Adrienne Simpson, *The Greatest Ornament to Their Profession: The New Zealand Tours by the Simonsen Opera Companies, 1876–1889* (Christchurch: University of Canterbury, 1993). See especially the references to Frances Simonsen (Saville).

21. Both the Miranda sisters and Ada Crossley have substantial entries in McKenzie, *Singers of Australia* (Melbourne: Landsdowne, 1967), 80–87.

22. Max Harris, "The Singing Bikie," in *The Unknown Great Australians* (Melbourne: Sun Books, 1983), 26–31.

23. Melba's attention to the young singer is well documented, particularly offering the use of her private box at the Royal Opera House, Covent Garden, and use of her house on the Thames.

24. Melbourne correspondent for *Table Talk*, 10 June 1899.

25. See *Bulletin*, 17 June 1899. A copy of this article can be found in the Castles scrapbook preserved on microfilm in the State Library of Victoria.

26. In characteristic publicity following Amy's London debut much effort went into gathering and creating text to support the view that the concert there had been a triumph. Published in, for example, the *British Australian*, 28 November, 1901, page 2114. Australian periodicals mined the rich vein of news that seemed to confirm Amy's stature.

27. The Melbourne *Age* and the *Argus*, both of which had promoted the young singer with considerable energy, agreed that, by September 1899, Amy's voice had lost its quality. The *Bulletin* agreed, but added that the *Bulletin* commentators had not heard much "quality" in the first instance. The change was put down to extensive touring and the singing of "big" bel canto arias by a singer who was not properly trained to do so. The result was strain and possible serious damage to the voice.

28. Henry Havelock Ellis, *Kanga Creek*, (Sydney: Nelson, 1970), 11.

9

The Doctrine of Corroboration in Sexual Assault Trials in Early Twentieth-Century Canada and Australia

CONSTANCE BACKHOUSE

Canadian and Australian scholars have increasingly begun to search each other's historical legal records for evidence of similarity and difference. The two countries have much in common. They were birthed as colonies by the same mother country and share roots in the British commonwealth tradition. Both countries were bestowed with virtually identical common law and legislative heritages. Both share a history of patriarchy, of political, social and economic imbalances between men and women that resonate in law. The comparative analysis of women's legal history in Canada and Australia is potentially a remarkably rich field, which will contribute to the task of articulating what is unique or particular about the historical foundation of the two nations.

This paper seeks to determine what the law of sexual assault in the early twentieth century illustrates about the similarity and distinctiveness of Canadian and Australian legal traditions. Both countries inherited a criminal law that was premised upon British common law traditions of judicial precedent. The constitutional framework in Canada located the criminal law power within the federal sphere, while the Australian nation placed it under the jurisdiction of the individual states. Canada departed from British example by codifying its criminal law in 1892.[1] Some Australian states, such as Victoria, remained true to the common law tradition, but others, such as Western Australia in 1902, codified their criminal law as well.[2] All of the codifications were substantially influenced by the work of the British jurist Sir James Fitzjames Stephen, whose draft code failed to secure enactment in Britain, but obtained currency within the larger commonwealth.[3] Most importantly, Canadian and Australian judges remained highly deferential to British judicial pronouncements in the field of criminal law, citing British appellate rulings regularly, often in preference to local appellate decisions, and occasionally in spite of their own country's statutory departures from the British law concerned.

The focus of this article will be two early twentieth-century trials, *R. v. Sullivan* decided in Perth, Western Australia in 1913,[4] and *Hubin v. The King* decided in Winnipeg, Manitoba in 1927.[5] These cases offer useful illustrations of the judicial reasoning spawned by sexual assault proceedings in the two countries during this period. The issues concerned, the types of evidence adduced, and the legal arguments raised typify the sexual assault trials that focused on the doctrine of corroboration in the early twentieth century.[6] Both cases involved thirteen-year-old complainants, and accused men charged with the offence of "carnal knowledge" perpetrated upon women under the age of consent. Both decisions focused on the legal framework for assessing female credibility, both dwelled on the doctrine of corroboration in depth, and both resulted in convictions at trial, which were quashed on appeal. Both cases also present a wealth of factual detail. *Sullivan* is richly documented in the surviving archival records and the contemporary press, allowing examination well beyond the contours of the reported judgment.[7] Although *Hubin* is less well-documented in the press, the judicial records contain scrupulously detailed accounts of the types of evidence introduced – and rejected – as corroboration.[8] The timing of the two cases is also fortuitous. The case of *R. v. Baskerville*, decided by the English Court of Appeal in 1916, articulated a set of corroboration criteria that came to hold sway across the British commonwealth for the next half a century.[9] *Sullivan* presents a unique opportunity to scrutinize early Australian law prior to the trend-setting English decision, at a point in time when the rules of corroboration were quite fluid and unsettled. *Hubin* provides a glimpse into the immediate post-*Baskerville* era, at a time when commonwealth courts were making their own precedential rulings about how the doctrine of corroboration should be articulated in the wake of *Baskerville*.

The cases are also well suited to comparison because the statutory foundations of the crime of "carnal knowledge" were identical in Canada and Australia. The British Parliament passed an imperial statute in 1861 making it a crime to have sexual intercourse with a girl younger than twelve, and raised the age limit to sixteen in 1885.[10] Although many of the young women whose cases were heard under this provision were forcibly and coercively assaulted, it was not strictly necessary to prove that the victim had been raped by means of force, fear or fraud, as was required for adult females. Sexual relations with underage women could generate conviction simply upon proof that the accused had had sexual connection with the female concerned, with or without her consent. Both Canada and Western Australia inherited the 1861 statute, but both went on to enact their own legislation thereafter. Canada retained the age limit of twelve in its 1869 statute, raising it to fourteen in 1890 and sixteen in 1920.[11] Western Australia put the age limit for carnal knowledge at fourteen in 1892, and increased this to sixteen in 1900.[12]

One of the criminal law ideas that seems to have taken firm root in both countries was the belief that women and children were inherently untrustworthy when they testified about sexual assault. There has never been any empirical basis for such presumption, which appears to have sprouted from pervasive and long-standing misogynistic perspectives.[13] Judges and text writers in Canada and Australia routinely cited eighteenth-century English jurist Sir Matthew Hale, for the adage that rape "was an accusation easily to be made, and hard to be proved, and harder to be defended by the party accused, though never so innocent."[14] In deference to Lord Hale, special evidentiary rules were constructed for sexual assault trials, with judges urged to caution juries that it was dangerous to convict upon the uncorroborated testimony of female rape complainants.[15] Canadian and Australian legislators expanded upon the common law rules, fortifying many of their criminal law statutes with additional requirements for corroboration in cases of sexual assault. For some offences, the statutes went well beyond the common law *preference* for corroboration, making it *mandatory*, and stipulating that no one could ever be convicted "upon the uncorroborated testimony of one witness." The offence of "carnal knowledge" under which the accused men were charged in the *Sullivan* and *Hubin* cases was such an offence in Canada[16] and Australia.[17] A review of the legislative debates that accompanied the introduction of mandatory corroboration provisions indicates that the all-male legislators were worried about false complaints, the potential for extortion and blackmail, "seducers," "tempters," and "brazen females" of "vicious habits," who were wont to exhibit "hysterical," "wanton" and "wicked" practices, as well as "designing girls" and "libidinous women" who might "entrap" the "vigorous, active" and "foolish" young men of the country. The efforts of female reform groups to remind the politicians that "false charges of this kind" were of "very rare occurrence" failed abjectly.[18]

Ila Collins and Sophie Oleksiuk: Two Highly Credible Witnesses

Ila Collins was a mere slip of a girl just thirteen years old when she took the witness stand in Police Magistrates' Court in Perth, Western Australia in December, 1912. Observers described her as timid, embarrassed and reticent to speak about the intimate sexual details of her experience. However, after being duly sworn, Ila Collins told the court how Louis Sullivan, a fifty-year-old innkeeper who co-habited with her mother, had sexually assaulted her repeatedly for the past eleven months. She testified that Louis Sullivan had accosted her while they were out riding horses in the bush and when she was down at the paddock feeding the pigs. She spoke in a wavering, barely audible voice of her terror, of her efforts to resist, of Sullivan's persistent threats. She described her tears when he forced her to the ground, "hurt" her inside her "private parts," and left her "wet" and in great pain. She recalled how Sullivan had taunted her, saying, "If it hurts you, it will only hurt you once in your life."

Neighbours and acquaintances all characterized young Ila Collins as "very innocent," "a good, quiet, retiring girl," "babyish" and "reserved." She apparently struck everyone who knew her as proper, shy and subdued. Her demeanour in court was highly compelling, and the magistrate committed Louis Sullivan for trial on the strength of her statements. Ila Collins stood up equally well at trial before the Supreme Court in Perth three months later. Although she was cross-examined at length by defence counsel, she seems to have impressed those in the courtroom as unshakeable and "entirely believable." She convinced the jury beyond a reasonable doubt.[19]

Sophie Oleksiuk seems to have been equally compelling when she appeared before the County Court Judge's Criminal Court in Winnipeg, Manitoba in December, 1926. A few days shy of her thirteenth birthday, Sophie Oleksiuk explained that she had been walking along a country road around nine o'clock in the morning, to mail a letter at the nearest post office in Lockport, several miles southeast of her rural home. Leo Paul Hubin, a St Boniface man of undetermined age, had driven up alongside her in a McLaughlin coupe, and offered her a lift. She did not know him, but accepted the ride. She told the court how Hubin turned north on a cross-road, and drove her four miles out of her way despite her remonstrations. She explained that she tried to escape from the vehicle, but that Hubin followed her out of the car, grabbed her by the coat, and raped her on the side of the road. She also spoke of her resistance, her tears, how Hubin had ripped her bloomers when he tore them from her body. She testified that she refused to get back into the car with her attacker, and that he drove off and left her there, frightened, hurt and weeping.

The general assessment of Sophie Oleksiuk's testimony was also highly positive. The witnesses emphasized her youthful vulnerability, with the medical expert testifying that she was "still a child physically." She was described as "unhesitating," and her evidence was characterized as "true" and "convincing," ultimately constituting "a very strong case." Since this was not a jury trial, the trial judge was the ultimate trier of fact. He pronounced Sophie Oleksiuk's story to be "absolutely truthful," and emphasized that he "accepted" her word "absolutely." The judges of the Manitoba Court of Appeal who subsequently reviewed the case and upheld the verdict of guilty labelled her narrative "a convincing and well-connected one."[20]

In both instances, then, the primary Crown witness was deemed to be steadfast and highly convincing. The young girls' testamentary credibility was elevated even further by comparison with the manipulative and vacillating stories proffered by the accused men. Louis Sullivan initially denied having had any sexual contact with Ila Collins, but then confessed to her mother that he was surprised at the charge because he had never "got properly into" the girl. In the end, he was reduced to complaining to a neighbouring publican that he "was not the only one" to have had sexual relations with the girl. An arrogant and bombastic man, who angered the appellate judges by complaining that they were not making sufficiently detailed notes of his legal argument, Sullivan was also known to have advised one of his employees that "a little bit of vaseline" would prevent genital tearing during intercourse with young girls.[21] For his part, Leo Paul Hubin gave dramatically inconsistent statements to the police. Initially he claimed that on the day of the rape he had been playing pool in the Seymour Hotel in Winnipeg, and having his car fixed at a local garage, all of which he brashly asserted could be confirmed by multiple witnesses. Thinking better of the matter, Hubin later retracted this statement and advised that he had played pool only briefly, then spent the balance of the day with his mother and sister in St Boniface. Hubin's evidence was judicially characterized as "weak and quibbling," even "a tissue of lies."[22]

If the criminal trial had been constructed in accordance with the ordinary principles of evidence, it would have been a simple matter for the Crown attorneys in both cases to meet their onus of proof. It was an irrefutable rule of English law that in most criminal trials, the testimony of a single witness was sufficient to prove a legal case, provided that the trier-of-fact believed that witness beyond a reasonable doubt. The doctrine of corroboration was a marked departure from the general practice, an evidentiary hurdle that made it substantially more difficult to secure convictions despite the overwhelming ring of truth that seems to have suffused Ila Collins's and Sophie Oleksiuk's testimony.[23]

The "Back-Up Evidence"

What exactly did the term "corroboration" mean? What sorts of additional proof did the prosecution have to muster to secure convictions in cases of carnal knowledge of young girls? Turn-of-the-century English dictionaries defined the word with a list of equivalent phrases: "strengthening, fortifying, invigorating," "the confirmation (of a statement, etc.) by additional evidence," "to strengthen (a statement, etc.) by concurrent or agreeing statements or evidence," "to make more sure or certain."[24] As will become evident, the legal definition did not entirely accord with contemporary parlance. However, if the common understanding of the word had been taken as indicative, it would seem that judges and juries could have accepted a great many things as "corroborative" in sexual assault trials.

In the *Sullivan* case, there was a surfeit of "strengthening" and "confirming" testimony. A physician testified that he had examined Ila Collins and found "a considerable dilatation of the whole vaginal tract," leading him to conclude that she had had "repeated sexual connection" dating back several months. Various neighbours testified to having seen Louis Sullivan and Ila Collins out riding together in the bush and in the direction of the paddock, often late into the night. A police officer went out to investigate the paddock, and found the table and bundle of empty chaff bags upon which Ila Collins had reported that she was raped. The proprietor of a nearby saloon who had formerly trained as a nurse testified that Louis Sullivan had come over to ask her whether a medical man could "tell positively that a girl had been interfered with." This was the same conversation during which Sullivan complained that he was "not the only one."

Ila Collins's mother also testified that her daughter had reported to her the details of the sexual attack well before any formal charges were laid with the police. The mother told the court that when she confronted her co-habitee and accused him of sexually abusing her daughter, Sullivan had insisted that he "never got properly into her." Understood within the context of the conversation, most hearers would have taken this as an unwitting admission that Sullivan had indeed "got into" the young girl after some fashion. The Australian statute did not require the Crown to prove full sexual intercourse. The crime of "carnal knowledge of girls under sixteen" was defined as "having" or "attempting [to have] unlawful carnal knowledge of a girl under the age of sixteen." The crime specifically encompassed the "attempt" as well as the completed offence.

The "fortifying" evidence in the *Hubin* case was equally substantial. The medical practitioner who examined Sophie Oleksiuk reported that he found "the hymen ruptured and the vagina slightly injured" with abrasive swelling on the left side, that this condition was "of recent origin," and that it could have been "caused by sexual intercourse." Sophie Oleksiuk's oldest sister, fifteen-year-old Mary, confirmed that Sophie had returned to her home on the day of the rape in tears. Mary testified that her sister told her immediately what had happened. Mary had had the presence of mind to save the torn bloomers that Sophie showed her, and these were filed as a material exhibit in court.

Sophie Oleksiuk was a very observant young girl, and she was also able to describe an unusual cushion that was lying on the driver's seat in Hubin's car – a "little round one," one side of which was "black plush" and the other "a kind of sand colour." The car was tracked because Sophie Oleksiuk had been carrying a pencil in her pocket on the morning of the rape, and she had accurately written down the licence number of the car on the envelope she was bringing to the post office. The police traced the car to an automobile salesman who identified the McLaughlin coupe as one he had earlier sold to Hubin. Sophie Oleksiuk was able to identify the car while it was sitting at a garage, by its appearance, licence number and the cushion that remained on the driver's seat, identical to the one she had described. The police brought Hubin down to the police station and placed him in a line-up with four other men. Without hesitation, Sophie Oleksiuk pointed him out as the man who had raped her. Hubin also admitted that he was the owner of the car, and that he was driving it on the day the offence was committed. Although the police cautioned Hubin that any statement he might make would be taken down and could be used against him at trial, he offered two dramatically inconsistent statements as to his whereabouts on the day in question.

Whittling Down the Scope of Legal Corroboration: The Australian Example

When eighteenth-century judges first dreamed up the need for corroboration, they did not provide a detailed or systematic code to regulate what sorts of evidence should be called. Theoretically, any additional evidence beyond the complainant's testimony could have sufficed. When Western Australian legislators first enacted their *Criminal Code*, they took a major step back from this potentially wide interpretation. The 1902 *Code* set out a statutory definition that described "uncorroborated testimony" as "testimony which is not corroborated in some material particular by other evidence implicating the accused person."[25] This narrowed the scope of the doctrine to encompass only certain kinds of evidence – that which related to a "material particular" rather than less critical elements of the case – and that which implicated the accused, rather than simply increased the credibility of the complainant's testimony. This went well beyond the simple concept of "strengthening" or "confirming" evidence.

The legislators had made a decision to codify the doctrine of corroboration, mandating additional evidence before the sexual assault victim could be believed. Then they had stipulated that not just anything would suffice. In the hands of the lawyers and judges in Australia, the statutory definition would be pulled apart, probed and pinched still further, until the legal doctrine came to resemble but a fraction of the original, theoretically-broad concept. The *Sullivan* case provides an ideal vehicle for examining this winnowing process, as judges dismissed certain types of evidence and narrowed the scope of corroboration to a thin band of qualifying data. The Supreme Court of Western Australia rejected all of the evidence led by the Crown, finding none of it sufficient to meet the legal burden of corroboration, and quashed the conviction of the jury that had believed Ila Collins.

The medical evidence was the easiest to dismiss. The doctor's findings might have proved that the young girl had been sexually assaulted, but the report did not solely "implicate the accused." This was because the testifying physician was unable to state whose penis had caused the "considerable vaginal dilation" he had observed. With one stroke of the pen, the new statutory definition had rendered meaningless a swath of otherwise confirmatory testimony. What was theoretically a remarkably affirming piece of evidence, a medical finding that the complainant had been sexually violated, was now nugatory.[26] This rule would largely eviscerate the utility of most medical evidence in sexual assault trials, at least until the advent of DNA-testing three-quarters of a century later.

The corroborative value of the statements of the multiple witnesses who had seen Ila Collins out riding with Louis Sullivan late at night and in the vicinity of the paddock was also denied. This seems slightly more difficult to understand, since the evidence placed Louis Sullivan at the scene of the crime. Unlike the doctor's testimony, this presumably "implicated the accused." However, Australian courts had rejected evidence of "mere opportunity" as insufficiently corroborative without some further "inference of impropriety."[27] Presumably merely going horse-back riding in the vicinity of the assaults was taken to be lacking such an inference. A similar fate befell the police evidence. The scene of the crime looked just as Ila Collins had described it, but her ability to describe the physical surroundings that attended the location in which the assault occurred did not "implicate the accused" either.

The complaint that Ila Collins made to her mother was potentially more useful, at least at this point in Australian jurisprudential development. Australian law was still somewhat unclear as to whether the complainant could corroborate her own story by divulging the sexual assault to a third party. None of the reported decisions prior to *Sullivan* had ruled categorically whether this type of evidence was sufficient. The main case on the point had caused considerable disagreement between two judges. *R. v. Gregg*, an 1892 decision of the Victoria Supreme Court, had involved a charge of indecent assault on an eight-year-old girl. The court heard evidence that the child had returned to her mother "in a state of distress," and described the assault, the place where it was committed, the appearance of the place and the appearance and garb of her assailant.[28] Chief Justice Higinbotham held that the conversation was "forcible evidence" of corroboration, stating:

> Corroboration may be easily supplied in most cases by our law, though not by the English law. Our law admits that a statement by a

child to its mother, made after the commission of such an offence, is admissible, not as part of the res gestae, but as evidence confirming and corroborating the testimony which the child gives in the box; and in a very large number of cases I am not aware of any kind of corroboratory evidence more satisfactory than that of a female child suffering under a shock of this kind, and indicating by appearance, manner, words, and acts the distress caused by the assault.

In the peculiar circumstances of the case, however, the Chief Justice went on to hold that the evidence did not meet the qualifications of legal corroboration. In *Gregg*, the conversation between mother and child had taken place before the child identified her assailant pursuant to a police investigation. The Chief Justice held that the statement thus failed to "implicate the accused":

... under the present law such corroboration can only be given so as to implicate the accused person, if the child knows at the time of the assault the person who has assaulted her, or if some other testimony exists independent of that of the child by which the assailant can be identified.

While agreeing with the outcome of the case, Judge Hood was in marked disagreement with his Chief Justice over the utility of complainants' statements to third parties. Dismissing this type of evidence as generally insufficient, Judge Hood noted:

There was evidence to support the girl's story and to confirm her credibility and to show that she was telling what she believed to be the truth. But I think that the Legislature has in these cases required something more. There must be some other material evidence implicating the accused; that is, something proved altogether apart from the child's story tending to establish the guilt of the prisoner. It seems to me that the intention was that no man should be convicted upon the unsworn testimony of a child of tender years unless other facts were established which would raise a suspicion of the accused's guilt, even if the evidence of the girl had been absent.[29]

Judge Hood's interpretation was draconian in import. Essentially he was demanding that "corroboration" be restricted to evidence that originated entirely separate and apart from the complainant's words and actions. The statutory wording did not mandate this. What was required was testimony that was corroborated "in some material particular by other evidence implicating the accused person." Judge Hood had taken the phrase "other evidence" and equated it with evidence that was completely "extrinsic" or "independent" of the complainant.

In Louis Sullivan's case, the legal authorities seem to have preferred Chief Justice Higinbotham's sense of the issues over Judge Hood's. There was no legal argument over whether Ila Collins's mother's testimony about her daughter's description of the sexual assaults could potentially qualify as corroboration. Counsel on both sides of the case seem to have taken the recent complaint to fit within the legal criteria for potential corroboration. The defence lawyer argued instead that Ila's mother could not corroborate her daughter's story because she was simply not a credible witness. He pointed out that this was a woman blatantly living in sin, a "mistress" to Louis Sullivan. As it turned out, Ila Collins's mother had also held herself out as a widow, claiming that Ila's father had died six months after the child's birth. Yet Ila's birth certificate was blank where the father's name should have appeared. The marital history created additional problems when it was revealed that Ila's mother had sworn to be a widow while making application for a hotel licence in 1906. Sullivan's defence lawyer accused the mother of perjury, birthing an illegitimate child, extra-marital cohabitation, and alcoholism. The Supreme Court judges who heard the appeal were strongly influenced by this disparaging evidence, and quick to dispense with Ila's mother's testimony. Rattling off the reasons why no jury should ever have relied upon such a woman's evidence, Chief Justice Sir Stephen Henry Parker noted that Ila's mother had falsely sworn to be a widow in order to obtain a hotel licence, that she "had been living with the accused for years as his mistress," and that she was "a drunkard." What more could one possibly imagine to destroy the reputation and credibility of a woman? The judges did not dispute that the recent complaint that Ila Collins had made to her mother fell within the legal parameters of the doctrine of corroboration. Instead they dismissed the mother's testimony as incredible.

The conversation that Louis Sullivan had had with the saloon proprietor and former nurse, in which he had grilled her about the accuracy of medical assessments of female virginity and grumbled that he was "not the only one" was inexplicably never put forward as legal corroboration before the Supreme Court. These statements might have been construed as incriminating admissions, and it is difficult to know why the Crown chose not to include this evidence as potential corroboration. It is true that Australian courts had been very cautious about drawing implications from statements of the accused, giving them every benefit of the doubt before accepting such evidence as corroborative.[30] However, it is hard to see how Sullivan's statement was not a full-fledged admission of sexual intercourse. How often was similar evidence disqualified, without any records left to offer analysis or rationale? The other admission Sullivan had made, to Ila Collins's mother, that he had "not properly got into" Ila, was put before the Supreme Court by the Crown. It was rejected on the same ground as the rest of Ila Collins's mother's evidence, on the basis that she was an inherently untrustworthy witness.

In the end, the case faltered entirely over corroboration. Judge Robert Bruce Burnside was at pains to articulate the long-standing rationale behind the evidentiary barrier to conviction: "The policy of the law from time immemorial has been to require that in cases of offences against women and female children the evidence of the prosecutrix should receive some corroboration." Paraphrasing the indomitable Sir Matthew Hale, he went on: "It was commonly put before juries in criminal cases that it was a charge very easily made and most difficult to disprove, and the wisdom of the legislators has in the statute under review enunciated that policy, namely, that the prisoner cannot be convicted merely upon the testimony of one witness."[31]

Chief Justice Parker was equally quick to emphasize the importance of corroboration, taking care to support the statutory underpinning of the doctrine:

> Her [Ila Collins's] story may be quite true, and in all probability the jury, having seen her in the box and observed the mode in which she answered the questions and her demeanour when cross-examined, may have rightly come to the conclusion that they entirely believed her story, but it is necessary that there should be corroboration as defined by the statute. ... Now I venture to think that the jury did believe the girl – it may be that they rightly believed her – and that they entirely overlooked the question that they must find corroboration in the manner defined in the Code, before they could convict the accused.[32]

Here was a blatant recognition that the legal rules requiring corroboration ought properly to override the conviction of guilty men.

The appellate court confidently applauded the "wisdom of the policy of the Legislature in requiring corroboration" in trials such as these. "It is not sufficient that she should be believed," the court ruled, "although the jury may have believed her." The jurors had satisfied themselves "of the truth of the girl's story" and "determined to convict" the accused.[33] But in their haste to see justice done, they had ignored the requirement for corroboration. Even where the complainant was "entirely believable," even when a jury "rightly" decided that she was telling the truth, even where the complainant gave evidence in a completely honest and compelling manner throughout her testimony-in-chief and cross-examination, the verdict must go to the accused unless legal "corroboration" was available. And what sort of evidence would qualify as "corroboration" was to be rigorously and tightly controlled. In the tug-of-war between the need to protect young girls from sexual abuse and the need to protect men from untrustworthy females, it was incontestably Australian men who came out on top.

Three years later, the *Baskerville* decision of the English Court of Appeal would tighten the formula still further. The court equated the definition of corroboration at common law and under statute. In both situations, corroboration would now require "independent testimony which affects the accused by connecting or tending to connect him with the crime." In the hands of the Australian judiciary, the *Baskerville* decision would also come to stand for the rule that corroboration must always emanate from a source other than the complainant. This would ultimately place off-limits the details of any complaints made by sexual assault victims to third parties.[34]

Strangling the Doctrine of Corroboration: The Canadian Example

The first legislative requirement for corroboration in carnal knowledge cases surfaced in a Canadian statute in 1890. At the start, Canadian legislators did not mandate corroboration as a prerequisite for conviction in all carnal knowledge offences, but only when the female complainant had been too young to swear her evidence under oath.[35] With the passage of the first Canadian *Criminal Code* in 1892, Parliament saw fit to make corroboration a prerequisite for a variety of sexual offences, although carnal knowledge was not initially included.[36] In 1920, when the age of consent was raised to sixteen for girls of "previous chaste character," corroboration finally became mandatory.[37] Carnal knowledge of girls under fourteen escaped such compulsory treatment until 1925.[38]

Two statutory definitions of corroboration were provided. The general definition, applicable after 1925 to all carnal knowledge trials, provided that no person could be convicted "upon the evidence of one witness, unless such witness is corroborated in some material particular by evidence implicating the accused."[39] The slightly different version, which applied to the unsworn evidence of children of "tender years" in charges of carnal knowledge, prevented conviction unless the testimony "given on behalf of the prosecution" was "corroborated by some other material evidence thereof implicating the accused."[40] Sophie Oleksiuk had been duly sworn when she gave her testimony, so the former definition was applicable to her case.

The statutory definitions enacted in Canada suffered from the same restrictive formulation that beset Australian criminal law. This unnecessarily narrow formula eviscerated the value of the medical examination that had been conducted on Sophie Oleksiuk. The doctor's testimony about her "ruptured hymen" and "swollen" vagina failed to "implicate the accused" in much the same way that Ila Collins's "vaginal dilation" had failed to corroborate her evidence in the earlier trial.[41] A similar fate befell Sophie Oleksiuk's torn bloomers. An item of concrete evidence that undeniably attested to the violence of the sexual assault was rejected because the rent undergarment failed to disclose who had ripped it.

The matter of the complaint that Sophie Oleksiuk had made to her fifteen-year-old sister Mary was somewhat more complex. "Recent complaint" was the legal term frequently used to describe the complainant's first disclosure of the assault. Allowing a witness to take the stand to testify that the complainant had divulged information about the sexual assault was a departure from the ordinary rules of "hearsay" evidence. The Ontario High Court had explained the anomaly in *Hopkinson v. Perdue* in 1904, as a survival of the practice which "prevailed in early times" of receiving evidence of previous statements of witnesses not under oath similar to their testimony in court for the purpose of "confirming" that testimony. Although such evidence had long since ceased to be admissible as a general rule, the "ancient practice" had survived as an "exception" in cases of rape, probably in line with legal expectations that women who were truly raped would raise a "hue and cry."[42] The relationship between this "confirming" testimony and the legal requirement for corroboration was not entirely clear. Early cases stipulated that "recent complaint" evidence should not be construed to be "independent or substantive evidence to prove the truth of the charge," but as "corroborative evidence" that could "confirm the injured party's testimony."[43] Although Canadian courts often used the terms "corroborative" and "confirmatory" within the same judgment, many judges seemed loath to accept recent complaints as constituting full legal corroboration that a sexual assault had in fact occurred.[44]

The Canadian courts had also constructed a series of restrictions on the admissibility of "recent complaint" evidence. If the recent complaint was not made at the first reasonable opportunity, it could be excluded.[45] The timeliness factor was a potential problem in the *Hubin* case. During cross-examination, Sophie Oleksiuk had admitted that she had seen a number of people after the alleged rape had occurred, before she confessed the details of the attack to her sister. As she was walking back along the highway, she passed by a woman named Mrs. Lipsick, two boys driving along on a threshing machine, and two female school chums. Before returning home, she had stopped off at her grandmother's home for about fifteen minutes, where she spoke briefly with her grandmother, aunt and uncle who were out in the field picking potatoes. She had also gone into the store where she spoke with a female salesclerk, and to the post-office where she mailed a letter to Eaton's Department Store. Both Crown and defence counsel demanded to know why Sophie Oleksiuk had not blurted out the story of the rape immediately. The young girl replied that she hadn't told the children "because the kids they go and tell everybody and I didn't want them to know." As for her reluctance to complain to the older people, she explained that she was too "ashamed."

Another potential problem involved the circumstances under which the complaint had been extracted. Canadian courts refused to admit evidence of recent complaints if they were not made in a voluntary and spontaneous fashion.[46] Mary Oleksiuk had testified that about five minutes after Sophie returned home, she noticed that her younger sister was crying. Mary asked her what was the matter, and why it had taken her so long to go to the post office. That was the point at which Sophie first told about the rape.

At the trial, County Court Judge Stacpoole did not allow these potential problems to deter him. He did not characterize the complaint as lacking in spontaneity or voluntariness, or dismiss it as given in response to a suggestive or leading question. He also ruled that Sophie

Oleksiuk had "explained her reason for the delay quite satisfactorily." Judge Stacpoole permitted the Crown to introduce the evidence of Sophie's complaint to her sister, Mary Oleksiuk. He did not specifically state whether he accepted the recent complaint as legally corroborative under the requirements of the *Criminal Code*, or whether he took it as simply confirmatory of credibility. On appeal to the Manitoba Court of Appeal, Walter Harley Trueman speaking for the majority, made mention of the story told to the elder sister in his decision confirming the conviction, although he too failed to indicate whether he was treating the complaint as corroboration or something less. Dissenting Manitoba Court of Appeal Judge James Emile Pierre Prendergast also took note of the recent complaint, stating that "the fifteen-year-old sister corroborated her younger sister's evidence as to being informed by her of the occurrence, adding that she was crying at the time." But Judge Prendergast then explicitly refuted the classification of such evidence as corroboration in law. "Nothing she said," he wrote, "however much [it] may strengthen her version, can be corroboration." The difficulty, according to Judge Prendergast, was that complaint originated with Sophie Oleksiuk. The fact that her sister, Mary, could testify to the details of Sophie's complaint did not make it sufficiently "independent." By the time the case reached the Supreme Court of Canada, all mention of the recent complaint was gone. There was no reference whatsoever to this "fortifying" piece of evidence.

Sophie Oleksiuk's identification of Leo Hubin and his car provoked a substantial degree of judicial disagreement until, in the final result, these items of potentially corroborating evidence were also jettisoned. Sophie had testified, apparently completely credibly, that she had never seen Leo Hubin before the morning of the attack. She was able to advise the police of the licence number of the car, and to give a full description of the car and its contents, including the plush black and sand coloured cushion on the driver's seat. When the police traced the ownership of the car to Hubin, he admitted driving the car on the morning of September 20. He was brought down to the police station, where Sophie Oleksiuk confidently identified him from the police line-up.

At the lower trial level, Judge Stacpoole was prepared to accept the identification evidence as legally corroborative. He stated in his oral judgment:

> I accept [the girl's] story absolutely – I think her story is absolutely truthful. The evidence I regard as corroborative is contained in the

statement of the accused whereby he admits the ownership of the car. The little girl claims that car was out there, and that was the car she was conveyed in to where the offence took place. The accused admits the ownership of the car, and that is a corroboration on a material point implicating the accused. ... [T]he girl swears that this was the car he drove her in, and identified the car, and I think that in itself is sufficient corroboration to support the girl's story. ...[47]

The majority of the Manitoba Court of Appeal judges who heard the appeal also took the identification evidence to be legally corroborative. Penning the lead opinion, Chief Justice William Egerton Perdue noted:

It was shown that the girl immediately identified the accused at the police office as the guilty man. It was clearly established that he owned the motor car and was driving it on the day on which the offence was committed. He himself admitted these two facts. After the offence had been committed the girl took the number of car and by this number the accused was traced and arrested. These facts fully corroborate the girl's identification of him as the man who committed the crime.[48]

Manitoba Court of Appeal Judges Prendergast and Fullerton thought differently. Judge Prendergast began with the seemingly obligatory reference to the long-departed Sir Matthew Hale, noting that the Canadian Parliament had not been "content with the protection given an accused by Lord Hale's dictum now become a Rule of Court." Indeed, as Prendergast emphasized, Parliament had "judged proper to go further and require corroboration in such cases as this one as a matter of law." And as a matter of law, Prendergast and Fullerton both concluded that the identification evidence could not serve as statutory corroboration.

The difficulty was traceable, according to the dissenting judges, directly to the legal test. "The proper question," they stipulated, was whether there was "any material particular in the main witness' testimony that is corroborated by independent evidence implicating the accused." The formulation of the test differed a bit from the statutory language, although the dissenting judges professed to be simply "following the wording" of the corroboration section of the *Code.*[49] In fact, Section 1002 of the *Criminal Code* stated that "no person accused of an offence [including carnal knowledge] shall be convicted upon the evidence of one witness, unless such witness is corroborated in some material particular by evidence implicating the accused."[50] The word "independent" was nowhere in sight. Section 1003 came somewhat closer. It set forth the corroboration rule that applied to prosecutions for carnal knowledge where the child was of such tender years as to be unable to give testimony under oath. Evidence admitted without the safeguard of an oath had traditionally been viewed as more suspect than properly sworn testimony. In cases such as these, the *Code* provided that no person could be convicted unless the evidence was "corroborated by *some other* material evidence in support thereof implicating the accused."[51] It is an arguable point whether the word "independent" is precisely equivalent to the phrase "some other." But neither the word "independent" nor the word "other" appeared in Section 1002, the corroboration provision that governed Sophie Oleksiuk's sworn testimony.

Judge Prendergast failed to stipulate from where he took the concept of "independent evidence." He claimed to be simply interpreting Section 1002 of the Canadian *Criminal Code*, but it is likely that he was drawing upon the 1916 English case of *Rex v. Baskerville.* Judge Trueman, who wrote a majority concurring opinion in *Hubin,* did quote from the English Court of Criminal Appeal's ruling in *Baskerville* that "evidence in corroboration must be independent testimony which affects the accused by connecting or tending to connect him with the crime."[52] Judge Trueman, however, did not focus any further upon the "independent" requirement. He was more than content to confirm the conviction of Leo Hubin upon the evidence tendered. And it should have remained an open question whether *Baskerville* applied to the case at bar. The English decision related to the evidence of accomplices, which required corroboration at common law and not as a result of a statutory formulation. There was no reason to apply the "independence" language from *Baskerville* to the statutory corroboration rules attached to the crime of carnal knowledge under the Canadian *Criminal Code*. The "independent" criterion set the evidentiary burden for rape victims one step beyond where the legislators had already gone. It practically necessitated third party evidence in crimes of sexual assault where the judges must have known that separate witnesses would rarely exist.[53]

Prendergast and Fullerton's judicial decision to import the concept of "independent evidence" into the doctrine of corroboration turned out to be critical to their holding that Leo Hubin's conviction should be quashed. Under the new formulation, Sophie Oleksiuk's testimony that Hubin's car had been on the road near Lockport on the morning of September 20th was a "material particular" that needed to be corroborated by "independent evidence." But the evidence that qualified as "independent," in the sense that it did not emanate from Sophie Oleksiuk, did not go to a "material particular." Neither the car vendor's testimony that Hubin owned the car nor Hubin's admission of car ownership corroborated the "location" of the car at the particular moment in question. And the evidence that went to a "material particular" was not "independent." The note upon which Sophie Oleksiuk had jotted down Hubin's licence number was Sophie's evidence alone:

> It does not serve any purpose to observe that she gave the police at the station a paper on which she stated she had noted the plate number, nor that she repeated the same thing under oath at the trial. Nothing that she said and no document that proceeded from her, however much they may strengthen her version, can be corroboration.

The same difficulty beset the identification of Hubin in the police lineup:

> If, as she says, she had never seen him before the 20th (and the accused, on his part, says that he saw her at the station for the first time) such identification undoubtedly adds further value to her testimony. ... [S]till the statement, as true and convincing as it may be in itself, remains wholly unsupported. That the identification was made in the presence of police officers, adds nothing to it. It is still her evidence and that only, just as it would be if the identification had been made at the trial for the first time.

With a sense of certitude that almost lent itself to a lecturing tone, Judge Prendergast continued:

> It is the purpose of corroboration to communicate its own independent virtue to the primary evidence. To follow the reverse process of looking for something in the primary evidence to bolster up and energize the corroboration, is to travel in a circle, and corroboration then becomes meaningless. No degree, however high, of plausibility or certainty in the primary evidence, is a substitute for corroboration,

which must stand by itself and be judged on its own independent value.[54]

Judge Trueman, who had obviously read the dissenting judges' opinions before writing his own, upbraided his colleagues for the irrational result that attended their narrow interpretation of the doctrine of corroboration. His decision, issued as a concurring majority opinion, noted:

> No one on the evidence which I have above detailed can reasonably have any view other than that the prisoner is guilty. That some one had carnal knowledge of the complainant is corroboratively shown. The theory that the complainant seeks to connect the prisoner, a person she did not know and never saw before, with the commission of the act, in order to shield another person, is too barren to have a moment's consideration. She gave not only the number of the car – something it is true she could have got from any passing car driven by an unknown man, if there would have been the slightest sense or object in doing it – but she shows through her familiarity with the cushion in the back of the driver's seat that she had been in the car. This is a detail it is likely she would not have given if her story was an invention. ... Its nature differs from cumulative or supporting statements resting solely upon the veracity of the complainant. It relates to facts she was powerless to invent.

Judge Trueman ridiculed the theory that Sophie Oleksiuk could have concocted the identification of Hubin and his car, linking her testimony to Hubin's sworn statement that he had been driving his car that morning nowhere in the vicinity of alleged rape:

> If the prisoner's statement is true that during the whole of the forenoon of the 20th he was not at Lockport because he was elsewhere, then the number was a fictitious one invented for no earthly reason, and which on investigation by the police might be found not to belong to anyone or to belong to a person who weeks before had left the country. The conclusion, in my opinion, is unavoidable that the car was in Lockport on the 20th and that the complainant was in it. It is pointless to suggest that the complainant could have got the number when it passed her on some former occasion. ... If it was not in Lockport on that date, then the incredible supposition is made that

before the act in question was committed, the complainant in anticipation that the act would be committed on the 20th, and to protect the
person who was to commit it, obtained the number of the car at an
earlier date for the purpose of fastening the crime on the prisoner, a
person she did not know, and who, if her story was to hold together,
she had to assume would be in Lockport on the 20th.[55]

Given the division of opinion from the provincial appellate bench,
the Supreme Court of Canada agreed to consider the prisoner's appeal.
The Supreme Court judges unanimously sided with the dissenting
appellate decision, finding that the identification evidence was tainted
by its connection with Sophie Oleksiuk:

> While the verification of the details given by her no doubt adds to the
> credibility of the story she tells, everything in that connection, includ-
> ing the admitted facts of ownership and driving (not at or near the
> scene of the offence, but in and about Winnipeg) depends, for its evi-
> dentiary value, upon her statement that a certain license number was
> that carried by the car in which she was conveyed to the scene of the
> crime and her subsequent identification of a cushion found in the car
> bearing that number. That is not, in a proper sense, independent evi-
> dence tending to connect the accused with the crime. In themselves
> these facts and circumstances merely "relate to the identity of the
> accused without connecting him with the crime."

Citing *Rex v. Baskerville*, Chief Justice Francis Alexander Anglin
decided to reject the identification evidence because it implicated the
accused "solely by reason of the complainant's statement." Without the
"additional factor" of her testimony, the identification evidence was
"quite irrelevant." Summing up, Anglin concluded: "Nor can any multiplication of such facts amount to corroboration. They are all admissible only by reason of the girl's own story connecting them with the
crime. They lack, therefore, the essential quality of independence."[56]
    There was nothing that irrevocably dictated this final result. The
Criminal Code did not stipulate that corroborating proof had to issue
from a source separate from the complainant. There was no need for
the judges to tighten the doctrine of corroboration still further than the
legislators had formulated. To import the criteria of "independent"
evidence constituted a rude and unnecessary dismissal of the veracity
of sexual assault victims, to the point that not only were they rejected

as trustworthy witnesses, but everything that even remotely stemmed from their evidence was summarily disregarded.

Even if it were correct to interpret the statutory wording as incorporating some element apart from the victim herself, there was no need to take the concept of "independent evidence" to such an extreme point as the judges ultimately did in the *Hubin* case. One might have located the "independent" criterion within the concrete existence of the identified motor vehicle and the peculiar cushion. Sophie Oleksiuk may have written the note with the licence number that identified the car, and she may have identified the cushion, but the material objects belonged to a man she did not know, who independently admitted he was driving in that motor vehicle, which contained that cushion, at the time in question. Hubin's admission was what implicated him, quite apart from Sophie's testimony. Sophie Oleksiuk may also have been the individual who identified the accused as the man who raped her. But the man she identified turned out to be the owner of the car she had identified earlier. And the fact of his ownership was proven by the car dealer and Leo Hubin himself, both sources independent of Sophie Oleksiuk.

The final items of evidence that came under scrutiny as potential corroboration were the two inconsistent statements that Leo Hubin gave to the police upon his arrest. Hubin was duly cautioned in the police station that anything he might say could be taken down and used against him in court. Heedless of the risk, Hubin signed a written statement purporting that he was at least twenty miles distant from the country road on which Sophie Oleksiuk was raped on the morning of September 20. He swore that he had been driving his car in Winnipeg, conversing with pool hall mates at the Seymour Hotel, and consulting with a garage mechanic at the City Dray Garage. Almost immediately after signing this statement, Leo Hubin asked to withdraw it and to make a second statement. This time he swore that he drove his car directly from the Seymour Hotel to his mother's home in St Boniface, stayed there until 10:30 a.m., drove to his sister's home and brought her back to his mother's, and then departed for his own apartment in Winnipeg where his wife was waiting, arriving there about noon.

Both statements constituted denials on the part of the accused. The denials were internally inconsistent. It was arguably open to the court to draw an adverse inference regarding the credibility of the accused man, a finding that could offer some corroboration "implicating the accused." What was more, there was no quarrel that Leo Hubin's statements to the police were "independent" of the complainant. At trial, Judge Stacpoole made no mention of the inconsistent statements. He had already found the identification of Hubin and his car to be sufficient corroboration, and he went no further in his oral judgment. The majority of the judges at the Manitoba Court of Appeal canvassed the whole of the evidence and ruled the statements to be fully corroborative in law. Chief Justice Perdue was quick to characterize the statements as incriminating admissions, noting that they were clearly made "for the purpose of founding an alibi upon them." Perdue suspected that after Hubin made the first statement, he "feared that the persons he mentioned as in conversation with him that forenoon might not support his statements." He then shifted his statement "in the expectation that his mother and sister" would vouch for him. Judge Trueman was even more scathing:

> These statements carry nothing but conviction that they are a tissue of lies. Each completely contradicts and refutes the other. It is not necessary to examine or compare them in detail. ... That both statements are false I have no doubt. That one is assuredly false need alone be stated.[57]

Although Leo Hubin did not testify at the trial, Judge Trueman indicated that it was open to the trial judge to come to the conclusion that the accused was lying when he gave the inconsistent denials to the police. This, entirely on its own, could constitute legal corroboration.[58]

Judge Prendergast in his dissent came to a remarkably different view. Like the Australian judges who exhibited distinct caution in reviewing statements of the accused, he was prepared to extend every feasible excuse to explain the apparent inconsistencies in Leo Hubin's police statements. First he suggested that the discrepancies might be explained on the basis that Leo Hubin was trying to account for his whereabouts a full four days after the events in question. Hubin had been quite busy on September 20, ferrying around between home, pool hall, city garage, his mother's home, his sister's home and so on. Perhaps Hubin had simply "made a mistake" when he signed the first statement, and immediately decided to make a second statement. According to Prendergast, there was nothing "suspicious" in the "bare fact of his stating that [the first statement] was not correct." Dissecting the two statements for discrepancies, Prendergast deduced that the account of Hubin's movements early that morning was the same. The divergent information related to what had transpired after 10:00 a.m., all arguably irrelevant to a sexual assault that allegedly occurred shortly after 9 a.m. Hubin's effort was to establish an alibi with his mother and sister was legally inconsequential, because he did not need an alibi for the latter portion of the morning or the afternoon. Prendergast was prepared to overlook the inconsistencies, noting that they did not "necessarily show such bad faith as would be ground for holding that they constitute corroboration."[59]

The Supreme Court of Canada was somewhat less charitable concerning Hubin's possibly faulty memory. Chief Justice Anglin indicated that Hubin's conduct "in voluntarily making the two inconsistent statements" was such that "the trial judge might infer from it some acknowledgment of guilt." This was a "finding of fact" that properly lay within the jurisdiction of the jury, or in cases tried without a jury, with the trial judge. The problem was that Judge Stacpoole had not specifically cited Hubin's inconsistent statements in his trial judgment. He had stopped prematurely once he identified the identification of the car as corroborative. Anglin summed up: "There is no finding by the trial judge as to the inference to be drawn from the conduct of the accused, already adverted to, nor any adjudication that affords the requisite corroboration. We cannot, without usurping the exclusive function of the tribunal of fact, make such an adjudication."[60]

Here was a legal interpretation that finally accepted as "corroborative" one of the multiple items of evidence put forward by the Crown prosecutor. Yet in the final analysis it too was spurned. The Supreme Court quashed the conviction, and directed that a new trial should be held to relitigate the matter. There is no record of any second prosecution ever being instituted.[61] Leo Hubin, whom almost everyone connected with the case seems to have believed responsible for the sexual attack upon Sophie Oleksiuk, was judicially branded "not guilty." Even his defence counsel, J.M. Issacs, appears to have recognized his client's moral turpitude. In his written submissions to the Supreme Court of Canada, Isaacs noted: "Corroboration has been adopted by the Legislature as a matter of public policy and like all such enactments they must inevitably lead to injustices being done in individual cases. That is the price paid to secure public protection."[62] Here was a succinct articulation of the heavy costs associated with the demand for corroboration. Isaacs, the majority of the Canadian judges, and the legislators all seem to have been predisposed to believe that the "public protection" that required securing was the safekeeping of men who might potentially be falsely accused. The "public protection" of raped young girls went by the wayside, as something more intangible, more inconsequential, a mere "inevitable injustice."

Conclusion: A Case for Comparison?

The credibility of witnesses is fundamental to the process of legal adjudication. All legal systems recognize that some witnesses tell the truth, while others do not. However, the manner in which the trustworthiness of witnesses is assessed reveals a great deal about the judiciary, the legislators who shape the statutory framework of evaluation, and the wider society within which such findings of credibility are constructed. Where legal systems differentiate between witnesses on the basis of gender, this suggests grave sexual imbalances and inequalities. Where the law stipulates presumptions of incredibility that are applied to female witnesses, but not to males, this would seem to be reflective of patriarchal injustice.

The history of the legal doctrine of corroboration, as it was grafted onto the crime of "carnal knowledge" of young women, offers an exemplary opportunity to probe the evidentiary prescriptions constructed by legislators, lawyers and judges. The similarities between the corroboration rules promulgated in Australia and Canada were remarkable. Both countries took their lead from England in their decision to criminalize the offence of sexual intercourse with girls below the age of consent. Both countries borrowed from the common law traditions rooted in Sir Matthew Hale's unsubstantiated anxieties about the credibility of women and girls who reported coercive male sexuality. Legislators from both jurisdictions departed from English precedent in enacting statutory requirements that mandated corroboration for the crime of carnal knowledge of girls under the age of fourteen. The statutory formulations of the rules of corroboration set forth parameters that were substantially narrower than the ordinary usage of the word might have suggested. In the hands of the judiciary, the boundaries of what qualified as legal corroboration constricted still further.

The early twentieth-century cases of *Sullivan* and *Hubin* provide useful illustrations of the parallel development of corroboration doctrine in Australia and Canada. Crown prosecutors in both cases supplemented the testimony of highly credible complainants with a host of additional evidentiary material. The evidence that convinced judge and jury at the trial level of the guilt of the accused men, beyond a reasonable doubt, was dismissed out of hand by appellate judges. The convictions were quashed because of mandatory statutory corroboration provisions that were interpreted extremely narrowly by judges who professed greater concern over the plight of men potentially falsely accused than they did over sexual crimes involving females.

Medical evidence that attested to the sexual assault of the young girls was rejected in both cases as failing to "implicate the accused." One witness's torn bloomers were ignored for the same reason. Recent complaints made by the two girls to family members were also thrown out. The rationale in one case was that the recipient of the recent complaint was "inherently incredible." In the other case, the appellate court failed to articulate its reasons. Evidence that one of the accused men had been seen in the vicinity of the crime location was dismissed as "mere opportunity" and insufficiently probative. The incriminating statements made by the two men also did not secure their convictions. In one case, the admissions made to the complainant's mother were dismissed because of extenuating circumstances related to the mother's reputation. Incriminating statements made to a neighbour were ignored, with no rationale offered. In the other case, the accused's contradictory alibis were thrown out because the lower court judge had forgotten to stipulate that he found this evidence to be corroborative at trial. One witness's description of the paddock in which she had been violated was rejected as unable to "implicate the accused." The other witness, whose identification of the accused's car certainly met that test, had her evidence dismissed because it did not issue from an "independent" source.

Were there apparent distinctions between the corroboration law in Australia and Canada? To the extent that these leading cases[63] document diversity, the disparity is but slight. The phrasing of the statutory definition of "corroboration" was not identical in the Western Australian and Canadian Criminal Codes. Since judges in neither country seemed to pay much attention to the niceties of the statutory phrasing, whether the small discrepancies in wording might have resulted in different legal findings was never put to the test. The introduction of the concept of "independent" evidence, a judicial importation that was not apparent on the face of any of the legislative formulations, had not taken hold in Australia in 1913. The Australian courts would await the 1916 English *Baskerville* decision before beginning to insist that corroboration must emanate from an entirely separate source other than the complainant. The unnecessarily restrictive "independent" rule was in full swing in Canada by 1927, when Canadian courts unreflectively transported the rule from an English court that was ruling on common law corroboration applied to an entirely different offence. The *Hubin* approach, a colonial acceptance of the English precedent without further consideration of the distinctions codified in Canadian statute, or a purposive interpretation flowing from such legislative language, foreshadowed what would ensue in Australia in the future.

Deeply suspicious of the testimony of women and girls, Australian and Canadian authorities were historically loath to receive their evidence at face value, or to leave it subject to the ordinary tests for veracity. Without any perception of embarrassment, hesitation or remorse, early twentieth-century legislators and judges wielded the doctrine of corroboration as a club to assail women and girls who dared to seek criminal sanction against men accused of sexual offences. Fashioning corroboration as the *sine qua non* for conviction was calculated to ensure that the testimony of guilty men would receive more credence on the scales of justice than the testimony of female victims of sexual assault. The promulgation of restrictive and stilted definitions of corroboration tilted the balance still further. The application of such doctrines in the hands of the judiciary whittled down the scope of qualifying evidence, and served to skewer the credibility of young women complaining of sexual intercourse. The doctrine of corroboration made a mockery in both countries of the ideals of even-handed justice and gender parity. For Ila Collins and Sophie Oleksiuk, raped half way across the world from each other, the end result of such discriminatory legal treatment was precisely the same. In this shameful record, there was virtual parity, and no apparent divergence in the legal history of the two sister colonies.

I would like to thank the following individuals for their assistance: Pascal-Hugo Plourde, Brian Hubner, Rosemary Morrissette Rozyk, Bruce Feldthusen. Financial assistance from the Social Sciences and Humanities Research Council of Canada, the Bora Laskin Human Rights Fellowship and the Law Foundation of Ontario is gratefully acknowledged.

Notes

1. *The Criminal Code*, 1892, S. C. (1892, c.29).
2. *Criminal Code*, (1902), (WA).

3. Desmond H. Brown, *The Genesis of the Canadian Criminal Code of 1892* (Toronto: Osgoode Society, 1989).

4. *R. v. Sullivan*, State Archives of Western Australia "Depositions in *R. v. Louis Sullivan*" Criminal Indictment Files, Cons. 3473, Item 427, Case 4475 (Perth, 913); (1913), 15 WAR 23.

5. *Hubin v. The King*, Archives of Manitoba, Manitoba Court of Appeal No. 3/27 (1927); Supreme Court of Canada Archives RG 125, Part 2, Box 483–1192 (1922–1962), Vol. 556, File 5369, Series A; (1927), 36 Man. R. 373 (C.A.), 47 C.C.C. 237 (Man. C.A.), [1927] 1 W.W.R. 705 (Man. C.A.), [1927] 2 D.L.R. 593 (Man. C.A.); [1927] S.C.R. 442, 48 C.C.C. 172 (S.C.C.).

6. The Sullivan and Hubin cases were selected after reviewing all of the reported sexual assault cases from Canada between 1900 and 1950, a sample of unreported Canadian cases during this period from the archival records of Nova Scotia, Ontario and Saskatchewan, and all of the reported sexual assault cases from Western Australia and Victoria, Australia published between 1900 and 1950.

7. *R. v. Sullivan*, State Archives of Western Australia "Depositions in *R. v. Louis Sullivan*" Criminal Indictment Files, Cons. 3473, Item 427, Case 4475 (Perth, 1913); "A Serious Charge" *Perth Daily News* 16 December 1912; "A Serious Charge" *Perth West Australian*, 13 December 1912.

8. The Provincial Archives of Manitoba holds the appeal files for *Hubin*, but not the lower court files. The Supreme Court of Canada Archives contains portions of the trial transcript, as well as the written arguments of appellate counsel. I am indebted to Brian Hubner of the Provincial Archives of Manitoba for his efforts to locate the surviving records. The press coverage is sparse on detail: "Four Years For Serious Crime" *Winnipeg Tribune* 8 December 1926; "City and District" *Winnipeg Free Press* 8 December 1926; "Supreme Court Reserves Judgment in Hubin Case" *Winnipeg Free Press* 4 May 1927; "Supreme Court Gives Manitoban New Trial" *Winnipeg Free Press* 31 May 1927; "Circumstantial Evidence Must Be Corroborated" *Winnipeg Tribune* 31 May 1927.

9. *R. v. Baskerville*, [1916] 2 K.B. 658 (C.A.). On the dominance of the *Baskerville* analysis, see A.B. Clarke "Corroboration in Sexual Cases" *Criminal Law Review* (1980): 362; A.E. Branca "Corroboration" in *Studies in Canadian Criminal Evidence*, eds. R.E. Salhany and R.J. Carter (Toronto: Butterworths, 1972) 133–4.

10. *Offences Against the Person Act 1861*, (Eng.), 24 & 25 Vict., c.100, s.50–51; *Criminal Law Amendment Act 1885*, (Eng.), 48 & 49 Vict., c.69, s.5. On the legislative history of these provisions, see Constance Backhouse "Nineteenth-Century Canadian Rape Law, 1800–92" in *Essays in the History of*

Canadian Law v.2 ed. David H. Flaherty (Toronto: Osgoode Society, 1983), 206–11.

11. *An Act Respecting Offences against the Person*, S.C. 1869, c.20, s.51–53; *An Act to Amend the Criminal Law*, S.C. 1890, c.37, s.3,7, 12. For discussion of the discrepancy in penalties between Canadian and British legislation, see Backhouse "Nineteenth-Century Canadian Rape Law." *The Criminal Code 1892*, S.C. 1892, c.29, s.269 provided: "Every one is guilty of an indictable offence and is liable to imprisonment for life, and to be whipped, who carnally knows any girl under the age of fourteen years, not being his wife, whether he believes her to be of or above that age or not." See also *Criminal Code*, R.S.C. 1906, c.146, s.301. The *Criminal Code Amendment Act*, S.C. 1920, c.43, s.8 added s.301(2): "Every one is guilty of an indictable offence and liable to imprisonment for five years who carnally knows any girl of previous chaste character under the age of sixteen and above the age of fourteen, not being his wife, whether he believes her to be above the age of sixteen or not. No person accused of any offence under this subsection shall be convicted upon the evidence of one witness, unless such witness is corroborated in some material particular by evidence implicating the accused." Section 17 of the 1920 statute added s.301(3): "On the trial of any offence against subsection two of this section, the trial judge may instruct the jury that if in their view the evidence does not show that the accused is wholly or chiefly to blame for the commission of the said offence, they may find a verdict of acquittal." See also *Criminal Code*, R.S.C. 1927, c.36, s.301.

12. See *Criminal Law Consolidation Ordinance 1865* (WA); *Criminal Law Amendment Act 1892* (WA); *Criminal Law Amendment Act 1900* (WA); *Criminal Code 1902* (WA), s.188(1). The latter section provided that "any person who has or attempts to have unlawful carnal knowledge of a girl under the age of sixteen years ... is guilty of a misdemeanour, and is liable to imprisonment with hard labour for two years, with or without whipping." There was no requirement for proof of "previous chaste character," as in the Canadian counterpart legislation. However, it was a defence to prove that the accused person believed, on reasonable grounds, that the girl was of or above the age of sixteen years. (This defence did not apply to charges of unlawful carnal knowledge of a girl under the age of thirteen years; s.185, 205). See also *Criminal Code Amendment Act 1911* (WA), s.2–4.

13. For some discussion of the absence of any empirical foundation to substantiate the claims that females often lie about rape, see Jocelynn Scutt, "Sexism and Psychology: An Analysis of the 'Scientific Basis' of the Corroboration Rule in Rape," *Hecate* 5 (1979): 35–48.

14. Matthew Hale, *Historica Placitorum Coronae* v.1 (London: Nott and Gosling, 1734), 635–6. On the frequency with which these statements were quoted, see *Harris's Principles of the Criminal Law* 7th ed., (London: Stevens and Haynes, 1896), 164. For some discussion of Hale's reputation as a misogynist and his notorious role in convicting women accused of witchcraft, see G. Geiss, "Lord Hale, Witches and Rape," *British Journal of Law and Society* 5 (1978): 26; Jocelynn Scutt, "Law Reform and Child Abuse in Australia," in *Childhood and Society in Western Australia*, ed Penelope Hetherington (Perth: University of Western Australia Press, 1988), 125–6, 134.

15. See, for example, *Halsbury's Laws of England*, Vol. 9 (London: Butterworths, 1909), 388; E.H. East, *Pleas of the Crown*, Vol. 1 (Abingdon: Professional Books, 1987 reprint), 445.

16. *An Act to amend the Criminal Code*, S.C. 1925, c.38, s.26; *Criminal Code*, S.C. 1927, c.36, s.301(2), 1002.

17. The *Criminal Code 1902* (WA), s.188(1) provided that "a person cannot be convicted of any of the offences defined in this section upon the uncorroborated testimony of one witness." Section 1 provided that the term "uncorroborated testimony" meant "testimony which is not corroborated in some material particular by other evidence implicating the accused person."

18. For reference to the debates, see Backhouse "Nineteenth-Century Canadian Rape Law"; Constance Backhouse, *Petticoats and Prejudice: Women and Law in Nineteenth-Century Canada* (Toronto: Osgoode Society, 1991), 69–80; Constance Backhouse "Skewering the Credibility of Women: A Reappraisal of Corroboration in Australian Legal History," *Western Australian Law Review* 29 (March 2000): 87.

19. For more details regarding this testimony and its characterization by witnesses, court officials and the press, see Backhouse "Skewering the Credibility of Women: A Reappraisal of Corroboration in Australian Legal History."

20. *Hubin v. The King* (1927), 36 Man. R. 373 (C.A.) at 374–5, 377–9; Supreme Court of Canada Archives (1927).

21. See Backhouse, "Skewering the Credibility of Women."

22. *Hubin v. The King* (1927), 36 Man. R. 373 (C.A.) at 375–6, 383, 385.

23. The requirement for corroboration under English law was attached primarily to allegations involving sexual violence, exploitation or immorality made by women and children. It encompassed criminal proceedings for a variety of sexual offences and civil proceedings for affiliation, breach of promise to marry and divorce. The unsworn testimony of children "of tender years" also attracted the need for corroboration, as did the evidence of

accomplices, and criminal prosecutions for perjury, treason, blasphemy and personation. Highlighting the peculiarities of such rules, *The Dictionary of English Law*, v. 1 (London: Sweet and Maxwell, 1959) 504 stated: "The general rule of English law, unlike that of other systems, is that the evidence of a single witness is sufficient to prove any case, civil or criminal. In certain cases, however, the court will not act on the evidence of a single witness unless that evidence is corroborated. This, in some cases, is a matter of practice, but in a few cases the court is precluded by statute from acting on the evidence of a single witness unless there is corroboration."

24. *A New English Dictionary* v.2 (Oxford: Oxford University Press, 1893) 1020.

25. This definition was first introduced in the Western Australia *Criminal Code 1902* (WA), s.1. There was no general statutory requirement for corroboration for carnal knowledge in England at the time. The only extant provisions were found in the *Criminal Law Amendment Act 1885* (Eng.), 48 & 49 Vict., c.69. Section 2 made it a crime to procure or attempt to procure any girl or woman under twenty-one years, not being a common prostitute or of known immoral character, to have unlawful carnal connection, or to leave the United Kingdom to become an inmate of a brothel. The section continued: "provided that no person shall be convicted of any offence under this section upon the evidence of one witness, unless such witness be corroborated in some material particular by evidence implicating the accused." Section 3, which made it a crime to procure such a woman to have unlawful carnal connection by threats, intimidation, false pretences or the administration of drugs, contained a similar corroboration provision. Section 4, which made it a crime to have unlawful carnal knowledge of a girl under the age of thirteen years, or to attempt to do so, did not contain the same provision. However, the section described how evidence of children "of tender years" might be taken pursuant to this charge without being sworn, "if the witness was possessed of sufficient intelligence to justify the reception of the evidence, and understands the duty of speaking the truth." Where this type of unsworn evidence was received, the section required a different sort of corroboration: "Provided that no person shall be liable to be convicted of the offence unless the testimony admitted by virtue of this section shall be corroborated by some other material evidence in support thereof implicating the accused." The phrasing of the corroboration requirement subsequently enacted in Western Australia appears to have been an amalgam of the two English sections. The only other statutory corroboration requirements in England were found in *An Act for the Prevention of Cruelty to, and better Protection of, Children* (Eng.), 52

& 53 Vict. (1889), c.44, s.8, which provided that evidence of children not given upon oath could not result in a conviction of an adult for ill-treatment or neglect of children, unless that evidence was "corroborated by some other material evidence in support thereof implicating the accused." See also 57 & 58 Vict. (1894), c.41, s.15; 4 Edw. VII (1904), c.15, s.15.

26. Prior to the introduction of the statutory definition, Australian law had been quite unsettled regarding the corroborative potential of medical evidence in sexual assault trials. See, for example, *R. v. Abbott* (1898), 9 QLJ 92; *R. v. Roys* (1898), 9 QLJ 47, and the unreported trial of Thomas Palmer in the Geelong Court of Assize in 1885 on the charge of raping his daughter, described in Jill Bavin-Mizzi "Writing About Incest in Victoria 1880–1890" in *Childhood and Society in Western Australia* ed. Penelope Hetherington (Perth: University of Western Australia Press, 1988), 49, 58–65.

27. *R. v. Walsh* (1905) 7 WAR 263, State Archives of WA, "Depositions in *R. v. John Walsh*," Criminal Indictment Files, Cons 3473, Items 3692 and 3701 (Perth, 1905) involved a charge of carnal knowledge of a nine-year-old girl. The girl's parents had sent her to the accused's residence with messages on three occasions, and each time she had come home complaining of injury. The sexual assault was medically ascertained some weeks later. The Supreme Court ruled that the fact that the girl had been at the accused's house, or in his company, was insufficient corroboration without further incriminating particulars. It was up to the Crown to prove something more to obtain an inference of impropriety – that they had been seen in an "indelicate position," that he was enticing her into his house, or shutting the door or pulling down the blinds. *R. v. McGee* (1894) 6 QLR 151 also ruled that the fact that the accused man and the child were alone together in the house in which the offence was alleged to have been committed did not constitute corroboration. See also *R. v. O'Brien* [1912] VLR 133, holding that "evidence that the accused had an opportunity to commit the act charged, the commission of which was clearly proved, was not sufficient." A Canadian case which seems to have taken a more relaxed approach is *Rex v. Elzear Pailleur* (1909), 15 O.W.R. 73 (Ont. C.A.), involving the charge of attempting to commit incest upon a daughter aged seven. A witness testified to seeing the accused go upstairs and call his daughter to come up to him, that the girl was reluctant but went, and that she came back later with her clothing in "disorder" and showing "signs of agitation." The court found such evidence corroborative, noting that the law did not require that every part of the evidence should be corroborated, but only that it must be corroborated by some other material evidence. See also *Rex v. Bowes*, [1910] 20 O.L.R. 111 (Ont. C.A.); *Rex v. Steele*

(1923), 33 B.C.R. 197 (B.C.C.A.), upheld in *Steele v. The King* (1924), 42 C.C.C. 375 (S.C.C.); *Rex v. Kramer* (1924), 20 Alta. L.R. 244 (C.A.); *Rex v. Bristol* (1926), 46 C.C.C. 156 (N.S.S.C.). But see *Rex v. McGivney* (1914), 22 C.C.C. 222 (B.C.S.C.); *Rex v. Drew* (1932), 60 C.C.C. 37 (Sask. C.A.); and *Rex v. Newes* (1934), 61 C.C.C. 316 (Alta. S.C.), where Canadian courts dismissed the corroborative potential of evidence suggesting that the accused had the opportunity to commit the offence.

28. *R. v. Gregg* (1892), 18 VLR 218 (Vic.Sup.Ct.F.C.).

29. *R. v. Gregg* (1892) 18 VLR 218 (Vic.Sup.Ct.F.C.) at 222–224. See also *R. v. Smith* (1901) 26 VLR 683 (Vic.Sup.Ct.F.C.), a charge of indecent assault on a girl of five years, where the court heard evidence that the girl had described portions of the assault to her mother. Ruling that the conversation between the girl and her mother had not revealed sufficient "circumstances of indecency," the court disqualified it as corroborative. Although nothing in the court's judgment suggests that such evidence could never be corroborative, the holding did note at 686 that corroboration constituted "extrinsic sworn evidence" that would "implicate the accused."

30. See, for example, *R. v. Rima* (1892) 14 ALT 138, where the accused gave statements to the arresting officer in which he admitted having "tampered with the child." The court held that this was insufficient to justify the conclusion that he had committed an indecent assault. In *R. v. Walsh* (1905) 7 WAR 263; State Archives of Western Australia, "Depositions in *R. v. John Walsh*," Criminal Indictment Files, Cons 3473, Items 3692 and 3701 (Perth, 1905), the accused, who was charged with carnal knowledge of a girl under the age of thirteen, told the police that the complainant was a "young hussy." He also admitted she had been in his place when he was undressing. Upon arrest, he added: "It would not do me any good to say anything." The court held these statements were insufficient to implicate the accused.

31. *Sullivan v. R.* (1913) 15 WAR 23 (W.A.Sup.Ct.F.C.) at 28–9. For press coverage of the appellate ruling, see "A Criminal Appeal" Perth *West Australian* 27 June 1913; "Court of Criminal Appeal." Perth *Daily News* 26 June 1913.

32. *Sullivan v. R.* (1913) 15 WAR 23 (W.A.Sup.Ct.F.C.) at 24–5.

33. *Sullivan v. R.* (1913) 15 WAR 23 (W.A.Sup.Ct.F.C.) at 25–26, 30.

34. J. A. Gobbo, (Australian edition) *Cross on Evidence* (Sydney: Butterworths, 1970), 221.

35. An Act further to amend the Criminal Law, S.C. 1890, c.37, s.13 provided only that when a child of "tender years" was tendered as a witness, who did not understand the nature of an oath, such evidence might be received

"if, in the opinion of the court or justices such girl is possessed of sufficient intelligence to justify the reception of the evidence and understands the duty of speaking the truth." In such cases only, s.13(2) provided: "But no person shall be liable to be convicted of the offence unless the testimony adduced by virtue of this section, and given on behalf of the prosecution, is corroborated by some other material evidence in support thereof implicating the accused."

36. The *Criminal Code 1892*, S.C. 1892, c.29, s.684 made corroboration mandatory for all charges under s.181–190, which included "seduction of girls under sixteen," "seduction under promise of marriage," "seduction of a ward, servant, etc.," "seduction of female passengers on vessels," "unlawfully defiling women," "parent or guardian procuring defilement of girl," "householders permitting defilement of girls on premises," "conspiracy to defile," "carnally knowing idiots" and "prostitution of Indian women," as well as the offences of treason, perjury, procuring feigned marriage and forgery. It did not cover "carnal knowledge of a girl under the age of fourteen," or "attempt to commit carnal knowledge of a girl under fourteen." The wording of the corroboration rule stated: "No person accused of an offence under any of the hereunder mentioned sections shall be convicted upon the evidence of one witness, unless such witness is corroborated in some material particular by evidence implicating the accused." Slightly different wording was retained in s.685(2), with respect to evidence of children of "tender years" received without an oath: "But no person shall be liable to be convicted of an offence [of carnal knowledge of a girl under fourteen or indecent assault] unless the testimony given on behalf of the prosecution is corroborated by some other material evidence thereof implicating the accused." See also the *Criminal Code*, R.S.C. 1906, c.146, s.1002, 1003(2).

37. *An Act to amend the Criminal Code*, S.C. 1920, c.43, s.8 amended s.301 of the Code by adding s.301(2): "Every one is guilty of an indictable offence and liable to imprisonment for five years who carnally knows any girl of previous chaste character under the age of sixteen and above the age of fourteen, not being his wife, and whether he believes her to be above the age of sixteen years or not. No person accused of any offence under this subsection shall be convicted upon the evidence of one witness, unless such witness is corroborated in some material particular by evidence implicating the accused."

38. *An Act to amend the Criminal Code*, S.C. 1925, c.38, s.26 expanded the list of offences requiring corroboration to include "seduction of girls between sixteen and eighteen," "seduction of step-child or foster child," "seduction

of female employee," "procuring," "carnal knowledge of girls under fourteen," "carnal knowledge of girls of previous chaste character between fourteen and sixteen," "attempted carnal knowledge of girls under fourteen," the abortion offences, "communicating venereal disease" and "bigamy." See also the *Criminal Code*, R.S.C. 1927, c.36, s.1002, 1003(2). The 1927 revision reprinted the corroboration provisions directly within s. 301(2), carnal knowledge of a girl between fourteen and sixteen and s.307, communicating venereal disease, an unusual duplication.

39. *Criminal Code* 1892, S.C. 1892, c.29, s.684, as amended by S.C. 1925, c.38, s.26.

40. *Criminal Code* 1892, S.C. 1892, c.29, s.685(2); *Criminal Code* R.S.C. 1906, c.146, s.1003(2); *Criminal Code*, R.S.C. 1927, c.36, s. 1003(2).

41. For examples of Canadian cases dismissing the corroborative value of medical evidence, see *Rex v. Turnick* (1920), 33 C.C.C. 340 (N.S.S.C.) *Rex v. Drew* (1932), 60 C.C.C. 37 (Sask. C.A.) and *Rex v. Terrell* (1947), 88 C.C.C. 369 (B.C.C.A.). For a case to the contrary, where the judge ruled that the medical evidence of a ruptured hymen might constitute corroboration in a charge of carnal knowledge, see *Rex v. Hyder* (1917), 29 C.C.C. 172 (Sask. C.A.). See also *Rex v. Drew (No. 2)* (1933), 60 C.C.C. 229 (Sask. C.A.).

42. *Hopkinson v. Perdue* (1904), 8 C.C.C. 286 (Ont. H.C.). See also *Rex v. Schraba* (1921), 35 C.C.C. 402 (Man. C.A.).

43. *The Queen v. Riendeau* (1900), 9 Que.B.R. 147 (K.B.).

44. For cases disavowing the use of recent complaint as corroboration of the facts in issue, see *Rex v. Schraba* (1921), 35 C.C.C. 402 (Man. C.A.); *Rex v. Gordon* (1924), 25 O.W.N. 572 (Ont. Div. Ct.); *Rex v. Everitt* (1925), 45 C.C.C. 133 (N.S.S.C.); *Rex v. Mudge* (1929), 52 C.C.C. 402 (Sask. C.A.); *Rex v. Stinson* (1934), 61 C.C.C. 227 (B.C.C.A.); *Rex v. Tolhurst* (1939), 73 C.C.C. 32 (Sask. C.A.); *Rex v. Reeves* (1941), 77 C.C.C. 89 (B.C.C.A.); *Rex v. Reardon* (1945), 83 C.C.C. 114 (Ont. C.A.). *Rex v. Calhoun* (1949), 93 C.C.C. 289 (Ont. C.A.) upheld as correct a trial judge's charge to the jury that a recent complaint was not evidence of the actual happening of the event, but testimony that pointed to the complainant's consistency, and that it could also be considered corroborative of the absence of consent.

45. On the importance of promptness, see *The Queen v. Riendeau* (1900), 9 Que.K.B. 147; *The King v. Smith* (1905), 9 C.C.C. 21 (Halifax Co. Ct.); *The King v. Akerley* (1918), 46 N.B.R. 195 (N.B.C.A.); *Rex v. Gordon* (1924), 25 O.W.N. 572 (Ont. Div. Ct.); *Rex v. Hall* (1927), 49 C.C.C. 146 (Ont. S.C.); *Rex v. Marsh* (1940), 74 C.C.C. 312 (B.C.C.A.); *Rex v. Jones* (1944), 84 C.C.C. 299 (P.E.I. S.C.) . For cases that showed more tolerance toward a delayed complaint, see *The King v. Barron* (1905), 9 C.C.C. 196 (Halifax Co. Ct.); *Rex v.*

McGivney (1914), 22 C.C.C. 222 (B.C.S.C.) in the majority decision; *Rex v. Hill* (1928), 61 O.L.R. 645 (Ont. C.A.).

46. For cases stipulating the importance of voluntary and spontaneous disclosure, and rejecting complaints that were made in response to questions, see *The King v. Bishop* (1906), 11 C.C.C. 30 (N.S.S.C.); *The King v. Dunning* (1908), 14 C.C.C. 461 (Sask. S.C.); *Rex v. Stonehouse and Pasquale* (1927), 39 B.C.R. 279 (B.C.C.A.). For cases illustrating a less rigid view on these matters, see *The King v. Spuzzum* (1906), 12 C.C.C. 287 (B.C.S.C.); *Rex v. Pailleur* (1909), 15 O.W.R. 73 (Ont. C.A.); *Rex v. Bowes*, [1910] 20 O.L.R. 111 (Ont. C.A.); *Rex v. McGivney* (1914), 22 C.C.C. 222 (B.C.S.C.) in the majority decision; *Shorten v. The King* (1918), 42 D.L.R. 591 (S.C.C.); *Rex v. Tolhurst* (1939), 73 C.C.C. 32 (Sask. C.A.); *Rex v. Ashley* (1944), 82 C.C.C. 259 (P.E.I.S.C.).

47. *Hubin v. The King*, Supreme Court of Canada Archival File, Oral Judgment of Stacpoole C.C.J., at 54–55.

48. *Rex v. Hubin* (1927), 36 Man. R. 373 (C.A.) at 375.

49. *Rex v. Hubin* (1927), 36 Man. R. 373 (C.A.) at 378.

50. *Criminal Code* R.S.C. 1927, c.36, s.1002.

51. *Criminal Code* R.S.C. 1927, c.36, s.1003, emphasis added.

52. *Rex v. Hubin* (1927), 36 Man. R. 373 (C.A.) at 383, citing *Rex v. Baskerville*, [1916] 2 K.B. 658 (C.A.) at 667.

53. The steepness of the evidentiary barrier this interpretation would impose was considered and explicitly rejected in the earlier case of *The King v. Burr* (1906), 12 C.C.C. 103 (Ont. C.A.), a prosecution for the seduction of a girl under sixteen, which also required statutory corroboration under s.1002. The court noted that the statute did not necessarily "make it incumbent upon the Crown to adduce testimony of another or other witnesses to the acts charged. To do so would be to virtually render a conviction impossible in the majority of cases like the present. It is enough if there be other testimony to facts from which the jury, or other tribunal trying the case, weighing them in connection with the testimony of the one witness, may reasonably conclude that the accused committed the act..."

54. *Rex v. Hubin* (1927), 36 Man. R. 373 (C.A.) at 378–9.

55. *Rex v. Hubin* (1927), 36 Man. R. 373 (C.A.) at 384–5.

56. *Hubin v. The King*, [1927] S.C.R. 442 at 444–5.

57. *Rex v. Hubin* (1927), 36 Man. R. 373 (C.A.) at 375.

58. The majority opinion cited no authority for this rule, either Canadian or English. Cases that had used similar reasoning include *Rex v. Daun* (1906) 12 O.L.R. 227 (Ont. C.A.) where the failure of the accused to deny responsibility for his fiancee's pregnancy was found to constitute corroboration

for the charge of seduction under promise of marriage. *The King v. Romans* (1908), 13 C.C.C. 68 (N.S.S.C.) located corroboration for a charge of seduction under promise of marriage in the testimony of the woman's parents as to admissions made by the accused regarding his promise to marry their daughter. See also *Rex v. Whistnant* (1912), 20 C.C.C. 322 (Alta. S.C.); *The King v. Wakelyn* (1913), 21 C.C.C. 111 (Alta. S.C.); *Rex v. Magdall* (1920), 33 C.C.C. 387 (Alta. S.C.); *Rex v. Stinson* (1934), 61 C.C.C. 227 (B.C.C.A.); *Rex v. Richmond* (1945), 84 C.C.C. 289 (B.C.C.A); *Rex v. Stelmasczuk* (1948), 93 C.C.C. 124 (N.S.S.C.) on the implied admission of guilt as implicating the accused. But see *Rex v. Goodfellow* (1927), 49 C.C.C. 268 (N.B.S.C.) which held that the mere failure of the accused to deny the charge and to take the stand in his own defence could not constitute corroboration.

59. *Rex v. Hubin* (1927), 36 Man. R. 373 (C.A.) at 379–80.

60. *Hubin v. The King*, [1927] S.C.R. 442 at 446, 449–50.

61. No record of a second trial against Leo Paul Hubin was found in a search of the following: Provincial Archives of Manitoba, Court of Queen's Bench and County Court Criminal Registers, Schedule A0107, Micro film #M1196 (from 1872–1949); Court of Queen's Bench Criminal Pockets, ATG0007A, Micro film #M1245 (from 1872–1989).

62. *Hubin v. The King*, Supreme Court of Canada Archives, Memorandum of Argument for Appellant at 91.

63. On the importance of *Hubin* to the development of Canadian jurisprudence in this area, see A. E. Branca "Corroboration," in *Studies in Canadian Criminal Evidence*, eds. Roger E. Salhany and Robert J. Carter (Toronto: Butterworths, 1972), 133 at 136, where he notes: "Unquestionably, the leading case in Canada is *Hubin v. The King*."

PART III

Citizenship Challenged

10

Citizenship Politics in Canada and the Legacy of Pierre Elliott Trudeau

LINDA CARDINAL

Pierre Elliott Trudeau is probably one of Canada's best known politicians internationally as well as one of the most controversial in the country's history. His attitude towards Quebec nationalists is well known as is his commitment to individual rights within the citizenship debate starting in the nineteen-sixties. Simply put, for Trudeau, Canada had to learn to see herself as a multicultural and bilingual society, multiculturalism being the right of every individual to his cultural heritage and bilingualism meaning the right of every Canadian to receive federal services in the official language of his choice. He premised his understanding of Canada on the idea that all individuals and cultures were equal; that there should be no official culture in Canada while the demographics of the country made it sensible to have two official languages.

Most studies of Trudeau's legacy imply that there is a Canada before and a Canada after Trudeau. Commentators refer to his radical liberalism and legalistic approach to language and culture.[1] They also insist on his anti-nationalism[2] and on his centralist approach to federalism[3] which was exacerbated, in 1982, by the adoption of the *Canadian Charter of Rights and Freedoms*.[4] To be sure, it is as if the ideas of one man had been enough to transform the destiny of a whole country.

In this chapter, I argue that Trudeau was a man of his times. Canadians associate the language of rights with the United States, a society which is founded on the notion of popular sovereignty and where using the courts is a normal way of asserting that sovereignty against the state.[5] It is assumed that Canada is a gentler country. It has a British parliamentary tradition in which politics is understood as an on-going dialogue within the walls of the House of Commons or the legislative assemblies. It is understood that rights are better protected by Parliament and not by the courts.[6]

This chapter is premised on the idea that Trudeau was the product of a society (Quebec and Canada) that, since the nineteen-sixties, tended to adopt more explicitly the American approach to rights.[7] The country's style of politics had already started to change in the nineteen-thirties with the development of a civil liberties movement and with the beginning of the welfare state.[8] Trudeau's politics were quite compatible with the language of social rights underlying the Canadian welfare regime as well as with the growing civil rights movement of the time. His accomplishment was to bring this new rights-based politics into the area of identity and citizenship. In other words, one of his major contributions to the politics of citizenship in Canada is to have succeeded in defining language and culture both as individual rights and as the main criteria of belonging to the Canadian nation. He was either criticized or celebrated for doing so but he was certainly not going against the current by promoting a rights discourse around language and culture. His politics were a reflection of the changing relations between politics and society and of a shift from a traditional parliamentary approach to a more rights-based approach.

Thus, my contribution to the Trudeau debate will be to move away from denunciations or celebrations of his liberalism and proceed with a more structural and historical approach to the analysis of his legacy on the debate on Canadian citizenship. So much emotion is involved when one discusses his politics, especially in Quebec and in the Western provinces, that the exercise of putting Trudeau into context may give us a better picture of the man while looking at an area which deserves more research, i.e. the history of rights politics in Canada.

This chapter is divided into three parts. First, I will present the context which has made the development of a rights-based politics in Canada possible. Second, I will show how Trudeau has contributed to the citizenship debate by building on that tradition and applying it to the discussions on language. Third, I will address more generally Trudeau's legacy and the future of the citizenship debate in Canada.

The Rights Tradition in Canada

Canadians are not strangers, historically, to the rights discourse and the appeal to courts. By the nineteenth century, the dialogue between rights and politics was already an on-going one. The understanding may have been that rights were better defended in a sovereign parliament than by the courts. But this did not prevent provincial governments from using the latter whenever they were fighting the centralist approach of the federal government. The language of rights served to re-assert what they believed were the founding principles of the Constitution – foremost among those was the federalist principle. More precisely, provincial governments appealed to the Judicial Committee of the Privy Council (JCPC) in London to fight the tendency of the then Prime Minister, John A. Macdonald, to disawow provincial laws even if they fell under their own jurisdiction. A case in point is how the government of Ontario used the language of individual rights in the area of natural resources in order to insist that the province was a political community in its own right.[9] The Quebec government was also strong in demanding that the central government respect its jurisdiction. For Quebec, it was also a matter of respecting the right to self-determination of the French-Canadian people.

As early as 1890, the French-speaking minority in Manitoba also appealed to the courts to fight restrictions imposed on the use of French by their provincial government and then in 1912, the French-speaking minority in Ontario did the same.[10] At the time, Macdonald supported Franco-Manitobans financially, hoping the courts would reject the prohibition of French in that province.[11] However, he refused to use his powers to disavow the new language legislation although he would not hesitate to use them in other areas.[12] At the time (and still today), language was too sensitive an issue to force provinces to be tolerant towards their French-speaking minorities even though their practices went against the spirit of the Constitution.

This vignette of Canadian politics during the nineteenth century should make us wary of interpretations that ignore the rights tradition in nineteenth-century Canada or that see the adoption of the *Charter of Rights and Freedoms* in 1982 as decisive in the development of a language of rights. Although it is not false to think of the nineteen-eighties as an important moment in the development of a legalistic politics in Canada, especially in the area of identity, one must not forget that Canada was already a legalistic society before 1982.[13]

During the thirties, the nature of federalism and of the Canadian federation continued to be debated as the Canadian government became more interventionist and centralist in the areas of economic and social rights. Provincial governments, notably Alberta, Ontario and Quebec, thought that Canada was taking a "collectivist" route.[14] They were opposed to state intervention in the economy and believed in a minimal liberal state.[15] But they were not alone in their struggle. Canadian business groups shared their concern and did not hesitate in asking the courts to limit state intervention.[16]

However, for civil libertarians, it was clear that the powers of the provinces had to be limited. This was certainly the opinion of Supreme Court Justice Rand who was the first to give the notion of a Canadian citizen a meaning which would be based on a doctrine of rights and freedoms.[17] His approach to rights and freedoms can be found in three cases especially: the *Alberta Bill Press* (1938), a case on the freedom of the press in the province of Alberta; *Saumur v. Quebec City* (1953) which determined the right of Jehovah Witnesses to freedom of expression; and the *Roncarelli* affair in 1957 which involved the right to distribute communist literature in Quebec.

Finally, in 1960, the adoption of a Bill of Rights confirmed Canada's commitment to rights and freedoms. For Bora Laskin, the Bill of Rights would allow the courts to become more active in the area of policy while hoping, in the near future, that the federal government would adopt a charter of rights and freedoms. It was understood that only through such means, even though in contradiction with the British tradition, would rights and freedoms evolve progressively in Canada.[18]

In the nineteen-sixties, this new language of rights and freedoms inspired largely the politics of new social movements even though they also saw themselves as radical or emancipatory groups. Feminists, civil liberties groups and many more demanded the right to choose in the area of abortion, the right to equal pay for work of equal value, the right to be free from discrimination based on sexual orientation, ethnicity, religion, race, gender, the right to speak French, the right to be educated in French, the right to self-determination. At the institutional level, in 1962, the Ontario government was the first provincial government to adopt a Human Rights Code in order to protect individuals against discrimination and to demand that they should all be treated as equals.

More needs to be said on the subject of rights politics in Canada since the nineteen-thirties. In the nineteen-sixties, civil rights and equality issues became more and more important and a reflection of growing concerns for more justice in Canadian society. Thus Canada's rights discourse was moving from a debate on the nature of federalism to one in which the protection of individuals would become the measure of a democratic government. It is within such context that Trudeau became committed to a politics of rights in the area of culture and language.

Trudeau and the Politics of Citizenship

Trudeau came to federal politics in the nineteen-sixties, influenced by the civil rights movement and the ideals of the welfare state. Such context informed the development of a rights-based politics in Canada, and Trudeau was there at the right time and the right place to add language and identity issues to the questions being debated. He was not alone in this enterprise. His opponents such as René Lévesque or Jacques Parizeau were as immersed in the language debate as he was except that their discourse was one of collective rights and the right of the Quebec people to self-determination.

In 1965, Trudeau co-authored a manifesto for a just and functional society in which individual or civil rights were key values to his ideal society.[19] Thus mediating the rights of individuals or citizens through their different governments would no longer be as relevant as under the "old" regime. For him, which government should govern would become a question of pragmatics, with his preference going to the federal government.[20]

In 1969, the legislation making French and English the official languages of Canada was his first attempt in implementing his ideas of a just society.[21] He believed that in a country like Canada, with two large linguistic groups, it was common wisdom that language, ethnicity and culture should be de-politicized and defended as individual rights.[22] He was mostly concerned with Quebec nationalists with whom he spent his whole career fighting. He wanted Quebeckers to identify with Canada, not with their province. He agreed that French was a minority language which needed protection and support but he was against the idea of a separate national state for Quebeckers. He then rejected the proposition by André Laurendeau and Léon Dion from the Royal Commission on Bilingualism and Biculturalism in Canada that French should be confirmed as the official language of the province of Quebec.[23] Any majoritarian principle was problematic to him. It was minorities which needed support from governments, not majorities. He was worried that such a law recognizing French as the official language of Quebec would only threaten the rights of the English-speaking minority. He was also concerned with the status of French speaking minorities living outside of Quebec.

Frank Scott, a member of the Royal Commission on Bilingualism and Biculturalism in Canada and whose ideas were close to those of Trudeau, thought that Canadians would be more open to a legislation which would make their country bilingual from coast to coast.[24] Therefore, no one would think that Quebec was receiving special treatment. Moreover, for Trudeau, it was important that French and English be equal at the federal level.[25] He wanted language to be entrenched in the Constitution because he did not believe, for historical reasons, that it was realistic to hope that politics would be sufficient in such matters as language rights.[26] He believed in the principle of reciprocity at the provincial level, which meant that in a province with a French- or English-speaking minority of more than 15 percent of the population, the legislative and judiciary should be bilingual.[27] However, only one province contained a linguistic minority of such proportion – New Brunswick, with 32 percent of its population being of Acadian descent – and the province did adopt a legislation on language similar to the federal one, but no other province did. In 1974, Quebec adopted Bill 22 which stipulated that French was the official language of the province. In 1977, the government adopted the *Charte de la langue française*, Bill 101, which extended Bill 22 in the workplace, giving the right to Quebec's francophones to work in their own language. A specific section of Bill 101 also stipulates the commitment of the Quebec government to the protection of the English-speaking minority and another section, which was never implemented, addressed the possibility of reciprocity agreements between governments which would give French-speaking minorities living outside of Quebec comparable rights to those of the English-speaking minority in Quebec.[28] It was understood that this would allow more cooperation among governments on language since a constitutional right could only prevent discrimination.[29] In 1975, the Quebec government also adopted a *Charter of Rights and Freedoms*, seven years before the one adopted federally.[30]

Ontario is the only other province with a generous language law towards its French-speaking minority even though it only represents 5 percent of the population. Adopted in 1986, the law on French services in Ontario recognizes institutional bilingualism; however all political parties in Ontario have always rejected any proposition towards official bilingualism.[31] In other provinces, French was not considered a language worthy of support by the provincial government. As a result, in Manitoba, French-speaking minorities did not hesitate to use the courts once more to have their rights recognized as a collectivity. The federal government was also quite active in financially supporting French- and English-speaking minorities who were taking their respective governments to court.[32] The Trudeau government favoured the legalization of language politics.[33] It contributed to depoliticizing the issue and defining the latter as a question of fundamental rights. Such an approach also explains why Trudeau, in 1979, was so much against the recommendations of the Pepin-Robarts Commission on national unity which wanted the provinces to be more involved in the protection of linguistic minorities. The Commissioners were hoping that Trudeau would call for more cooperation with provincial governments instead of entrenching language rights in the Constitution.

In 1982 when Trudeau unilaterally patriated the Constitution and entrenched in it a *Charter of Rights and Freedoms*, he gave constitutional status to language. He entrenched the right of every French- or English-speaking Canadian to an education in their language everywhere in Canada. He also gave constitutional status to gender equality, multiculturalism and native rights. He hoped that these elements of the identity debate would be understood as fundamental to Canadian unity. He also used the opportunity to increase financial support to linguistic minorities wishing to get even more involved in legal action against their governments. As a result, from 1982 to 1985, major cases were debated in the Supreme Court of Canada which helped make a case for language rights to be recognized as a fundamental right.[34]

However, Quebeckers believed that the Charter was an instrument which would make it forever impossible to recognize their rights as a collectivity.[35] There is no provision which allows for the recognition of their special status in Canada – neither was it the intention of Trudeau. Ever since his beginnings in federal politics he wanted to entrench such a document in the Canadian Constitution. The Charter should be acknowledged as an important step in the development of a citizenship politics based on the language of individual rights and of Canadians' renewed sense of nationhood, not as a compromise with Quebec's demands. It is true that during the nineteen-eighties and nineties, the different attempts to reform the Canadian Constitution are the closest we have come to implementing a multinational citizenship in Canada. In 1987, the Meech Lake Accord recognized Quebec as a distinct society. The 1992 Charlottetown Accord also recognized Quebec as a distinct society as well as the First Nations' right to self-determination. Had those proposed changes been ratified, Canada would in effect have instituted a form of multinational citizenship. But both Accords were rejected: we may have lost a unique opportunity to redefine citizenship.

Trudeau's Legacy and the Future of the Citizenship Debate

Trudeau's legacy in the area of language and Charter politics is blurred. After thirty years of politics in the area of language, most commentators seem to agree that Trudeau failed in making language rights the basis of a renewed sense of nationhood among the majority of Canadians, especially among those living in the Western provinces and in Quebec.[36] His policy on bilingualism is seen as unfair by many Canadians.

Commentators prefer his policy on multiculturalism because bilingualism still connotes collective rights and the Canada-Quebec debate, not individual rights.[37] In other words, language has not been the basis for a renewed sense of nationhood in Canada insofar as it has been too much perceived as a source of division among Canadians.[38] In fact, many observers have acknowledged that the rights-based politics of citizenship promoted by the Charter in the area of language has divided the country even more today than before.[39] Trudeau never managed to silence Quebec's nationalism. On the contrary, Quebeckers identify more today with Quebec than with Canada.[40] They believe Quebec is their nation and not just a province where they happen to be living as Canadians; Quebeckers have a strong sense of destiny as a group. Moreover, they are still not reconciled with the rest of Canada and more than 30 percent of them support a sovereigntist political party at both federal and provincial levels.

A majority of Canadians also believe that the rights of the English-speaking minority in Quebec are threatened even if Bill 101 makes provisions for their protection. It is a case in point that English-language signs were prohibited in Quebec in the area of advertising. The Quebec government made things even worse when it used the notwithstanding clause in the Charter to exclude itself from a judgment of the Supreme Court on the issue. However, for Will Kymlicka, the English-speaking minority has been much better served in the language debate than the French-speaking minority living outside of Quebec.[41] The language policy in Canada helped the English-speaking minority in Quebec because it gave the federal government the mandate to promote

English in Quebec. It is still not possible to live fully in French outside of Quebec except for some parts of the province of New Brunswick and Ontario whereas a unilingual anglophone can live quite well in Quebec, especially in Montreal. Moreover, 50 percent of all French-speaking children in Ontario still do not go to French school even though it is their constitutional right to do so.

Finally, according to Kymlicka, the language debate has given birth to a new pan-Canadian nationalism based on the sympathy of English Canada towards the English-speaking minority in Quebec.[42] It articulates itself around the idea that English in Quebec and in the rest of Canada is potentially threatened by French. Such movement also serves to legitimize the actions of groups such as the Alliance for the Preservation of English in Canada, which is explicitly francophobic, as well as Canada First, which is against hyphenated Canadians such as French-hyphen Canadian or Italian-hyphen Canadian.[43] These groups are especially active in Ontario, where in the nineteen-eighties, more than 110 municipal governments adopted English as their official language in reaction to Quebec's own policy towards its English-speaking minority.

Many observers have also criticized Trudeau's Charter based-politics because it has been perceived as a threat to Canada's political tradition of parliamentarism.[44] It has turned the politics of identity into a movement for the legalization of politics which has undermined the role of legislative assemblies. For David Smith, the Charter brings in a new element of popular sovereignty in the realm of Canadian politics which undermine the powers of the Crown.[45] Other commentators also perceive it as having reinforced a vision of national unity based on the subordination of the provinces to the central government.[46]

To be sure, most commentators seem to agree that the Charter has given the debate of citizenship and moreover, Canadian politics, an American flavor. But we should be wary of explanations which put too much weight on the Charter. In fact, what we have witnessed is an acceleration of a process which had started as early as the nineteen-thirties with the civil rights movements and the beginning of the Canadian welfare state. The Charter has allowed more groups to have access to the courts and it also gave more power to judges to interpret the law, in keeping with the hopes of Bora Laskin of a more active and normative Supreme Court. Among those groups, language minorities have made extensive use of the courts as have visible and religious minorities, women and native groups. As such, the Charter represents the extension of the logic of social and economic rights in the area of identity and culture. It is not at all at odds with the pre-Charter period. However, it has transformed Canadian politics in that it is now impossible for governments to avoid the language of human rights in the areas of culture and identity and the question is, was it a good thing? Have we progressed? This is obviously not a question specific to Canadian politics but one which is impossible to avoid in Canada given the extent to which we discuss identity politics.[47]

On the one hand, there now seems to be a consensus that the legalization of politics and citizenship issues into questions of human rights has its limits.[48] The judicialization of politics creates anomie and contributes to the fragmentation of citizenship.[49] It goes against the possibility of reciprocity among groups. But what could replace it?

On the other hand, even if we do not want to adapt the Canadian Constitution to the demands of First Nations and Quebec, a new language is necessary for future discussions with minority nations in Canada. The denial of the identity and nationhood of Quebec as well as of First Nations communities will not go on forever, and when the time comes to engage again in an inter-cultural dialogue in Canada, we should be able to propose a viable and credible alternative to the status quo. Such an alternative should be based on principles such as reciprocity, responsibility and pluralism, and a more in-depth understanding of First Nations constitutional traditions such as the two row wampum. We should also renew our understanding of Quebec's role as political actor in the development of constitutionalism in Canada and question the actual stereotype of Quebeckers as people manipulated by their elites.

Conclusion

What is left of Trudeau's legacy to Canadian politics? It is fair to say that the *Charter of Rights and Freedoms* gave English Canadians a renewed sense of pride in their country. They have acknowledged that individual rights, as well as multiculturalism and gender equality are at the core of Canadian identity. They are less comfortable with Quebec's demands as well as with those of Native peoples. In both cases, they refuse to acknowledge the legitimacy of their collective right to self-determination. In this respect, citizenship in Canada is not all that it could be. It may now no longer be possible to reconcile the ideal of citizenship with the demands for recognition of minority nations such as Quebec and First Nations. The contemporary language of inclusion or civic nationalism should make it possible that all citizens participate equally in the affairs of the nation, regardless of religion, language, gender, race, culture, etc. However, the language of civic nationalism seems to be incapable of accommodating the demands for recognition of other nations within the nation.

In many ways, Trudeau's legacy is in keeping with Canada's (both French and English) liberal and individual rights tradition. It is a politics which became more civil rights oriented in the nineteen-thirties and it is one which has not been absolutely faithful to traditional parliamentary principles. Such politics reached new heights in the nineteen-sixties and was confirmed in the nineteen-eighties with the Charter.

To conclude, we have to be wary of any whig interpretation of Trudeau's role in Canadian politics which would create a false sense of progress. His actions were possible because groups and individuals used institutional processes available to them in a successful way. Trudeau, the hero for so many Canadians, was also a man of his time, an actor among others, albeit an important one, in a general movement towards the development of a more popular based and American form of democracy in Canada. But Canada is still a constitutional monarchy and the possibility of a regime in which sovereignty would lie outside of the Crown is not yet foreseeable. Yet Canada is not characteristic of a traditional constitutional monarchy; it is a mixture of different approaches in search of a new equilibrium still to come.

Research for this paper was made possible with a grant from the SSHRC on the political culture of rights in Canada. I would like to thank Marie-Ève Hudon for her assistance.

Notes

1. Guy Laforest, *La fin d'un rêve canadien* (Montréal: Septentrion, 1992); François Houle, "Des identités nationales dans le régime fédéral canadien," in *Dislocation et permanence. L'invention du Canada au quotidien*, ed. Caroline Andrew (Ottawa: Les Presses de l'Université d'Ottawa, 1999), 229–281.
2. Claude Couture, *La loyauté d'un laïc. Pierre Elliott Trudeau et le libéralisme canadien* (Montréal/Paris: L'Harmattan, 1996).
3. Rainer Knopff and F.L. Morton, "Le développement national et la Charte,"

in *Le constitutionnalisme et la société au Canada*, eds. Alan Cairns and Cynthia Williams (Ottawa: Approvisionnement et Services Canada, 1986), 149–205; Kenneth McRoberts, *Un pays à refaire : L'échec des politiques constitutionnelles canadiennes* (Montréal: Les Éditions du Boréal, 1999).

4. François Rocher and Daniel Salée, "Démocratie et réforme constitution-nelle : discours et pratique," *Revue internationale d'études canadiennes*, no 7–8, (1993): 167–186.

5. Robert Vipond, *Liberty and community: Canadian federalism and the failure of the constitution* (Albany: State University of New York Press, 1991); Michael Sandel, *Democracy's Discontent: America in Search of a Public Philosophy* (Cambridge: The Belknap Press of Harvard University Press, 1996).

6. Janet Ajenzstat, "Reconciling Parliament and Rights: A. V. Dicey Reads the Canadian Charter of Rights and Freedoms," *Canadian Journal of Political Science*, vol. 30, (1997): 645–662.

7. Paul Cavaluzzo, "Judicial Review and the Bill of Rights: Drybones and its Aftermath," *Osgoode Hall Law Journal*, vol. 9 (1971).

8. Jacques Beauchemin, Gilles Bourque et Jules Duchastel, "Du providential-isme au néolibéralisme: de Marsh à Axworthy. Un nouveau discours de légitimation de la régulation sociale," *Cahiers de recherche sociologique*, no 24, (1995): 15–47; Susan D. Phillips and Jane Jenson, "Regime Shifts: New Citizenship Practices in Canada," *International Journal of Canadian Studies*, no 14, (1996): 111–135; Richard Fisk and Robert Vipond, "Rights Talk in Canada in the Late Nineteenth Century: The Good Sense and Right Feel-ing of the People," *Law and History Review*, vol. 14, no 1, (1996): 1–32.

9. Robert Vipond, "Citizenship and the Charter of Rights: The Two Sides of Pierre Trudeau," *International Journal of Canadian Studies*, no 14, (1996): 179–192.

10. Kent Roach, "The Role of Litigation and the Charter in Interest Advocacy," in *Equity and Community*, ed. Leslie Seidle (Montreal: IRPP, 1993), 159–188.

11. Jean-François Cardin et Claude Couture, *Le Canada. Espace et différence* (Quebec: Les Presses de l'Université Laval, 1995).

12. One had to wait for Sir Wilfrid Laurier, a decentralist, to help the franco-phone population of Manitoba arrive at a compromise with their provin-cial premier, the only case of the kind in the area of linguistic minority rights in Canadian history.

13. Miriam Smith, "Ghosts of the JCPC: Lessons for the Study of Law and Pol-itics in Canadian Political Science," paper presented at the joint meeting of the Canadian Political Science Association and la Société québécoise de science politique, Quebec, 29 July to 1 August 2000.

14. Doug Owram, *The Government Generation* (Toronto: University of Toronto Press, 1993).

15. In theory, they were adamantly opposed to the welfare state. However, in practice, the Ontario government was also more and more interventionist in the areas of economic and social rights. In 1952, it was the first government to adopt the *Female Remuneration Act* which promoted equality between men and women at work. The Quebec government was also forced to become more interventionist in the area of welfare.

16. Richard Fisk and Robert Vipond, "Rights Talk in Canada in the Late Nineteenth Century: The Good Sense and Right Feeling of the People," *Law and History Review*, vol. 14, no 1, (1996): 1–32.

17. Linda Cardinal, "Le pouvoir exécutif et la judiciarisation de la politique au Canada," *Politique et sociétés*, vol. 19, nos 2–3 (2000): 43–64.

18. Paul Cavaluzzo, "Judicial Review and the Bill of Rights: Drybones and its Aftermath."

19. Pierre Elliott Trudeau, *Le fédéralisme et la société canadienne-française* (Montréal: Éditions HMH, 1967); Thomas Axworthy and Pierre Elliott Trudeau eds., *Les années Trudeau. La recherche d'une société juste* (Montréal: Le Jour éditeur, 1990).

20. It is true that in 1965, Trudeau still believed in a Canadian federalism which respected provincial jurisdictions. However, once in power, he never hesitated to use the discretionary powers of the central government to impose his policies on the provinces.

21. Claude Couture, *La loyauté d'un laïc. Pierre Elliott Trudeau et le libéralisme canadien*, 122.

22. Pierre Elliott Trudeau, *Le fédéralisme et la société canadienne-française* , 391.

23. Léon Dion, *La révolution déroutée*, (Montreal: Boréal, 1999).

24. Ibid.

25. Pierre Elliott Trudeau, *Le fédéralisme et la société canadienne-française*, 56.

26. Ibid., 58.

27. Ibid., 58.

28. The reciprocity clause in Bill 101reads as follows: "Le gouvernement peut faire des règlements pour étendre l'application de l'article 73 aux personnes visées par une entente de réciprocité conclue entre le gouvernement du Québec et le gouvernement d'une autre province." (1977), c. 5, a. 86; 1993, c. 40, a. 34; José Woerhling, "Les aspects juridiques et la redéfinition du statut politique et constitutionnel du Québec," *Éléments d'analyse institutionnelle, juridique et démolinguistique pertinents à la révision du statut politique et constitutionnel du Québec* (Québec: Commission sur l'avenir du Québec. Document de travail, no 2, 1991): 1–111.

29. Normand Labrie, "La protection des minorités de langues officielles au Canada au moyen des accords de réciprocité: prospectives de l'aménagement linguistique," *Actes du colloque sur la problématique de l'aménagement linguistique: enjeux théoriques et pratiques* (Chicoutimi: Université du Québec à Chicoutimi, 1993), 73–89.

30. The adoption of the 1975 Quebec *Charter of Rights and Freedoms* is a case in point which reveals how the Canada-Quebec debate has been falsified by the adoption of the 1982 Canadian Charter. The Quebec government gives the impression, by opposing the Canadian Charter, that it is against the idea of rights. In fact, it would be more accurate to say that it is against the imposition of a language of rights from the federal government but it is not against the idea of rights *per se*. Since the nineteenth century, Quebec has been as immersed in the culture of rights as the rest of Canada with the difference that it accepts the language of collective rights. Interestingly enough, the rejection of a language of collective rights by the rest of Canada may just be another proof of the way in which a tradition of individual rights is also well entrenched in Canadian political culture. Moreover, individual rights in Canada have been defended by both Parliament and the courts, perhaps even in ways unprecedented in the United States.

31. Linda Cardinal, *Chroniques d'une vie politique mouvementée. L'Ontario francophone de 1986 à 1996* (Ottawa: Le Nordir, 2001).

32. In 1978, a courts challenge program was set up by the Privy Council which invited individuals and groups to appeal to the court for a clarification of their language rights provincially and federally. For more information see Cardinal, "Le pouvoir exécutif et la judiciarisation de la politique au Canada."

33. For an overview of the cases taken to the Supreme Court from 1978 to 1982 see Richard Goreham, *Les droits linguistiques et le programme de contestation judiciaire: Réalisations du Programme et incidence de son abolition* (Ottawa: Commissaire aux langues officielles, 1992).

34. Linda Cardinal, "Le pouvoir exécutif et la judiciarisation de la politique au Canada," 43–64.

35. Guy Laforest, *La fin d'un rêve canadien*; François Houle, "Des identités nationales dans le régime fédéral canadien."

36. Only one group seems to believe in Trudeau's language policy, Canadian Parents for French, which promotes immersion programs for young English-speaking Canadians; but times are changing. These programs were popular at one time but not anymore. For example, there are now more children in the Western provinces of Canada learning Spanish than

French; Robert Vipond, "Citizenship and the Charter of Rights: The Two Sides of Pierre Trudeau," *International Journal of Canadian Studies*, no 14, (1996): 179–192; Ray Conlongue, "English-Canadian Culture and the Absent French Canadian," *Inroads*, no 8 (1999): 87–97; François Houle, "Des identités nationales dans le régime fédéral canadien," 229–281.

37. Robert Vipond, "Citizenship and the Charter of Rights: The Two Sides of Pierre Trudeau."

38. Ibid.

39. Linda Cardinal, "L'illusoire nation civique à l'épreuve des francophones hors Québec," in *Nation, multination et supranation*, ed. Michel Seymour (Montreal: Liber, 2002).

40. Léon Dion, *La révolution déroutée* (Montreal: Boréal, 1999); Alain-G. Gagnon, "Québec-Canada: Circonvolutions constitutionnelles," in *Québec. État et société*, ed. Alain-G. Gagnon (Montreal: Quebec/Amériques, 1994), 85–106.

41. Will Kymlicka, "Le fédéralisme multinational au Canada: un partenariat à repenser," in *Sortir de l'impasse. Les voies de la réconciliation*, eds. Guy Laforest and Roger Gibbins (Montreal: IRPP, 1998), 15–54.

42. Ibid.

43. The group succeeded in pressuring Statistics Canada to use *Canadian* in the 1996 census dealing with ethnic origin. Traditionally such a question, just like in the USA, excluded answers such as Canadian. The purpose of a question on ethnic origin in the census is to measure patterns of discrimination based on ethnicity. The answer *Canadian ethnic origin* makes the measurement of discrimination more difficult, which can be damaging to affirmative action programs.

44. Charles Taylor, *Rapprocher les solitudes* (Quebec: Les Presses de l'Université Laval, 1992); Janet Ajenzstat, "Reconciling Parliament and Rights: A. V. Dicey Reads the Canadian Charter of Rights and Freedoms," *Canadian Journal of Political Science*, vol. 30, (1997): 645–662.

45. David E. Smith, *The Invisible Crown* (Toronto: University of Toronto Press, 1995).

46. Rainer Knopff and F.L. Morton, "Le développement national et la Charte," 149–205; Kenneth McRoberts, *Un pays à refaire. L'échec des politiques constitutionnelles canadiennes* (Montreal: Les Éditions du Boréal, 1999).

47. For a good survey of identity politics in Canada, see James Tully, *Strange Multiplicity: Constitutionalism in an Age of Diversity* (Cambridge: Cambridge University Press, 1994).

48. Gilles Paquet, "Le droit à l'épreuve de la gouvernance," *Gouvernance*, vol. 2, nos 1–2, (2001): 74–84.

49. Alan Cairns, "The Fragmentation of Canadian Citizenship," in *Belonging. The Meaning and Future of Citizenship*, ed. William Kaplan (Montreal: McGill-Queens University Press, 1993), 181–220; Jacques Beauchemin, "La question nationale québécoise: les nouveaux paramètres de l'analyse," *Recherches sociographiques*, vol. XXXIX, no 2–3 (1998): 249–270.

11

The Second Wave: Australia Transformed

SARA DOWSE

The question of citizenship is basically: who counts? I am a writer, more specifically, a writer of fiction, and it is the writer's way, as it is the scholar's, to try to get to the truth, but by the use of techniques such as dissociation, distillation and dramatic development. Moreover, the writer's landscape is the landscape of subjectivity rather than a strictly objective one.

I would like to begin, then, with a reference to a fairy tale, which was published in 1978 in an unusual place for fairy tales, unless you consider debate in the Australian parliament an exchange of fictions, a view for which a reasonable case might be made. The story I am referring to is a paper entitled "The Witch Who Came in from the Cold" which I wrote for a Women's Electoral Lobby conference soon after I resigned from the Australian Public Service, and which somehow appeared on the desk of Senator Brian Harradine, who tabled it during the Wednesday night adjournment debate of 4 March 1978. As far as I am aware it is the first time a fairy tale or indeed any short story was printed in the Hansard proceedings. It was especially pleasing to me because it was the first time I had published any fiction, and I considered it an unprecedented honour to have my debut as a writer occur in something as exalted as the Senate Hansard.

Because of my recent move to Canada it has been difficult for me to get a copy of this work, but I offer a precis from memory. Basically, it is the story of a white knight and a black knight and the white knight's lady-in-waiting – a thinly disguised allegory about the fall of the Whitlam Government and what happened to the feminists who had been working in it. It is not a particularly memorable piece of fiction, its chief interest to me lies in the part it played in my transition from a public policy adviser to a writer, and it was in fact written more or less as a joke, but its interest to Senator Harradine can be deduced from the 4 March 1978 Hansard. Senator Harradine, then an independent Senator from Tasmania, had formed the habit of delivering a speech every Wednesday night to a practically empty Senate chamber, for this was the time when he could air his reactionary views on a host of topics without impediment. His straight man in this was the president of the Senate, Senator Magnus McCormack, as he was obliged to be there. Incredible as it sounds, Harradine provided a full exegesis of the story, explaining that the white knight was Gough Whitlam, the black knight Malcolm Fraser, the lady-in-waiting was Whitlam's adviser on women's affairs, Elizabeth Reid – and so forth. The thrust of his argument, seconded with enthusiasm by Senator McCormack, was that it had been an unconscionable waste of taxpayers' money to have employed me to advise on matters of concern to women – or, indeed, of concern to anyone – the implication being that this was the sort of nonsense that I had served up routinely to Malcolm Fraser. In any case, the story proved conclusively that I never had been a Fraser supporter and that my views on the place of women in society did not accord with those of Senators Harradine or McCormack. All of which was perfectly true.

From memory, Harradine's closing rhetoric went something like this: *And this is the kind of woman who was advising the Prime Minister! How could such a thing have happened?*

With respect to the late Senator, I often ask the question myself. The superficial answer is that in 1974 I went to work in the Department of the Prime Minister and Cabinet to head what was then a new Women's Affairs Section.[1] My immediate brief was to provide bureaucratic back-up for Elizabeth Reid, the Prime Minister's personal adviser on women, whose correspondence had grown more voluminous than that of any other minister save the Prime Minister, and threatened to engulf his own.[2] In this position I also participated in the development of a range of new policies embracing child care, women's shelters, women's employment, women's film and broadcasting, and many other initiatives. In October 1975, soon after Elizabeth Reid resigned and just before the Whitlam Government fell, the Section was upgraded to a Branch, and fifteen months later under Malcolm Fraser it became an Office, pending its anticipated removal from the Prime Minister's Office in December 1977, after which I too resigned. I headed the Office in all its permutations throughout this period, and some of the problems I faced were dealt with in my first novel, *West Block*.[3] I will not comment further on the Office. What I want to do now is move on to an even more personal story, one which I think representative enough to illustrate a transformation that took place over the last years of the twentieth century.

It is blustery spring day in 1958. I am one of thousands of migrants to land by ship in Australia, a place I imagine, because of the Australian prominence in sport, to be something like a giant tennis court dotted with an occasional city. The only difference between me and the majority of other females who have been travelling is that I was born an American – the others come mainly from England and Europe.

I had some idea of what Australians were like from my husband and his Australian friends, but in no way was I prepared for the country. I spoke English, but a radically different kind. Much of the difficulty of my adjustment was due to my being a spoiled American girl: so many things I had taken for granted were prohibitively expensive or simply unavailable in Australia. Automatic washing machines were a luxury (in any case, many Australian women just did not believe that they could get clothes clean), and I learned to use a copper and later a wringer; there were no supermarkets, and I was introduced to the daily regimen of shopping by being handed a beautiful wicker basket by my mother-in-law. For the first few years I spent my afternoons pushing a stroller from the greengrocer's to the butcher's and then to the corner grocery – a routine that might seem delightfully simple and pleasurable today. But then it seemed that my life was being shaped to an extraordinary degree merely by dint of my being female – an experience I had not felt before so sharply.

To my eyes and from myriad other accounts as well, the social segregation of the sexes in Australia was astounding.[4] Although they could vote and run for public office, women scarcely seemed citizens at all, if what we mean by citizenship is full participation in adult society. My first home was my in-laws' Sydney pub, so from the start I was confronted by this most Australian institution, where women were forbidden to drink in the saloon and public bars, and sipped their "ponies" sitting on the steps outside, shelling peas into aluminum saucepans balanced on their knees, while toddlers tugged at their hems. I was taken to a party on Sydney's upper north shore; all the women there gathered round and I never saw a male again until my husband said it was time to leave. On another occasion I began talking to a friend of my husband's who abruptly excused himself when I unwittingly displayed an enthusiasm for politics. Thus, in thousands of small ways, I learned my place, but was never happy with it, and it seemed to me at the time that the whole of Australian society was maintained by the unacknowledged toil of unappreciated, undervalued women.

It was the beginning of the wholesale postwar introduction of married women into the paid workforce, but the convention held firmly that a woman's place was in the home. Woman did most of the domestic work, and a woman was savagely criticized if she failed to meet absurdly high standards of housekeeping. Two instances of this rigid social policing spring to mind. The first occurred when I was living in a block of flats with my husband and baby. The flats had been newly built to cater for the influx of migrants and to provide cheap housing for the elderly. The older women in the building considered it both their right and obligation to comment on the state of the washing pegged out by the young mothers living there. The second took place much later, when the Australian Security Intelligence Organization, the domestic arm of Australian intelligence, was checking me out for employment with the Prime Minister and Cabinet. The only questions they asked my nominated referees related to my housekeeping – how often did I sweep the floor and was I a good mother? This was in 1974 and already there were changes, although ASIO had yet to keep up with them.

The work of Edna Ryan and others has shown that, far from the conventional perception, Australian women had always worked in significant numbers outside the home, married women included, but this was in addition to rather than a substitute for their domestic labour.[5] And although many of these women were sole or significant breadwinners for themselves and/or their families, a woman's earnings were generally considered "extra," or as the phrase went, "pin money." This view of things was expressed most forcibly perhaps in the famous 1906 Harvester decision when Justice Higgins ruled that a woman's wages need only be half a man's, thus institutionalizing a legally sanctioned disparity of pay between men and women that was to operate well into the 1970s, and would continue to retard the achievement of pay equity long after the legal barriers were removed.[6]

As it was socially, so it was in the paid workforce. For many years Australia was considered to have the most gender-segregated labour force among OECD countries, and it was this segregation, arguably – even more than the legally enshrined pay disparity – that would act as a brake on any moves for equity. Women were corralled in a small number of low-paid occupations – mainly nursing, teaching, secretarial and, lower down the scale, food processing work – where the law of supply and demand alone would have kept wages and salaries down. The fact that women still held primary responsibility for the care of children also limited the work they could undertake and, for women, part-time, or more accurately, casual, employment could be as much of a trap as it was an opportunity.

Although it has its own distinctive culture, Australia has been continuously susceptible to overseas influences, whether social or economic. Largely because of its reliance on the export of primary commodities (wool and dairy products in the early part of the twentieth century, coal and other minerals later) Australia has always been part of the global economy and has suffered heavily, some would argue disproportionately, for it. The Great Depression of the 1930s hit Australia hard, and for a long time reactionary attitudes to women were reinforced by a generation of men who had suffered the ignominy of not being able to get work when their wives and daughters could.[7] (That this was yet another consequence of industrial and occupational segregation was little understood.) By the late 1960s these attitudes were so entrenched that it was estimated that women's unemployment was comparable to that of men during the Depression. Indeed, any harking back to the 1950s as the halcyon days of low unemployment must be tempered by the acknowledgement that unemployment was only low for men. Yet the high, largely hidden unemployment of women stood in contradiction to two significant contrary trends – firstly, the shortage of labour experienced in a burgeoning economy; and secondly, the growing number of tertiary-educated women who felt a keen frustration at not being able to find employment commensurate with their qualifications.[8]

So, when news of an overseas movement called Women's Liberation reached Australia, its ideas landed on particularly fertile ground. Beginning in Sydney, groups sprouted up all over the country. By that time I had moved with my husband and four children to Canberra, graduated from Sydney University, and wangled a part-time job as a publisher's representative. It was while I was on the rounds for this job that I met a woman who invited me to a meeting, and from the moment I stepped into that suburban house on a night in September 1970, my life was set on a different track.

Who speaks of Women's Liberation nowadays? Merely uttering the syllables takes one back to a wholly different zeitgeist. We tend to look back on the sixties and seventies as a time of great naivety, a time when personal liberation took precedence over personal commitment, and families and children suffered. I have no doubt that this was true. But neither do I doubt that the great welling up of women's aspirations that took place at that time was inevitable. Many of the hopes we had then have failed to materialize, and others did in ways we could not have predicted, given that they blossomed at a time when economic constraints were not quite as insistent as they are today. Yet despite these disappointments, I do believe that a revolution took place – remember "revolution," too, was a word often on our tongues – and for women, thankfully, Australia today is not the same country I migrated to forty-some years ago.

I am attempting to put the case that Australia was transformed because of what happened to women – a large claim but not insupportable. When you let loose the suppressed desires of half a population and channel that energy towards implementing a host of reforms, how can you avoid transforming a society? To give you an idea of what happened, I will recapitulate slightly, focusing this time more broadly on the position of women before the movement for liberation or, as we like to call it now, feminism's second wave, began.

In 1972, when the Whitlam Government was elected, there was not a single woman in the federal House of Representatives. Although Australian women were among the first to win the vote, since Federation there had been only a handful of women senators and fewer representatives; their participation in politics was, as it was in paid employment, poorly rewarded and virtually unacknowledged. Before the 1970s movement took hold, women were largely invisible.[9] You never saw a woman's face or heard a woman's voice delivering the news, you rarely saw a woman professor, fewer still were industry managers or represented on corporate boards. When I joined the public service a little over one percent of the senior officers were women – a woman head of department seemed as improbable as a woman prime minister. Well into the seventies, in order to take out a loan a woman required a male guarantor; in order to get an abortion a woman had to have her husband's permission. And a lawful abortion was only possible in the direst of cases – where the woman's physical or mental health was deemed to be at stake by at least two physicians. Until 1966 married women teachers and public servants, state and federal, were required by law to resign from permanent service. It was not until the 1970s that pubs began to open their doors to women, largely in response to women dramatically chaining themselves to the bars. There were no women bus drivers or airline pilots. In the arts, sciences and professions, women tended to be handmaidens to men, dropping out or severely curtailing their careers after giving birth to children. Apart from Norman Mackenzie, hardly anyone regarded it worth their while to study Australian women.[10]

The turning point was 1972. That was the year when the Women's Electoral Lobby, an offshoot of Women's Liberation, but more moderate and pragmatic, was established. The work of the Lobby coincided with the election of the Whitlam Labor Government, and rightly or wrongly, many Labor politicians believed that WEL indicated a shift from the traditional voting pattern of women, which tended to favor the conservative parties, and was responsible for the Australian Labor Party finally getting elected after twenty-three years in opposition.[11] One of the government's first acts was to re-open the equal pay case and lend its support to the argument for equal pay for equal work. The following year a single mother's benefit was introduced, planks on equal pay, part-time work and child care were inserted in the ALP platform, and Gough Whitlam appointed Elizabeth Reid to his personal staff.

Everything began to flow from that. The government machinery for the development of women's policy expanded, federal funding was obtained for a host of women's projects including refuges and child care. At the time we gave the highest priority to the establishment of high quality, government-supported child care, which we considered even more crucial in the struggle for equal employment opportunities than discrimination legislation, which was not introduced until a decade later.[12] Apart from the child care program, and funding for women's refuges (which was far less expensive and more politically acceptable and fell to us almost by accident), Women's Affairs consistently maintained that, as women constituted half the population, our input was required in the development and implementation of all government policy, and could not be contained in one narrowly defined area specific to women. This insistence led to two important, innovatory approaches: the first establishing what Marian Sawer has described as the "wheel" model of administration, with the Prime Minister's office functioning as the coordinating "hub" of a number of outposts in other key departments, the second establishing the Office's right to vet all Cabinet submissions for their impact on women.[13] This was further refined under the Hawke government in the 1980s with the requirement that all submissions include a gender impact statement and the institution of the Women's Budget Statement – one of the most effective tools of all.[14]

Most of these reforms occurred at the federal level, although given Australia's constitution, many profound changes in the delivery of services for women's health and education, for example, took place in the state and local governments. Here too, however, the impetus came largely from the federal government, and stemmed from that germinal period from the election of the Whitlam Government in 1972 to its dismissal in 1975. While it is evident, principally again through Marian Sawer's documentation, that many of these initiatives were undermined by the government, and by a conservative political and cultural climate generally, it is also obvious that the feminist reforms have changed what Australian women expect from their lives, whether they call themselves feminist or not.

How people see themselves can be telling, and it does seem that middle class women at least regard themselves a good deal more seriously than those of our generation did. They plan their careers and they put away money for their retirement. It falls a bit short of our ideas of revolution, and our notion of liberation has certainly been co-opted and corrupted, but I still maintain that Australia today gives women a better deal.

And it is obvious that if things change for one half of the population, changes will occur for the other, although perhaps not always so welcome. My sons give nearly as much time to cooking and to their children as their partners do, but have also expressed resentment over certain kinds of affirmation action, which they have regarded more as a devaluation of their gender than any well-considered special treatment for women. Certainly there is anecdotal evidence from schools that equal opportunity policies have often been insensitively applied, turning what should have been positive encouragement for girls into fierce competition between the sexes, frequently accompanied by the belittlement of boys.

Still, though Australia's social landscape has changed, with changes in gender roles a crucial part of this, women still battle some of the old demons, the subtle expectations that Australian society places on women that for all our emancipation we have not quite shaken off – like carrying primary responsibility for social obligations and the emotional well-being of the family, while assuming a larger share of the financial responsibility. At the same time, as a result of the continuing application of neoclassical economic policies and their adoption by both major parties as well as the monopolized media, the means by which women can effectively shoulder this responsibility are being incrementally whittled back, with strong class consequences as well as those for gender.

If citizenship means counting in a society, the recognition of unequal citizenship has led the disadvantaged to seek redress through state intervention, and in Australia women have constituted one of the most active and certainly the largest group involved in this. Our successes, in turn, have raised questions about equality, and how it can best be achieved, a far more complex task than any of us imagined in the 1970s. It has called for great experimentation, if you will, in trying to meet the differing needs of different social groups, even as they are represented among women. But while I am still strongly in favour of government intervention in the form of tailored policies, I am not at all certain that creating sets of separate rights really does confer citizenship effectively on the previously disadvantaged. In other words, though I have been an ardent proponent of affirmative action for women, I have never thought that women should be given rights to education, health, employment etc. that men cannot share. The distinction is fine, I know, but crucial. For citizenship to be truly inclusive, it is not enough just to "even" things up by enshrining an ideology of difference into law, for there is always the risk that policies to support one group may become new orthodoxies disadvantaging others. We need to look at society as a whole, as it is today and, given our increasingly permeable boundaries, what citizenship is not only in a national but in a global context. That women and men can truly form part of this process remains a goal for us all.

Notes

1. Officially, the Department of the Prime Minister and Cabinet (PM&C). Until Gough Whitlam's prime ministership, the department functioned largely as a "post office" between ministers, but was strengthened as a policy department, especially vis-à-vis Treasury, in the 1970s, a process Whitlam began but his successor, Malcolm Fraser, took further.

2. In April 1973 Elizabeth Reid was chosen in a highly publicized selection process to become the first Australian prime ministerial adviser on women. Reid's appointment was political – it was made by Gough Whitlam with the help of his personal staff – and she was not a permanent public servant, a distinction that was important at the time but is less so today. On her appointment she announced that she wanted to hear from every woman in Australia, and they more-or-less took her at her word.

3. In the early 1980s the Office of Women's Affairs was renamed the Office of the Status of Women, and was restored to PM&C in 1983 by the Hawke Labor Government. It remains there today, albeit much weakened. See Marion Sawer, "The Watchers Within: Women and the Australian State," in *Women, Public Policy and the State*, ed. Linda Hancock (Melbourne: Macmillan, 1999), 36–53.

4. The "boys around the keg" syndrome was often commented upon in the popular culture. It featured, among other things, in a book I read while sailing to Australia on the P&O liner Orcades in 1958. See Mulaka Corben, *Not to Mention the Kangaroos* (London: Hammond, 1956).

5. See in particular Edna Ryan and Anne Conlon, *Gentle Invaders* (Melbourne: Nelson, 1975).

6. Harvester Judgment (Ex parte H. V. McKay), Commonwealth Law Reports 2:2–18 (1906).

7. The "last hired, first fired" rule has been often countered in the case of women as a result of gender segregation. In the Depression women were often able to get work in food processing, for example, when heavier industry, employing men exclusively, was laying off workers. On the flip side, women did not benefit from "susso" or other government employment schemes. See Muriel Heagney, *Are Women Taking Men's Jobs?* (Melbourne, Status of Women Committee, 1935).

8. The Women's Bureau of the Department of Labour and National Service published regular bulletins on women's employment and unemployment in the late 1960s and 1970s, and were the first to point to women's hidden unemployment.

9. Women's Liberation came relatively late to Australia. The first meeting took place in Sydney at the end of 1969, a public meeting was held early the following year, then the movement quickly spread to other capital cities.

10. Norman Mackenzie, *Women in Australia* (Melbourne: F. W. Cheshire, 1962).

11. Opinion varies as to whether the 1972 shift in the women's vote towards the ALP was significant enough on its own in getting it elected, and no one knows how influential WEL really was. But as it often is in politics, it was the perception that mattered.

12. Although Reid did attempt to get the Whitlam Government to introduce contract compliance provisions for federal programs she was never successful. Nor were such provisions included in the legislation passed by the Hawke Labor Government in the 1980s.
13. For convenience, I refer to the unit as the Office, although the approach was developed and implemented before it became such. For example, it began vetting all Cabinet submissions for their impact on women in 1974, when it was still the Women's Affairs Section.
14. Marian Sawer, *Sisters in Suits* (Sydney: Allen & Unwin, 1990).

12

The Nations of Australia

MARCIA LANGTON

The enthusiasm of Australians for celebrating the Centenary of Federation expresses the pride many Australians have in being counted as members of this remarkable modern nation and its birth in a constitution building process. Great claims have been made of the creation of the Commonwealth of Australia, and one of them that we celebrate is the nature of our present society as a peaceful democracy. While some may believe that there can be only minor quibbles with that proposition, it falls to me to present an Aboriginal view of our place in the nation. We have more than a few quibbles, the principal of which can be stated in this way: The racialized Aboriginal citizen is an unacceptable and inappropriate replacement for the absence of the Aboriginal person that our Constitution required for six decades. Some concept more appropriate than the reference to a "race" in the Constitution should acknowledge our existence in the nation.

The background to the apparently parliamentary manner of the conventions was a world of violence, racist violence. The modern nation constituted at Federation in 1901 excluded Indigenous people from the state; unable to vote until 1962, Aborigines inhabited a political no-man's land for sixty-one years. The drafting of the Constitution of the Commonwealth of Australia occurred at the end of the nineteenth century when the intensifying ideological grounds for racism were bolstered by the new body of racial theory, often now called Social Darwinism, that posited Aborigines as the lowest form of evolution among the human "racial" types.

Australian nationhood was founded in racism. Alfred Deakin judged that the strongest motive for Federation was "the desire that we should be one people, and remain one people, without the admixture of other races."[1]

The concept of race became a key constitutional issue in this country in 1900 when the drafters of the Australian Constitution constructed the "race power," which, in conjunction with the provision for the national census, excluded Aborigines from the ambit of this founding document in order to prevent surviving post-frontier Aboriginal populations from affecting the parliamentary representation of the states and financial distributions by the Commonwealth to the States.[2] The High Court of Australia in a recent case has found that one of its provisions can be read to permit government acts to cause detriment to Aboriginal people. Neither nations nor citizens, Aboriginal peoples have been the subject of an extraordinary history of policy experimentation, much of it predicated on the belief that the first Australians would disappear, according to the absurd logic of Social Darwinism that posited the "survival of the fittest" as racial theory.

Since Federation, public debates about the place of Aboriginal people in the nation have focused on the problem of how to incorporate Aboriginal people within the framework of the Australian nation-state by various means: assimilation, integration, self-management, self-determination, reconciliation, but always on the proviso that they would never be equal.

There is a persistent unwillingness to acknowledge that in Australia, the rights of Indigenous people are inferior to those in the United States, Canada and New Zealand.

It is wrong for Australians to claim that the nation was born of a peaceful process; at the very time that constitutional conventions were held as gatherings of the white colonial men who sought to federate the six colonies into a single commonwealth, their brothers were still engaged in savage frontier campaigns to take territory from Aboriginal peoples, territory that the men at the conventions assumed a new authority over. The frontier wars were not yet over: Aboriginal people were being incarcerated at settlements to separate them from the white settlers, and the Chinese people then living in Australia, many near the gold mining fields that had brought riches to the colonial masters, were still under attack. Historian Stuart Macintyre has explained,

There had been earlier explosions of racial violence, most notably against the Chinese on the goldfields. Antagonism revived in 1888 with the arrival of a vessel from Hong Kong carrying Chinese immigrants who were turned away under threat of mob action from both Melbourne and Sydney. The controversy touched national sensitivities because Hong Kong was a British colony and the Colonial Office was antagonistic to immigration restriction based on overt racial discrimination. For nationalists, the alien menace therefore served as a reminder of imperial control; hence the adoption by the *Bulletin* in this same year of the slogan "Australia for Australians."[3]

Many Australians have planned thoughtfully for these celebrations, encouraging multiple narratives of the history of the nation and of its Constitution. Historians Stuart Macintyre and Helen Irving, for instance, have published works, *A Concise History of Australia*, and *To Constitute a Nation*,[4] respectively, which detail the evolution of the nation since Federation from White Australia to a multicultural Australia. These accounts make it difficult to sustain the nostalgic, jingoistic characterizations of Australian history by Geoffrey Blainey and Prime Minister John Howard as one of brave, white pioneers, and difficult to tolerate their refusal to accept an Australian history that narrates the story of what happened to the indigenous peoples. The "black armband" view of history, according to Blainey and Howard, "takes things too far."

One of the first legislative acts of the new Parliament of the Commonwealth of Australia was the Immigration Restriction Act of 1901. This Act was the basis of the "White Australia" policy, which dictated the national ethnic mix for sixty years and brought Australia into disrepute among all those nations whose citizens were excluded from Australian naturalization on the basis of its racially discriminatory intent. The intentions of the legislation – particularly how it should be used by immigration officials to discriminate – was set out in section 3, which refers to "prohibited immigrants" as being, amongst other things,

> any person who when asked to do so by an officer fails to write out at dictation and sign in the presence of the officer a passage of fifty words in length in a European language directed by the officer.[5]

White Australia was "an essential condition of the idealized nation the Commonwealth was meant to embody."[6] Deakin spelt it out during the debate on the Immigration Restriction Act:

The unity of Australia is nothing, if that does not imply a united race. A united race means not only that its members can intermix, inter-marry and associate without degradation on either side, but implies one inspired by the same ideas, and aspiration towards the same ideals, of a people possessing the same general cost of character, tone of thought ..[7].

Much was said during the Centenary about the exclusion of Aboriginal people from the Commonwealth in 1901, an exclusion that persisted until the 1960s when Aboriginal people were gradually enfranchised by state legislatures, and as a result of the 1967 Referendum, permitted for the first time to be counted in the national census.

It is worthwhile here to reiterate the history of Aboriginal disen-franchisement. Since the nineteenth century, confusion about the Aboriginal right to vote in Australia has been typical in debates about the Australian polity, and the details of Aboriginal rights of citizenship poorly understood. Discussions of the details of Aboriginal citizenship rights – or, more to the point, lack of such rights – have been largely confused by the effect of the 1901 Constitution on the franchise statutes of each of the States. Patricia Grimshaw has described how the confu-sion about Aboriginal voting rights arose:

When the British government first established constitutions for each colony as they handed over most administrative functions to the set-tlers, they set in place gender and property qualifications for voting and holding office, but not a colour bar. The new settler governments of the south-eastern colonies, now with the power to change the elec-torate, moved swiftly to widen voting rights to all men. Similarly, these settler governments did not at first erect a colour bar, and a very few Aboriginal men, especially in the vicinity of mission stations, reg-istered and cast their votes over the next decades. The South Austra-lian Act that gave women the vote in 1894 also enfranchised Aboriginal women, even if this went unremarked. By contrast, how-ever, Queensland's and Western Australia's settler governments, pre-siding over the colonies where most surviving Aborigines lived, did move explicitly to exclude Aborigines from the franchise. By the time women received the vote in Western Australia, Aboriginal men had been debarred from voting (unless by remote chance [they were] property holders) and hence Aboriginal women were similarly excluded from the vote. These states' interests would affect the rest in the federation settlement. [8]

In the twentieth century, the idea of citizenship, and whether or not it extended to Aborigines, was further confused by the effect of one provision of the 1901 Constitution on state franchise acts. Again, Grimshaw clarifies this issue:

The clause in the 1901 Constitution of the new Commonwealth of Australia that excluded Aborigines from enumeration in the census appeared to deal a blow to their citizenship, but one clause held out some possibilities for the Aborigines of the south-east. Section 41 declared that if a person already were an elector in a state, then that person automatically had the right to vote in Commonwealth elections. Section 41 owed its existence to the insistence of South Australian representatives present at intercolonial meetings to draft the Constitution, that South Australian women should retain the vote federally. South Australian women voted therefore in the first federal election. Aboriginal men in the south-eastern states, and Aboriginal women in South Australia, ostensibly should have also become Commonwealth electors by virtue of the same provision, but this right would swiftly be ignored or eroded. [9]

There was no protest at the effect of the new Constitution on Aboriginal voting rights, such few as then existed.

The Constitution they drafted did not formally exclude Aborigines from Australian citizenship or the vote. However, two sections did discriminate against Aborigines and establish the conditions – and powers – for the States to deny Aborigines the franchise among many other rights of citizenship. Section 51 of the Constitution provided that the federal Parliament had the power to make laws with respect to "the people of any race, other than the aboriginal race in any State, for whom it is deemed necessary to make special laws. Section 127 disallowed Aborigines to be counted in reckoning the numbers of people of the Commonwealth or of a State or other part."[10]

As Attwood et al. point out, it was section 41 that guaranteed the right to vote in federal elections to those who had that right in their state of residence. Thus those States that denied Aborigines the right to vote under State franchise acts thereby disenfranchised them in federal elections as well. The legal rights of Aboriginal people were severely limited by Commonwealth and State legislation, such that, even given the variation between the jurisdictions, the majority of Aboriginal people could not vote, receive social welfare such as the old-age pension and unemployment benefits, move freely from place to place, choose their place of residence, make basic decisions concerning their own lives such as where to work, what to do with their earnings and any property they acquired, and whom they might marry. Their children could be – and were in the thousands – removed and placed in institutions, in employment, or in the custody of strangers.[11]

Section 41, as already noted, provided that:

> No adult person who has or acquires a right to vote at elections for the more numerous Houses of the Parliament of a State shall, while the right continues, be prevented by any law of the Commonwealth from voting at elections for either House of Parliament of the Commonwealth.[12]

Attwood et al. relate that, in 1925, an Indian resident of Melbourne, Mitta Bullosh, challenged the ruling of the Solicitor General on Section 41 of the Constitution who had advised that "the constitutional guarantee applied only to those who had 'acquired' the vote prior to the passing of the Commonwealth Electoral Act in 1902."[13] A magistrate ruled that the Commonwealth interpretation was incorrect. The Commonwealth lodged an appeal with the High Court but withdrew the action for reasons of international diplomacy, deciding instead to pass legislation enfranchising Indian residents whilst ignoring the legal rights of Aboriginal people. The Solicitor-General advised that "the question of whether, following the case of Mitta Bullosh, enrollment should be accorded to persons in like circumstances, appears to be a matter of policy for the Government to decide." Attwood et al. conclude that:

> The government simply decided to do nothing, and Aboriginal people were neither sufficiently informed nor in any position to challenge the matter in the courts. Clearly, in this case, on the basis of the only judicial interpretation available, Aboriginal people were entitled to vote; the discrimination they faced was not based upon legislation but resulted from capricious government action. Some Aborigines, enrolled before 1902, even lost their voting rights in the 1920s and 1930s as the states and the Commonwealth adopted a joint electoral roll.[14]

It was not until 1949 that the Commonwealth Electoral Act was amended to give the vote to:

an aboriginal native of Australia ... [who] is entitled under the law of the State in which he resides to be enrolled as an elector of that State and, upon enrolment, to vote at elections for the more numerous Houses of Parliament of that State ...[15]

In 1962, the national Aboriginal association that spearheaded the fight for Aboriginal citizenship rights distributed a pamphlet that set out the rights of Aborigines in five states and the Northern Territory. In Western Australia and Queensland, Aborigines did not have voting rights.

Table 1 Rights enjoyed by Aborigines on settlements & reserves in 5 States & the Northern Territory

	NSW	VIC	SA	WA	NT	QLD
Voting rights (State)	Y	Y	Y	N	Y	N
Marry freely	Y	Y	Y	N	N	N
Control own children	Y	Y	N	N	N	N
Move freely	Y	N	N	N	N	N
Own property freely	Y	N	Y	N	N	N
Receive award wages	Y	N	N	N	N	N
Alcohol allowed	N	N	N	N	N	N

(as cited in Attwood et al. 1997:13)

Aborigines were denied the vote, not by the letter of federal law, but by the administrative practices of the Aboriginal "protection and welfare" regimes in most state jurisdictions, and in the two most numerous states, by statutes.

The overwhelming "Yes" vote in the 1967 Referendum also enabled the Commonwealth for the first time to legislate for Aborigines as a race. Those first six decades of White Australia left a legacy of Aboriginal inequality and disadvantage, of white hatred and fear, and tears in our civil fabric. While it is important to acknowledge that two racist provisions of the Constitution were removed in 1967 with the overwhelming support of Australian voters, it remains the case that our Constitution contains two provisions that permit racist or detrimental acts to be taken against the people of any race.

The "race power" allows the Federal Parliament to pass laws with respect to "the people of any race for whom it is deemed necessary to make special laws." In 1998, the Federal government used its "race power" to implement John Howard's so-called "10-point Wik plan" to extinguish native title in all pastoral leases and it also used it to allow the Hindmarsh Island Bridge in South Australia to be built. The Ngarrindjeri women, who asserted that they are custodians of a sacred site on the island affected by the bridge proposal, lodged a case in the High Court seeking to overturn that legislation.[16]

The central issue, answered by the six Judges sitting on the High Court, in the Hindmarsh Island case, is whether the "race power" can be used to pass laws to the detriment of Aboriginal people or whether it can only be used to pass laws for their benefit. Because Mr. Justice Callinan removed himself from the Bench in this case because of his previous involvement in the matter, the answers provided by the remaining six Judges do not clarify the matter sufficiently to provide guidelines for other legislation. While it was acknowledged that Australia's Constitution was conceived with racist purposes, two Judges found that governments could not act with manifest abuse of power, and one, Kirby, found that no act could be racially discriminatory. The other three found that legislation enacted by a state could be amended.

Before 1967, when a referendum on this issue succeeded in removing racially discriminatory clauses from the Constitution, the "race power" contained the words "other than the Aboriginal race in any State." This left the power to deal with Aboriginal issues with the State Parliaments. The 1967 referendum changed two aspects of the Constitution. First, it amended the race power to allow the Commonwealth to pass laws for the Aboriginal people.

Secondly, it deleted section 127 of the Constitution, which had stated that in taking the census, "Aboriginal natives were not to be counted." Few constitutional referenda have succeeded in Australia. Thirty years later, it is difficult for one to believe that the 1967 referendum was passed by almost 90 percent of Australian voters, easily the highest "yes" vote ever.

Until the Hindmarsh case, the objective of the 1967 referendum has been read as removing discriminatory references to Aboriginal people from the Constitution and allowing the Commonwealth to take over some responsibility for the welfare of those people.

According to George Williams, barrister and senior lecturer in constitutional law at the Australian National University, the purpose of the race power as originally drafted was expressed by Sir Edmund Barton, Australia's first Prime Minister and later High Court judge. At the 1898 convention on Federation and the then-proposed Australian constitution in Melbourne, he argued that the power was needed so that the Commonwealth could "regulate the affairs of the people coloured or inferior races who are in the Commonwealth."[17] The power enables the Commonwealth to enact laws that, for example, restrict where the people of a certain race can live or what employment they can take. It is a power to pass laws such as those in force at the turn of the century, which provided that "no Asiatic or African alien can get a miner's right or go mining on a goldfield."[18]

The national soul-searching about this history was reflected in the Reconciliation Marches joined by well over a million Australians in 2000 as the work of the Council for Aboriginal Reconciliation was coming to an end. The purpose of Australians who support Reconciliation between indigenous and non-indigenous Australians is to find common ground for our respective membership of this nation beyond the old prejudices and beliefs of the frontier culture.

Soon after the establishment of the Council for Aboriginal Reconciliation in 1990, the five volume *National Report of the Royal Commission into Aboriginal Deaths in Custody,* its contents agreed to by all the Commissioners, including Johnston Q.C., Wootten and Wyville, was presented to the Australian Government and published. The Report explained that:

> ... Aboriginal people and others often believe that police or gaolers have killed those who died in a serious indictment of Australia's colonial past, as well as proof that the present society has yet to provide reassurance that that past is over.
>
> 10.4.3. Aboriginal perceptions of threat by various forces in non-Aboriginal society have been perpetuated by a long heritage of control, with often harsh means of enforcement ...
>
> 10.4.4. In order to make way for British rule and its law to take effect, flagrant disregard of this same law was popularly accepted ...
>
> 10.4.5. The frontier period indicates the type of "law and order" first imposed on Aboriginal people, which set the tone. In most parts of Australia during its various frontier eras, force or its threat became the key means of establishing British "law and order."

As far as the whites were concerned, the general view by the end of the century was that there was a direct relationship between colonial progress – the fulfillment of their mission – and the destruction of Aboriginal society. It was in itself a proof of progress.[19]

The National Commissioner, in concluding his five-volume report, considered the then newly established reconciliation process. He wrote:

> If it is recognized that the cause of distrust and disunity is the historical experience of Aboriginal people and their continuing disadvantage, then, plainly, good community relations cannot be achieved without elimination of the disadvantage and the recognition of Aboriginal rights, Aboriginal culture and tradition. There must be a complete rejection of concepts of superiority and inferiority. Unless the wider society gives the most tangible proof of on-going and substantial efforts to achieve those objectives, there can be little prospect of permanently and substantially improving community relations.[20]

The project of reconciliation was a brave attempt to overcome the historical legacy of the frontier – the racially founded society. That project has failed because it has been reframed in the "currency of the absolute." Reconciliation has been viewed by the government as a process for normalizing the natives, for dismissing any difference which cannot be tolerated in their idea of the nation.

The "currency of the absolute," the term used by Bourdieu and Darbel[21] in their study of European art museums and their public in *The Love of Art*, is useful in grappling with ideas such as the supremacy of British traditions of civil society held by Australian conservatives. The concept is particularly useful because it is relevant to the visual appropriation of Aboriginal culture for the purposes of creating the myth of the new nation. Bourdieu and Darbel write:

> Thus, the sanctification of culture and art, this "currency of the absolute" ... fulfills a vital function by contributing to the consecration of the social order. So that cultured people can believe in barbarism and persuade the barbarians of their own barbarity, it is necessary and sufficient for them to succeed in hiding both from themselves and from others the social conditions which make possible not only culture as a second nature, in which society locates human excellence,

and which is experienced as a privilege of birth, but also the legitimated hegemony (or the legitimacy) of a particular definition of culture... They derive the justification for their monopoly of the instruments of appropriation of cultural goods from an essentialist representation of the division of their society into barbarians and civilized people.[22]

This partly explains why Australians allow Aboriginal cultural symbols to represent the idea of Australia as they did in the opening ceremony of the Olympic Games. But, how can we explain why Australians hold such ideas in the late twentieth century, after all that has happened to people "of colour," and in Australia, to Aborigines?

It is, I propose, as Richard Dyer, a white American scholar, puts it so succinctly in his book, *White*:

> As long as race is something only applied to non-white peoples, as long as white people are not racially seen and named, they/we function as a human norm. Other people are raced, we are just people.
>
> There is no more powerful position than that of being "just" human. The claim to power is the claim to speak for the commonality of humanity. Raced people can't do that – they can only speak for their race. But non-raced people can, for they do not represent the interests of race.
>
> The point of seeing the racing of whites is to dislodge them/us from the position of power, with all the inequities, oppression, privileges and sufferings in its train, dislodging them/us by undercutting the authority with which they/we speak/act in and on the world.[23]

Dyer gives examples of this core cultural concept of whites as non-raced showing that it is most evident in its absence – conspicuous absence of almost any reference to whiteness in the habitual speech and writing of white people in the West. He exposes a key corollary of the assumption that white people are just people, which is that "it is not far off saying that whites are people whereas other colours are something else" and that these twin pre-ideas "are endemic to white culture."[24]

This also explains why that harmless document, *The Draft Document of Reconciliation*, to which thousands of Australians made a contribution in a nation-wide consultative process, was rejected by the Prime Minister at the final Council of Aboriginal Reconciliation Convention,

Corroborree 2000. Through 1990 and 1991, cross-party support developed for a formal process of reconciliation to be led by a council of prominent Australians, and the Council for Aboriginal Reconciliation was formally established on 2 September 1991. The ten years of educative and consultative work of the three terms of the Council, two under the Chairmanship of Patrick Dodson, and the last under Evelyn Scott, have created a fundamental change in the terms of the debate. "Reconciliation" is a key word in Australian political and social life, and a significant proportion of Australians support the idea. In September, Prime Minister John Howard made it clear that any kind of agreement that his government would consider would be a reiteration of the policy of assimilation and make no mention of an apology to the "stolen generations," a continuing right of occupancy, or any special rights or measures.

The frustration and anger of many Aboriginal people at the relentless efforts of governments to dispossess Aboriginal people were heard clearly in Patrick Dodson's summary of the outcome of the recognition of common-law native title. Patrick Dodson first introduced the idea of a "framework agreement" in his Vincent Lingiari Memorial Lecture at the Northern Territory University in 1999, some months after the passage through the federal Parliament of the Native Title Amendment Bill.

Patrick Dodson set out the idea of a Framework Agreement as a process for the settlement of the outstanding inequalities in the relationship between the first peoples and the settler state. This proposal was communicated by a delegation of Aboriginal leaders, including Dodson, to Prime Minister John Howard following his rejection of the *Draft Document of Reconciliation* at Corroboree 2000. The Prime Minister likewise rejected the idea of the Framework Agreement.

His rejection of yet another offer from Aboriginal people for resolution of our outstanding grievances is only of minor historical importance, however. History will record and future generations will know that Aboriginal people have continued to assert the right to negotiate just terms and conditions of the seizure of their territories and resources and the proscription of customary laws, governance and ancestral jurisdiction.

Despite the formal rejection of a document of reconciliation by the Prime Minister, the outcome of the reconciliation process pursued in the last ten years is a review of how to progress postcolonial community relations between settler Australians and the Indigenous peoples.

This then leaves us with a future of "unfinished business," with a similar legacy as was considered ten years ago when the Reconciliation movement started. How are our children to live with this history? Many of our children have no commitment to the old ideas of the Empire, to its core values of the supremacy of the white man, but its effects remain. These effects of inequality, including formal Constitutional inequality, and disadvantage will continue to engender division and dispute.

Our children will not live in what Asians even now call "the White Tribe of Asia," reminded as they are by populist figures, such as Pauline Hanson,[25] of the racialist history of our nation.

Stuart Macintyre reminds us that forty percent of present Australians have at least one parent who was born overseas:

> The insistence on a common culture has yielded to the acceptance, even celebration, of many cultures ... For all the difficulties in accepting its implications, the Aboriginal renaissance is an indisputable feature of contemporary Australia.
>
> True, this rearrangement has left the dominance of the ethnic majority intact – the descendants of those who claimed exclusive possession continued to define the comfortable limits of pluralism. The gradual, piecemeal manner in which they have done so has in turn allowed for their own reconstitution, so that they now partake of the very characteristics that were once alien and threatening ... The problem with this slow, often grudging, transition is that it provides no clear break that would settle the ghosts of White Australia. Perhaps the Australian republic, which must eventually come, will allow a final settlement.[26]

The idea of an Australian republic, I suggest, must be based in a commitment to be rid of the formal racism of our Constitution and of the ideas that created "Australia for the White Man," as the header of Australia's oldest magazine, *The Bulletin*, put it.

Conclusion

It is still the case that Indigenous people have neither a clear nor a just place within the ambit of the Australian polity. This fact, and the continuing disputes over the status of Indigenous people within the political discourse of the nation, are fraught hanging threads in the fabric of the contemporary Australian state. Unlike either Canada or New Zealand, no treaties or agreements were concluded with Aboriginal people.

Still today, the right of Aboriginal people is inferior to that of other Australians. For Aboriginal people in Western Australia it is not compulsory to vote, while for other Australians it is. Historically, settler Australians have always refused to permit either full equality for Aboriginal peoples or a separate equality.

The calls for a treaty go to the heart of the juridical denial, in Australian case law, of the existence of Aboriginal nations in Australia prior to the seizure of the land and consequent dispossession of Indigenous people by the British Crown. This denial has in effect accorded our nations the status of an anomaly among the settler colonial states. The monstrous injustice of the seizure of, and establishment of dominion over, Aboriginal lands by the Crown, and the lack of agreements or treaties, remains a stain on Australian history and the chief obstacle to constructing an honourable place for Indigenous Australians in the modern nation-state. That place must now be found both through, and beyond, the limits of a legal discursive framework that de-humanizes and de-historicizes Aboriginal people, rendering us as the mere wandering brutes of Hobbesian and Rousseauian mythology.

The calls for a treaty also go to the heart of what the Aboriginal lawyer Noel Pearson has termed the "moot point" of the acquisition of sovereignty over Australia by the British Crown.[27] Pearson argued in his 1993 Evatt Lecture that "there is no way that the issue" of sovereignty "will ever be entertained at the international level," given the *Mabo* judgment's confirmation of *Coe v. The Commonwealth* (1979).[28] That earlier judgment had found, in essence, that the acquisition of sovereignty is an Act of State that cannot be reviewed and consequently is not justiciable in municipal courts. However, Pearson conceded in the Evatt lecture that:

> A concept of sovereignty inhered in Aboriginal groups prior to European invasion insofar as people have concepts of having laws, land and institutions without interference from outside of their society. This must be a necessary implication of the decision in Mabo against *terra nullius*.[29]

Thus, in accordance with the Mabo finding on native title arising from particular "traditional laws and customs," Pearson suggested that, with the development of human rights standards relating to Aboriginal people at international law, "recognition of 'local Indigenous sovereignty' could exist internally within a nation-state, provided that the fullest rights of self-determination are accorded."[30]

Since the first agreements signed under the provisions of the Aboriginal Land Rights Act in the Northern Territory more than twenty years ago, there has been an astonishing proliferation of agreements between Australian Indigenous people and various corporations and branches of government.

These developments in relations between Indigenous and non-Indigenous Australians are evidence of creative thinking by those involved in grappling with the legacy of the Australian frontier. Corporations such as Comalco,[31] signatory to the Western Cape York Communities Co-existence Agreement, are readily prepared to treat with Aboriginal nations, noting in their agreements their ancient identities, the Wik, the Thaayorre, the Alngith, and many others. Corporations acknowledge that preexisting aboriginal polities exist as a profound reality in our political and economic landscape. The Constitution does not.

While the many attempts at treating with Aborigines in colonial times and in the early twentieth century were not translated into enduring outcomes it is clear that the agreements negotiated since the 1970s are evidence of a willingness to do what the "colonial settlers" were unable to countenance: that is, to acknowledge that another group of people were the owners and custodians of the lands and waters of Australia; that their descendants have a right to possess, use and enjoy those lands and waters; to govern, within the limits of Australian law, their use and access by others; and to reap any benefits arising from that use and access by others, as would any other group of people in rightful possession of a place.

I propose that our children will benefit from a serious consideration of these issues, in particular, proposals for referenda questions that would deal with removing the offending racist provisions of the Constitution and replacing them with an acknowledgement of the pre-existing Aboriginal polities, or Aboriginal nations, and the necessity to make agreements with these groups in order to achieve peace and good order.

Notes

1. As cited in Stuart Macintyre, *A Concise History Of Australia* (Melbourne: Cambridge University Press, 1999), 141.

2.   The sections of the Australian Constitution referring to Aborigines, repealed or amended in the March 1967 referendum, do not, according to J.A. La Nauze *The Making of the Australian Constitution* (Melbourne: Melbourne University Press, 1972), reflect in any way a concern with Aborigines. It was only by careful scrutiny of the succession of drafts and other documents that La Nauze could reconstruct the origins of these sections, because there was no substantial debate about Aborigines in the Constitutional Conventions. La Nauze explains the origins of these two sections as follows:

> Two of the Lucinda innovations have a curious interest, for in 1967 they were to be cancelled by one of the few constitutional amendments made since 1901. Griffith's clause concerning an exclusive Commonwealth power to make "special laws" for people of any race had been devised for the case of the Polynesian labourers in Queensland though he later made it clear that it could apply to Indian coolies or other groups needing special protection or contractual arrangements. Presumably on 26 March, the New Zealander Russell had objected that the terms could be applied to the Maoris. Australians would not have wished to intervene in this matter, and the draftsmen now added: "but so that this power shall not extend to authorize legislation with respect to the Maori race of New Zealand." This, to anticipate, led to the next alteration, made by the Constitutional Committee on Monday 30 March. The specific exclusion of Maoris became irrelevant. In 1897–8 the Aborigines were therefore left by themselves as a specific exception to the Commonwealth's power to make "special laws." Perhaps not one of the electors who voted in 1967 to remove this reference from the Constitution could have explained how it ever got there in the first place.

At the same referendum of 1967 a second Lucinda insertion was cancelled. This was Section 127: "In reckoning the numbers of the people of the Commonwealth, or of a State or other part of the Commonwealth, aboriginal natives shall not be counted." That, too, had originally linked references to the Australian Aborigines and the Pacific Islanders. As it emerged from the Lucinda revisions it read: "In reckoning the numbers of the people of a State or Territory aboriginal natives of Australia or of any Island of the Pacific shall not be counted." Again to anticipate (for now this is indeed a mere curiosity), the clause was struck out by the Constitution Committee before it came to the Convention. But why was it inserted, and why was it first struck out and then, in the full Convention, restored in a rather different form? As Griffith explained, it was struck out because the clauses to which it referred had been struck out by the Constitutional Committee. Now these were the financial clauses concerning the apportionment of surplus Commonwealth revenue among the States "in proportion to the numbers of their people." As they were now restored by the Convention it was necessary that the original definition of the mode of reckoning "the numbers of the people" should also be restored, and Griffith so moved, though no mention was now made of the Pacific Islanders. The exclusion of the Aborigines from the reckoning was not based on the impossibility of counting nomads, nor on views about their inferiority, nor on any of the reasons alleged in 1967.

In a note he adds:

> The evolution of Sec. 127 (now cancelled) requires very complicated explanation which must be closely based on Griffith's successive drafts, and since it is now irrelevant it will not be traced here. Briefly, it is quite clear that the origin of the exclusion of aborigines from the reckoning of "the numbers of the people" lay in the requirements of the finance clauses, including the cancelled clause concerning federal direct taxation. Not until a late stage of drafting was it decided to place this exclusion in the "Miscellaneous" chapter, so that it would apply not only to the financial clauses but to the "numbers" on which each State's membership in the House of Representatives would be based. Although the origin of the section was a good deal more complicated than is implied by Geoffrey Sawyer ... he is completely justified in holding that it had no relevance at all to the taking of the census.

3. Macintyre, *A Concise History of Australia*, 141.
4. See also Helen Irving, ed., *The Centenary Companion to Australian Federation* (Cambridge: Cambridge University Press, 1999); Idem., *To Constitute a Nation: A Cultural History Of Australia's Constitution* (Cambridge: Cambridge University Press, 1997).
5. Immigration Restriction Act of 1901, Section 3 (a). See Stuart Macintyre, *A Concise History of Australia*, 142:

> In 1897 the Colonial Office persuaded the Australian premiers at a conference in London to drop explicit discrimination against other races in favour of an ostensibly non-discriminatory dictation test

for immigrants, a device used by other British dominions to achieve the same result. Since a foreigner could be tested in any European language, the immigration official need only select an unfamiliar one to ensure failure. This was the basis of the Immigration Restriction Act passed by the new Commonwealth parliament in 1901, but by then Asian immigration was negligible.

6. As cited in Macintyre, *A Concise History Of Australia*, 141.
7. Ibid., 141.
8. Patricia Grimshaw, "Reading the silences: suffrage activists and race in nineteenth century settler societies" in *Citizenship, Women and Social Justice: International Historical Perspectives*, eds. Joy Damousi and Katherine Ellinghaus (Melbourne: History Department, The University of Melbourne, 1999), 39.
9. Ibid., 39.
10. Bain Attwood et al., *The 1967 Referendum, Or, When Aborigines Didn't Get the Vote* (Canberra: Aboriginal Studies Press, 1997), 1–3.
11. Ibid., 14.
12. Ibid.
13. Ibid., 14.
14. Ibid., 14–15.
15. Ibid.
16. *Kartinyeri v. The Commonwealth* HCA 22, (1988) (1 April, 1998).
17. George Williams, "A double edge to races power," *The Sydney Morning Herald*, Thursday, May 29, 1997, Opinion, 17.
18. Ibid., 17.
19. Elliot Johnston, Commissioner QC, *National Report of the Royal Commission into Aboriginal Deaths in Custody,* Vol. 2 (10.4), Frontier Period: Disease and Violence (Canberra: AGPS, 1992).
20. Elliot Johnston, Commissioner QC, *National Report of the Royal Commission into Aboriginal Deaths in Custody* , Vol. 5 (Canberra: AGPS, 1992), 57.
21. Pierre Bourdieu and Alain Darbel, with Dominique Schnapper, *The Love of Art: European Art Museums and their Public* (Cambridge: Polity Press, 1997), 111–112.
22. Ibid., 111–112.
23. Richard Dyer, *White* (London: Routledge, 1997), 2–3.
24. Ibid., 4.
25. Pauline Hanson was a disendorsed Liberal Party candidate in 1995 when she was voted into federal Parliament by the electors of a rural Queensland seat on a platform of racism and nationalism. She established the One

Nation Party, lost her seat in the following election, and in 2001 was charged with electoral fraud. She was a candidate in the 2001 federal election in Australia. She is now in prison.

26. Macintyre, *A Concise History of Australia*, 278.
27. Noel Pearson, "Indigenous Peoples and International Law," Address to the Evatt Foundation Annual Dinner, 28 July, 1995.
28. Ibid.
29. Ibid.
30. Ibid.
31. Comalco operates the bauxite mine at Weipa in Cape York Peninsula, Queensland, Australia, and was a party to the High Court case brought by the Wik peoples and others for recognition of their native title. (See *Wik Peoples v. Queensland* 187 CLR 1 [1996].) Comalco is a supplier of bauxite, alumina and primary aluminum to world markets, with sales in 1999 of over $2.3 billion. It is a wholly-owned subsidiary of Rio Tinto and provides about 22 percent of Australia's total production of bauxite, 8 percent of its alumina and 24 percent of its primary aluminum. It is the world's eighth largest aluminum company.

13

Citizenship and Aboriginal Governance: The Royal Commission's Vision for the Future

JUSTICE RENÉ DUSSAULT

As former co-chair of the Royal Commission on Aboriginal Peoples, I thought it would be interesting to address this issue of Citizenship and Aboriginal Governance from the perspective of the Royal Commission's vision for the future.

Let me point out, first, that in a country like Canada where Aboriginal peoples are dispersed and do not have substantial political clout during elections, there is a need for reform: one that would open the doors to their participation in the main Canadian institutions and another that would recognize that they have a large measure of self-government based on an inherent right. In regard to the latter, room should now be made in the Canadian legal and political framework for Aboriginal nations to resume their self-government status.

Except in urban centres where we propose a community of interest model of Aboriginal government with voluntary membership, by and large the Commission proposes that Aboriginal self-government be developed around a nation model.

We consider an "Aboriginal nation" to mean a sizable body of Aboriginal people that possesses a shared sense of national identity and constitutes the predominant population in a certain territory or group of territories.

From our point of view, only nations have a right of self-determination and only at the nation level will Aboriginal people have the numbers necessary to exercise a broad governance mandate and to draw from a large pool of expertise.

According to this vision, Aboriginal people are both Canadian citizens and citizens of their particular nations. Thus they hold a form of dual citizenship, which permits them to maintain loyalty to their nation and to Canada as a whole.

Citizenship in Canada

For a long time, Aboriginal people in Canada were not seen as people whose voices mattered, as people to whom the franchise could be entrusted. Deprived of this essential attribute of citizenship, it was difficult for them to see themselves as citizens of Canada, a country that had no legitimacy in their eyes. In fact, despite their direct relationship with the federal government, the majority of the Aboriginal people living on reserves could not vote in federal elections until 1960.

In the period before Confederation it was widely assumed that Aboriginal people were simply inferior or were to be excluded on grounds of their lack of "civilization" and that they had to become assimilated before they could enjoy the benefits of citizenship. After Confederation, provincial voter eligibility requirements determined who could vote in federal elections and generally involved property ownership provisions that reserve-based Aboriginals could not meet unless they enfranchised. From 1920 to 1960, the ground for exclusion appeared to reflect the belief that Aboriginal people enjoying certain types of tax exemption should have no representation in the House of Commons.

In 1960, the federal franchise was finally extended without qualification to all Aboriginals. In the same year, Inuit, legislatively barred from voting from 1934 to 1950, also started to be enumerated for federal elections. Métis people had also faced problems of enumeration and had limited opportunity for exercising their franchise.

When the provinces dropped the property qualification and adopted universal male suffrage in the late nineteenth and early twentieth century, many provinces passed legislation explicitly to exclude Aboriginals. The provincial franchise was then re-extended to Aboriginals at different times: British Columbia in 1949; Manitoba in 1952; Ontario in 1954; Saskatchewan in 1960; Prince Edward Island and New

Brunswick in 1963; Alberta in 1965; and Quebec in 1969. Inuit and the Innu of Labrador, like other citizens, received the right to vote in 1949 when Newfoundland joined Confederation.

It's no wonder that Aboriginal people themselves have resisted participating in Canadian institutions of government. Since Aboriginal people played no role in the design of Canadian government institutions or the Confederation agreement, many see these as "settler" institutions. In some cases, treaty nations view their relationship with Canada as one of nation-to-nation only, and they want their relationship mediated by their own governments and leaders through their treaties – not by another institution. In other cases, Aboriginal people think that they should have their own distinct institutions, leaving Parliament to non-Aboriginal people. This lack of participation by Aboriginal people in Canadian institutions has been a growing problem in Canadian federalism and undermines the legitimacy of our system of government.

The extent of under-representation of Aboriginal people in Canadian governing institutions is startling. At the time of the publication of the final report of the Royal Commission on Aboriginal Peoples in November 1996, almost 11,000 members of Parliament had been elected to the House of Commons since Confederation. Of these, only 13 members had self-identified as Aboriginal People. The record for the Senate was not much better, at one percent of all senators appointed since Confederation. This is far from proportional to the Aboriginal population of Canada.

Be it as it may, there remains one fact. As citizens of Canada, Aboriginal men and women are entitled to enjoy the protection of the Canadian Charter of Rights and Freedoms in their relations with all governments in Canada. In its application to Aboriginal governments, the Charter should be interpreted in a manner that allows considerable scope for distinctive Aboriginal philosophical outlooks, cultures and traditions. This interpretive rule is found in section 25 of the Charter. It applies with particular force where distinctive Aboriginal perspectives on human rights have been consolidated in Aboriginal charters of rights and responsibilities.

Citizenship in Aboriginal Nations

Many concepts of Aboriginal governance centre on territorial jurisdiction. They envisage governments that exercise mandatory jurisdiction over a definite territory and all the people located there. However, there is a good deal of variation in the particular arrangements envisaged. Under some of them, the right to vote and stand for public office is available to all residents (Nunavut); in others, it is restricted to individuals who meet citizenship or membership requirements (the Nisga'a Treaty).

From the Commission's point of view, the right of an Aboriginal nation to determine its own citizenship is an existing Aboriginal and treaty right within the meaning of section 35(1) of the *Constitution Act, 1982*. At the same time, any rules and processes governing citizenship must satisfy certain basic constitutional standards flowing from the terms of section 35 itself. The purpose of these standards is to prevent an Aboriginal group from unfairly excluding anyone from participating in the enjoyment of collective Aboriginal and treaty rights guaranteed by section 35(1), including the right of self-government. In other words, the guarantee of Aboriginal and treaty rights in section 35 could be frustrated if a nation were free to deny citizenship to individuals on an arbitrary basis and thus prevent them from sharing in the benefit of the collective rights recognized in section 35.

The most obvious of these constitutional standards is laid down in section 35(4), which states that Aboriginal and treaty rights are guaranteed equally to male and female persons. Since Aboriginal and treaty rights are generally collective rather than individual rights, an individual can have access to them only through membership in an Aboriginal group. It follows that the rules and processes governing membership cannot discriminate against individuals on grounds of sex, for to do so would violate the guarantee embodied in section 35(4).

Section 35 embodies a second basic standard. In our view, the Aboriginal peoples recognized in this section are political and cultural entities rather than racial groups. This fundamental principle has implications at two levels. It lays down a basic standard governing individual membership in such groups. It prevents an Aboriginal group from specifying that a certain degree of Aboriginal blood (what is often called blood quantum) is a general prerequisite for citizenship. On this point, it is important to distinguish between rules that specify ancestry as one among several ways of establishing eligibility for membership, which are acceptable, and rules that specify ancestry as a general prerequisite, which are not.

In offering this opinion, the Commission recognizes the sensitive nature of the subject and the existence of strongly held opposing views. We also acknowledge the legitimate concerns that underlie these views. After all, birth is the normal way to acquire citizenship, and descent is the normal way a nation's culture and identity are perpetuated. The citizenship codes of most countries, including Canada, reflect that reality. None of this leads us to believe, however, that a minimum blood quantum is an acceptable general prerequisite for membership in an Aboriginal group. In our view, such a specification would be an impediment to the future development of Aboriginal peoples as autonomous political nations within Canada and inconsistent with the historical evolution and traditions of most of them.

It should be remembered that, under the traditional practices of most Aboriginal groups, birthright was not the only method by which group membership could be acquired. Methods such as marriage, adoption, ritual affiliation, long-standing residence, cultural integration and group acceptance were also widely recognized. As Rene Lamothe has noted with respect to Dene:

> In the traditions of the Dene elders, because The Land is the boss and will teach whoever She wants, they will accept as Dene anyone who comes to know and live as they know and live. At that time they will be only too eager to share their responsibility for jurisdiction and governance. This is not a note on racial relationships, it is a statement to the belief of the Dene that The Land is the boss of culture, that culture is inextricably tied to The Land, and that people are required to adapt their way of life to the teachings of The Land.[1]

Recommendations

The Commission recommends that:

2.3.8
The government of Canada recognize Aboriginal people in Canada as enjoying a unique form of dual citizenship, that is, as citizens of an Aboriginal nation and citizens of Canada.

2.3.9
The government of Canada take steps to ensure that the Canadian passports of Aboriginal citizens
(a) explicitly recognize this dual citizenship; and
(b) identify the Aboriginal nation citizenship of individual Aboriginal persons.

2.3.10
Aboriginal nations, in exercising the right to determine citizenship, and in establishing rules and processes for this purpose, adopt citizenship criteria that
(a) are consistent with section 35(4) of the *Constitution Act, 1982* (no discrimination on grounds of sex);
(b) reflect Aboriginal nations as political and cultural entities rather than as racial groups, and therefore do not make blood quantum a general prerequisite for citizenship determination; and
(c) may include elements such as self-identification, community or nation acceptance, cultural and linguistic knowledge, marriage, adoption, residency, birthplace, descent and ancestry among the different ways to establish citizenship.

2.3.11
As part of their citizenship rules, Aboriginal nations establish mechanisms for resolving disputes concerning the nation's citizenship rules generally, or individual applications specifically. The mechanisms are to be
(a) characterized by fairness, openness and impartiality;
(b) structured at arm's length from the central decision-making bodies of the Aboriginal government; and
(c) operated in accordance with the *Canadian Charter of Rights and Freedoms* and with international norms and standards concerning human rights.

Note

1. Rene Lamother, " 'It Was Only a Treaty': A Historical View of Treaty 11 According to the Dene of the Mackenzie Valley," (research study prepared for Royal Commission on Aboriginal Peoples 1993), 58–59.

14

Canadian Citizenship and Multiculturalism

FRANÇOIS HOULE

The Canadian policy of multiculturalism is perceived either as a great Canadian contribution to the world, or as a Canadian aberration that undermines the idea of belonging to a political community and reduces the inclusive character of citizenship. These two views are to be found in magazines and in academic journals. For instance, an article in the French magazine *L'Express international* describes how Canadian society is divided by an identity crisis. The journalist points out that during the last decade, Canada has welcomed 2.4 million immigrants. Moreover, he adds that 4 out of 10 immigrants in Vancouver are from China and that 50 percent of Toronto residents were born outside of Canada. The Canadian multiculturalism policy is presented as "aiming to recognize and to encourage the cultural diversity of the different communities which live in Canada."[1] Furthermore, the article continues by stating that in Canada the hiring of people who are members of visible minorities is ensured by means of "positive discrimination." Canadian state and society are seen as being the ones that have to adjust to the new immigrants. The Canadian nation also tries to promote the myth of being a "nation of minorities."[2] According to *L'Express*, Canada is a post-national society. The author agrees with Neil Bissoondath's critiques and concludes that Canada is a communitarian state and as such is unique in the world. The journalist argues that this leads to a communitarian conception of rights and that Canada will inevitably face a political crisis.

The combined effect of the multiculturalism policy and the *Charter of Rights and Freedoms* is that they encourage communitarian claims which the Canadian courts receive positively. Canadian multiculturalism is contrary to integration according to *L'Express international*.

In a long study of Canadian multiculturalism, *Canadian Geographic* proposes a completely different point of view. Canada is not different from other developing countries, with the exception of the U.S.. In most countries there is an "easygoing acceptance of diversity." However, Canada is seen as being far ahead of the rest of the world. Canada is increasingly becoming a more ethnically diverse society, and this has contributed to a "detribalized Canada" which is making less central "the historic confrontation between French Canada and English Canada which depended on an ethnic uniformity and collective memory."[3] These old conflicts are gradually being eroded by ethnic diversity. The fact that being Canadian no longer implies a particular ethnicity and that many Canadians have little memory of the history of ethnic rivalry "has probably been the salvation of the Canadian state." Canada is in a position to become "the world in one country."[4]

These two diametrically opposed perspectives on the Canadian multiculturalism policy and Canada's ethnic diversity are nothing new. They have dominated the debate in Canada for the last decade. In my article, I will try to show that Canadian multiculturalism has been seen in the 1990s as undermining Canadian unity and that the federal government was brought to modify the main orientations of its multiculturalism policy. Canada has not been the only country in the 1990s to worry about social cohesion. This questioning has been an important fixture in many countries. However, in Canada the question was associated with both the Quebec question and multiculturalism policy.

Ethnic renewal in many liberal democracies questions the implicit link between liberal citizenship and shared values. Those values are often central in allowing for the full participation of all citizens. Since the nineteenth century, ethnic homogeneity has become part of our understanding of what defines a political community. Clearly, ethnic diversity questions it.

A group of individuals without any intellectual or moral unity would not compose a society able to govern itself. Neither would it be able to come to any practical decisions by means of rational deliberation. Democracies require an encompassing community that can inspire its members with a feeling of belonging. Therefore, a political community should inspire people with feelings that go beyond diversity and allow them to share goals and values.

Political Theory and Cultural Pluralism

Contemporary liberalism, particularly the ideas of John Rawls, tends to reduce what citizens share to a few ideas in their political culture. In order to accommodate the diversity of comprehensive doctrines, conceptions of the good life are excluded from the political principles of justice. In reducing the conception of an inclusive community to the sole shared conception of justice, political liberalism aims at allowing for a larger expression of cultural pluralism in the non-public sphere. As for the public sphere, liberalism sees it as being at arm's length from the dominant culture. Citizens share only the ideals and values associated with political liberalism. The liberal state should have no role to play in the preservation of culture. Claims linked to identity should be received only if they aim to eliminate obstacles which prevent the full participation of all citizens in the public sphere. The feeling of belonging to the political community depends only on the shared conception of justice. As we will see, Trudeau's conception of multiculturalism was considered to fit within this view of liberalism.

For a liberal nationalist such as David Miller, there is a positive link between national identity and political autonomy. A shared national identity can ensure a common loyalty, which then facilitates the collaboration of all citizens towards common public goals. Solidarity is easier among individuals who have a feeling of a shared identity, and this plays an important role in allowing them to determine their common destiny.

National identity is defined as a shared public culture that includes not only liberal principles, but also social norms and values. This common identity contributes both to ensuring equality among citizens and to reducing feelings of alienation. For liberal nationalists, citizens must be attached to their political community and not attached solely in terms of shared universal values, such as liberty, justice and democracy. Political identity must have a cultural meaning. The common identity that is ideally shared in order to facilitate political participation and solidarity is defined as an inclusive identity, that is, an identity that is transformed by the recognition of cultural pluralism. Contrary to rawlsian liberalism, the public space is not perceived as being neutral towards cultural identity. However, if the state attempts to protect the national identity from all the effects of cultural pluralism, members of minority groups would have no other options than assimilation or marginalization. A common public identity might mean that newcomers should learn the language, and, for instance, respect gender equality in their communal practices and participate in an educational system that teaches people the value of individual autonomy.

As we will see with our study of the Canadian experience, the liberal proposal of a purely political conception of belonging to a political community does not ensure the development of a shared identity and of a sense of belonging.

Liberal citizenship has always insisted on the equality of rights of all citizens, and has associated values and conceptions of the good with the private realm. Ethnocultural identity should be left to flourish in the private sphere and be separated from the public sphere.

However, if solidarity and feelings of belonging exist in a liberal democracy, it is often because citizens share certain values, which in most countries are related to the dominant group. There is nothing wrong with such a situation per se. However, quite often, this culture presents itself as the common culture and contributes to the definition of the common public culture, which in turn plays an important role in defining the frontiers between the public and private spheres. Therefore, justice in a multicultural society demands some forms of recognition, and that some distance be put between the dominant and the public cultures. One must, however, never go as far as to pretend that the state and the public sphere should be neutral towards the public culture.

Canadian Multiculturalism and Shared Citizenship

I will argue that, starting at the end of the 1980s and into the early 1990s, the Canadian policy of multiculturalism has been seen by the federal government as impeding the fostering of a new Canadian political identity, because it is perceived as undermining equal citizenship and leading to radical cultural pluralism, the reason being that multiculturalism praises differences and autonomy between ethnic groups. This, we will see, has never been the goal of the multiculturalism policy; on the contrary, integration has always been its aim, not assimilation or radical pluralism.

Since its inception in 1971, Canadian multiculturalism policy can be divided into three periods:

- The first period was marked by an emphasis on the preservation of culture.
- During the second period the emphasis was on integration. Multiculturalist policy was seen as an important means of fighting diverse forms of discrimination that were severely limiting the full participation of members of visible minorities in Canadian society. The main core of the multiculturalist policy had become an active policy of integration, both into society and into the economy.
- The third period has been marked by the notion of shared values and shared citizenship. If values are now at the forefront of the multiculturalism debate in Canada, it is because social cohesion appears to have been eroding. It is partly for that very reason that Canadian citizenship has been increasingly defined as implying certain shared common values. But, as we will see, the federal government has not been able to define with any precision what those common values should be, with the exception of those closely related to any liberal democratic regime.

The introduction of a discussion on common values is seen as a way to limit tolerance, which should not be boundless, and to establish a framework for social recognition.

How is it that Canadian multiculturalism, which was introduced in order to facilitate integration and to recognize the equality of all Canadians, has been perceived since the early 1990s as undermining our shared political identity and consequently undermining social cohesion, and contributing to a feeling that Canadians are not all equal? The reason is the way Canadian multiculturalism has been associated with Trudeau's liberalism.

Trudeau's critique of nationalism was framed within a strict liberal ideology. For Pierre Elliott Trudeau any government that puts an emphasis on the idea of a nation "is necessarily brought to define the common good in relation to the dominant ethnic group rather than in relation to the whole citizenry."[5] According to Trudeau, "a truly democratic government cannot be 'nationalistic' because its aim ought to be the pursuit of the good of all citizens, regardless of their ethnic origins."[6] As most democratic countries are becoming more polyethnic, the state's aim should be the safeguard "of the cultural liberty of Canadians." For Trudeau, within a democratic state "[no] ethnic group [should] take precedence over any other" and therefore, a policy of multiculturalism assures "the cultural freedom of Canadians."[7] Allegiance to a country should have nothing to do with cultural identity; individuals should be left free to maintain their cultural identity.

Trudeau's liberal conception of citizenship and of the role of a modern state resulted in the affirmation that the links between state and culture should be broken; they should simply vanish. The Canadian state, Trudeau said, "[has] no official culture."[8] One of the main objectives of the 1971 policy on multiculturalism was to redefine Canadian political identity by replacing the anglophone conception of political identity not with a two-nations conception, but rather with cultural diversity. Cultural pluralism is defined as the essence of Canadian identity and Canadian unity is to be found in its diversity.[9]

The almost ad nauseum assertions that Canadian unity is in its diversity and that the allegiance to Canada does not imply certain shared values were not counterbalanced by an active promotion of liberal principles. Of course, for Pierre Elliott Trudeau, the preservation of cultural identity could not be realised at the expense of liberal principles and values such as negative freedom. However, the result has been that citizenship has increasingly been perceived as a passive notion and as such cannot be the basis for full participation in society. This is contrary to the understanding of citizenship in a liberal democratic society. Because it did not expressly link multiculturalism policy with democratic principles and shared values, the policy was more often seen as promoting cultural separation than integration. In the 1970s this situation was not considered to be a problem for Canadian unity because most ethnic groups the policy addressed were already well integrated into Canadian society. It was a policy of recognition that was threatening neither to Canadian identity nor to solidarity. Trudeau presumed that most Canadians subscribed to liberal values and on this point he was more right than wrong in thinking so at the time. I would dare say that it has always been the case in Canada. Trudeau rejected any essentialist conception of a nation and any homogenising conception of minority groups. For Trudeau, belonging to a group does not depend upon an ethnic origin or a mother tongue, but upon a feeling of belonging. Trudeau's conception of multiculturalism should reinforce liberty, not curtail it. In this sense, Trudeau asserts that "we should not forget that individuals in a democracy may choose not to be concerned about maintaining a strong sense of their ethnic identity."[10]

The patterns of immigration to Canada changed drastically during the 1970s. If 90 percent of immigrants to Canada before 1961 came from Europe, in the 1970s this was the case for only 35 percent of immigrants.[11] During this time, the large majority of immigrants arrived from Third World countries. Subsequently, the share of Canada's immigrant population born in Asia and the Middle East increased from 14 percent in 1981 to 31 percent in 1996.[12] In 1996, roughly five million individuals living in Canada were born abroad and more than 26 percent of Ontarians (by far the most populous province in Canada) were immigrants (2.7 million Ontarians were born outside of Canada). Therefore, during the seventies, Canadian multiculturalism ceased to be primarily European. The consequence of this change in immigration patterns has been to considerably enlarge the scale of pluralism and of communitarian values present in Canadian society. Racism and discrimination became pressing problems and multiculturalism had to make these issues its main concern.

During the 1980s, statements such as "minority groups which are only concerned with multicultural programs have a tendency to remain isolated" became more frequent in federal publications and academic journals. The multiculturalism policy of the 1970s was designed with the interests and preoccupations of the ethnic groups which had been in Canada for a long time and whose origins were European in mind. The federal government recognised that the radical modification in the origin of immigrants made it inevitable that the main goal of multiculturalism should now be integration, not the preservation of culture. According to the permanent Committee of the House of Commons on Multiculturalism, "in the late seventies and early eighties, issues of social integration, harmonious race relations, support for Heritage Languages and political involvement also gained importance."[13]

In 1985, Otto Jelinek, then Minister of State for Multiculturalism, said that the government "was looking for more efficient means to ensure equality of opportunity and ways to promote a rich and homogeneous society .Equality should not only concern the cultural sphere but also the economic, political and social spheres."[15] In order to achieve such equality, the minister thought that the multiculturalism policy should aim at fighting discrimination and social prejudices. The 1971 policy is viewed as not having met its goal of social integration in addition to potentially reinforcing isolation of groups. Academics including Leslie Pal, Philip Resnick and Garth Stevenson agree with the foregoing conclusion.

The government no longer considers contributing to the promotion of diversity and to the maintenance of Canadian cultural patrimony to be within its mandate. Its role rather is to ensure the full participation of all Canadians in Canadian society and to ensure equality of opportunity. The goals of the 1988 law on multiculturalism were the reaffirmation of the fundamental values of individual rights and liberty. Multiculturalism aims at "removing the barriers of discrimination and ignorance which stand in the way of acceptance and respect."[15] In the 1970s the federal government stated that it was ready to play an active role in cases where individuals and groups wished to preserve their culture. However, in the 1980s this became the sole responsibility of individuals and groups, because the government began to worry about the development of a "vertical mosaic." To this end, the Special Committee on Visible Minorities in Canadian Society wrote in its report that "a greater emphasis on race relations and the concerns of visible minorities should be given a high priority in federal multicultural policy in the near future."[16] In order to ensure integration into Canadian society one needs more active policies in order to ensure equality. The preservation of cultural heritage is left to individual choice and to the responsibility of ethnocultural groups.

But even then, ethnocultural diversity continued to be presented as a basic element of pan-Canadian identity. While the federal government insisted during the 1970s and part of the 1980s on the right of Canadians to preserve their culture and to value their origins, it was never specified how this right could be meshed with other basic values of Canadian society. During the Meech Lake debate the majority of leaders of ethnocultural groups criticised the Accord for giving special status to one group, the francophones, and thereby not ensuring the equality of all cultures. Diversity no longer appeared to get along with unity anymore. The federal government has never claimed that the promotion of diversity could threaten Canadian unity or citizens' commitment and sense of belonging to the Canadian political community. However, it did recognise that many Canadians were concerned about a perceived lack of sense of belonging to the political community. Canadians perceived multicultural policy as pushing many neo-Canadians to turn their backs on a Canadian identity. Multiculturalism "does not mean celebrating the fact that we are different from each other and have differences, but rather celebrating the fact that we can be comfortable with our difference and yet live together in a harmonious manner."[17] In order to overcome this problem of "misperception," the federal government did not propose what would have been the logical answer to the perceived problem, that is to say to better explain to Canadians the goals of multicultural policy. Instead, it proposed to change the emphasis, and to further stress the links and values that unite all Canadians. One should promote "national values," and "we must be prepared to take part in building a strong society that truly reflects the values, visions and hopes we share."[18] According to the new governmental discourse, Canadians should focus "on the traditions and shared values through which we express our citizenship."[19] Multiculturalism must, therefore, contribute to the promotion of those values and traditions.

Social cohesion and solidarity necessitate a collective identity that relies on "shared values and goals." It is by now quite obvious that cultural diversity does not appear sufficient to cement the Canadian political identity.

The House of Commons has recognised many times that Canadians "share essential values" and that those values should transcend diversity. The Department of Citizenship and Immigration has insisted in the past that "there is virtually no mention of integration."[20] The department says that

> We have heard general concern about what is perceived to be the devaluation of Canadian citizenship; the requirements for citizenship are perceived to no longer reflect any obligations to the country or to promote integration into Canadian society. To achieve greater social cohesion through integration and to place a higher value on citizenship, it is necessary to identify immigration criteria which in fact reflect Canadian core values and principles in more practical terms.[21]

However, the federal government has never been very successful in determining what these Canadian values are. Although one can find various lists in different governmental publications, liberal democratic principles such as fundamental rights and liberties, equality, tolerance, the rule of law, democracy and equity emerge as a common to each of them.[22] Diversity is presented as one value among others and not as the defining characteristic of the Canadian identity.

The important modifications in the discourse of multiculturalism have never been officially associated with a change in the federal government's conception of integration. If this policy has been presented from the mid-1980s on as promoting an infinite tolerance and a profound diversity, this has always been associated with a misperception by Canadians. The government often assumes that Canadians see the links between a feeling of belonging and their political identity as having been broken. This situation undermines our social cohesion and makes it more difficult to integrate immigrants. Unity needs certain shared values that transcend diversity; social cohesion requires a sense of belonging.

Cultural diversity did change Canadian citizenship substantially; it has put some distance between Canadian identity and British culture. It has certainly pluralized and somehow neutralized the common public culture. But multicultural policy has also been one of the main focal points for questioning what appears to be an important cause of fragmentation in Canadian society. There are limits to tolerance and diversity; social integration, political participation and respect among groups are the goals of the Canadian policy of multiculturalism.

Conclusion

Canadian multicultural policy has played an important role in explaining to Canadians that integration in a multicultural society can appear to be just only if it goes along with the transformation of a number of historical characteristics of the dominant culture. However, as the current debate and the changes in governmental discourse show, the necessary transformation of the common public culture should not threaten the support and participation of everybody in the democratic principles. Our study also shows that the very notion of citizenship implies that all citizens share a common public culture and therefore that the state cannot pretend to be neutral towards it, as Trudeau and the many liberal theorists believe. Integration is an adaptive process that touches not only the members of minority groups, but the welcoming society as well. However, this having been said, if certain values will be transformed, others are understood to be non-negotiable. Gender equality has that status in Canada. Most Canadians agree on these prerequisites for citizenship and their public affirmation would facilitate the recognition of cultural pluralism. Besides, members of the majority who are reticent towards multiculturalism would have difficulty arguing that the preservation of cultural heritage is a threat to the continued existence of a common Canadian political identity when these shared values are affirmed. One cannot ignore the importance of a common public culture without putting the social cohesion and solidarity of the political community at risk. One should not think, however, that the existence of shared values results automatically in national unity. Canada is a good example that this is not necessarily true.[23]

Multiculturalism policy has been a very efficient means to engage Canadians in the transformation of the Canadian public culture and to redefine the Canadian political community. But it has also shown that a political identity cannot "exist" without a substantial collective identity, what the federal government now refers to as a shared citizenship based on values such as mutual respect, responsibility and diversity. Therefore, Canadians must learn the values and institutions of civic life. However, there is no one value that cannot be questioned or pretend to perpetuity. The federal government now appears to be arguing that the manner in which liberal principles are institutionalised in a society depends on the public culture, which is associated with the history and culture of the political community. A paradox of liberal democratic societies lies in their need for a common public culture, but a culture that possesses no sacred characters.

Notes

1. Jean-Michel Demetz, "Les nouveaux Canadiens," *L'Express international,* no 2577 (November 2000): 55.
2. Ibid., 54.
3. Gwynne Dyer, "Visible Majorities," *Canadian Geographic* (January-February 2001): 47.
4. Ibid., 49.
5. Pierre Elliot Trudeau, "La nouvelle trahison des clercs," *Cité libre,* vol. 13, no 46 (April 1962): 11.
6. Ibid.
7. House of Commons, *Debates* 8 October 1971, 8545.
8. Ibid.
9. Ibid., 8580.
10. Ibid., 8581.
11. Statistics Canada, *The Daily, 1996 Census: Immigration and Citizenship,* (Ottawa, Statistics Canada, 4 November 1997), Internet Document. http://www.statcan.ca/Daily/English/971104/d971104.htm.
12. Ibid.
13. House of Commons, Standing Committee on Multiculturalism, *Multicultur-*

alism: Building the Canadian Mosaic (Ottawa: The Queen's Printer, 1987), 19.

14. House of Commons Standing Committee in Multiculturalism, Testimony (Ottawa: Goods and Services Canada, 26 November 1985).

15. Multiculturalism and Citizenship Canada, *The Canadian Multiculturalism Act : A Guide for Canadians* (Ottawa: Supply and Services Canada, 1990), 1.

16. House of Commons, *Equality Now*, Report of the Special Committee on Visible Minorities in Canadian Society (March) (Ottawa: The Queen's Printer, 1984), 55.

17. House of Commons, *The Ties that Bind*, Report of the Standing Committee on Communications and Culture (Ottawa: The Queen's Printer, 1992), 10.

18. Multiculturalism and Citizenship Canada, *Canadian Citizenship: What Does it Mean to You?* (Ottawa: Minister of Supply and Services Canada, 1992), 10.

19. Ibid., 24.

20. Advisory Group: Immigration Legislative Review, *Not Just Numbers: A Canadian Framework for Future Immigration* (Ottawa: Public Works and Government Services Canada, 1997), 13.

21. Ibid., 39.

22. House of Commons, *Canadian Citizenship: A Sense of Belonging*, Report of the Standing Committee on Citizenship and Immigration (June, 1994) (Ottawa: Public Works and Government Services Canada, 1994); Department of Canadian Heritage, *Annual Report 1993–1994 on the operation of the Canadian Multiculturalism Act* (Ottawa: Supply and Services Canada, 1995); Citizenship and Immigration Canada, *Building on a Strong Foundation for the 21st Century. New Directions for Immigration and Refugee Policy and Legislation* (Ottawa: Public Works and Government Services Canada, 1998).

23. Will Kymlicka, *Finding Our Way: Rethinking Ethnocultural Relations in Canada* (Toronto: Oxford University Press, 1998).

PART IV

The Future of Citizenship

15

Governance and Emergent Transversal Citizenship: Towards a New Nexus of Moral Contracts

GILLES PAQUET

> *Liberalism is a doctrine about the external organization*
> *of society. It is silent on the more important question:*
> *How shall we live?*
> Michael Lind

Pluralism is a world view that defines societies as fragmented and discontinuous, composed of different complementary/conflictive parts or spheres that are incommensurable, and therefore cannot be reduced to a single logic. In plural societies, there is a constant and active process of reconciliation, harmonization and effective coordination of the logics in these different spheres to ensure a minimal degree of coherence, resilience and effective learning.

Citizenship is a covenant based on the values, principles and reciprocal privileges and responsibilities that define our ways of living together. Therefore, in a plural society, citizenship cannot be anything but *plurielle* – i.e., limited and multiple – for the citizen in such a world has multiple and limited relationships, and multiple, limited and overlapping identities.[1]

Many political scientists and jurists are critical of this notion of limited/multiple citizenships. To bring commensurability to the incommensurable, they routinely reduce this rich and variegated nexus of values, principles, privileges and responsibilities connoting citizenship to a common denominator, for the purposes of governance, by granting politics a transcendent role. Through a sleight of hand, they invent a projection of this n-dimensional socio-economic reality (that citizenship synthesizes) onto a single transcendent plane where all agents are defined as equivalent and equipotent, and make it the sole locus of citizenship. The citizen becomes an *être de raison* operating in the transcendent plane of politics, a sort of smallest common denominator *soul* in all agents.

In such an ethereal world, there is a denial of diversity, no possibility of considering any differences within the n-dimensional world, and a refusal to establish lucid and responsible rankings among dimensions. This reductionism is even presented as the essence of democracy: inferring that without the transcendence of politics, democracy would not prevail.[2]

I argue that plural societies need a much richer notion of citizenship. The argument is developed in four stages. First, I describe in a cursory way the stratagem of the "public sphere" as a sanitized locus for agent-state intercourse, and show the limitations of this strategy on which politics has built its purported dominium. Second, I suggest an analytical framework to explore various crucial dimensions of citizenship. Third, I develop a broader notion of citizenship, one rooted in civil society and in the notion of moral contracts, and I show how it is likely to be better adapted to pluralist contexts. Fourth, I consider rapidly the different ways in which Canada and Australia are drifting towards this position.

Pluralism and the Perils of Transcendent Politics

The notion of open society[3] suggests societies that have escaped the dominance of holistic values, and have managed to put the individual at the centre of the stage. In the traditional stylizations of this open society, one finds a private sphere for the individual, where his negative freedom (freedom from constraints) is guaranteed through arrangements like private property, and a public sphere where an *État de droit* regulates the relationships among individuals and between the individuals and the state.[4] The restricted power of the state is meant to ensure that the society will never be allowed to be closed.

A pluralist society is a much richer concept than open society. It goes beyond this notion of negative freedom and calls for "un ensemble composé (à compartiments) librement aggloméré" where the constituent parts maintain a good portion of their original autonomy. These sectors are regarded as "autant de domaines irréductibles, en interaction permanente ... chaque sphère particulière trouve son expression dans un pouvoir à part ... à la division des pouvoirs correspond ... une véritable démultiplication des allégeances."[5]

Plural societies are societies that explicitly recognize that individuals and groups are motivated by different values, and that they can legitimately have different value systems. To pursue their different objectives, they require positive freedom: capacity and opportunity to pursue these values actively and effectively, and the elimination of the constraints or unfreedoms that prevent them from doing so. Moreover, plural societies deny that there is any constantly overriding value.[6] This entails the inevitability of conflicts, and the need to develop reasonable conflict-resolution mechanisms based on some core credo (however minimal) that the disputants may share. While the plurality of conceptions of a good life increases the range of valued possibilities, not all possibilities are reasonable. So there is also a need for limits, and for the justification for such limits as excluding unreasonable possibilities, or unreasonable ways of pursuing them, or ways that might simply maximize conflicts.

The central strategy of many political scientists and jurists in the face of "plural" societies has been to focus on finding complexity-reducing devices for the purpose of governance.

One favorite stratagem has been the reductive assumption that there are only two sectors: the private and the public sphere. According to this device, there is a private sphere relying on a right to privacy, and a public sphere where individuals interact under the aegis of the state. It is in this public space that citizenship is nested, and that the citizen participates in a restricted way (through representation in Parliament) to give a voice to "la volonté générale."

For those who defend such a dichotomy, the two spheres represent the private and public faces of the lifeworld of individuals. Groups and communities are simply considered as insignificant symbolic markers; citizenship pertains to the public sphere, and is dominated by state-agent relations. This occluding of communities, and the emphasis on the private-public dichotomy and the vertical notion of citizenship associated with it, are both altogether too Manichean and unduly reductive.

The real plural world is much more complex and characterized by deep diversity: it is filled with communities (real and imagined), there are many more spheres, and they all overlap to such an extent that it is of little use to build any analysis on the assumption of tightly compartmentalized spheres.[7] Consequently, citizenship cannot be restricted to the public sphere. State, market, private and public spheres – and there may be others in the material and symbolic orders – overlap to such a significant degree that it is unreasonable to limit the ambit of citizenship to the state sphere. Indeed, as T.H. Marshall[8] would put it, the development of the nexus of privileges and obligations defining citizenship has evolved sufficiently that it has invaded all spheres (market, state, private, public, etc.).

Moreover, citizenship cannot be reduced to state-agent relations. At a certain level of generality, political scientists and jurists recognize that citizenship is fundamentally a dual relationship – *vertical*, between the members of the political community and the political authority and the state, and *horizontal* amongst members of the community. But they overemphasize the former relation to such an extent that the notion of citizenship becomes therein totally absorbed.[9]

The bias toward the vertical is based on the special importance of the public sphere, and of politics and state within it, through the process of political representation. Politics and state are purported to play a transcendent role as the agent of transfiguration of society – "une élévation tranfiguratrice de la société."[10] And there is a quasi-doctrinaire belief that it is a *necessary* elevation, since only politics, through the process of conflicts among parties and collective adversaries, can lead to a meaningful taking-into-account of the common good.[11] For those holding that view, the state is the centre of the public sphere and the privileged locus of the conflicts between power groups. Consequently, any relativization of the role of the state can only be regarded as a deplorable erosion of the political, even though the state is said, by the same persons, to have generated a "primat de la représentation des acteurs sur la résolution des problèmes qu'ils posent."[12]

It is our view that in a modern, pluralist, knowledge-based socio-economy, there is no privileged or transcendent locus of conflict, and, therefore, that the valence of politics and state is considerably overstated. In a more realistic approximation of the socio-economy, the horizontal (community) relationships are as important as (or perhaps even more important than) the vertical ones. The reduction in the relative importance of the stato-political, any disenchantment with the political, or any drift toward a reduction of the intermediation role of the political,[13] or its implosion or its reconfiguration in new sites – all this means a shift from government to governance.[14]

Governance may be defined as effective coordination when resources, information and power are distributed. Citizenship – in a context of governance – means the ensemble of values, principles, reciprocal privileges and responsibilities that define the nexus of moral contracts. These contracts constitute the necessary social technologies of coordination capable of bringing forth good life in all its various senses for the different agents. The perils of maintaining a fixation on the stato-political are clear. Since citizenship is a nexus of relationships dominated not by the state but by a much richer array of relations throughout the socio-economy, the fixation on the political can only rob the notion of citizenship of much of its meaning.

An Analytical Framework

Refusing to reduce citizenship to the realm of the political does not suffice, however. One must suggest an alternative and broader framework within which citizenship might be usefully analyzed. While there are many monist schemes playing up one dimension of citizenship or the other, none of the efforts at producing an acceptable synthetic scheme has been totally successful. This is ascribable to the very nature of the societies that have become plural through historical times: no single template would appear to be applicable to all. At this stage of the debates, one can only hope to identify an "analytical framework" – "a set of relationships that do not lead to specific conclusions about the world of events ... (but) may be looked upon as the mould out of which the specific types of theories are made"[15] in response to demands by diverse groups, and in order to temper the behaviour of groups by reframing their representations and perceptions.[16]

This more inclusive framework helps to provide the basis for interpretations encompassing "material" and "symbolic" dimensions, and in probing the growing centrality of "recognition capital." Membership and identity are simply less structured forms of social and symbolic life, but they naturally either progress through the development of culture and institutions or fade away.

We have identified three major dimensions to be taken into account in a classificatory scheme, presented in Figure 1.[17]

1.   The first dimension pertains to the dichotomy between material and symbolic orders. This *notion* has emerged clearly from the works of Raymond Breton, among others, and has contributed to broadening

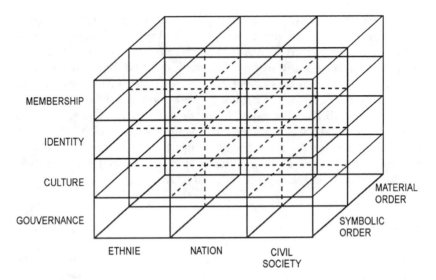

Figure 1: Dimensions of Citizenship

the debate on culture in Canada.[18] The insistence on the importance of the symbolic order has allowed the discussion to escape from the traps of traditional analyses of interest groups' demands for material or financial gratifications. The broader analysis has focused on problems of collective identity (traditions, customs, norms, way of life, etc.) that are embedded in the forms and styles of private and public institutions. It has re-affirmed something that is often forgotten, i.e., that the symbolic order underpins the workings of the material order and is also a prime target of government interventions.[19]

For Breton and others, the construction of the symbolic order is as important as the construction of the material socio-economy. Citizens traditionally have sought a certain concordance between their private way of life (their "culture") and the style of their public environment (their "national identity"). Their demand for status (that is, for recognition) will often be as vociferous as their demand for access to economic and political resources.[20] Indeed, recognition and redistribution are often alternative ways of transferring different sorts of capital. Governments of plural democracies must be increasingly involved in monitoring and understanding the symbolic order, and in intervening in it, both in response to demands by diverse groups, and in order to temper the behaviour of groups by reframing their representations and perceptions.[21]

2. The second broad axis of the analytical block defines an increasing degree of formality in social arrangements: from membership, which may be regarded as a minimal set of conditions to belong to a club (the difference between members and strangers); to identification/identity, which is the subjective recognition of some salient features as the basis for self-categorization; to culture, which represents a somewhat formalized set of rules, laws, customs and rituals; to governance, which amounts to the development of a stable pattern of social interaction and institutions.[22]

The notions of membership, identity and culture are extremely difficult to define precisely. Essentialist definitions of belonging are anchored in certain traits. Others have insisted on some primordial features as determinant. A third group has fundamentally defined these notions in a relational way: shared differences that are the result of negotiated arrangements.[23] In the first two instances, a number of ethnographic features are said to provide the basic or dominant characteristics necessary to qualify for membership.[24] In the last case, membership, identity and culture are in the nature of a *persona*, which is the result of a creative and interactive process through which relationships are constructed and evolve in a manner that makes them a matter of conventions and agreements with outsiders.[25]

In that sense, membership, identity and culture may be regarded as increasingly more complex forms of "social glue" or social capital.[26] This sort of capital simultaneously provides the basis for differentiation, structuration and integration: i.e., it serves to provide a basic partitioning based on negotiated differences, but also as a basis for assembling those disparate elements into a coherent whole.[27]

Since *de facto* heterogeneity may generate a segmentation of the social space in disconnected groups, and since such segmentation may well degenerate, through multiplex relationships, into cumulative processes accentuating and crystallizing such a segmentation, an increasing degree of balkanization and anomie of the segments may ensue.[28] Consequently, it is crucial that we spell out these conventions, along with the pattern of rights and obligations of each party, if active and vibrant citizenship is to ensue, and not a mosaic of disparate groups in conflict on all fronts.

Membership will be easier to negotiate than identity, and identity easier than culture, but corresponding to these different degrees of cohesion, there are different types of "moral contracts."[29]

3.   The third broad axis of the block identifies three complementary and yet intricately interwoven terrains of social integration: ethnos, nation and civil society. These are the different grounds in which these moral contracts, however loosely negotiated or otherwise arrived at, are embedded. They are alternate/joint foundations for moral contracts.

The case of ethnos used to be regarded as quite distinct because of the fact that membership was perceived as rooted *primarily* in physical characteristics and the material order. But even ethnicity has tended to become more and more symbolic, so that growing importance has been given to symbolic recognition in defining ethnic boundaries.[30]

Ethnos, nation and civil society are different ways of anchoring membership and identity, and may be regarded as tending to become substitutes (or at least the basis for a complex compound) rather than being the basis of absolutely non-intersecting realities. Ethnos, nation and civil society are valid bases for discussing membership, identity, culture and governance, but depending on which one is the hegemonic terrain, the "moral contracts" will contain a different set of collective rights and obligations. Determining the valence of each terrain has therefore become crucial.

Such determination is difficult, and fraught with Manichean dogmas and nasty discussions that reveal the full powers of naivety and political correctness. Ethnos has become the target of many attacks because it is a source of exclusion. Indeed, the dichotomy between "bad" nationalism (ethnic based) and "good" nationalism (territorially, constitutionally based) has become a mantra. Connection between government and an ethnocultural nation upon which the nation-state is based has become regarded as "xenophobic, nativist and even fascist."[31]

In its place, the politically correct conventional wisdom has proposed a sort of "civic" nationalism as "progressive because it is committed to a political ideal." This represents a subtle but futile stratagem to capture the "psychological economies of scale" of the nation-state, without having to pay the price of ethnocultural commonality broadly defined. For, unfortunately, it would seem that "the ethnic nation is the largest community with which ordinary beings can have an emotional attachment" and that civic patriotism is simply an *être de raison*.[32]

So far these attempts to exorcize ethnocultural dimensions completely have failed the test of reality – for ethnocultural nations and nationalisms thrive. There has been a recent attempt to salvage the civic nationalism paradigm by insisting that ethnocultural dimensions may be factored in, but only as subsidiary/secondary features. These features are regarded as important only at the symbolic level, as a support system for the "liberal-civic-nationalist" citizen whose "liberalism" remains the only fundamental value. Michael Ignatieff has undergone such a minor conversion between 1993 and 2000.[33]

This has led to the emergence of a form of "boutique multiculturalism" – i.e., a multiculturalism one can invoke only in matters inconsequential, for as soon as there is an effort to leverage or parley these ethnocultural values into anything significant, the dominant liberal view of the individual-without-ethnocultural-qualities is used forcefully to trivialize forcefully the ethnocultural dimensions.[34]

This analytical block leaves a great deal of room for a wide variety of complex notions of citizenship, anchored in quite different terrains. This captures the central fact that citizenship as a set of ligatures (values, principles, reciprocal privileges and responsibilities) is an essentially contested concept – i.e., one about which reasonable persons may never agree[35] because it is a multidimensional concept, and different persons may legitimately put more emphasis on one aspect or another within the citizenship analytical block. What crystallizes as the relevant notion of citizenship is a set of ligatures or moral contracts defining a transversal syncretic entity within the citizenship analytical block: a mixture of values, principles and reciprocal privileges and responsibilities that provides citizenship with its broad diffuse base and its syncretic unity.

Terms of Integration and Emergent Transversal Citizenship

In the process of defining citizenship as ligatures of all sorts, it is easy to understand how different groups may focus on different cells of the block. Ethnic membership may be regarded as the essential feature by some, while others may elect to emphasize symbolic identity in civil society exclusively. But in a world characterized by much spectrality – multiple memberships, limited identities, a mélange of ethnic/national/civil society identification and cultures, layered governance structures and a most fluid boundary between the symbolic and the material world – citizenship is unlikely to be captured in one cell or dimension of the block. Indeed, and this is our main argument, citizenship is a transversal concept: it is nested in a diagonal cluster within the analytical block.[36]

This means that citizenship might be regarded as a nexus of ligatures defining a covenant or pact cutting across the block, across the many boundaries, and attempting to reconcile in an evolutionary way the many different perspectives that coexist, within a given society or at the intersection of many societies, through a nexus of fluid "moral contracts."[37] Moral contracts are more or less informal arrangements and conventions that embody values and norms on which people agree. They define mutual expectations, legitimate entitlements and obligations, and the corridor or boundary limits within which people have agreed to live.

Only such a transversal notion of citizenship, based on moral contracts, can capture the array of ligatures capable of meeting individuals' complex needs for autonomy and belonging, the needs for responsibilities, and opportunities for participation in an active democracy, and the challenges of a spectral society with its new type of sociality based on weak ties. This notion of citizenship need not be univocal, since there are multiple citizenships anchored in different terrains, and there may be differentiated citizenships – in degree and in kind.

For instance, one can easily imagine a basic set of minimal norms corresponding to basic citizenship, but also differential levels of rights-cum-obligations that individuals and groups might choose in order to equilibrate their entitlements with the sort of responsibilities they are willing to accept.[38] In the same manner, in a world of limited identities and multiple citizenships, one can imagine layers of citizenship corresponding to different pacts entered into by individuals or organizations. These may echo either different degrees of rootedness, or complementary ensembles of commitments, or, in some cynical scenarios, flags of convenience that can be used alternatively or strategically by individuals or organizations, depending on circumstances.

In this context, the multiplication of citizenships has called for some ordering (strong or weak) if the notion is not to be trivialized. The notion of primary and subsidiary citizenships connotes a sense of priority among the different limited affiliations. This ordering cannot be embodied in a formal legal arrangement. At best, it would correspond to an always emergent and never fully crystallized meta-moral contract defining the relative valence of the different ligatures that make up individuals' and organizations' citizenships of all sorts.[39]

1. Coordinates

To facilitate the discussion, one might identify some important dimensions of citizenship – citizenship as legal status, as participation in governance, and as belonging – as illustrations of the range of meanings that might be attached to a transversal concept within the block, and of the wide array of flavours that can emerge as layers are multiplied, and one dimension or the other is emphasized. This is presented in Figure 2.

At one apex of this citizenship triangle is the liberal notion of citizenship, fundamentally rooted in the notion of legal status – a notion that is in good currency in the Anglo-Saxon world. Here, citizenship inheres in individuals, who are seen as the bearers of rights, and it is couched in a language of rights and entitlements. Citizens do not have to do anything, or at least not much, to become or remain citizens. It minimizes participation requirements and expects little sense of identification. This notion emphasizes the centrality of negative freedom (i.e., protection against interference with individual choices).

At a second apex is the civic republican view of citizenship. It is largely couched in terms of duties, and defines citizenship as a notion with a high valence to practice and participation – the citizen is a producer of governance. It calls on individuals to become members of the community, to participate in the culture and governance of the community. This concept emphasizes positive freedom (i.e., the person's being able to do this or that, and the duty to help others in that respect).

A third apex emphasizes neither status nor participation, but the process of belonging. In this zone of the triangle, what is of central importance is the "recognition," respect and esteem given to the individual-and-his-circumstances. There are two important variants of this polar case: one in which recognition is simply a "mise en visibilité" of some basic characteristics that are already there; and the second which focusses rather on the "construction" of status and differences by activism designed to transform the symbolic order.[40]

These three ideal-type conceptions are only meant to illustrate the broad range of different notions of citizenship in good currency. One may find countries having anchored their notion of citizenship all over the terrain of the citizenship triangle, corresponding to different mixes of status, participation and belonging. In any concrete real-world situation, citizenship in a plural society is a transversal mix of these three components. Indeed, a given notion of citizenship condenses some of these dimensions, and represents a nexus of moral contracts that deals with these different dimensions in a particular way. Consequently, citizenship may cover a whole range of possible meanings with all sorts of intermediate cases giving different weights to each of these dimensions.

Moreover, one may easily imagine, as was suggested earlier, different layers of citizenship within which the individual may be embedded through his/her membership in different organizations, and a variety of families of citizenship within which individuals and organizations are nested as they take part in the different arrangements pertaining to different countries.

Belonging

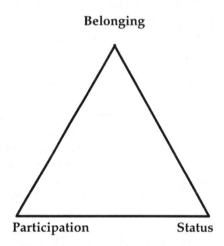

Participation   **Status**

Figure 2: The citizenship triangle

2.   Guideposts

Over the last few decades, the dynamics of the debates about citizenship have led to an evolution of the concept. From the original formulation of T.H. Marshall[41] emphasizing the development of citizenship entirely in terms of rights (civil rights in the eighteenth century, political rights in the nineteenth century and social rights in the twentieth century), one has seen it evolve towards an ever-greater importance being given to the participation aspects of citizenship, but also in ways that give more import to the whole dimension of belonging and symbolic recognition.

Moreover, there has been a tendency for the notion of citizenship not only to change the valence of these three components, but also to react to the ever greater "liquidity" and complexity of modern societies[42] by an increase in the degree of "informality" in the normativities embedded in the moral contracts, and by a multiplication of the contracts dealing with these more complex relationships.[43]

Instead of being absorbed into a simple, formal and legal linkage between the citizen and the state, the citizenship relationship has evolved into a looser but more encompassing covenant covering a web of relationships among members of the community, but also between them and the state.

Finally, the proliferation of multiple citizenships has heightened the complexity of these arrangements, and has generated a whole new set of problems for persons or organizations purporting to hold membership in many clubs at the same time. This has led both to ugly abuses of power (when a group of citizens has been branded by a paranoid state as likely to collaborate with the enemy as happened to Japanese Canadians during the Second World War), and to individuals and organizations using their "citizenship of convenience" to take opportunistic advantage of all possible entitlements while shirking the responsibilities of citizenship.

This should have led to debates about meaningful arbitrages among competing allegiances or at least to the emergence of a dominant logic acting as lodestar to guide collectivities in such choices. However, not all countries have had the fortitude to deal squarely with such problems. Many have found it politically incorrect to even raise these issues.

The emergence of the loose covenant that ensues faces many challenges. In two recent documents, Jenson and Papillon[44] have identified some of them. One may underline a few of these challenges as a way of probing the process of construction of citizenship underway in all countries.

The first challenge has to do with the increasing *diversity and spectrality* of the populations. It would appear that nothing less than a recognition of differential and asymmetric citizenships can do the job in a world where diversity and spectrality entail a multiplicity of limited identities that may be complementary or competing.[45] Unless one can define some rank ordering among these attachments, citizenship becomes meaningless.

The second one has to do with the multiplication of the *sites of citizenship*. While the power and legitimacy of the nation-state would appear to be lessened, there are reasons to believe that this proliferation of sites of power is even more important when the ethnocultural basis of the society is more diverse.

When new entities at the supra-national and infra-national levels become meaningful actors, and alliances and joint ventures blur the old distinction between the state sphere and the rest of society, one must either firmly re-establish the state sphere to salvage the old notion of citizenship, or transform the notion of citizenship to deal with the new realities.[46] This latter route calls for citizenship to be broadened, and for new social ligatures and arrangements to be negotiated. While different groups may wish to obtain symbolic recognition, others may want some political autonomy or a portion of the economic surplus. This is true for groups at the local and regional levels, but particularly for ethnocultural groups.

The third challenge has to do with the evolving nature of *solidarity*. The old notion of citizenship associated with rights has simply been driven to extend rights to cover all sorts of social entitlements on the ground that social and political equality are linked. This has often been discussed in complete ignorance of a citizen's responsibilities, and is often rooted in the basic assumption that only the state could be trusted to take action with a view to the common good.

This has led to a strong emphasis on redistribution as a way to ensure that the so-called collective rights of communities would be honored, and on a reiteration of the importance of a strong central government as a source of redistribution – for only a centralized state can bring the requisite resources to the centre, and redistribute them to lessen inequality. However, it is far from clear that redistribution (be it of material or symbolic resources) is the way.

A return to the principles of insurance might be a more appropriate response in a world of weaker ties and greater turbulence, where what one wants to encourage is a more efficient allocation of risk-taking through a wider use of risk-sharing.[47] And this refocusing may be all the more important if one accepts (even only in part) the argument of René Girard, who contends that reducing inequality by redistribution may increase the danger of envy and violence.[48]

A final challenge has to do with *participation*, i.e., taking part in the governance process. Again, this may take two forms – either opening the political process through stratagems of inclusion, or accepting that citizenship does not necessarily have to be restricted to the political. This latter approach would require a broadening of the notion of citizenship to encompass more than individuals and communities, and the design of appropriate mechanisms to define and enforce the rights and responsibilities of these other "organizational entities."[49]

There are daunting challenges in eliciting the requisite participation and engagement for a society to thrive and prosper when faced with a more and more variegated population in a more and more turbulent world.

The mix of negative and positive freedoms likely to provide the optimal integration (i.e., one capable of providing ample possibilities for differentiated citizenship while ensuring the minimal rules of engagement for the society to succeed) need not necessarily have evolved organically. One must therefore identify the ways in which the state wittingly or not is influencing the "terms of integration."

Australian and Canadian Musings

It is only since 1947 (Canada) and 1948 (Australia) that the members of these societies can claim Canadian or Australian citizenship. Before that time, these persons were either British subjects or without citizenship. One may reasonably ask whether this discontinuity per se has made any difference. The answer is not clear. It has obviously entailed the creation of some symbolic capital around the new label, but it is fair to say that, in and by itself, this re-labelling has done little to effect the instant crystallization of a new identity. It has only triggered the process of learning about what it meant to be a citizen, for citizenship always remains *en émergence*.

This process of social learning has been experienced quite differently in Australia and Canada. Australia has tackled the issue more openly, frontally and transparently. In Canada, the birth of citizenship came just a few years after a very divisive fracture in Canadian society created by the Conscription Crisis.[50] This crisis split Canada along ethnic lines right at the core of the Second World War when the federal government tried to escape from a promise made to Quebec that it would not invoke conscription as a quid for the quo that constituted the agreement of Quebec to support Canada entering actively into the war effort. This particular experience was so traumatic (Quebec leaders being jailed) that it had quite a chilling effect on the post-war debates in Canada.

This has led both countries to enter these citizenship debates in quite different circumstances. In Australia, debates and documents registered progress in the emergence of a syncretic notion of citizenship. In Canada, the debates were muffled, the arguments less vibrant and the documents not very clear as markers.

A preliminary examination of the two experiences suggests that the Australian approach has led to faster progress toward a clear definition of the meaning of citizenship. Most certainly, this issue has received more attention, has generated more debates, and has led to a much sharper sense of what constitutes the nexus of moral contracts making up citizenship in Australia than in Canada.

Yet, one should not conclude too hurriedly that the Canadian way has proved dysfunctional. A closer examination reveals that a slower process of social learning in Canada was not only well suited to the Canadian circumstances and ethos, but also a strategy not necessarily unhelpful in dealing with ever more complex citizenship issues in countries that do not have the robust debating culture of Australia – a strategy of small steps and ad hocery.

In this section, some hypotheses are put forward about the different routes that these two countries would appear to have followed over the last fifty years, about the different nexuses of moral contracts that have emerged as a matter of consequence, and about the paradoxal efficiency of the Canadian approach.

1. A few contrasts

One might suggest the following differences between Australia and Canada as deserving some probing:

- the importance of "citizen commitment" in Australia, and its relative unimportance in Canada; the centrality of discussions about the moral contract embodying this commitment in Australia, and the diffidence vis-à-vis any such discussions in Canada; and the consequent sense of the limits to tolerance that ensues in Australia as a result of the debates about the emergent moral contracts, while almost unlimited tolerance prevails in Canada because no norms have been agreed upon so a no-norm convention has emerged by default;

- a carefully constructed bottom-up social cohesion built on commitment in Australia, and a top-down mechanical social glue supposedly generated through redistribution of resources in Canada;
- a capacity and taste for robust national debates in Australia, while in Canada there is a "sociality of consensus" and a taste for obfuscation, irony and bricolage in the public sphere; and a certain differential in the degree of political correctness (higher in Canada than in Australia) which stunts seriously social debates in Canada and is a source of differential social learning between the two countries.

a.   From the "white Australia" policy of yesteryear to the "commitment to Australia" expected from citizens today, there has been significant clarity in Australia's position. In Canada, on the contrary, much has been done to equivocate. Canada's immigration policy was almost as quasi-racist as Australia fifty years ago, but without being stated as bluntly as the Australians did. There is still great difficulty in Canada even today in accepting that this ever was the case. This hypocritical policy of obfuscation about an era when soft but effective discrimination was in force is easy to understand and is ascribable to the Quebec factor. It is not possible to debate openly the rights, responsibilities, values, participation, appartenance, etc. underlying the moral contracts of citizenship when a significant segment of the Canadian population of different ethno-cultural extraction has not been persuaded that such moral contracts are internally acceptable and provide for the identity and lifeworld of communities.

Indeed, as a result of the Quebec factor, the conditions for becoming a Canadian citizen have had to remain strategically ill-defined: at first, admission was based on opportunistically defined norms rooted in no clear principles; then it evolved toward the present situation where any person putting one foot on the tarmac at any Canadian airport is automatically granted almost all the rights of long-term Canadians except the right to vote.

The granting of a "Canadian citizenship" to Nelson Mandela by the Parliament of Canada has gone further and expanded the definition of citizen to include someone who meets none of the standard criteria for citizenship. Whatever the merit of this particular individual, the Canadian Parliament admitted into "our community of fate" someone who has only the most tenuous possible reciprocal relationship of obligation with other members of our community, and through this gesture, all but declared that there are no firm conditions for becoming a Canadian citizen, and did much to establish that it is simply an honorific title.

b.   Canadians as individuals are inclined to be much more demanding in their definition of citizenship than Canadian officials. They define it not only in terms of a bundle of rights and liberties, but also in terms of responsibilities, attitudes and identities. But public officials (for whom pragmatism is the dominant value)[51] claim to have no concern about defining any such set of expectations about the terms of integration for newcomers on the ground that one cannot ask anything from newcomers that one does not require explicitly from native born. Making any additional demands from newcomers is branded automatically as intolerance, chauvinism or racism. As a matter of consequence, officials are not concerned much either about ensuring that newcomers are provided with the requisite help to make them capable of participating fully in the host society, and feel that they have no legitimate basis to refuse to modify the Canadian ways in response to requests by newcomers claiming that such ways constitute a discriminatory stance against them.

The result is not only a lack of debates in Canada about limits to tolerance and diversity, but a natural drift, as the jurisprudence cranks out case after case, towards a refusal to recognize that there are any limits. This is no longer pluralism but a leap of faith that if some form of limits proves necessary, it will emerge organically. This is quite a gamble since the required terms of integration are in fact likely to emerge only from a continuous renegotiation as the expectations and environments change, and to coalesce into an explicitation of rights and responsibilities but also of the limits to tolerance of the host society, and of the obligations this entails for the newcomers to adapt somewhat. This challenge, Canadian leaders refuse to confront.

To clarify these expectations, Australia has spelled out the content of the "Australian Compact" – seven basic principles based on "commitment" that Australian citizens must accept:[52]

- to respect and care for the land we share
- to maintain the rule of law and the ideal of equality under the law
- to strengthen Australia as a representative liberal democracy

- to uphold the ideal of Australia as a tolerant and fair society
- to recognise and celebrate Australia as an inclusive multicultural society
- to continue to develop Australia as a society devoted to the well-being of its people
- to value the unique status of the Aboriginal and Torres Strait Islander peoples.

Moreover, the community consultations conducted by the Australian Citizenship Council revealed that it was perceived by a majority of respondents that "Australian citizenship should be valued emotionally rather than purely as a way of gaining certain legal rights and responsibilities ... should also signify a commitment to Australia and to shared civic values."[53]

c. The present Canadian refusal to engage in an exercise of definition of terms of integration is understandable but not inconsequential. The lack of a clear notion of the responsibilities of citizenship can only lead to a great fuzziness in the definition of the limits of tolerance. More than any other factor, the very reluctance of the Canadian government to foster debates leading to a clear articulation of what the guideposts are in this fuzzy land is probably the main source of concern for those who would like tighter controls on immigration to Canada.

Australia has chosen to establish these limits clearly. They are defined in terms of acceptance of the basic structures and principles of Australian society (the Constitution, the rule of law, parliamentary democracy, English as a national language, equality of the sexes, etc.), of the responsibility to accept the right of others to express their views and values, and of an overriding and unifying commitment to Australia, to its interests and future first and foremost.

While Canada is reluctant to develop any such "moral contract" defining the responsibilities of citizens, this is a matter that has been explicitly raised and discussed by the Quebec Government in the Gagnon-Tremblay report on immigration.[54] Quebec has stated clearly the basis of the "moral contract" it would wish the newcomers to accept: recognition of French as the language of public life, respect for liberal-democratic values, respect for pluralism, etc. This was not well-received by the Canadian federal government, and Quebec has fought for these principles without much success. Of late, the creation of a separate Quebec citizenship has been proposed as a way to clarify

these citizenship requirements. There is obviously some danger in trying to overformalize such contracts and covenants, but there is also
much merit in providing a statement of some substantial principles on
which to build these arrangements.

The danger of this unwillingness to establish clear conditions of
admission and terms of integration is that it has allowed extreme
forms of erosion of trust as significant groups have found it opportune
to take advantage of the Canadian benefits without accepting any of
the obligations that constitute the flip side of this "amoral contract" of
citizenship. This can only lead in the longer run to greater exclusion
than would otherwise be desirable, and both old and new Canadians
are consequently bound to be worse off.

d.   The last two hypotheses mentioned at the beginning of this section
are less closely related to citizenship per se. They pertain to the ethos of
the two countries – Canada and Australia – and underline the fact that,
on two important fronts, the different perspectives of the two communities have resulted in the social learning process evolving differently.

First, the sort of social glue that is regarded as binding the citizenry
together is quite different in Canada and in Australia. While Australia
builds on commitment of the members bottom-up, to construct the
identity and the commonalities, Canada has proven unable to follow
this route and bets on inter-regional and inter-group redistribution
schemes as the foundation of citizenry. This is done on the basis of the
assumption that egalitarian rights yield belonging.[55] This has generated, maybe unwittingly, an instrumental view of citizenship – citizenship being viewed as a way to get access to the privileges of being a
member. Some observers[56] pretend that Canada's perspective is not
strictly instrumental but this is a most unpersuasive argument; they
also suggest that the only way to generate solidarity is by inter-
regional and inter-group laundering of money, but this is also questionable, even though it may understandably be regarded as a defensible stratagem to generate social cohesion if all else fails.

Secondly, Canada has developed a sociality of consensus that has
made public debates and harshly critical appraisal of opposing views
most unwelcome because they are likely to be both painful and divisive. This most un-Australian modus operandi has led to undue
restraint in public debates, and greater timidity in tackling difficult
policy issues.[57] This modest approach and the omnipresent search for
appropriate compromises have had important positive impacts on the

socio-economic performance of the country. Some, like Joseph Heath, even say that it is a particularly apt approach that has generated a very successful society.[58]

This oblique and timid approach to crucial policy issues has been strengthened considerably by the extraordinarily high degree of political correctness that has marred public debates in Canada. A few years ago, Judge John Sopinka, of the Supreme Court of Canada, even suggested that political correctness in Canada had become the greatest enemy of free speech. It is most certainly a powerful enemy of vibrant debates on issues like citizenship.

This Canadian timidity has stalled the process of social learning by suppressing or stunting national debates. For instance, one is not allowed to discuss the required transformation of the costly and inefficient health care system in Canada – this is a taboo topic because medicare is purported to be the social glue that forges Canadian citizenship. One is only allowed to pay homage to the Canada Health Act as an untouchable icon despite its inadequacies.[59]

The fact that public debates are more robust and political correctness less crippling in Australia has accelerated social learning and made it possible to generate national debates on many fundamental aspects of Australian society – even the possibility of becoming a republic. In Canada, such debates have not been possible very often, and the painful experience with Meech and Charlottetown has made such initiatives even less likely in the future.

Finally, there has been much done explicitly in Australia (as in Switzerland) to root citizenship in sites at the local and state levels. This was part of a process that wished to ensure membership's being felt bottom-up. Citizenship has been an active and emotional commitment built in consort with local authorities. In Canada, the federal government has hijacked the citizenship file. It has forcefully defined it as a status bestowed passively by the federal government as the monopoly agent entitled to do so. Citizenship has therefore degenerated into a federal gratification.

Moreover, to the extent that citizenship has come to be used as a federal instrument of Canadian unity, and used as an instrument of propaganda by the federal government to promote its view of the good life in the federation, this was bound to generate reactions on the part of fragments of the population that had a different point of view on what is the good life. And indeed, this is now happening. Quebec, being unable to find a place to locate its identity, its participation or its sense of belonging within the federal discourse, is searching for a new site where it might be easier to do so. This has led to the recent proposal for the construction of a Quebec citizenship that would attempt to articulate separate rules of the game in Quebec. Australia, on the contrary, has used citizenship as an integrative feature involving state and local authorities, and has chosen to promote explicitly the involvement of local and state authorities in the liturgy of national celebration, especially at the time of public ceremonies to confer citizenship.

2. Different emergent transversal ligatures

In both Australia and Canada, the notion of citizenship has not fully crystallized yet – it is still *en émergence,* but the nature of the moral contracts also appears to evolve quite distinctly in each case.

a. Canadian citizenship is fundamentally anchored in the notion of legal status, and gives scant attention to participation. Australia, by contrast, emphasizes the participation dimension. Both countries pay attention to belonging but in a starkly different manner: in Australia, belonging is an emotional force to be emphasized as the foundation for commitment and participation; in Canada, belonging is looked upon with suspicion, for it is an echo of sub-national communities (national, ethnic or other) that evokes emotional forces likely to undermine the integrity of the "national" political collectivity. Belonging is not abstract but visceral, and in Canada belonging is feared because it is seen as pertaining primarily to sub-Canadian communities. Yet outbursts of emotion on the occasion of Canada Day reveal the depth of this untapped "national" resource.

b. Another important difference is in the relative importance given to the vertical and horizontal relationships (between state and citizen, and among citizens) in the definition of citizenship in Canada and Australia. In Canada, the emphasis is clearly on the vertical dimension, and citizenship is rooted fundamentally in the entitlements of the citizen from the state. The social glue integrating the groups is supposed to emerge from the inter-regional, inter-groups, and inter-personal redistribution of resources effected top-down by a centralized state. This has bolstered the instrumental notion of citizenship as a one-way contract to gain access to certain rights. In Australia, citizenship is more truly emphasizing the relationships among Australians, and the commitment to other members of the community by citizens them-selves. There is some hostility to the instrumental notion of citizenship, and a strong emphasis on an emotional commitment, on the recognition of obligations, and on an agreement to participate actively as a condition of entry.

c.   Australia and Canada have explicitly recognized the constraint of diversity in some formal way. However, in the case of Canada, there has been a stronger reluctance to accept primary communities like Quebec (or Aboriginal groups) because of the very size of the Quebec fragment (and because of the multitude of smallish Aboriginal groups) for it might entail a significant balkanization of the country. In Australia, the existence of aboriginal communities has been acknowl-edged, and there has been a genuine attempt to reconcile unity and diversity through a composite citizenship. Canada has been nervous about following the same strategy, so it has done so, in general, in a rather timid way, but sometimes in a bold way locally as in the case of Nunavut.[60]

d.   The debate about the nature of the "civic" deficit has been robust in Australia since 1995. It is still inert in Canada. Instead of dealing forcefully and explicitly with this need to square the circle – ensure national unity while fully legitimizing the diversity of the civil society and fostering community participation – as was done in Australia, the debate on citizenship has remained moot and less explicit in Canada.

e.   Despite the differences in approach, both countries are still grap-pling with some important challenges that are likely to materialize in each country in the form of moral contracts defining:

- the way in which one can recognize a multiplicity of citizen-ships and some order among these different allegiances;
- the way in which citizenship can accommodate some priority among the multiplicity of allegiances to different ethno-cultural or sub-national communities within a nation-state;
- the way in which to define in a congruent manner the degree of ease of entry and the power to deport – it being understood that the easier the entry is, the more powerful the instruments of expulsion might have to be;
- the way in which communities can be provided with a demo-

cratic voice in the governance of the country either through some form of self-government or some sort of effective community representation as the way of ensuring the requisite mix of status / participation / belonging in a world of multiple and limited identities through an explicit recognition that "ethnos" may well be forging the largest possible site of belonging[61]; the narrow interpretation of ethnicity as a static entity instead of a form of cultural practice has led to a very narrow definition of community and to a demonization of ethnicity: what is required is a capacity to recognize the social need for difference and a democracy of communities deriving from it, while not mandating that this should be the case for all communities, and therefore running the risk of balkanizing the country;[62]

- the way in which one might be able to use differentiated citizenship as a way to reconcile the multiplicity of allegiances and the different levels of commitments;
- the focus on "recognition" and the redistribution of symbolic resources and the extent to which it can be a substitute for the sharing of real resources or the protection against real contingencies.

3.   The paradoxes of the Canadian way

The Canadian ethos would appear to make it more difficult than in Australia to face squarely the need to negotiate explicitly the terms of integration for citizens and newcomers, and to determine what these terms might be in the new world of citizenship. Yet the task is clear: what is needed is a nexus of moral contracts (1) that ensures the requisite degree of rights, obligations, participation, appartenance and identity necessary for the country to prosper; (2) that ensures that all the stakeholders retain their basic freedoms (political, economic, social) as a way to increase their capabilities; and (3) that the appropriate tradeoffs are defined between these two sets of priorities.

The more timid and *étapiste* Canadian way is not necessarily an inferior strategy, since it fits the Canadian ethos. However, it entails a complex and somewhat erratic process of social learning, where progress comes most of the time by fits and starts, locally, by trial and error rather than as a result of broadly debated revolutionary transformation. This often means that social learning is fractured and slower.

This fundamental Canadian conservatism could prove extremely costly in an evolutionary learning sense.

But this way of gauging the opportunity cost of the Canadian way may be somewhat unreasonable for it presumes that Canada has the choice of doing it otherwise. While theoretically such is the case, de facto, it is not. Compulsory debates imposed on a Canadian citizenry that has neither a taste for them nor a capacity to sustain them does not represent a meaningful alternative.

Canada can no more adopt the Australian way than the Swiss or the Japanese way in defining its moral contracts of citizenship. Even if Canada has to face many of the same challenges as these other countries (globalization, growing polyethnicity and multiculturalism, etc.), it is forced to confront these challenges with a different habitus.[63] This habitus constitutes Canada's idiosyncratic propensity to deal with issues in a particular way that has been inherited from its history and experience.

Canada's habitus is its organized reaction capability, its *manière de voir*, a sum of its dispositions, and it has to be taken as a given at least in the intermediate run. Changing it amounts to changing Canada's culture. The peculiar Canadian habitus is undoubtedly a source of slower learning and of a lesser ability to confront these challenges head on. But, Canada is condemned to deal with these challenges in ways that are congruent with its habitus.

This Particular Way Is Not Without Some Advantages.

However frustrating and ineffective the Canadian way may appear by radical standards, it is not only efficient in its own way but it may even constitute a truly attractive strategy for polyethnic, multicultural and plural societies in general when they do not have the capacity to orchestrate the sort of open and vibrant debates that Australia has seemingly managed to conduct in a legitimate and peaceful way. It may well be that Australia is unique, i.e., not representative of the social capabilities of most societies and that Canada, with its crab-like, oblique mode of operations, is a more realistic approximation of what is observed generally – i.e., a fractured and somewhat disconcerted socio-economy incapable of anything but ad hocery. As a result, the slow, scattered, unfocussed and small-stepped approach that Canada has been known for might not be an unreasonable strategy for most countries.

De facto, Canada is slowly moving toward a supra-national and community-based federalism, while fruitless "official" debates continue unabated in a manner that appears very unpromising.[64] This de facto modest and oblique way to get there is obviously a roundabout way of tackling the unity-diversity problem, but, in many cases, it may be the only practical way to proceed. Unwittingly, then, Canada may have invented an approach useable by many small nations to engineer the right strategy to preserve their cultural identity in a globalized world while allowing their component communities to maintain both their integrity and their capacity to be heard. This Canadian approach is characterized by a two-tracked strategy – a cacophonous public forum where the powers of disconcertion are modulated by a systematic avoidance of general, ambitious and all encompassing debates, while, in parallel, difficulties are resolved *in situ* most imaginatively even if it is in an ad hoc manner.

This social technology to square the unity-diversity circle is exportable, and citizens of most small and medium-sized countries may well come to the conclusion when they reflect on it that, in this sense, "ils sont tous Canadiens."[65]

Conclusion

Australian and Canadian citizenships are emergent idiosyncratic realities. These complex institutions are the result of the on-going interaction between values and environment. The sort of social armistices and moral contracts embodying the workable notion of citizenship at any moment, and the sort of adaptive learning process defining the dynamics of the terms of integration over time, are different from one society to another.

First, this paper has suggested that the syncretic notion of citizenship may be usefully analyzed through a prism that reveals its complexity, its fundamental transversality, and its essentially emergent nature. A two-stage process has been sketched to identify the basic dimensions of interest, and to suggest the mix of ligatures that would appear to be useful to compare different types of citizenship.

Second, these templates have been used to contrast the Australian and the Canadian ways of evolving their notion of citizenship. In the Australian case, the nexus of moral contracts defining citizenship would appear to have been arrived at through more vibrant national debates and to have elicited a more explicit and proactive set of moral contracts. In Canada, a more ad hoc and pragmatic process avoiding national debates has generated a more tacit and passive set of vague arrangements.

While the former experience appears to be more satisfying from an intellectual point of view, it depends much on the existence of a national ethos and habitus that carry the capacity to underpin such national debates. Canada's ethos would appear to be unable to promote and support such robust debates without generating much divisiveness. It is not unreasonable to suggest, however, that Canada may be more typical of most pluralist societies, and that, in such societies, the low road of ad-hocery appears to be the only way to avoid divisive, destructive and perilous national debates.

The paper is therefore led to conclude that the slow and erratic road to citizenship adopted by Canada might be a useable model in our post-modern world. While one might deplore Canadians' incapacity to conduct a high road debate on such issues, and bemoan the ad-hocery of citizenship construction in Canada, the extraordinary excesses and violence that would appear to ensue when such broad national debates are engineered or simply experienced in contexts that are not suited to them would appear to favour the more modest Canadian way.

This conclusion should not be interpreted however as condoning the centralized mindset that underpins the current federal "liberal constitutional project"[66] in vogue in Canada nor its top-down, heavy-handed, arrogant efforts to devoice communities, and to use citizenship as a way to smother deep diversity.

Canada may be right in general but wrong in particulars on this front. Hopefully, we have made the case for it being right in general. As to the ways in which one might be able to use the citizenship debates to correct some of the most destructive particulars, this is a topic for another paper.

The assistance of Anne Burgess, Daniel Hubert and Christopher Wilson and the financial support of the Social Sciences Research Council of Canada (410–97–0899) are gratefully acknowledged.

Notes

1. Alan C. Cairns et al., eds., *Citizenship, Diversity and Pluralism: Canadian and Comparative Perspectives* (Montreal: McGill-Queen's University Press, 1999).
2. Marcel Gauchet, *La religion dans la démocratie* (Paris: Gallimard, 1998).
3. Henri Bergson, *Les deux sources de la morale et de la religion*, 3rd ed. (Paris: Alcan,, 1932); K. Popper, *The Open Society and Its Enemies* (London: Routledge and Kegan Paul, 1942).
4. André Reszler, *Le pluralisme* (Genève: Georg, 1990).
5. Ibid.
6. John Kekes, *The Morality of Pluralism* (Princeton: Princeton University Press, 1993), 19.
7. Thomas Janoski, *Citizenship and Civil Society* (Cambridge: Cambridge University Press, 1998); Gilles Paquet, "Gouvernance distribuée, socialité et engagement civique," *Gouvernance* 1(1), (2000): 52–68; Gilles Paquet, "Le droit à l'épreuve de la gouvernance," *Gouvernance* 2(1/2), (2001): 74–84.
8. Thomas H. Marshall, *Class, Citizenship and Social Development* (Chicago: The University of Chicago Press, 1964).
9. Alan C. Cairns et al., eds., *Citizenship, Diversity and Pluralism: Canadian and Comparative Perspectives*; Jane Jenson and Martin Papillon, *Citizenship and the Recognition of Cultural Diversity: the Canadian Experience* (Ottawa: CPRN, 2000).
10. Marcel Gauchet, *La religion dans la démocratie* , 112.
11. Chantal Mouffe, *The Return of the Political* (London: Verso, 1993).
12. Marcel Gauchet, *La religion dans la démocratie* , 123.
13. Alain Touraine, "Le désenchantement de la politique," *Le Monde des Débats*, (December 1999): 39.
14. Gilles Paquet, *Governance Through Social Learning* (Ottawa: University of Ottawa Press, 1999).
15. Harvey Leibenstein, *Beyond Economic Man* (Cambridge: Harvard University Press, 1976), 17–18.
16. Joseph Tussman, *The Burden of Office* (Vancouver: Talonbooks, 1989).
17. Gilles Paquet, "Le kaléidoscope de l'ethnicité: une approche constructiviste," in *L'ethnicité à l'heure de la mondialisation*, eds. Caroline Andrew et al. (Ottawa: ACFAS-Outaouais, 1992); Idem, "Betting on Diversity: The Problématique of Cultural Diversity" in *Building Plurality*, ed. Robin Higham (Ottawa: University of Ottawa Press, 2001).
18. Raymond Breton, "The Production and Allocation of Symbolic Resources: An Analysis of the Linguistic and Ethnocultural Fields in Canada," *Canadian Review of Sociology and Anthropology*, 21, 2 (1984): 123–144.

19. Joseph Tussman, *Government and The Mind* (New York: Oxford University Press, 1977).

20. James Tully, "Struggles over Recognition and Distribution," *Constellation*, 7(4) (2000): 469–482.

21. Joseph Tussman, *The Burden of Office*.

22. Michael Walzer, *Spheres of Justice* (Oxford: Martin Robertson, 1983); John Edwards, and Lori Doucette, "Ethnic Salience, Identity and Symbolic Ethnicity," *Canadian Ethnic Studies*, XIX, 1 (1987): 52–62; Lance W. Roberts, and Rodney A. Clifton, "Exploring the Ideology of Canadian Multiculturalism," *Journal of Canadian Studies*, 17, 1 (1982): 88–94.

23. Lee Drummond, "Analyse sémiotique de l'ethnicité au Québec," *Questions de culture*, No. 2 (1981–2): 139–153.

24. Manning Nash, *The Cauldron of Ethnicity in the Modern World* (Chicago: University of Chicago Press, 1989).

25. Victor P. Goldberg, "Relational Exchange: Economics and Complex Contracts," *American Behavioral Scientist*, 23 (1980): 337–352.

26. James S. Coleman, "Social Capital in the Creation of Human Capital," *American Journal of Sociology*, 94, Supplement (1988): 95–120.

27. James N. Porter, "On Multiculturalism as a Limit of Canadian Life," in *The Canadian Alternative: Cultural Pluralism and Canadian Unity*, ed. H. Bouraoui (Downsview: ECW Press, 1979), 64–79; B. Lussato, *Le défi culturel* (Paris: Nathan, 1989).

28. Max Gluckman, *The Judicial Process Among the Barotse of Northern Rhodesia*, 2nd ed. (Manchester: Manchester University Press, 1967); Paul Laurent and Gilles Paquet, "Intercultural Relations: A Myrdal-Tocqueville-Girard Interpretative Scheme," *International Political Science Review*, 12, 3 (1991): 173–185.

29. Gilles Paquet, "Betting on Moral Contracts," *Optimum*, 22, 3 (1991–1992), 45–53.

30. Herbert Gans, "Symbolic Ethnicity," *Ethnic and Racial Studies*, 2 (1979): 1–20.

31. Michael Lind, "National Good," *Prospect*, 56 (October 2000): 44–49.

32. Ibid.

33. Michael Ignatieff, *Blood and Belonging* (New York: Viking, 1993); Idem., *The Rights Revolution* (Toronto: Anansi, 2000).

34. Stanley Fish, *The Trouble with Principle* (Cambridge: Harvard University Press, 1999).

35. W. B. Gallie, *Philosophy and the Historical Understanding* (London: Chatto & Windus, 1964).

36. Gilles Paquet, "Pour une notion renouvelée de citoyenneté." *Transactions of the Royal Society of Canada*, Fourth Series, Volume XXVII (1989), 83–100;

Idem., "Citoyenneté dans une société de l'information: une réalité transversale et paradoxale," *Transactions of the Royal Society of Canada*, Sixth Series, Volume V (1994): 59–78; Idem., "Political Philosophy of Multiculturalism," in *Ethnicity and Culture in Canada*, ed. J. Berry and J. Laponce (Toronto: University of Toronto Press, 1994), 60–80.

37. Gilles Paquet, "Betting on Moral Contracts," 45–53.

38. Gilles Paquet, "Pour une notion renouvelée de citoyenneté," 83–100.

39. Gilles Paquet, "Canada as a Disconcerted Learning Economy: A Governance Challenge," *Transactions of the Royal Society of Canada*, Sixth Series, Volume VIII (1998), 69–98.

40. James Tully, "Struggles over Recognition and Distribution," 469–482; P. Markell, "The Recognition of politics," *Constellation*, 7(4) (2000): 496–506.

41. Thomas H. Marshall, *Class, Citizenship and Social Development*.

42. Zygmunt Bauman, *Liquid Modernity* (Cambridge: Polity Press, 2000).

43. Gilles Paquet, "Le droit à l'épreuve de la gouvernance," *Gouvernance* 2 (1/2) (2001): 74–84.

44. Jane Jenson and Martin Papillon, *The Changing Boundaries of Citizenship: A Review and a Research Agenda*; Jane Jenson and Martin Papillon, *Citizenship and the Recognition of Cultural Diversity: the Canadian Experience* (Ottawa: CPRN, 2000).

45. Herman Van Gunsteren, *A Theory of Citizenship* (Boulder: Westview Press, 1998); Gilles Paquet, "E-gouvernance, gouvernementalité et État commutateur," *Relations Industrielles/Industrial Relations*, 55(4), (2000b): 746–769.

46. Gilles Paquet, "E-gouvernance, gouvernementalité et État commutateur," 746–769.

47. Gilles Paquet, "La gouvernance en tant que conditions auxiliaires," in *Gouvernance et démocratie*, eds. Linda Cardinal and Caroline Andrew (Ottawa: Les Presses de l'Université d'Ottawa, 2001c), 213–237.

48. Paul Laurent and Gilles Paquet, "Intercultural Relations: A Myrdal-Tocqueville-Girard Interpretative Scheme," *International Political Science Review*, 12, 3 (1991): 173–185.

49. Gilles Paquet, "Canada as a Disconcerted Learning Economy: A Governance Challenge," *Transactions of the Royal Society of Canada*, Sixth Series, Volume VIII (1998), 69–98.

50. André Laurendeau, *La crise de la conscription 1942* (Montréal: Les Éditions du Jour, 1962).

51. In a survey of members of the Institute of Public Administration of Canada conducted by Iain Gow, it was found that respondents held a common outlook that included as basic tenets pragmatism and suspicion of theory. J. I. Gow, *Learning from Others* (Toronto: IPAC/CCMD, 1994); O. P.

Dwivedi and J. Iain Gow, *From Bureaucracy to Public Management* (Toronto: Broadview Press/IPAC, 1999).

52. Australian Citizenship Council, *Australian Citizenship for a New Century* (Canberra, 2000), 82.

53. Ibid., 92–93.

54. Guy Rocher, "Du pluralisme à l'égalitarisme," *Le Devoir*, 18 December, 1997.

55. Robert C. Vipond, "Citizenship and the Charter of Rights: The Two Sides of Pierre Trudeau," *International Journal of Canadian Studies*, 14 (1996): 179–192.

56. Keith G. Banting, "Social Citizenship and the Multicultural Welfare State," in *Citizenship, Diversity and Pluralism: Canadian and Comparative Perspectives*, eds. Alan C. Cairns et al. (Montreal: McGill-Queen's University Press, 1999), 108–136.

57. Gary Caldwell, *La culture publique commune* (Quebec: Éditions Nota bene, 2001).

58. Joseph Heath, *The Efficient Society* (Toronto: Penguin/Viking, 2001).

59. Gilles Paquet, "Pepin-Robarts *redux*: socialité, régionalité et gouvernance," in *Le débat qui n'a pas eu lieu: La Commission Pepin-Robarts, quelque vingt ans après*, ed. J.-P. Wallot (Ottawa: Les Presses de l'Université d'Ottawa, 2002).

60. Gilles Paquet, "Innovations in Governance in Canada," *Optimum* 29, 2/3 (1999): 71–81.

61. Michael Lind, "National Good."

62. Rhoda E. Howard-Hassmann, "Canadian as an Ethnic Category: Implications for Multiculturalism and National Unity," *Canadian Public Policy*, 24 (4) (1999): 523–537.

63. Pierre Bourdieu, *Esquisse d'une théorie de la pratique* (Genève: Droz, 1972).

64. Gilles Paquet, "Innovations in Governance in Canada," 71–81.

65. Gilles Paquet, "Pepin-Robarts Redux: socialité, régionalité et gouvernance."

66. Stephen P. Carter, *The Dissent of the Governed* (Cambridge: Harvard University Press, 1998).

16

Debating Citizenship in Canada:
The Collide of Two Nation-Building Projects

MICHELINE LABELLE and FRANÇOIS ROCHER

Debates about the meaning of citizenship have been fundamentally altered following the *Forum national sur la citoyenneté et l'intégration* held in Quebec in September 2000. The focus of discussion is no longer mainly on the formal-legal definition of citizenship. In the debates on citizenship, there has been a shift away from outlining and defining the rights of citizenship towards a more substantive discussion on the symbolic meaning of citizenship. Central to this debate is the term citizenship, which is often understood in these discussions as referring to a sense of belonging to a national-political community. Yet, recognizing that this understanding of citizenship is not accepted by all, it is not surprising that the initiatives put forth by the Quebec government were not well received by a variety of individuals. First, these initiatives were rejected by those individuals who do not approve of the Quebec's government political project. Second, they were also rejected by those who view initiatives by the Quebec government in the realm of citizenship as intrusions in an area of federal responsibility, resulting in the undermining of the role of the federal government in the promotion of a Canadian citizenship.

The concepts of national identity and citizenship push us to reflect simultaneously upon what unites those who share a territorial and political space, the criteria of inclusion and exclusion in citizenship, and the social and political power relations that lead to the construction of the symbolic borders of citizenship.[1] The multiple identities that exist in the nation-state develop as much in reference to an identity group defined by language, ethnicity, nation, religion, culture, etc., as through the co-existence of these groups within the same political community. According to Gamberale, a national or ethnic identity precedes any form of political association. A national identity refers to a sense of belonging to a particular community. It is defined through temporal and spatial representations from nationals. These representations can be political, though not necessarily. In contrast, citizenship is the result of a political project that is based upon a social contract defined by a set of rights.[2] Political institutions serve as mechanisms that allow the participation (or non-participation) of the various individuals who find themselves within the political boundaries governed by the rules of citizenship. These institutions serve to determine the space for public deliberations as well as the conditions and mechanisms through which these public debates become possible.[3]

Necessarily, this political space does not exist in a vacuum. The nation does call upon the political without being limited to this realm, while citizenship remains strictly political in nature. This brings forth the issue of how the concepts of national identity and citizenship coexist. How can various national identities coexist in a political space that contains more than one nation? How are the nation and nationalism defined when more than one nation is found in a given political space? Do these definitions change over time? In a multinational political community, what becomes of minority groups who are not or do not want to be considered nations? These are the issues with which the national and political identities in the Canadian context are faced.

The relationship between Quebec and the rest of Canada entered a new era in the 1990s. Especially following the 1995 Quebec referendum, citizenship became the privileged political and symbolic battleground where the concepts of what constitutes a nation, who are its members, and what are its attributes have been highly debated. The Canadian government worked towards redefining the concept of national belonging by revising its multiculturalism policy, its immigration and refugee legislation, and the Canadian citizenship law, and through the promotion of Canadian symbols, such as the flag. At the same time, the Quebec government made significant changes to its strategy of integration and interculturalism with the transformation in 1996 of the *ministère des Communautés culturelles et de l'Immigration* into the *ministère des Relations avec les citoyens et de l'Immigration*. This change in the structure of government is significant for it reflects a policy shift that wants to encourage every Quebec citizen, those born in Quebec as well as those who have immigrated to Quebec, to develop a sense of belonging to the *peuple québécois*. The *peuple québécois* is presented here as a civic identity that should be endorsed as a pillar of any democratic society.

This paper addresses two questions: How are the federal and Quebec policies on citizenship set forth? And, how is citizenship debated in Canada and in Quebec? After outlining the initiatives undertaken by both the federal and Quebec governments in terms of citizenship, we will explore how the debates on this question have come about. Our main focus will be on the *Forum national sur la citoyenneté et l'intégration*.

As the debates on citizenship in Canada substantiate, despite the fact that in theory it is possible to disassociate citizenship and national identity, in the political realm, the two concepts are ultimately intertwined. Thus, both Canada and Quebec attempt to present a civic understanding of their national identity. However, neither can completely avoid the context in which the "civic" identity comes into being. Moreover, when examining issues of citizenship in Canada and Quebec, we cannot overlook the fact that the Canadian and Quebec policies on the integration of newcomers are in contradiction with each other.

The New Offensive on Citizenship and Identity in Canada

In terms of citizenship, Canada is pursuing an ideology of shared values that emphasizes the following as its main points: responsible citizenship, a sense of belonging to Canadian society and state, endorsement of Canadian cultural codes and values, and the promotion of national unity. These ideas are conveyed in numerous texts put forth by the Departments of Canadian Heritage, and of Citizenship and Immigration Canada and by various committees that have been concerned with the renewal of the Constitution or the renewal of the Canadian immigration and citizenship laws.[4]

This renewed interest on the question of Canadian citizenship is inscribed in an effort to redefine the boundaries of the political space in which the members of the Canadian political community must evolve. This came about in the 1990s, a period during which Canada was threatened by fragmentation and polarization that led to the undermining of the consensus upon which the social cohesion of Canadian society was built throughout the twentieth century.[5] To the issues of poverty and economic segmentation were added the problems of regional balkanization, nationalist claims by the people of Quebec and Aboriginal peoples, as well as demands from *Charter* groups (groups mentioned in Section 15) who are putting forward claims against a state that wants to be less interventionist than it has been in the past.[6]

In conjunction with attempts to control the source and quality of immigration to Canada, the Canadian state currently insists upon putting forth the idea of Canadian citizenship as bestowing a privilege. It presents Canadian citizenship as a precious asset that is to be earned and given serious consideration. This vision is enunciated in a series of informational documents put out in 1996 by Citizenship and Immigration Canada. According to these documents, being a Canadian citizen is "to be loyal towards Canada; to be loyal towards the Queen of Canada and her representatives; to obey Canada's laws; to respect public and private property; to take care of Canadian heritage; to uphold the ideals of Canada." From that point on, new immigrants and all citizens are asked to take on the task of safeguarding and promoting the unity of the Canadian nation-state. The failure to do this brings about accusations of disloyalty.

The federal approach on the issue of citizenship is also brought about by the challenge of immigration. Can Canadian society continue to integrate its newcomers harmoniously? While still open to immigration, the Canadian state is concerned that, as "resources once plentiful are now dear,"[7] immigration may put a stress on Canada's ability to integrate newcomers in a viable and equitable manner. Apart from this concern, a number of issues have become an important focus of the federal government's concerns with citizenship. These include: the federal government's insistence on welcoming mainly financially independent immigrants and, if need be, genuine refugees and asylum seekers; its emphasis on responsible immigrants; and concerns over some of the perverse effects induced by the globalization of immigration (security, terrorism, criminality, abuses of the welfare state). In sum, concerns over these issues indicate that the Canadian state intends to control more closely the "quality," volume and sources of immigration flows to Canada. The underlying assumption behind these recent orientations regarding immigration is to ensure that immigrants become fully integrated Canadian citizens.

In 1997, the federal government made public documents from a committee that revised the immigration legislation. The *Trempe* report,[8] as it came to be known, focused mainly on the ins and outs of citizenship and the selection criteria for immigrants.[9] This report is part of the new federal strategy on immigration that consists of making the federal government more visible throughout the selection and integration processes. As it was stated in the report, the federal government must recognize that it will always have a role in the establishment and integration of immigrants, as well as in the funding and establishment of services to oversee this integration process.[10]

Fearing that Canadian citizenship has lost some of its prestige and value and that it no longer reflects a commitment to Canada and an endorsement and promotion of its heritage, the *Trempe* report proposes to strengthen the selection criteria for immigrants and the granting of citizenship.[11] The report encourages active and responsible citizenship. An active citizen would be one who is informed, responsible and takes part in public life (politics, community actions) as well as private life (family). Access to citizenship should be more limited by increasing the time of residency, fiscal responsibilities, knowledge about Canada, fluency in one of the official languages, lack of criminal record and active participation.[12]

Without fully endorsing the *Trempe* report, the new orientations on immigration outlined in *Building a Strong Foundation for the 21st Century: New Directions for Immigration and Refugee Policy and Legislation* that aim ultimately to redefine the Canadian immigration legislation are definitely inspired by this report.[13]

The changes in policy content around multiculturalism and citizenship in recent years have emerged largely in response to public and official admonitions that the people interested in taking up Canadian citizenship must be made to understand that "loyalty to Canada must be given pride of place."[14] With this in mind, the ongoing renewal of multiculturalism is focused on a three-pronged approach that clearly emphasizes values to be associated with citizenship: *Canadian identity* – people of all backgrounds should "feel a sense of belonging and attachment to Canada" – *civic participation* – they must be "active citizens," concerned with shaping "the future of their communities and their country" – and *social justice* – they must be involved in "building a society that ensures fair and equitable treatment and that respects the dignity of and accommodates people of all origins."[15] The federal government is trying to reconfigure this policy by emphasizing notions of integration and participation rather than cultural diversity.

In other words, the underlying logic of the federal government's approach to immigration and multiculturalism aims to promote an understanding of citizenship that does not limit itself to a set of rights, but rather highlights the close relationship between citizenship and national identity. As it was said in a document published by the Privy Council Office as early as 1991, citizenship is first and foremost "an emotional tie, a sense of shared values and commitments to our country. Our shared Canadian citizenship provides a focus for unity that encompasses its parts, and brings our people together."[16] In sum, the federal government's discourse on citizenship is far from neutral. It endorses an identity closely tied to that of a national (Canadian) identity.

In 1998, a new legislation, Bill C-63 (*Citizenship of Canada Act*) was introduced in the House of Commons.[17] This bill has as its goal the reevaluation of Canadian citizenship by enforcing stiffer criteria for residency, and by the primacy of allegiance to Canada and its fundamental values, notably the Canadian *Charter of Rights and Freedoms*. In recent debates in the House of Commons following the second reading of the legislation on citizenship (reintroduced as Bill C-16), the parliamentary secretary of the Department of Citizenship and Immigration restated the rules upon which the federal legislation is based. These are as follow: 1) children born in Canada are automatically granted Canadian citizenship; 2) children born outside of Canada from parents who have their Canadian citizenship also receive Canadian citizenship; 3) immigrants must obtain their permanent residency status prior to making a request to obtain Canadian citizenship; 4) immigrants must prove their loyalty to Canada to obtain their citizenship; 5) immigrants must prove their knowledge about Canadian society and values; 6) immigrants must be knowledgeable about at least one of Canada's official languages.[18] The values to which the parliamentary secretary was referring to are the five founding constitutional principles defining the Canadian state: equality of opportunity, freedom of speech, democracy, basic human rights and the rule of law.

Within this same debate, the spokesperson for the government party expressed clearly the fusion between citizenship and national identity. He said:

> To me and to so many Canadians from whom I have heard, "citizenship" is about truly belonging to this society. It is anchored in allegiance to the values that Canadians share. It is a concept with real meaning and it is a proud celebration of what it means to be Cana-

dian. That makes "citizenship" far more than just a piece of paper, more than just some box to be checked off on a form, more than a convenience for international travel. It makes the law on "citizenship" one of our most fundamental laws. Our "citizenship" law sets the ground rules for those who can truly call themselves Canadian. It captures the common understanding among Canadians about what it means to be one of us.[19]

This suggests that for one to integrate truly into Canadian society, it is not sufficient for citizens simply to conform to the civic practices established through political institutions. It is also necessary that citizens embrace and demonstrate their loyalty and allegiance to the Canadian state. On another occasion during the debates in the House of Commons, the parliamentary secretary emphasized that:

It is important to note that what has never changed is a sense that "citizenship" is about joining the Canadian family, and a great family it is. It is about sharing in the values, traditions and institutions which define us as a people and unite us as a nation and which made us the finest country in the world according to the United Nations *Human Development Report* for six years in a row. That's no coincidence. It is because of who we are and what we represent and the "citizenship" of Canadians is part of that greatness that is ours.[20]

Finally, since the 1995 referendum, the federal government has spent large amounts of money on the promotion of symbols of Canadian national identity. These include the free distribution of Canadian flags and huge budgets put towards Canada Day celebrations (in 1999–2000, the Canadian Heritage Department's budget for Canada Day was 5.4 million, 65 percent of which was disbursed in Quebec). Moreover, the federal government has promoted the visibility of certain of its initiatives, including some that are in areas of provincial responsibility (e.g. Millennium student scholarships, research grants and partnerships). The goals driving these initiatives are apparent. These initiatives are aimed at opposing the increasing inclination for the people of Quebec to identify first and foremost as Quebeckers of various origins and, furthermore, to promote the perception that the federal government represents the true national government.[21]

From the federal government's perspective, the endurance of Quebec nationalism and the affirmation of Aboriginal People's identity (and nationalism) threatens the structural integrity of the Canadian state and social cohesion of its national-political community. Consequently, the current initiatives on citizenship are the federal government's response to these threats, aiming to reaffirm the primacy of Canadian citizenship and undermine the impact of those other forms of identification.

Despite the fact that citizenship is usually discussed with respect to the naturalization of newcomers, by making the claim that this issue is of interests to all Canadians, it is hoped that a by-product of these discussions will be the enhancement of Canadian pride or a renewed attachment to Canada felt by all Canadians including the people of Quebec. It is not insignificant that the number of people in Quebec who identify primarily as Quebeckers has grown from 21 percent to 59 percent over the last 20 years;[22] 29 percent consider themselves first and foremost as Quebeckers and then Canadian, while 28 percent consider themselves as equally Canadian and Quebeckers. Another research group has found that for Francophones in Quebec, 63 percent identify as Quebeckers, 26 percent as French-Canadian and 11 percent as Canadian. In contrast, 70 percent of Anglophones in Quebec identify as Canadians and 5 percent as Quebeckers.[23] According to Lisée, 51 percent of Allophones identified as Canadians in 1979, a number that had increased to 70 percent by 1999. The number of Allophones who identified as Quebeckers increased from 0 percent to 12 percent by 1995, but decreased to 10 percent by 1999.[24]

The federal strategy, first elaborated in the 1990s, which aims to strengthen Canadian citizenship and identity, while undermining other forms of national identification perceived as threats to the Canadian social cohesion, is considered to be effective according to some experts. For example, Will Kymlicka, in *Finding our Way,* stated:

> we know that were it not for the "ethnic vote," the 1995 referendum on secession in Quebec would have succeeded. In that referendum, ethnic voters overwhelmingly expressed their commitment to Canada ... More generally, all the indicators suggest that immigrants quickly absorb and accept Canada's basic liberal-democratic values and constitutional principles, even if their home countries are illiberal or non-democratic."[25]

According to Kymlicka, the high level of naturalization rates of immigrants is a strong indicator that immigrants identify with Canada and of the successful political integration of newcomers into Canadian society. This understanding is of course open to other interpretations.[26]

Turning Towards Citizenship in Quebec

The new emphasis on citizenship in the Quebec state's discourse represents an attempt to assert the symbolic hegemony of the Quebec state in the fields of politics and identity. The term hegemony is used here to suggest a process of appropriation of political and ideological autonomy by the state of Quebec that has been emerging ever since the Quiet Revolution. This process puts the Quebec state at odds with the Canadian state in areas such as multiculturalism and integration of immigrants. Despite the fact that there are numerous similarities between the Quebec and federal policies on immigration and diversity, the two diverge in significant ways. Thus, although respect for pluralism, emphasis on social justice and civic participation of all citizens of all origins are central to both the Quebec and federal policies, the two differ in terms of defining the nation, especially the Quebec nation.[27]

Over the last three decades, the Quebec state discourse and practices have aimed to open up the definition of citizenship to pluralism while simultaneously maintaining a particular recognition for Quebec society. For example, several government initiatives uphold French language and culture in the following manner:

- The francization of public spaces through the adoption, in 1977, of the *Charte de la langue française* (Bill-101) that officially made French the language to be used by the state and its citizens;
- The involvement of the Quebec government in the selection of immigrants and refugees as a result of bilateral negotiations with the federal government to allow Quebec to play a role in the selection of independent immigrants as well as in the integration of newcomers;
- The establishment of a new juridical framework to work towards countering discrimination, promoting equality and recognizing diversity. This includes the Quebec *Charte des droits et libertés de la personne*, adopted in 1975, which prohibits discrimination as a result of one's race, ethnic or national origins, etc. (article 10) and which furthermore guarantees to individuals from ethnic minorities the right to maintain and further

their own cultural lives with other members of their group (article 43), and the *Déclaration sur les relations interethniques et interraciales* adopted in 1985;

- The recognition, in 1981, of eleven Aboriginal Nations;
- The passage of initiatives that aim to have various institutions accommodate or account for the cultural diversity of society. These include programs to promote equal access to employment, intercultural training, accommodations within social services and public institutions to help towards the integration of diverse cultures;
- Active involvement in international initiatives.

Moreover, in 1981, the Quebec government of the Parti Québécois elaborated a policy of *convergence culturelle* that stated that the *peuple du Québec* constitute a nation. Notions of a common public culture and of a moral contract between immigrants and the host society began to come to the fore in Quebec during the 1990s, with the new Policy Statement on Immigration and Integration[28] elaborated under a Quebec Liberal government. It produced significant referents in the Quebec discourse on integration and interculturalism. Considered as equal in terms of rights and obligations, immigrants were invited to adhere, in spite of their differences, to a common public culture defined by the democratic character of its institutions, the equality of all citizens before the law, the commonalty of the French language, the embracing of a diverse heritage and pluralism. The policy then referred to the Quebec society as a *société distincte*. The notions of *peuple québécois* and *nation* disappeared.

In 1996, following the election of the Parti Québécois, the *ministère des Communautés culturelles et de l'Immigration du Québec* was restructured and renamed the *ministère des Relations avec les citoyens et de l'Immigration*.[29] Needless to say, it occurred in the post-referendum context and had a decisive political impact. It encouraged the whole Quebec citizenry, including new immigrants, to develop a sense of belonging to the *peuple québécois* and the Quebec political community (rather than to the francophone majority) and to embrace a common civic framework. The new ministry defines Quebec citizenship as a political attribute common to all people residing in the territory of Quebec. Citizenship is rooted in the sense of belonging that is shared by individuals who have rights, freedoms and responsibilities with respect to the society of which they are a part. This citizenship recognizes differences and plurality of belonging while basing itself on the endorsement of common civic values.[30]

As in the Canadian context, Quebec state discourse on citizenship is marked by symbolic events. For example, a Citizenship Week, a Citizenship Prize and Certificates of Civic Merit are steps undertaken by the Quebec state to deepen notions of belonging to a common public culture. These initiatives undermined the perverse dichotomy in which all citizens were trapped, a dichotomy undermining the social cohesion of a common public culture: "we, the Quebecois; you, the cultural communities – we, the cultural communities; you, the Quebecois."

This new discourse on Quebec citizenship engendered immediate reservations. In a notice made public in 1997, the *Conseil des relations interculturelles du Québec* (CRI), an organization that has as a mandate the task of advising the government on various issues with respect to immigration and interculturalism, questioned whether people should be strictly recognized on the basis of their status as citizens or future citizens, or if multiple identities or senses of belonging to given cultural communities should also be acknowledged. The CRI notes that the government's new directions with respect to citizenship are somewhat worrisome. The CRI felt that the government, in its new citizenship policy, did not take into account the various issues at stake in terms of immigration, cultural diversity and the specific needs of newcomers and ethnic minorities. Considering that some of the requirements for a modern Quebec citizenship include diminishing inequalities linked to national or racial identity as well as the accommodation of diversity through political institutions, it is problematic that the new policy ignores these issues.[31]

The *National Forum on Citizenship and Integration* that was held on 21 and 22 September 2000 has sparked more heated debates on this issue. This forum was held in a particular context structured by two marking events. First, it was held in the aftermath of the debates in the House of Commons on Bill C-20 (or the federal *Clarity Bill*). These debates were significant for they discussed the issue of secession of Quebec using only the terms "province" and "population," rather than "state" and "people." Second, the *Forum* was held following the debates on *Bill 99 (An Act respecting the exercise of the fundamental rights and prerogatives of the Quebec people and the Quebec State.)* This legislation put forth by the Quebec government affirms the national diversity of Quebec society. It describes this diversity as follow: a Francophone majority, Aboriginal Nations with ancestral privileges and treaty rights, an Anglophone community that has acquired a given number of minority rights, and minority groups that have established themselves, some recently, others a long time ago, following international immigration to Canada and who also contribute to Quebec society.

During the opening keynote address for the *Forum*, the minister of the *ministère de Relations avec les citoyens et l'Immigration du Québec* clearly stated the reason for debating issues of citizenship and integration: the people of Quebec constitute a nation. The *peuple québécois* has a history, its own democratic institutions, its laws, a common language and a *Charte des droits et libertés de la personne*. This *peuple québécois* is represented in its national assembly. Thus, it constitutes a nation. According to the minister, the challenge before the *peuple québéois* is to find projects and initiatives that can unite all citizens, including those who are not part of the Francophone majority. As he said: "Nous avons le défi de rechercher les voix d'une citoyenneté pleinement partagée."[32]

Therefore the underlying challenge is that of the coexistence or the tension between the political project of Quebec citizenship and the vision put forth by the federal government. The federal government denies the right to self-determination as it is expressed by the Quebec National Assembly. The Quebec National Assembly is the pinnacle of the democratic representation of the *peuple québécois*, or in other words, the democratic voice of the citizens of the nation of Quebec. Ultimately, the concept of citizenship as put forth by the Quebec government is directly opposite to the federal understanding. The Quebec government aims to represent a Quebec society as a full entity, while the federal government recognizes the people of Quebec as a sub-set of Canadian citizenship.

However, citizenship is not simply defined through political, social and cultural rights. Citizenship is also defined through a dynamic process that delineates inclusion, integration and participation in public life. Moreover, issues of social justice or the prevention of economic, social and political marginalization of large segments of society are closely linked to questions of citizenship. Citizenship is also about responsibilities. In this sense, citizenship is based on a civic contract that aims to define Quebec citizens' relations to political institutions. Although voluntary, this civic contract aims to strengthen one's sense of belonging to the national-political Quebec society. Oblivious to the inherent conflicts in society, according to the minister responsible for citizenship, this approach aims to reiterate the needed consensus in society to develop a modern Quebec. This consensus can only come into being if the society it aims to define shares a set of values.[33] More precisely, the ministerial document that was the basis for the public consultation states that there exists a specific Quebec citizenship that transcends any sense of belonging, whether political, ideological or ethnic in kind. This citizenship is expressed through democratic institutions, democratic life, laws and a set of shared values. It introduces the concept of civic contract at the centre of Quebec citizenship. It demarcates itself from the concept of the moral contract which was proposed by the Quebec Liberal government to newcomers in the *Policy Statement on Immigration and Integration* of 1991. The civic contract addresses itself to all Quebec citizens, not only to new immigrants. It speaks of citizenship by delineating its parameters in the following manner: democratic values and principles; respect for the legitimacy of laws; French as the common public language; recognition of the Quebec-Anglophone community; recognition of First Nations; recognition of the contribution of immigrants; active participation in the political, social and cultural life.

The civic heritage outlined in this contract takes into account issues of rights and freedoms and the political institutions that have been adapted to accommodate the various social elements that are part of Quebec society. This civic heritage is the sum total of the contribution of successive generations born in Quebec or who have come to establish themselves in Quebec. It is and continues to be a dynamic process, a synthesis of everyone's contribution.[34] However, because the boundaries of Quebec and Canadian citizenship are not clearly distinguished, we are confronted by a situation in which two identity-making processes that are in conflict with each other are operating simultaneously towards ends that are at odds with each other.[35] This makes it more difficult for citizens to participate fully in public life.

The preliminary documents to the *Forum* put forth a three-pronged definition of citizenship. This definition of citizenship is anchored in a set of rights and obligations at the basis of all liberal democracies; in a society that is defined territorially (Quebec) as well as symbolically or socially (*peuple québécois*); and finally through the willingness to participate and contribute to this society, a demand which requires more than a simple endorsement of shared values. However, this definition is counter to how the federal government defines the parameters of the national community. This issue is rarely acknowledged in the debates on citizenship.

It is not surprising that the initiatives on citizenship revealed by the Quebec government in the Fall of 2000 brought forth some opposition. The 350 participants at the *Forum*, most of whom were part of community organisations (women's groups, ethnic community representatives, social rights activists), labour organizations, and governments, as well as some academics, examined the document at hand. The comments and criticisms emerging from this consultation also revolve around the three dimensions of citizenship defined in the preliminary document.

The first set of criticisms focuses on how the model of citizenship presented in the document revolves around a theoretical understanding of citizenship. These criticisms focus more specifically on the chapters dealing with principles and shared values. It was suggested that there was not enough emphasis on the real conditions of exercising citizenship and especially the obstacles that limit the participation of various groups in society. Moreover, it was argued, the struggles against marginalization and socioeconomic exclusion (poverty, illiteracy, discrimination) should be accompanied by a formal recognition of the role of community organizations. The contribution of these organizations is not recognized in the ministerial document. In this respect, the civic contract depicted is sharply criticized because it makes demands upon individuals to take on responsibilities linked to citizenship, making individual citizens carry the burden of the perverse effects of globalization and of the state's withdrawal from social welfare. For a number of the participants, this focus on the struggles against marginalization needs to preceed any discussion on the political implications of citizenship. Without this focus on social justice and marginalization, citizenship can only be understood in terms of formal-legal rights, a vision in which the more substantive understanding of the social and symbolic elements emphasized by the government is not recognized.

A second line of criticism focuses on the definition of *peuple québécois*. For example the *Conseil des relations interculturelles* (CRI) argues that the ministerial document keeps on failing to acknowledge fully the cultural diversity of Quebec society and the responsibilities of the state as a result of this diversity. The CRI perceives the endorsement of the proposed vision of citizenship as detrimental to interculturalism. Here, diversity needs to be understood as beneficial to society rather than a threat to the social cohesion. The fact that newcomers are asked to integrate into the institutions of the French majority[36] obliterates the pluralism of Quebec society. Moreover, the CRI does not view Canadian and Quebec citizenship as projects with goals counter to each other. Rather, the CRI feels that it is unfortunate that Quebec is not willing to put forth a vision that is complementary to that of Canada. As the CRI mentions, the multiplicity of identities that emerge from these different visions of citizenship is not understood by most citizens of Quebec as conflicting or as a clash of loyalty between two entities. The CRI is even doubtful that these two models of integration for new-comers are sources of tension or confusion. The CRI therefore does not view Canadian and Quebec citizenship as political projects that negate each other.[37]

Claude Bariteau, an anthropologist and founder in 2000 of the *Rassemblement pour l'indépendance du Québec*, is also critical of the definition of the *peuple québécois* put forward by the department. He raises three objections. First, the department position is oblivious to the formal-legal framework of citizenship. The people of Quebec are Canadian citizens. Canada is the one that naturalizes immigrants, sees to law and order and has prerogative on the international scene. In this sense, there is no Quebec citizenship. Second, the ministerial position favors the political institutions that were defined through a monarchical understanding of democracy. These institutions have reduced Quebec's responsibilities towards its citizens. To uphold the constitutional framework is to accept the diminished role of Quebec. Finally, by insisting that there are two opposite national dynamics, a Canadian one and a Quebec one, the department is putting forward a nationalist understanding that remains within the concept of the "two-nations theory." Yet, a Quebec citizenship does imply the creation of a state and the creation of a different frame of reference, one that directly defines a political nation.[38]

A third set of criticisms emphasizes the hidden political agenda of the Quebec government. A number of participants disagree that the motivations of the Quebec government are limited to protecting a Francophone minority in North America. As they stated: "Le projet de vouloir vivre ensemble ne doit être emprisonnée par une volonté de régler notre problème constitutionnel."[39] Others fear that this process of consultation is aimed at reviving sovereignist enthusiasm.[40] This criticism is what brought the federal Intergovernmental Affairs Minister to suggest that this *Forum* was simply an exercise in propaganda. In one reply, he insisted that this was an attempt to pull Canada out of Quebec, while waiting for Quebec to secede from Canada. Citizenship is not a zero-sum game: "They [immigrants] know that identities add on to each other, they never subtract."[41]

Similarly, Danielle Juteau, a sociologist, attacks the Quebec policy by arguing that this policy emphasizes a move away from multiple identities and the possibility of having more than one allegiance. She is critical of the fact that both citizenship and national identity are intertwined in this project. She asks whether one needs to identify as *Québécois* to be a responsible citizen and goes on to stress that making access to the rights of citizenship dependent upon developing a sense of belonging to Quebec society is highly problematic. She explains that what she perceives as emerging from this document is an emphasis on creating and reinforcing the role of the Quebec government. While omitting to discuss the federal offensive on citizenship and national identity, she stresses that the Quebec offensive is a willingness to institutionalize the Quebec national identity and to subordinate to it all other identities. And finally, it is an attempt to favour a universal identity and suppress diversity.[42] In sum, there is an attempt to anchor Quebec citizenship in a territorialized vision of cultural belonging, an understanding that is counter to the more trendy model of postnational citizenship as advanced by Yasmin Soysal.[43]

Similar criticisms were expressed by various public personalities (including the leader of Quebec's Action démocratique Party, the spokesperson for Quebec's Liberal party, the leader of *Alliance Quebec* and a few academics) insisting that multiple allegiances and identities are the norm and not the exception.[44] Reacting to the passages in the document that focused on the unwillingness of the federal government to recognize the *peuple québécois* and the issue of allegiances to Canada and Quebec, the leader of the Anglophone group *Alliance Quebec* wrote:

> For English-speaking Quebeckers and indeed many other Quebec federalists to buy into this process, these political references will have to be removed from the document. Indeed, if the government is acting in good faith, it should be made clear at the beginning of the document that the Quebec government's desire to instill pride in living in Quebec is not in any way meant to diminish the attachment most Quebeckers have to being citizens of Canada or to diminish the important symbols of being part of Canada, including the *Charter of Rights and Freedoms* and the Canadian flag.[45]

Similarly, while recognizing that French is the language most commonly spoken in Quebec, he questioned the assumption that French should be the common public language, especially in a Canada that is officially bilingual and where obtaining services from the state should be possible in either language.

The Montreal English newspaper *The Gazette* stated that:

> The government should not still behave as though non-francophone groups are by definition threatening to Quebec's continued existence as a French state. It is time the government recognized that it should not even try to mould the increasingly pluralistic society of contemporary Quebec into a single shape. The value of diversity must be affirmed.[46]

The editorialist of the Montreal French newspaper *Le Devoir* proposed similar objections and denounced this desire to make Quebec a national state with which all citizens must identify exclusively.[47]

All in all, the arguments deployed in the media attack mainly the nationalist and partisan nature of the government text. Whether or not it is perceived as a public relations operation or a gimmick better to sell the sovereignist cause, what is being expressed is a profound discomfort with the assertion made by the government in that document that there are conflicts of legitimacy between the federal and Quebec government's competing visions of citizenship (rather than between one or several citizenship identities or one or several ethnic, religious or immigrant identities) as well as conflicts between the federal and Quebec policies of diversity management. Many have accused the Quebec government of promoting an exclusive Quebec national identity. Others assert that the Quebec government does not have the right or the legitimacy to discuss Quebec citizenship, for a Canadian citizenship is the only formal and legal form of citizenship possible.[48] For example, the Montreal West-Island newspaper *The Suburban* denounced the fact that immigrants, as a pre-condition to their acceptance as Quebec citizens, will be expected to take a separate oath of allegiance to the Quebec state and abide by the values and rules outlined in the civic contract.[49]

These criticisms incited by the *Forum* highlight four main issues. First, these highlight the inability to locate the Quebec government's discourse in the context of the federal offensive on citizenship and national identity. Second, these highlight the inability to locate the Quebec government's discourse within the whole of its policies since the beginning of the 1980s. This new direction fails to highlight the tensions among civic nationalism, ethnic nationalism and communitarian tendencies that exist within each of these entities: the MRCI, the CRI and the sovereignist movement. Third, these criticisms also highlight the disquieting double-standard with which the federal government's discourse and that of the Quebec government are evaluated, a double-standard that merits further study, for it reveals the different ways neo-racism – *le racisme différentialiste*[50] – is concealed and propagated, especially through the media. Finally, they highlight the difficulty of locating Quebec and Canadian discourses in a world context. Currently, all Western states are elaborating a discourse on citizenship with diverse functions, such as dealing with issues of violence and terrorism, or functions of social cohesion through policies of multiculturalism or even calls for partnerships with organizations in civil society. The federal and Quebec discourses, which are based on social cohesion, belonging and allegiance point to problems associated with the limits of nation-building projects and the dislocation of social solidarity in many societies, while omitting to address these world issues.

Conclusion

In Canada, debates on citizenship take on the important issue of symbolism. These debates are framed by a context in which the legitimacy of the society to which citizenship refers is contested, where tensions around power relations are not limited to the demands by rights activists, but also include demands made by the state, and which are also affected by the impact of economic and social forces. Political institutions are confronted by the demands of minority groups that want to be recognized by the state. Moreover, the multinational character of Canada is also a challenge to citizenship, especially since the federal structures offer one nation (Quebec) a political space in which it is able to develop its own political institution and voice. Hence, Canadian citizenship is confronted with the reality and challenge of a Quebec nation. Thus, despite the fact that the preferred model of citizenship in the academic literature is a post-national model, both Canada and Quebec advance a model of citizenship that is anchored in a national space. The federal and Quebec understandings of citizenship are far from endorsing a model of citizenship that is not anchored in territory and cultural belonging. Although some lament this fact, we are only commenting that this is the case. To endorse a model of post-national citizenship is to suggest wrongly that the nation-state no longer plays an important role in citizenship. It is also to endorse an understanding of citizenship that presents itself as free from universalizing aims, but which remains nevertheless normative. The debates on citizenship, whether in Canada or Quebec, put forth an understanding of the citizen as attached to a national community. In both cases, citizenship and national identity are intertwined concepts. The real Canadian citizen proves his loyalty and allegiance to Canada first and foremost. According to Morton, Canadian citizenship is a "soft" form of citizenship ("une citoyenneté faiblarde"), weaker than the European models. In contrast, Quebec citizenship is a "hard" form of citizenship for it attempts to develop a civic and linguistic solidarity without nuances: "Une citoyenneté québécoise titille ceux et celles qui recherchent une solidarité civique et linguistique sans trop y mettre de nuances. Elle perturbe les autres qui se sentent à l'aise avec des allégeances multiples ou qui refusent de marcher au pas derrière les fifres et les tambours de qui que ce soit d'autre."[51] As this confirms, the debate on citizenship is extremely normative and politicized. What seems acceptable in the Canadian discourse is often condemned in the Quebec case by those who oppose the idea of Quebec citizenship.

It should be said that those who criticize the Quebec government on its citizenship initiatives often turn a blind eye to how the Canadian government deals with this issue. It would be wrong to suggest that neither Canada nor Quebec allows for multiple allegiances and identities or even pluralism. Canada and Quebec both recognize the legitimacy of hyphenated identities. Quebec even mentions cultural rights. However, it should be noted that while Canada presents itself as having a fully developed political and national community, Quebec remains open as it struggles to gain recognition. It should also be noted that Quebec citizenship defines Canadian citizenship.[52] Citizens of Quebec always remain citizens of Canada, even when they identify with the Quebec political space. The project is therefore truncated. And most participants at the *Forum* did come to this realization, as their criticism clearly demonstrates. They have attacked each of the tenets of the government's proposal from the references to the national character of Quebec, to the use of French as a common public language, the idea of the civic contract and even the conflicting models of integration. If citizenship is essentially anchored in a political association, the ambiguity of the political status of Quebec, which is always defined as a sub-set of the Canadian political space, can only undermine a model of Quebec citizenship.

Notes

1. Bryan Turner, "Citizenship Studies: A General Theory," *Citizenship Studies*, vol. 1, No 1 (1997): 5–18; Carlo Gamberale, "European Citizenship and Political Identity," *Space & Polity* vol. 1, no. 1 (1997): 37–59.
2. Carlo Gamberale, "European Citizenship and Political Identity," 37–59.
3. François Rocher, "Repenser le Québec dans un Canada multinational. Pour un modèle fonctionnel de la citoyenneté," *Globe. Revue internationale d'études québécoises*, vol. 1, no. 1 (1998): 77–113; Idem., "Citoyenneté fonctionnelle et État multinational: pour une critique du jacobinisme juridique et de la quête d'homogénéité." in *Droits fondamentaux et citoyenneté. Une citoyenneté fragmentée, limitée, illusoire?*, eds. Michel Coutu, Pierre Bosset, Caroline Gendreau, and Daniel Villeneuve (Montreal: Les Éditions Thémis, 2000), 201–235.
4. Micheline Labelle and Daniel Salée, "La citoyenneté en question. L'État canadien face à l'immigration et à la diversité," *Sociologie et sociétés*, vol. 31, no 2 (1999): 125–144; Idem., "Immigrant and Minority Representations of Citizenship in Quebec," in *Citizenship Today: Global Perspectives and Practices*, eds. T. Alexander Aleinikoff et Douglas Klusmeyer (Washington: Carnegie Endowment for International Peace, 2001).
5. Privy Council Office, *Shaping Canada's Future Together: Proposals* (Ottawa: Minister of Supply and Services Canada, 1996).
6. François Rocher and Daniel Salée, "Libéralisme et tensions identitaires: éléments de réflexion sur le désaroi des sociétés modernes," *Politique et Sociétés*, vol. 16, no. 2 (1997): 30.
7. Citizenship and Immigration Canada, *Into the 21st Century: a Strategy for Immigration and Citizenship* (Ottawa: Supply and Services Canada, 1994), viii–ix.
8. This report contained no fewer than 172 recommendations on the main juridical, political and social strategies of Canadian immigration. It focussed on the legislative framework, on the federal government's relations with the provinces, municipalities and non-governmental organizations that are involved in the integration of newcomers, the role of the family, the selection of financially independent immigrants, political asylum and, finally, rules and regulations for the administration of this law. This report did consider the values and principles privileged by Canadians over the last fifteen years as revealed in various studies and opinion polls. Moreover, national consultations were held in the cities that are the principal destinations for newcomers (Vancouver, Montreal and Toronto). The committee also received over 500 written statements.

9. Groupe consultatif sur la révision de la législation, *Au-delà des chiffres. L'immigration de demain au Canada* (Ottawa: Travaux publics et services gouvernementaux, 1997).

10. Ibid., 16.

11. Ibid., 39.

12. Ibid., 39–40.

13. These new orientations are based upon the following principles: accountability and transparency (principles and policies must be clearly set out in legislation); supporting family reunification by responding to new social realities (family life outside of marriage and same-sex couples); upholding Canada's humanitarian tradition while supporting greater effectiveness in decision-making; balancing privileges and responsibilities (i.e. greater responsibilities for sponsors, actions against people who fail to meet their obligations under the law or abuse of the refugee determination process); enriching the country's human resources (Canada's selection system for independent immigrant applicants needs a sharper focus on flexible and transferable skills); promoting public safety as international crime becomes more pervasive and sophisticated; fairness, effectiveness and integrity of the system. See Citizenship and Immigration Canada, *News Release no. 98–59* (Ottawa: Citizenship and Immigration Canada, 1998). Citizenship and Immigration Canada, *News Release no. 98–64* (Ottawa: Citizenship and Immigration Canada, 1998). Citizenship and Immigration Canada, *Building on a Strong Foundation for the 21st Century: New Directions for Immigration and Refugee Policy and Legislation* (Ottawa: Public Works and Government Services Canada, 1998).

14. Standing Senate Committee on Social Affairs, Science and Technology, *Canadian Citizenship: Sharing the Responsibility* (Ottawa: Senate of Canada, Standing Senate Committee on Social Affairs, Science and Technology, 1994).

15. Canadian Heritage, *Multiculturalism Program: The Context for Renewal* (Ottawa: Canadian Heritage, 1997).

16. Privy Council Office, *Shaping Canada's Future Together: Proposals* (Ottawa: Supply and Services Canada, 1996).

17. Citizenship and Immigration Canada, *Citizenship of Canada Act* (Ottawa: Public Works and Government Services Canada, 1998).

18. House of Commons, *Debates*, no 52, 18 February 2000.

19. Ibid.

20. Ibid.

21. For more information on this offensive and propaganda, see Daniel Turp, *La nation bâillonnée* (Montréal: VLB éditeur, 2000).

22. Robert Bernier, Vincent Lemieux and Maurice Pinard, *Un combat inachevé* (Ste-Foy: Presses de l'Université du Québec, 1997).

23. Léon Bernier, "Recherche sur l'américanité des Québécois: l'assurance identitaire se conjugue avec l'ouverture sur le monde. La conscience nationale des Québécois est fortement associée à l'espace géopolitique qu'ils occupent," *Le Devoir*, 15 July 1998, A–7.

24. Jean-François Lisée, *Sortie de secours. Comment échapper au déclin du Québec* (Montréal: Boréal, 2000), 189.

25. Will Kymlicka, *Finding our Way* (Toronto: Oxford University Press, 1998).

26. Micheline Labelle, "Intégration et multiculturalisme: discours et paradoxes," in *Définir l'intégration*, Actes du colloque de l'Association internationale d'études québécoises et Institut d'Études politiques, ed. Yannick Resch (Montréal: XYZ, 2001).

27. Micheline Labelle, François Rocher and Guy Rocher, "Pluriethnicité, citoyenneté et intégration: de la souveraineté pour lever les obstacles et les ambiguïtés," *Cahiers de recherche sociologique*, no. 25 (1995): 213–245; François Rocher, "Pluralisme et multiculturalisme: Le rôle des langues dans la quête des identities," in *Les droits linguistiques au Canada: collusions ou collisions? – Linguistic Rights in Canada: Collusions or Collisions*, ed. Sylvie Léger (Ottawa: Centre canadien des droits linguistiques, 1995), 159–193; Micheline Labelle, "Politiques québécoises et diversité," *Cahiers du programme d'études sur le Québec* (Université McGill, no 13, 1998); Micheline Labelle, "La politique de la citoyenneté et de l'interculturalisme au Québec: défis et enjeux," in *Les identités en débat: intégration ou multiculturalisme*, eds. Hélène Greven and Jean Tournon (Paris: L'Harmattan, 2000), 269–293; Kenneth McRoberts, *Misconceiving Canada* (Toronto: Oxford University Press, 1997).

28. Ministère des Communautés culturelles et de l'Immigration du Québec, *Let's Build Québec Together: A Policy Statement on Immigration and Integration* (Québec: Direction générale des politiques et programmes, Direction des communications, Ministère des Communautés culturelles et de l'Immigration du Québec, 1990).

29. Assemblée nationale, *Projet de loi n° 18 (1996, chapitre 21). Loi sur le ministère des Relations avec les citoyens et de l'immigration et modifiant d'autres dispositions législatives* (Québec: Éditeur officiel du Québec, 1996).

30. Ministère des Relations avec les citoyens et de l'Immigration, "Allocution de Monsieur Ernst Jouthe, sous-ministre adjoint aux relations civiques," *Colloque Mondialisation, multiculturalisme et citoyenneté* (Montréal, Musée des beaux-Arts, 29 March 1998).

31. Conseil des Relations interculturelles, *Un Québec pour tous ses citoyens. Les défis actuels d'une société pluraliste* (Quebec: Editeur officiel, 1997).

32. Ministère des Relations avec les citoyens et de l'Immigration, *Le Forum national sur la citoyenneté et l'intégration. Recueil.* Les documents de consultation et textes importants du Forum (texte inédit), (2000).

33. Ibid., 8.

34. Ibid., 14.

35. The ministerial document states that: "À l'heure où les démocraties ont besoin d'une plus grande cohésion sociale et politique, le dédoublement des cadres de légitimité, parce que porteur de confusion et de conflits de loyauté, risque de rendre plus ardue la participation des citoyens à la vie publique. Parce que les sphères de citoyenneté québécoise et canadienne ne sont pas clairement démarquées, deux processus identitaire entrent en conflit, posant du même coup l'opposition des cadres de référence et d'interprétation." Ministère des Relations avec les citoyens et de l'Immigration, *La citoyenneté québécoise. Document de consultation pour le Forum national sur la citoyenneté et l'intégration* (Quebec: Editeur officiel, 2000).

36. Conseil des Relations interculturelles, *Intégrer tous les citoyens dans un Québec démocratique et pluralist,* Éléments de réflexion et pistes d'action en vue du Forum national sur la citoyenneté et l'intégration (texte inédit), (2000) 19.

37. Conseil des Relations interculturelles, *Intégrer tous les citoyens dans un Québec démocratique et pluralist,* 4.

38. Claude Bariteau, *Citoyenneté canadienne à la québécoise ou citoyenneté québécoise* (Quebec: Université Laval: texte inédit, 2000).

39. Centre Justice et Foi, "La citoyenneté ne doit pas être emprisonnée dans le problème constitutionnel," *Le Devoir,* 20 September 2000, 11.

40. Desmond Morton, "La citoyenneté, une notion un peu complexe," *Le Devoir,* 2 October 2000, A6.

41. David Gamble and Kevin Dougherty, "Dion Slams PQ on Integration," *Montreal Gazette,* 22 September 2000, internet edition.

42. Danielle Juteau, "Ambiguïtés de la citoyenneté au Québec," *Les grandes conférences Desjardins, Programme d'études sur le Québec* (Université McGill, no. 7, 2000), 6.

43. Ibid., 20.

44. Philip Authier, "Citizenship Forum Called PQ Gimmick," *Montreal Gazette,* 21 September 2000, A9.

45. Anthony Housefather, "Defining Quebec Citizenship," *Montreal Gazette,* 29 August 2000, B3.

46. Philip Authier, "Citizenship Forum Called PQ Gimmick"

47. Michel Venne, "Citoyen ou loyal sujet," *Le Devoir*, 22 September 2000, A8.

48. Philip Authier, "Citizenship Forum Called PQ Gimmick"

49. Ed Arzouian, "Do you have your Quebec Passport?" *The Suburban*, 9 August 2000, A6.

50. By *racisme différentialiste* we mean a tendency to to hierarchize, essentialize and generalize cultural traits attributed to the Other. For instance, Quebec nationalists are constantly accused of ethnicism, xenophobia and tribalism in the English press, particularly outside Quebec.

51. Desmond Morton, "La citoyenneté, une notion un peu complexe."

52. Claude Bariteau, *Citoyenneté canadienne à la québécoise ou citoyenneté québécoise.*

17

Canadian Culture and Canadian Identity

JAMES R. MITCHELL

The question I wish to explore in this essay is that of the relationship between culture and the citizen's sense of identity.[1] Or, to put it another way, I am interested in the importance of a distinctive culture to the expression and preservation of a distinctive national identity. I want to make a point about why culture matters to Canada in some rather special ways, and what this means for public policy. My remarks apply in large part to English-speaking culture in Canada, though in some particular ways they also apply to culture produced in the French language in this country.[2] The relationship between culture and identity is not a trivial matter in the modern world. In the information age, American popular culture is ubiquitous, and it has begun to affect (some would say submerge) national and local cultures throughout the globe. For Canadians, who share a continent and one of their two official languages with the United States, the issue of culture and identity has been at times almost a national obsession.[3] Canadians have debated and they have legislated to protect their culture and their cultural institutions; they have used public funds to subsidize artists and artistic endeavours in every domain of cultural activity. To a considerable extent, as we shall see below, these efforts have succeeded – despite the fact Canada's increasing economic integration with the U.S. has intensified the pressures on a distinctive Canadian culture and identity.

Identity and Citizenship

It is widely agreed that identity is not simply a function of citizenship. Who you are, who you *feel* you are, is not necessarily reflected in the passport you carry. Like the people of Catalonia or Brittany, French-speaking Quebeckers know this; so do Newfoundlanders and Acadians. Most Canadians recognize it too – identity is about *who* you are and *what* you are; it is about how you see yourself and the group with which you identify yourself by virtue of language, culture, kinship or even sexual orientation.

Identity in this collective sense is something that is partly self-determined and partly a matter of whether the other members of the group acknowledge you as one of them. One can describe and analyse the criteria that would justify an attribution of a particular group identity to an individual. One can also debate them: what is it to be a "real Quebecker"? What is it to be Aboriginal? What is it to be a westerner? These questions are asked in Canada, and not always answered by everyone in the same way.

Identity in this collective sense may have legal consequences and may carry with it certain rights. For example, Canadian courts are beginning to take the view that if you identify yourself as a Métis,[4] and if your self-identification is acknowledged by the Métis National Council according to its criteria for "membership" in the group commonly known as Métis, then you have certain entitlements to hunt and fish that are not enjoyed by non-Métis Canadians. Similarly, if you "self-identify" as a visible minority in the Canadian Public Service, you will enjoy access to programs for employment and professional development that are not open to employees who are not visible minorities. By contrast, the concept of citizenship describes membership in a class that is defined entirely in legal terms: you are a citizen of a country if the government of the country accepts you as a citizen. In every case, that acceptance depends on satisfying much stricter criteria of birth, residence or kinship than are required for the mere assertion or recognition of group identity. Those criteria for citizenship are invariably expressed in law and regulations. Citizenship confers rights on individuals and it entails, in most cases, certain obligations. Citizenship can be associated with a particular national culture but the connection is not necessary. That is, you can be a citizen even if your sense of personal or cultural identity lies elsewhere. Citizenship is about the individual's relationship to the state rather than to the group. Citizenship is something over which the individual may have no control, in the sense that a state may assert and enforce the obligations of citizen-ship over an individual[5] irrespective of the wishes of that person.

Culture and Identity

Does this mean the state has no role to play in identity (in the sense we are using the term)? In an obvious sense, the answer must be no. After all, for many people their sense of collective identity is closely connected with their citizenship. This is most obviously the case in the United States and in France, two countries where the citizen's sense of group identity is primarily with his or her fellow citizens. Yet in both these obvious cases, there are exceptions, whether racial (African-Americans and Hispanic-Americans in the U.S., North Africans in France), reli-gious (Muslims in France) or geographic (Bretons in France, Southern-ers in the U.S.) Governments cannot create or determine the individual's sense of collective identity, but they can do a lot to encourage and sustain it through what they do in relation to national culture. This has been the Canadian experience, and it is that experience, particularly in relation to a country with a dominant culture, that has prompted Canadian govern-ments to play a larger role in the encouragement of a distinctive national culture in support of a distinctive national identity.

Canadian Culture

There is today in Canada a dynamic, creative culture in which Canadi-ans can take pride. It is, I would argue, a distinctive culture, in spite of its obvious connection to the cultures of the U.S. and other countries where Canadians have their ancestral or artistic roots.

My first proposition is that Canadian culture is flourishing – despite the fact that Canadians live next door to the United States, a cultural as well as an economic superpower whose largest export is cultural products. Moreover, Canadian culture is flourishing notwithstanding that many foreigners cannot easily distinguish Canadian cultural products from those of our neighbour to the south. It is flourishing in two languages[6] and in a hundred forms of expression that draw upon the diverse roots of Canada's population. There was a time – it was only thirty years ago – when it was said that Canadians may read and write poetry, but they were unable to establish a place for themselves in prose. Then came writers like Alice Munro and Mavis Gallant. It was then said that Canadians could write short stories, but, unlike Britain or the U.S., Canada had no novelists worthy of international recognition.

Then came Robertson Davies and Margaret Atwood, and then Michael Ondaatje and Timothy Findlay, and now Rohinton Mistry and Alistair MacLeod and others whose names deserve mention. Today Canadian novelists occupy a place on the world stage that is far out of proportion to Canada's population or political or economic influence in the world.

Was it a surprise when Margaret Atwood won the Booker prize in 2000? No. The debate was over *whether she had won it for her best book.* Canada's culture – in books and music and art and almost every other form of creative expression – is thriving in the information age. It is thriving despite the fact that Canada is becoming ever more economically integrated with the United States.

Why Government Matters

Culture is also something that Canadians have long seen as a proper subject for government to worry about. Canadians have expected government to care about it because they do not enjoy the same tradition of private patronage of the arts, or more recently, of world-scale industrial excellence (in film and music) that has characterized contemporary culture in sister democracies. Canada has a relatively small population, and no significant history of private wealth that has seen fit to endow artists and the arts.

So governments, and especially the federal government, have always seen a role for themselves:

- in direct support to artists and artistic endeavours (via the Canada Council and other federally-funded granting programs such as book publishing).
- in the creation of national cultural institutions like the CBC, the National Arts Centre and the Canada Council.
- in law and regulation (e.g., the Canadian content rules on radio, the cultural property export review law, the laws on ownership of newspapers and TV/radio).

The theory was, if government didn't act, nothing would happen. And to a large extent, that was true. It was obviously government action that led to the creation of the CBC in the 1930s. This was a positive step, yet thirty years later, before government acted on the issue of Canadian content in popular music[7] there was almost no Canadian popular music on the radio. Today Canada's popular music industry is flourishing. Consider, for example, what an extraordinary achievement it was when, just a couple of years ago, the world's top-selling female vocalists in every category of popular music were Canadian:

- Celine Dion (Diva)
- Alanis Morissette (Pop)
- Shania Twain (Country)
- Sarah McLaughlin (New Age)
- Diana Krall (Jazz)

In a world in which American popular culture is seen to be overpowering virtually every other national culture, this is an extraordinary achievement. It means far more than most non-Canadians can imagine. Most importantly, it means that when young Canadians turn on the radio, or watch a video on television, they see themselves.

More prosaically, it also means there is a healthy recording industry in Toronto, and in Halifax and Montreal and Vancouver. It means that as a society Canadians are not just consumers of foreign culture, they are creators of cultural products that are finding a worldwide market. To a considerable extent, this achievement is a consequence of government policy. Government stepped into the marketplace of ideas and regulated a place for Canadians – and it worked!

Interestingly, the same thing has not happened to the same extent in television, where, through the CRTC, government acted in a similar fashion as it had in the music business. But regulation of Canadian content in television has not been a failure, either. Note, for example, that because of the requirement to create Canadian content for TV, a substantial film and TV industry has grown up here, especially in Toronto and Vancouver, both to create products for Canada and for export abroad, and also (significantly) to serve the immense U.S. market.

It must be acknowledged that, in the latter respect, Canada's film and television industry is largely a branch plant of the vastly larger American television and film industry. But one must be patient. Just as in sound recording, the Canadian television and film industry has grown from nothing to something quite substantial (Canada is the world's third or fourth largest exporter of television products) in less than thirty years. It would be foolish to bet against the eventual emergence of a distinctive national cinema in Canada, as has occurred, for example, in Australia.

Why Culture Matters

Why do culture and cultural industries matter to Canada? They matter because the preservation of a distinctive, creative, successful Canadian culture is the key to the preservation of a distinct Canadian identity in an economically-integrated North America.

As is well known, Canada is becoming ever-more integrated into a single, U.S.-dominated North American economy:

- over 80 percent of Canada's exports go the U.S.;
- two-thirds of Canada's foreign investment comes from the U.S.;
- Canada and the U.S. share what is essentially a common labour market for high-end talent;
- politicians and editorialists in Canada are debating whether NAFTA ought to lead to some closer form of economic union, ranging from a customs union to a common currency.

Canada's economic future is clear and it is unavoidable. Canada is part of the American economic space. What is open for debate, and where governments can play a role, is *whether it will be possible to preserve a Canada that is politically and culturally distinct within that economic space.*

This is where public policy gets interesting. For many years, Canadian governments sought, through law, regulation and direct intervention (subsidies, grants, etc.) to carve out a distinctive *economic* space, while devoting comparatively less attention, and much less money, to the more nebulous challenge of investing in identity. *My second proposition is that the Government of Canada should do precisely the reverse.* That is:

- it should invest in culture and cultural institutions;
- it should carefully consider how to use regulation to ensure access by Canadians to Canadian cultural products such as film and video; and
- it should made appropriate changes to the tax system to

encourage private giving and investing in culture and cultural institutions.

The federal government must do what only a national government can do – it must invest in national (and local) cultural infrastructure because the cities and provinces either do not have the money or simply won't spend it. And it must do this in support of a distinctive Canadian identity within a larger North America dominated by the U.S.

In making these investments, what the government of Canada should *not* do is create a "state" culture. In spending money on artists and on particular artistic projects, government should not act directly but rather through arm's length bodies that are not part of government. The so-called "Canada mark" – the half-flag that is beginning to be seen on everything from stationary to public buildings – should never appear on an artist's work. Nor, in particular, should it appear on the CBC.[8] Perhaps most importantly, in an age where cultural expression is the most significant expression of national identity, and in which cultural products are becoming ever more important elements of our national output, government must help Canadians to understand why public spending in this area is as important to our national interest as public spending in critical areas of social infrastructure such as health care.

Conclusion

In a hundred years, the world has gone from a time in which cultural expression was largely local, to one in which that same expression must be national or international in its reach if it is to survive. Culture, whether we think in terms of the visual arts or literature or music, may have its roots in the community but today it finds its *audience* outside that community – via television, sound recording, film, video and the printed word. If Canadian writers or singers or filmmakers are to survive as creators, they must sell into a market larger than Canada. The same holds true for virtually every other form of creative expression in Canada and indeed everywhere in the world.

In this context, what government can do is to provide a national environment in which creators can grow and take root, and then it can help ensure they have access to that larger stage. This, I submit, is one of the key functions of public policy in the information age.

Notes

1. I am using the term "identity" in the sense of membership in a group that is generally recognized as a group, both by members and by non-members. That is, I am referring to identity in the collective rather than the individual sense.
2. As well as the Canadian culture that I am going to talk about, there is also a Quebec culture, and distinctive cultures in Newfoundland and Cape Breton. There are not similarly distinct cultures in the other provinces, though the Acadian *people* do have a distinctive culture.
3. Quite by contrast with their American neighbours, for whom neither issue has ever been terribly important.
4. That is, a person of mixed aboriginal and non-aboriginal descent.
5. e.g., military service.
6. The issue of protecting and promoting French-speaking culture in Canada is one that both the federal government and the government of Quebec have taken very seriously over many years, for obvious reasons. Indeed, that issue – the role of government in the protection of culture – constitutes one of the key planks in the political platform of the separatists in Quebec. And as is well known, the question of whether French-speaking culture in English-speaking North America is better protected by a sovereign Quebec or within a larger Canada committed to the protection of the French language and culture is one of the great questions in the enduring political debate in Canada.
7. Pierre Juneau, Canadian Radio-Television Commission, (1972).
8. Which is a *public* broadcaster, not a *state* broadcaster.

18

Persistence of Vision: Memory, Migration and Citizenship – Free Trade or the Failure of Cross-Culturality?

GERRY TURCOTTE

> *It is possible that there is no other memory*
> *than the memory of wounds*
> Czeslaw Milosz

In my new novel, *Flying in Silence*, set in both Australia and Canada, my principal character is a French-Canadian man torn between landscapes, languages and allegiances. To represent what was for me the central dilemmas of the novel – reconciling memory and migration – I used the metaphor of persistence of vision, that process in film through which we physiologically make sense of, or hold together, what should be a blurred, segmented and impartial sequence of frequently unrelated images.

Persistence of vision is all about the eye, the way it follows a film, remembers an image, holds on to it, until the next one appears to replace it, so that we are never conscious of the stutter of frames – the space between. Image after image flows past us leaving ghostly fingerprints on shell-shocked retinas. Our mind races, slower than light, and we see through the past into the present, just as that present no longer exists. And so we imagine the future.

With the old projectors, a glitch could shake that sequence free.

Suddenly, we might glimpse a momentary stutter that we'd sup-pressed – a mother, torn and fractured by a creeping darkness, a loved one felled by another's lifelong expectations, violence inflicted on a child so that he turns himself inward and disappears.

Persistence of vision works through memory – a remembrance of forgetting, and inevitable return. There is no journey forward without ghosts; there is no telling without fear. We tread lightly through the stories, but leave prints wherever we happen to go.

I wrote this section of the novel as I travelled – to new lands, through different voices, through different social classes. I wrote what follows as I journeyed back and forth between Canada and Australia. I scribbled it on napkins, on coasters, in a diary. I tried to ask myself questions about identity as I enacted my own version of persistence of vision – travelling into my cultural past, in order to see into the future.

I wondered, in this context, what it meant to be post/colonial? To be French-Canadian. To be Canadian *and* Australian simultaneously. To be hybrid. And if a hybrid, why I privileged a part of myself over another.

What are these blindnesses we champion? Are they political fraud? Political correctness? Are they a way to give ourselves cur-rency?

Why is Walter Mosley African-American instead of Jewish? When I ask him this he says he thinks there are enough Jewish crime writers but that there aren't as many African-American ones.

So why do I choose the experience of the French-Canadian over the experience of the Scot which is also distantly in me? My father couldn't speak English until quite late in life, my mother couldn't speak French. And yet they met, they loved, they married. They tortured language religiously and I translated badly in between. At the dinner table we spoke a strange mixture of French and English – or *Franglais*. My mother would ask a question in English, my father would answer in French, and I would flutter between them: "Pass *le sel*. *Veux-tu* some water?"

My unilingual friends always felt somewhat exhausted when they visited. They blinked in confusion as familiar phrases slipped sud-denly out of their grasp, so that they'd reach for the salt shaker, but then weren't sure what to do with it, or accepted a glass of water not realizing they'd asked for it.

Why did I come away with the passion of my father's silencing? Why was this the cause I clung to even as I travelled further and further from the language – even as the words began to blur as I stopped writing, reading, speaking. So that as my father aged, and lost the English he had slowly learnt, and as my accent changed over the years, it became harder and harder for us to speak to one another.

He said he was going deaf. In fact I was becoming mute.

When he died, we hadn't spoken in years – I realized suddenly that all I knew of him, all that we had become, was through my mother's translations, across the miles, through telephone lines and static; through datelines. When he died, I failed to return to him in time. I wondered, who was he? And who was it I knew?

In France the taxi driver is rude to me because he thinks I'm Belgian. Until I stand my ground and he realizes that I'm Québécois. Then he is all smiles. "Oh, that's okay then," he tells me, and I can barely escape the cab.

Soon after my arrival in Australia, a bartender rudely slams a drink in front of me and scowls, "bloody American." "But I'm Canadian," I stutter, and he smiles half-heartedly. I become invisible. In that moment, I am Canadian, wholly, simply Canadian, without nuances, without hyphens – whatever that might mean. My cohesion, in that moment, makes me suddenly invisible, silent. Later the publican will say to a patron sitting next to me, in terms of general disdain, "Don't worry about him, mate. He's Canadian," and the fight will leave them.

In Eastern Europe, long ago, officials emptied our train carriage at gunpoint, and everyone was scrutinized, searched. When they saw my Canadian passport they threw it at me quickly, dismissed me with a half-hearted wave of the wrist. So that I wanted to shout, "Canadians can be terrorists too. We can smuggle drugs." I wanted trouble. I wanted to be someone.

Until a German couple were beaten before me and dragged away – and there were consequences. It wasn't funny. Identity has consequences – but they aren't always clear.

To be tongue-tied. It isn't a moment's faltering. It tears your mouth apart – it rips the walls of tissue down.

When I attended English high school, with a French accent, I was sent to the school psychiatrist, and forced to attend speech therapy to bring my pronunciation into line – in Montreal, in a French province. My accent was a medical deficiency. An illness.

I got my revenge secretly. Swear words, in French, are all religious. Eucharist, Sacristy. These are the stuff of the best exhortations. Since my father had forced me to go to English school, I delighted in filling my homework with these words, a perpetual rebellion. "A bit religious," one of my teachers commented in the margins, "but a lovely story." How could she know that my words were not what they seemed? That as she read other words emerged. "It must be lovely to be bilingual," she said. "Yes," I answered. Tabernacle, I thought. Chalice.

Years later, when the language laws descended upon Quebec, forcing businesses to remove all English signs from windows, façades, billboards, the city seemed to hum beneath the unspoken phrases. Ghosts were suddenly everywhere in Montreal. Buildings were scarred with the absences of letters – Eaton's became Eaton – possessives became obscene. You could see the outline of unwanted words – unwanted thoughts – etched into the surface of the stone – a type of braille that spoke of intolerance and weakness.

"When I worked in the lumber yard," my father told me, "I couldn't speak a word of English. When I finally got a promotion I was asked to chase up all the orders. I would call the customers and no one would speak to me – even when I tried to use English. 'What language are you talking?' customers said to me, 'Put your father on the line little boy.' That was their favourite joke. So that I had to walk upstairs and ask my boss to call the companies. He had to transfer me. 'What can I do?' he said. 'I know it's not your fault. But I can't do both our jobs, eh?'"

We pulled the English language signs out of the window display and threw them on the cutting table. The words stared up at us with blank, sacrificial faces. "But this," he said. "It's the same thing. An eye for an eye ..". He shook his head angrily and grabbed the brush from my hand. He painted out the English words with short, vicious strokes. I could see them there, waiting to surface. "Don't ever give in to ignorance," he said, in his deep, French syllables. "Anyone who's had their language taken away should know better than to do the same."

To be tongue-tied. It's only a trendy metaphor when it's a slip of the tongue and not a signature. It's only a slip of the tongue when you control the tongue, not the other way around. It's only an affectation when you can leave it all behind. Migrate. Move. But not everyone has the luxury of moving. Not everyone wants to move.

And when you do you take it with you anyway.

In Australia, when I published my first work there – in a magazine called *Outrider*, a journal of migrant writing – I was asked on several occasions, by a number of writers, how dare I publish there? That I wasn't a *real* migrant. So that I wondered what *fake* migrants were – and how I had become one. It's your accent, someone else explained patiently. Ah yes, my vocal fingerprint – this English sign I had learned to hide behind, which inadequately sheltered me in my new world. Who knew, back then, that there were different Englishes, and that they weren't all equal or the same?

Persistence of vision. You see forward through the past. The steps you take you place in footprints that are probably no longer there – they're ghostly images, suggestions for paths to take or paths taken – for identities formed once, for words spoken, but which are only echoes, not the words themselves. Sometimes you are brave to step into those moments, those signatures, to keep the film intact.

Often you are braver not to.

This paper incorporates passages from *Flying in Silence*, published by Cormorant Books (Canada) & Brandl & Schlesinger (Australia), 2001.

19

The Impact of Globalization on Citizenship: Decline or Renaissance?

PETER J. SMITH

Globalization is the catchword of our time. While some praise it, claiming it has brought a new era of wealth, freedom and democracy, others decry it, claiming that globalization brings the opposite – poverty, environmental devastation and corporate domination. The only point of concurrence seems to be its inexorability. Both sides agree that globalization, economically and technologically, is an irresistible and unstoppable force imposing its will on anyone or anything that might stand in its way, including the nation-state.[1] In sum, as states, of necessity, open themselves up to the global economy, they suffer a loss of political and economic authority. "Diminished," "narrowed," "hollowed out" are some of the adjectives used to describe the state's reduced capacity and scope of policy action. In this portrayal of globalization as a *deus ex machina*, structure triumphs over agency, citizenship, a phenomenon of the nation-state, loses its relevance, and globalization becomes our fate. Or so it seemed until lately.

Recently, however, there has come an increasing awareness that globalization can be contested. The controversies over the Multilateral Agreement on Investment (MAI), the World Trade Organization (WTO), the International Monetary Fund (IMF) and the World Bank are an indication of increasing concern about, if not hostility towards, globalization. As objects of discussion the primary instruments and agencies of globalization have moved from corporate boardrooms to the kitchen tables of everyday citizens, and governments have had to take notice. What seemed so certain now seems less so as globalization becomes a political, not just an economic, phenomenon. While politics still matter, however, the status of the state as the sole container of politics, public spaces, citizenship and identity is put in doubt. Politics and citizenship, like the market, have burst the borders of the nation-state. The very processes and means of communicating that made globalization possible, I argue, are making globalization contestable. Information and communication technologies (ICTs), primarily the Internet, have facilitated new forms of expression and connection among groups and the growth of new public spaces, which are not easily controlled by states and ruling elites. Citizenship is becoming a *vita activa* that can be practiced at all levels, locally, nationally and globally.

In particular, ICTs are facilitating the growth of what may be described as alternative or counter-publics that are challenging important aspects of globalization, in particular the top-down, state-driven processes of international governance and multilateralism as embodied in the MAI and WTO. Increasingly, as questions of global governance intersect with the state, they create new spaces in which citizens may act, contest and inject alternative values into what is becoming a worldwide debate over globalization. Canadians, I intend to demonstrate, are among the most active users of ICTs in the creation of new public spaces and possibilities for citizen engagement, both within the nation-state and beyond it, in an emerging global civil society. Indeed, the confidence with which Canadians engage in global political activity serves to remind us that Canadian citizenship, itself, is a contested notion. The recent neo-liberal attempt to reduce citizens to mere consumers is but an interlude in, not the culmination of, the Canadian debate over citizenship.

In the first part of the paper I briefly articulate the traditional state-centred view of politics and citizenship in Canada. As social constructs, both the state and citizenship have always been contested, and globalization has intensified this process. I then explore other dimensions of globalization, in particular the capacity of the Internet to facilitate the growth of networks of citizens, non-governmental organizations, and social movements opposed to globalization. Here, particular attention is paid to the contributions of Hannah Arendt and Nancy Fraser to public sphere theory.

These insights are then applied to the activity of a number of Canadian non-governmental organizations (NGOs) in contesting the MAI and the Third Ministerial meeting of the WTO in Seattle in 1999. Finally, I argue that the neo-liberal discourse of economic globalization is being resisted and, contrary to popular perception, that the Canadian state still retains capacity to act. The result is that the meaning of citizenship may be broadening and deepening in the era of globalization, rather than contracting and narrowing as is commonly claimed. Increasingly, citizenship as a political activity has meaning both within and outside the container of the state.

The State-Centred View of Politics and Citizenship

Economic globalization certainly has brought into question the Westphalian model of the modern state and politics. According to this model the political universe is composed of sovereign states – specific territorial/political units with their own populations and exclusive authority within their boundaries.[2] This model privileges a certain view of politics. State sovereignty structures a spatially delimited territory and political community, but in the absence of any overarching community the relations between states are characterized by anarchy and chaos. Today, state forms delineate virtually all territorial spaces. According to Walker:

> It is this proliferation, affirmed by accounts of the modern state as an institution, container of all cultural meaning and site of sovereign jurisdiction over territory, property and abstract space, and consequently over history, possibility and abstract time, that still shapes our capacity to affirm both collective and particular identities.[3]

Such, then, is the power of this image of the state that it grounds our political identity as citizens. According to this view, politics and citizenship are possible only within the boundaries of the state. To be a citizen means to be a member of a polis, that is, a member of a political community functioning within the territory of a state. Historically, the civic republican and the more legal, juridical views of citizenship implied rights that could only be recognized in a community and backed by the state or some form of political authority. Civic republicanism draws on the Aristotelian notion of citizenship as participation in self-rule, the freedom to participate in public decisions. Today, political theorists continue to insist that civic virtue can only be practiced effectively within the nation-state.[4] The liberal or civil view of citizenship conceives of citizens as individuals who are equally entitled to the due process and the equal benefit and protection of the law, in essence, a private, personal and economic view of citizenship. In the twentieth century, a third strand of citizenship, social citizenship, emerged. Social citizenship refers to the rights to a minimum standard of welfare and income without which other forms of citizenship have little meaning.[5] All three elements of citizenship were claimed to be intertwined and given definition by state authority.

The hold that the modern territorial state has on our imagination is enormous and seems to be a constant in human affairs. We assume that politics and citizenship have always been and can only be state-centred. Recently, however, there has been a growing literature arguing that state sovereignty and the concepts of politics and citizenship constituted by it are not timeless but socially constructed, heavily normative and constantly undergoing change and transformation.[6] What seems "natural," "historical" and "timeless" is, in effect, uncertain and historically contingent.

Canadian Citizenship Contested

It is with this realization of uncertainty and contingency that Canadian scholars have examined the social construction of Canadian citizenship. What is apparent is that the Canadian state and sovereignty have never had a defined and certain status, and therefore the construction of Canadian identity and citizenship is an unfinished and contested project. Only when Canadian citizenship and identity are placed within a historical context can we see that economic globalization is but one, and certainly not the last, formative influence on Canadian citizenship.

There is no doubt, however, that since the Second World War the Canadian federal state has played an instrumental role in attempting to construct a pan-Canadian state-centric citizenship. It has done so in a variety of ways, including the creation of Canada-wide communication and cultural institutions – the CBC, Radio-Canada, the National Film Board and the Canada Council – all designed to break down sectional differences.[7] Social citizenship was promoted by the creation of social programs in the 1950s and 1960s, such as unemployment insurance and public health care. Canadians began to identify themselves as Canadians because they possessed "positive" social welfare rights.

Yet, this pan-Canadian construction of citizenship was contested, particularly in Quebec where French-Canadians did not feel comfortable in the new Canadian nation. According to Louis Balthazar, the Quiet Revolution can be seen as a reaction to the conception of the welfare state and its corresponding nationalism emanating from Ottawa in the post-war years. Thus, claims Balthazar: "A Canadian national enterprise turned out to be instrumental in fostering Quebec nationalism. Quebec nationalism is the illegitimate child of Canadian nationalism. The Canadian nation-state gave rise to the Quebec nation-state."[8] In essence, Quebec, by engaging in its rival modernist project of state building and identity creation, was merely the first to have contested the notion of a universal pan-Canadian society composed of undifferentiated Canadian citizens. Speaking of Canada's Aboriginal peoples, Joyce Green writes: "Failure to acknowledge profound identity and rights collectively within the state leads to confrontation with the state when it seeks to impose a universal undifferentiated citizenship."[9]

Both the Ottawa and Quebec modernist projects were intended to create activist, secular states constructed around a left-right distributional politics. Canada's Aboriginal peoples have been less enamoured of modernity and the state. They have been joined by a host of new social movements (NSMs) – student, peace, environmental, women's, gay and lesbian and disabled movements – that have arisen to contest the state-centred construction of Canadian citizenship. Variously described as post-materialist or post-modern movements for their pursuit of particular "lifestyle paradigms," these movements tend to view state and market institutions with suspicion. They also tend to have a broader and more participatory concept of politics, focusing their activities within the institutions of civil society. NSMs possess more loosely structured and non-hierarchical organizations, eschew mainstream political organizations such as parties and pursue non-conventional actions that "take place outside of the institutions of representative democracy and 'normal' politics."[10]

The view of civil society as represented by NSMs, it must be noted, is but one view. As Louis Hunt notes, civil society is "as contested as the social and political institutions it purports to describe."[11] One common view of civil society is exemplified by Alexis de Tocqueville. Tocqueville viewed civil society as composed of a wide variety of voluntary associations, which, he thought, were free schools of democracy that inculcated the habit of attending to public concerns. Today, as Robert Cox notes, civil society has been given a Tocquevillean interpretation as a "mobilized participant citizenry juxtaposed to dominant economic and state power."[12] NSMs, in fact, are representative of the

Tocquevillean interpretation of civil society. This interpretation must be distinguished from another common view of civil society as liberal, as an apolitical or pre-political space organized around the market economy. Today, this interpretation is embodied in neo-liberal globalization.

The growth of NSMs is emblematic of a more critical public that arose in advanced industrial societies in the 1960s, 1970s and 1980s. This public was characterized by "declining confidence in both governmental and non-governmental institutions and the emergence of non-traditional forms of political participation."[13] While Canadian NSMs were similar to their counterparts elsewhere in being anti-institutional and suspicious of capital and state institutions, they developed a much closer relationship to the Canadian state than has generally been the case in other countries, receiving federal government funding so they could better perform their role as democratic citizens.[14] This approach to state funding of NSMs was not accepted by all Canadians, however. With a slowdown of economic growth in the 1980s and the rise of populism and neo-liberalism, the argument from the ideological right was that Canadians should relate to the state as self-sufficient individuals and not through advocacy groups. State-funded groups became identified as "special interests" and were depicted as exercising excessive influence on social policy and government expenditures in contrast to business and corporate interests. Beginning first with the federal Conservative government in the 1980s and then with the Liberals from 1993, the relationship between advocacy groups and the government was transformed. Substantial cuts to advocacy groups were made and instead of the government acting as the champion of marginalized groups and encouraging their participation in the formation of public policy, groups are now expected to act as service providers and conduits of information from the government to Canadians.

This change is representative of the change in the expected relationship of Canadians to governments. No longer were Canadians expected to relate to government as democratic citizens; rather, they were perceived as customers. As democratic citizens we have the right to participate, to shape the decisions that affect us. As customers we are judged to be self-interested, atomistic consumers of government services, the quality of which we judge by the information government provides.

The attempt to transform Canadians from democratic citizens to customers, with its movement from the public to the private and from the state to the market, is part and parcel of neo-liberalism and globalization. In the neo-liberal model, the market replaces the state and the individual, the community. Rather than accept citizenship as a political and social status, neo-liberals reassert the role of the market, rejecting the idea that citizenship confers a status independent of economic standing.[15] Increasingly, the protection of the rights of property owners was given emphasis over the participatory rights of citizens, nationally as well as globally.

This is usually where most analyses end – with neo-liberalism and globalization ascendant and the state and citizenship in crisis; however, there is growing evidence that economic globalization and the neo-liberal agenda, with its limited and unbalanced view of citizenship, are being contested. Moreover, the very means that have made globalization possible, ICTs, are helping to make globalization contestable. In effect, our capacity to act as participatory citizens is spilling beyond the borders of the Canadian state. While public spaces inside the Canadian state and public sphere appear to have shrunk, they are opening up elsewhere. They are doing so in a way that challenges the conventional understanding that politics and citizenship are confined to states and that the relations between states are characterized by anarchy and chaos. Now, however, through the means of the Internet "unmediated dialogue and information exchange between citizens from around the world occurs twenty-four hours a day."[16] Moreover, Canadians have become highly adept at using these new technologies to challenge the "consensus" of neo-liberalism and globalization. ICTs allow the creation of alternative spheres in which citizens may be active, receive information and organize against and challenge what, until recently, had been a one-sided debate about globalization. In essence, ICTs lend themselves to agonistic politics, the challenging of vertical power structures and the creation of alternative identities.

One theoretical grounding for this form of combative politics can be found in the work of Hannah Arendt. Arendt's theory of politics involved both association and contestation. Politics, for Arendt, is not only the action of people in concert but also a site of struggle in which we act both with and against our peers.[17] Moreover, Arendt argued that politics and public spaces are plural and not tied to any particular place or set of institutions – they can occur in a variety of social spaces. The political realm, then, comes into being when people act together in concert to gain power through the sharing of words and deeds.[18] Arendt contended that: "The *polis*, properly speaking, is not the city-state in its physical location, it is the organization of the people as it arises out of acting and speaking together for this purpose, no matter where they happen to be." Consequently, claimed Arendt, "wherever you go, you will be a polis." These words, wrote Arendt, "expressed the conviction that action and speech create a space between the participants which can find its proper location almost anytime and anywhere."[19]

Arendt's conception of politics and public spaces has an open and contingent quality not found in state-centric conceptions of the political and lends itself to transnational political activity. The political and the public may occur in specific locations and institutions, but they do not have to. Political and public spaces may be anywhere but not necessarily everywhere. Indeed, in Arendt's analysis, the terms "public" and "private" are always embedded in a complex web of power relations and are always the subject of discursive negotiation and contestation.[20]

Globalization, New Technologies and New Public Spaces

Until recently the idea that new technologies might provide a critical means by which globalization could be contested received scant attention. Because of their close connection with economic globalization, the new technologies tended to be viewed deterministically, often negatively, as a monolithic or homogenizing system in support of the dominance of global market capitalism. More recently, however, the new technologies have been seen to serve as instruments either of corporate and state domination or of democratization and empowerment.[21] In other words, ICTs, particularly the Internet, represent contested forms of social and political space. The Internet not only facilitates e-commerce, it facilitates other individual and group forms of social exchanges, including political and cultural activities.[22] According to Shields, the

> Internet is a network, linking interactants across space and time, not a "thing" or set of computers communicating autonomously without human actors. It is essential to foreground the human in the Net. This resets the Internet as a phenomenon of social and political interest, not just a bright and technical toy for engineers.[23]

The very features of the Internet, especially its decentralized, anarchic form, facilitate the expression of alternative and contesting voices capable of transcending the borders of states. In short, the Internet is a contradictory feature of globalization capable, at one and the same time, of promoting homogenizing forces of sameness and uniformity, and of heterogeneity, difference and hybridity.[24] Suddenly, then, economic globalization no longer seems to be monolithic or inevitable. As globalization spreads so does a possible means of resistance. They are two sides of the same coin.

The Internet has several features that promote democratization and alternative spaces of citizen expression and activism. First, it is characterized by its interactivity. Unlike the telephone, however, which is interactive but usually only on a one-to-one basis, the Internet facilitates both one-on-one communication (e.g. e-mail) and also one-to-many (e.g. putting up a web site or sending a message to an e-mail list). In effect, the Internet is many-to-many, for "many" people can speak to "many others."[25] This also distinguishes it from mass media, such as television and newspapers, which usually emanate from one centre and are not interactive. The result is that the Internet permits its users to be producers of content, not just passive consumers, thus allowing the creation of competing narratives.

The Internet is also open and flexible. Anyone who has access to the Internet can enter and its digital format (representation of information in binary form) means that large amounts of information can be compressed, manipulated and copied very easily and quickly, thus fundamentally altering the economics of long-distance interaction and communication. Information, whether words, numbers, audio or video, can easily be copied and transmitted around the world, thereby overcoming barriers of time and space. The overall effect is to put considerable control of the means of communication in the hands of many more people.

The Internet thus poses a challenge to existing political, economic, class, race and gender hierarchies. Individuals and groups can express themselves directly and not through agents, representatives, gatekeepers or middlemen, a process known as "disintermediation."[26] Increasingly, our communication links to others become horizontal. The consequence is that Canada's existing parliamentary and bureaucratic institutions are ill-suited, it can be argued, to operate in this new environment. The Westminster model with, its domination by cabinet and the public service, depends on secrecy and control of information. How, for example, does one govern when information increasingly leaks and citizens can be equally informed as cabinet ministers and bureaucrats? How does Canada's adversarial parliamentary system accommodate and mediate the newly emerging and diverging voices made possible by the Internet? The potential impact is enormous. According to former Clerk of the Privy Council Arthur Kroeger, the big challenge for politicians and public servants is "how to reconcile contemporary demands for direct participation with traditional representative democracy."[27]

In many senses, then, the Internet is highly advantageous to citizens, activists, non-governmental organizations and new social movements that seek to challenge existing authority and prevailing discourses. In brief, the Internet facilitates the growth of new public spaces in which citizens can participate. These new public spaces, I would argue, also pose a challenge to the contribution of the leading theorist of the public sphere, Jurgen Habermas. Habermas's early work, *The Structural Transformation of the Public Sphere*, provides the best-known account of how, during the era of the Enlightenment and eighteenth-century democratic revolutions, public spheres emerged in Europe where individuals could discuss and debate issues of common concern. According to Habermas's account of the ideal of the bourgeois public sphere, the public sphere represented space distinct from the state and the economy yet from which the state could be criticized. It was a space in which arguments, not status or traditions, were to be decisive, a space where citizens deliberated and debated about the common good.[28]

Habermas's interpretation has had a powerful influence on scholarship but has been criticized for a number of reasons, foremost among them being that the "official public sphere rested on, indeed, was importantly constituted by a number of significant exclusions" – most significantly, women of various classes and ethnicities, working-class men, and virtually everyone else of non-European origins. According to Nancy Fraser, "Habermas not only idealizes the liberal public sphere but he also fails to examine other non-liberal, non-bourgeois, competing public spheres."[29] Moreover, the relations between bourgeois publics and other publics, for example, elite women publics and working-class publics, were always conflictual as these counter-publics challenged the power and influence of the dominant public sphere.

What the Internet facilitates is not so much the growth of a Habermasian global public sphere of disinterested discussion and deliberation, but the proliferation of alternative public spaces, of counter-public spheres that contest the prevailing discourse of globalization and neo-liberalism. The Internet promotes oppositional discourses complete with sophisticated systems of networking and communication. They possess a much wider variety of options than possessed by earlier nineteenth- and twentieth-century counter-publics – organizational web sites that offer a vast amount of information in the form of documents, reports, critiques, press releases, alternative magazines and newspapers, audio, video, list serves, chat groups and links to other relevant sites. For those who feel excluded from the dominant media and public sphere, the Internet offers rapid access to an alternative world of expression, networking and organizing. In effect, the Internet intensifies the post-modern challenge to authority structures that was well under way before the current wave of economic globalization broke.

Even so, critics of the Internet repeatedly claim that it is exclusionary, biased in favour of young, white, middle- or upper-class males. While this was no doubt true in Canada not long ago, recent Canadian surveys indicate that other categories of the population are becoming increasingly active. Today, Canada has one of the highest concentrations of Internet users in the world. According to a survey conducted by the Angus Reid Group, 56 per cent of Canadians or 12.5 million adults used the Internet in November 1999.[30] Moreover, the male-to-female ratio of those who access the Internet at least once a month is nearly even in Canada.[31] The Angus Reid survey of 28,374 Internet users and consumers around the world forecast that in 2000, for the first time ever, women would lead global Internet growth. In Canada, the percentage of women intending to log on this year is 60 per cent. According to the study, "women and households with children represent the fastest growing segments of the online market in the developed countries." These new groups access the Internet not so much for e-commerce as for information/research, communications and general curiosity.[32] The critical barriers to access in Canada remain the large initial cost of owning a home computer, which is continuing to decline, and monthly on-line connection costs, which in Canada are among the lowest in the world. Outside of Canada, particularly in poorer countries, the digital divide is most acute.[33]

Finally, the fact that one does not have access to a computer or cannot go online does not mean complete exclusion from the Internet world. Increasingly, what occurs online penetrates the popular media or is diffused by other means, for example, via printouts of documents, reports or other information. Overall, then, the Internet is becoming a key means by which Canadians obtain information and communicate with one another.

Canadians Contest the MAI and the WTO

Given their high connectivity, Canadians were well positioned to take advantage of the Internet to mobilize against the MAI and the WTO. Canada had both of the ingredients crucial to the formation of critical publics – access to information and a well-educated population. Evidence indicates that many Canadians were also highly active as citizens both within and beyond their borders. While Canadian use of the Internet to resist neo-liberalism and globalization first became evident with the MAI, Canadian experience of networking using the Internet has its roots in the Canada-United States Free Trade Agreement (FTA) and the North American Free Trade Agreement (NAFTA).

While the debate over the FTA in 1988 was front and centre in Canada, dominating the 1988 federal election, subsequent trade and investment negotiations were increasingly shrouded in secrecy and depicted as largely technical in nature even as they evolved in an increasingly intrusive manner into a broad range of domestic policies.[34] Those activists opposed to these negotiations were steadily marginalized while the proponents of neo-liberalism became more bold. The opposition of a number of citizens to the succeeding rounds of negotiations on freer trade have tended to be mediated through social movements and NGOs. In each successive round of negotiations these social movements and NGOs have built broader international opposition coalitions. In the process they have moved the debate over globalization from the margins into full public view.

Beginning with NAFTA, Canadian activists have made extensive use of new communications technology. While the transnational networking failed to stop NAFTA, participants learned from their experiences. As Nick Witheford notes: "The movement created a powerful pedagogical crucible for cross-sectoral and cross-border organizing. And it opened pathways for future connections, including electronic ones."[35]

Since NAFTA there has been increasing recognition of the role played by the Internet in mobilizing opposition to international trade and investment agreements. For example, when the MAI failed in the fall of 1998, the Dutch secretary to the chair and vice-chair of the MAI negotiating group pointed out that the negotiators were ill-prepared for a challenge from political activists, and concluded that the Internet was the "worst enemy of the MAI."[36]

Initially, the MAI negotiations had begun in the fall of 1995 with little attention or public fanfare. It was only when a draft of the February 1997 text was leaked and ended up on the web sites of two public advocacy groups – the Washington-based group, Public Citizen, and Tony Clarke's Canadian-based Polaris Institute – that opposition to the MAI began to spread rapidly, greatly facilitated by the Internet. A survey shortly after the conclusion of the MAI negotiations on the presence on the Internet of MAI-related web sites and a number of interviews of web activists on the advantages and disadvantages of the Internet indicate how the web was used to mobilize and organize against the MAI. It is particularly noteworthy how robust Canadian participation was in this campaign.[37]

The 400 MAI web sites reflected a wide array of non-governmental organizations, political parties, governments, international organizations, individuals and student groups. Of the 400 sites, seventy-one (17.6 per cent) were Canadian, a number superseded only by the United States, with ten times Canada's population, which was the source country for 129 sites (31.9 per cent).

Moreover, the Canadian web sites were highly influential in spreading information against the MAI around the world. Through the use of hypertext links, information may be reproduced and shared in a very cost-effective manner. This sharing of information helped redress the monopoly of complex, technical information that large corporations, governments and the media typically have. With information comes potential empowerment. Virtually all sites had links to other sites. As Table 1 indicates, ten organizations accounted for over half of all the hypertext links on the 400 MAI sites.

Of these ten sites, six were Canadian. The most frequently linked Canadian site, MAI-Not Flora, was a bootstrap operation by two Carleton University students working through Ontario Public Interest Group Carleton and the OPIRG Ottawa. We found MAI-Not Flora links around the world. In turn, those Canadians who logged onto the MAI-Not web site received encouragement from other international activists via e-mail in support of their anti-MAI campaign. From New Zealand came this response:

New Zealanders are talking about the tremendous fight Canadians are putting up against the MAI every day ... Each day I switch on my email and there you are, carrying the flag of freedom and democracy,

TABLE 1 Top 10 Organizations Appearing as Links of Web Sites

Name of Organization	Frequency	Rank
OECD	95	1
MAI-Not (Flora) – OPIRG – Carleton U.	87	2
National Centre for Sustainability (Victoria, BC)	25	3
Appleton (law office, Toronto)	23	4
YUCC (personal site of York U. law student)	22	5
Public Citizen (Washington, DC)	21	6
Preamble Centre (Washington, DC)	21	6
Friends of the Earth – U.S. (Washington, DC)	19	7
Multinational Monitor (U.S. – linked to Public Citizen)	17	8
Council of Canadians	16	9
Canadian Centre for Policy Alternatives (Ottawa)	12	10
Stop MAI – Australia	12	10

Source: Peter J. Smith and Elizabeth Smythe, "Globalization, Citizenship and Technology: The MAI meets the Internet," *Canadian Foreign Policy* 7, 2 (1999): 83–107.

and we're encouraged all over again to keep going. Here's smiling at you Canada.[38]

Canadian web sites penetrated not only the Canadian debate but also international debate over the MAI. In the case of Austria, for example, even negotiators admit that media coverage and active, growing opposition to the MAI in the spring of 1998 were a result of the 1998 Internet campaign, including, prominently, information gathered from Tony Clarke's web site.[39]

Follow-up interviews revealed that the Internet was used in a variety of ways – to co-ordinate the global campaign, to provide draft faxes and open letters that could be used to lobby decision-makers or sent to members of Parliament, and to offer press releases that local groups could use in an effort to gain more media coverage and announce local meetings on the MAI. In sum, the Internet must be seen as a means to organize and to penetrate and facilitate broader public debate. Importantly, virtually all groups interviewed, including Canadian ones, continued to use traditional lobbying methods with their national legislators and officials, including phone calls and face-to-face meetings, which they regarded as more personal and more effective.

What this indicates is that the anti-MAI campaign was highly complex. It was not a choice between the global or the local, the inside or the outside, but a campaign that occurred at all levels, global, national and local. The targets included state actors, parliamentarians and members of the executive and the broader Canadian public. While it would be too much to claim that the Internet was primarily responsible for the defeat of the MAI – there were very significant differences among member states of the OECD – the Internet contributed to two remarkable accomplishments. First, those counter-publics marginalized by the dominant public sphere, including the mass media, emerged from the shadows to frame the anti-MAI debate in Canada and elsewhere. Second, a potentially far-reaching international treaty emerged from the realm of technical, bureaucratic discussions into the full glare of publicity. From this it was clear that the environment of global trade and investment negotiations had radically altered. Globalization was now contestable and citizens did not have to be passive bystanders.

In a sense, the furor over the MAI was just an episode in the increasingly contentious politics over globalization. Within a Canadian context the federal government, Parliament and Canadian non-governmental organizations and social movements drew on their MAI experiences to try to position themselves as the authentic and legitimate spokespersons for Canadians in anticipation of the Millennium Round of trade negotiations to be launched at the World Trade Organization meetings in Seattle in December 1999. The critical difference this time was that *all* participants, including government and international organizations, began to use a mixture of hearings, reports and the Internet to tell their stories directly to, and consult with, Canadians.

First, in September 1998 the Minister for International Trade, Sergio Marchi, in an unusual move, invited the House of Commons Standing Committee on Foreign Affairs and International Trade to undertake public consultations on issues relating to the WTO, a process that took place in March and April 1999. In September 1998 the Council of Canadians, representing the forty Canadian NGOs that had organized to defeat the MAI, began a cross country tour to hear the concerns of Canadians about globalization. In February 1999, the Department of Foreign Affairs and International Trade (DFAIT) established its own web site, with the stated intent of hearing directly from Canadians on trade issues and the unstated intent of providing information that would present its own point of view. Later, on 20 May 1999, DFAIT held consultations with business representatives and NGOs on Canada's trade policy agenda. This was followed by a country-wide series of Round Table Sessions on Investment Policy that took place from 21 June 1999 to 29 July 1999.

The most extensive consultations were those of the Standing Committee which held thirty public sessions across Canada and heard from over 400 witnesses, many of whom submitted substantial written briefs. Those testifying reflected a wide diversity of business organizations (88), NGOs (85), academics (61), government officials (26) and other concerned citizens (64). The Committee's ensuing report and accompanying testimony reveal the later schism over trade policy so evident in Seattle.[40] Given its control by the governing Liberal Party, the Committee did not challenge the government's trade liberalization agenda. The Committee's summary of the common themes of the testimony, however, echoes the views of most NGOs concerning trade negotiations – the need for greater public participation and the need to recognize other values in support of social justice, environmental sustainability, human rights, the public interest, fairness, openness, transparency and accountability.

Both during the hearings and after, NGOs repeatedly voiced scepticism that parliamentary and other representative institutions, such as an international association of parliamentarians, might provide the vehicle for oversight of trade negotiations. The NGOs, as was to be expected, preferred direct input from civil society organizations.[41] Such was the scepticism about Parliament being capable of representing the concerns of civil society that on the very day the Committee released its report, the Council of Canadians released its own inquiry report, "Confronting Globalization and Reclaiming Democracy."[42] The report stressed five principles that should govern all international trade and investment agreements: (1) upholding the rights of citizens; (2) protecting the common good; (3) promoting the development of sustainable communities; (4) guaranteeing the sovereignty of democratically elected governments over corporations; and (5) ensuring effective citizen participation in the development of trade and investment policies.

Canadian NGOs did not limit their activities to Canada. In the summer of 1999, over forty Canadian NGOs signed the on-line Civil Society Declaration, "No New Round, instead Turnaround," joining more than 1,100 organizations from eighty-seven countries calling for a halt to the proposed new talks at the WTO. The global mobilization campaign reveals how complex the efforts to stop the WTO negotiations had become. NGOs and many individual Canadians were active at the local, national and global levels, an effort co-ordinated via the Internet. The impact of the Internet on the global movement against the WTO has been acknowledged by Susan George:

> The civic movement's success in Seattle is a mystery only to those who had no part in it. Throughout 1999, thanks primarily to the Internet, tens of thousands of people opposed to the World Trade Organization ... united in a great national and international effort of organization. Anyone could have a front seat, anyone could take part in the advance on Seattle. All you needed was a computer and a rough knowledge of English.[43]

The movement was all the more potent because old social movements such as labour and new social movements such as the environmental movement had joined in common cause.

Canadians again had prominent visibility on the web. An analysis in early winter 2000 revealed 4,089 web sites with material specific to the Seattle round of the WTO, a tenfold increase over the MAI. Analysis of 513 indicated that organization and commercial sites were predominant.[44] Some of these were Canadian but most were American. Canadian web sites made up the next largest category, comprising 6.23 per cent of the total. This time, however, the only Canadian site in the top twenty organizations appearing as links of other web sites was not an NGO but the Department of Foreign Affairs and International Trade (see Table 2).

The top Canadian sites in terms of links are listed in Table 3. Most of these are well-known organizations. Second to DFAIT was the International Institute for Sustainable Development, which, given the prominence of environmental and developmental issues at the WTO, is not a surprise.

One difference from the MAI is the appearance of more union sites, such as the Canadian Union of Public Employees and the Canadian Labour Congress, which had an active presence on the web. Another difference is the prominence of A-Infos, which, in turn, was linked to tao.ca, a regional federation of local autonomous collectives and individuals involved in communications and media, radical activism and social work. TAO organizes networks in order to defend and create public space. In some ways TAO, along with Cross-Canada WTO Caravan and Citizens on the Web, represents the new breed of web sites, a hybrid of communications and activism. Particularly noteworthy on TAO is DAMN, Direct Action Media Network, which both organizes and provides media coverage, including on-line video, of protests, marches, strikes and other direct actions. In a sense, however, trying to classify Canadian participation on the web by means of links provides an incomplete picture of Canadian participation. Given the anarchic, horizontal structure of the Internet, Canadians, like everyone else hooked up to the web, can and do go everywhere they want to obtain information, tell their stories and participate in activity and debate on globalization.

The appearance of TAO, DAMN and several other on-line activist communication networks, many complete with journalists, magazines and audio and video, demonstrates the potential of on-line organizations to make an end run around the mass media to tell their story directly. Indeed, the Internet is the medium of choice for those opposed to economic globalization. Figures for Canada per se are not available, but of the 513 web sites we coded, 51 per cent expressed opposition to the WTO, 14 per cent supported it, while most of the remainder were neutral (33 per cent) or provided a means for public discussion and dialogue (2.53 per cent).

While those opposed to globalization have taken most readily to the web, Canadian governments also had a prominent presence on the web. Departments such as DFAIT are also finding it advantageous to tell their story directly. DFAIT echoed the opposition to globalization in trying to reach Canadians directly through the web, soliciting their comments, stating "it's important to listen to you, to draw on your wisdom and take your concerns to heart, before solidifying our negotiating position."[45] How seriously DFAIT listened is questionable. Surveys done on behalf of the G-8 and the OECD indicate that most governments still see the web as a means of sending messages rather than receiving them.[46]

Web sites and e-mail are only part of the politics of contestation and clearly have not replaced face-to-face meetings and traditional methods of protest. The Internet, though, has bolstered and even altered contentious processes of behaviour and provided new spaces for political activity. What the data do not indicate, however, is who actually accessed the web sites and what the impact was in terms of individual citizens. We do know that groups relied on sites to educate, organize and mobilize people and to co-ordinate opposition on the ground in Seattle.

Did the anti-WTO forces make a difference? Accounts vary. Those

TABLE 2 Top Twenty Organizations Appearing as Links of Web Sites

Name of Organization	Frequency	Rank
World Trade Organization	2129	1
Seattle Post-Intelligence	732	2
OECD	322	3
OneWorld Online	348	4
Washington Council on International Trade (host organization to wtoseattle.org)	127	5
Financial Times	125	6
Seattle Times	123	7
Institute de recherche pour le développement (IRD)	122	8
Third World Network	116	9
Institute for Global Communications	111	10
Le Monde diplomatique	107	11
Trade and Development Centre (joint initiative of WTO and World Bank)	99	12
United States Mission to the European Union	98	13
Seattlewto.org (sponsored site of NGO coalition against WTO)	92	14
International Centre for Trade and Sustainable Development	85	15
Corporate European Observatory	83	16
Corporate Watch	74	17
Southbound (Penang)	73	18
Institute for Agriculture and Trade Policy	71	19
DFAIT-MAECI (government of Canada)	70	20

opposed see the anti-globalization campaign as instrumental in turning the WTO talks in Seattle into a fiasco.[47] Others point to differences among member states as the reason the talks collapsed.[48] Moreover, while anti-WTO forces may have challenged trade liberalization, they have not defeated it. Talks on the General Agreement on Trade in Services (GATS) are going ahead, and in another venue the Canadian government is pursuing an agreement on the Free Trade Area of the Americas (FTAA). Indisputable, however, was the success of those opposed to the WTO in turning it from an obscure agency into one the world knows and talks about. An Angus Reid poll indicates that 79 per cent of Canadians were aware of the protests in Seattle against the WTO (Table 4). Clearly, trade liberalization policy and agencies have moved from the margins and become very public, no small victory to those opposed to economic globalization.

TABLE 3 Top Canadian Organizations Appearing as Links of Web Sites

Name of Organization	Frequency	Rank
DFAIT-MAECI	70	1
International Institute for Sustainable Development	55	2
Government of Quebec	40	3
TAO — The Anarchy Organization	23	4
Parliament of Canada	20	5
Canadian Union of Public Employees	19	6
Canadian Centre for Policy Alternatives	19	7
Flora (Ottawa Community Web)	17	8
Agriculture Canada	15	9
Anarchist News Service	15	9
Cross-Canada WTO Caravan (sponsored by coalition of NGOs)	14	10
Sierra Club of Canada	14	10
Canadian Labour Congress	8	11
Government of Ontario	7	12
International Centre for Human Rights and Democratic Development	6	13
Citizens on the Web	5	14
Government of British Columbia	4	15
Canadian Chamber of Commerce	3	16
Council of Canadians	2	17

Conclusion

Politics and citizenship still matter. The question dividing theorists of citizenship and globalization is: Which city are we citizens of? David Held, for example, argues that globalization is undermining the capacity for meaningful political participation at the national level as nation-states decline in importance and become "decision-takers," not "decision-makers."[49] Held consequently promotes the idea of a transnational democratic legal order circumscribed and legitimized by democratic public law. Will Kymlicka, however, rejects the view that globalization has deprived politics of its meaningfulness. He contends that nation-states still possess considerable autonomy that citizens – or their representatives – exercise and prize. Furthermore, argues Kymlicka, territory as a basis of politics and determination of political identity is not being undermined, and he rejects the idea that collective participation and deliberation are possible in transnational institutions and organizations.[50]

TABLE 4 Impact of World Trade Organization
"Did you see, read or hear anything about public protests being held at a WTO meeting in Seattle, Washington in December?"

Country	Percentage Yes
United States	82
France	81
Canada	79
New Zealand	74
Hong Kong	72
Australia	67
United Kingdom	64
Sweden	57
Thailand	57
Germany	57
Malaysia	52
Spain	50
Netherlands	50
Singapore	48
Mexico	44
Japan	41
Brazil	28

Source: Press Release, "The Face of the Web Wave One, 2000," Angus Reid Group Inc., 19 April 2000.

Kymlicka is right in defending the continuing relevance of the nation-state, yet he too easily dismisses people's desire and ability to participate politically at a global level. Decisions of the World Trade Organization now intersect with and have considerable impact on areas of domestic policy. Concerned citizens are increasingly acting at both the national and global levels to counteract the power of such international institutions; however, contrary to both Held and Kymlicka, citizens feel increasingly alienated from any representative assembly – provincial, national, global, territorial or non-territorial.[51] Citizens increasingly possess the technological capacity to overcome barriers of time and space and want to participate directly whether anyone likes it or not. So far there is no answer to the problem posed by political disintermediation and declining respect for representative institutions of any kind. In an era of critical citizenship, citizens realize that political power is held not so much by parliaments as by cabinets and bureaucracies, and they will go directly to those making the real political decisions – in global terms, for example, the WTO, the IMF and the World Bank. In effect, the public realm, which Hannah Arendt feared had "disappeared into the ... more restricted, impersonal sphere of administration," is gradually being recovered.[52]

Horizontal networks facilitated by new technologies and not limited to territory are providing an alternative to the vertical interaction citizens have traditionally had with governments. Acknowledgement of this change comes from an unlikely source. Pierre Pettigrew, Minister of International Trade, in a speech to the Global Forum 2000 in Washington, claimed:

> Today ... individuals no longer see themselves only as citizens of a given territory, of a given country. What characterizes individuals more and more is their sense of belonging towards all kinds of other networks that are not necessarily limited to their own territory – horizontal networks such as Greenpeace, Amnesty International, Médecins sans frontières. More and more people in today's world belong to such groups. As a result, more and more individuals' identities are becoming extremely complex.[53]

In a very important sense, then, neither Held nor Kymlicka has it right. To reiterate, Hannah Arendt was perhaps closer to the mark. "The *polis*, properly speaking," she wrote, "is not the city-state in its physical location; it is the organization of the people as it arises out of acting and speaking together ... no matter where they happen to be."[54] In today's world the *polis* can be almost anywhere – wherever decisions are made that affect our lives – and consequently, so can the activities of citizenship.

Thanks in part to ICTs, citizens can more readily act as citizens both nationally and globally. The spaces between states are no longer necessarily spaces of anarchy and chaos; increasingly, they have become spaces of discourse, action, politics. But this is not necessarily at the expense of the nation-state. Contrary to those who argue that the capacities of the nation-state are significantly reduced, a growing number of sceptics argue that nation-states still have significant room to manoeuver in domestic policies. According to Hoberg et al, "despite deeper economic integration ... Canada does retain far more capacity for distinctive policy choice than is widely believed."[55] Moreover, data indicate that Canadians still believe in government and rank social policy, not fiscal policy, as their top priority. Polling data, for example, show that they want their governments to be citizen-centred and feel that big business and the media have too much influence on govern-ment policy.[56]

Thus, despite the rhetoric of neo-liberalism, Canadians have not accepted the notion that they be defined as customers and not citizens with voices. The Canadian view of what a citizen means is changing and becoming more complex as Canadians take advantage of new technol-ogies to voice their concerns and tell their own stories, locally, nation-ally, globally. Canadian citizenship is not dying but its face is changing.

The capacity to participate will increase as ICTs improve and become more prevalent, thereby strengthening the ability of citizens to form networks and relate horizontally to government. Yet ICTs have their limitations. First, the quality of information is frequently uneven. Second, the immense quantity of on-line information can exceed our capacity to process and analyze it.[57] Third, the English language pre-dominates and only lately has the World Wide Web lived up to its name and become more multicultural. Fourth, a digital divide exists, so that significant portions of the population are left out of the digital world. Thus the Internet may serve to strengthen the voices only of Canadians or members of other nation-states with higher incomes. Not all voices may be heard.

Finally, while diversity is needed for a robust political sphere,[58] new technologies make it possible to create a customized environment of vir-tual communities and information where citizens do not have to listen to or confront one another. Those who operate on-line can create narrower and smaller worlds for themselves; however, unless citizens engage one another, unless we are exposed to a wide range of views – including speech we might not initially want to hear – we cannot make informed decisions about social and political issues. ICTs have the potential to intensify social and political fragmentation so that the capacity to find common ground disappears. This all points to the continuing need for trusted intermediaries, institutions and agencies that can bring people with differing points of view together, mediate differences, construct consensus and make decisions – in short, govern. Which ones they will be is the central question. This, not the disappearance of public spaces, is perhaps one of the biggest challenges we face in a global era. Agency is possible, and economic globalization can and is being resist-ed. The question is: What alternative values will shape its future path?

This article was originally published in the *Journal of Canadian Studies*, Vol. 16, No. 1, Spring 2001. I am grateful to the journal for granting permission to republish the article. The author wishes to acknowledge the research assistance of Leonard Stoleriu-Falchidi and the financial support of the Mission Critical Research and Academic Research Funds of Athabasca University.

Notes

1. See Kenichi Ohmae, *The Borderless World: Power and Strategy in the Inter-linked Economy* (New York: Harper Collins, 1990), and Susan Strange, *Retreat of the State* (Cambridge: Cambridge University Press, 1990).
2. Stephen D. Krasner, "Contested Sovereignty: The Myth of Westphalia" (paper prepared for presentation at the American Political Science Association, New York, NY September 1994).
3. R.B.J. Walker, "State Sovereignty and the Articulation of Political Space/Time," *Millennium: Journal of International Studies*, 20:3 (1991): 445.
4. See David Miller, "Bounded Citizenship," in *Cosmopolitan Citizenship*, ed. Kimberly Hutchings (London: Macmillan Press Ltd., 1999), 60–80 and Will Kymlicka, "Citizenship in an era of globalization: commentary on Held," in *Democracy's Edges*, eds. Ian Shapiro and Casiano Hacker Cordón (Cambridge, UK: Cambridge University Press, 1999), 112–127.
5. T.H. Marshall, "Citizenship and Social Class," in *Class, Citizenship and Social Development* (New York: Doubleday, 1964).
6. Thomas J. Biersteker and Cynthia Weber, "The Social Construction of State Sovereignty," in *State Sovereignty as Social Construct*, eds. Thomas J. Biersteker and Cynthia Weber (Cambridge: Cambridge University Press, 1996), 1–22.
7. Jane Jenson, "Fated to Live in Interesting Times: Canada's Changing Citizenship Regimes", *Canadian Journal of Political Science*, 30:4 (1997), 627–644.
8. Louis Balthazar, "The Faces of Quebec Nationalism," in *A Passion for Identity*, 3rd edition, eds. David Taras and Beverly Rasporich (Toronto: ITP Nelson, 1997), 75.
9. Joyce Green, *Exploring Identity and Citizenship: Aboriginal Women, Bill C-31 and the Sawridge Case* (Ph.D. Thesis, University of Alberta, 1997), 229.
10. Susan D. Phillips, "Social Movements in Canadian Politics," in *Canadian Politics*, 3rd edition, eds. James Bickerton and Alain-G. Gagnon (Peterborough: Broadview Press, 1999), 383.
11. Louis D. Hunt, "Civil Society and the Idea of a Commercial Republic," in *The Revival of Civil Society: Global and Comparative Perspectives*, ed. Michael G. Schecter (London: Macmillan Press Ltd., 1999), 11.

12. Robert Cox, "Civil society at the turn of the millennium: prospects for an alternative world order," *Review of International Studies*, 25 (1999): 6.
13. Neil Nevitte, *The Decline of Deference* (Peterborough: Broadview Press, 1996), 51.
14. Susan Phillips, "Social Movements in Canadian Politics," 383.
15. Will Kymlicka and Wayne Norman, "Return of the Citizen: A Survey of Recent Work on Citizenship Theory," in *Theorizing Citizenship*, ed. Ronald Beiner (Albany: State University of New York, 1995), 283–323.
16. David J. Rothkopf, "Cyberpolitik: The Changing Nature of Power in the Information Age," *Journal of International Affairs* (Spring 1998): 325.
17. Bonnie Honig, ed., *Feminist Interpretations of Hannah Arendt* (University Park, Penn: Pennsylvania State University Press, 1995), 189.
18. Hannah Arendt, *The Human Condition* (Chicago: University of Chicago Press, 1958), 198.
19. Arendt, *The Human Condition*, 198.
20. Catriona Sandilands, "Is the Personal Always Political? Environmentalism in Arendt's Age of 'the Social,'" in *Organizing Dissent*, ed. William K. Carroll (Toronto: Garamond Press, 1997), 80.
21. Douglas Kellner, "Theorizing Globalization Critically" (paper presented to the International Studies Association Annual Conference, Los Angeles, March 14–18, 2000), 9.
22. Gillian Youngs, "Boundary Breaking and Cyberspace" (paper presented to the International Studies Association Annual Conference, Washington, February 1999), 16–20.
23. Rob Shields, "Introduction," in *Cultures of Internet: Virtual Spaces, Real Histories, Living Bodies*, ed. R. Shields (London: Sage, 1996), 8.
24. Douglas Kellner, "Theorizing Globalization," 6.
25. Andrew L. Shapiro, *The Control Revolution* (New York: Public Affairs, 1999).
26. Ibid., 55.
27. Arthur Kroeger, "Notes for a Speech to the Canadian Newspapers Association," 23 November 1999, Canadian Policy Research Network, www.cprn.org/, 5.
28. Craig Calhoun, "Introduction: Habermas and the Public Sphere," in *Habermas and the Public Sphere*, ed. Craig Calhoun (Cambridge: MIT Press, 1992), 2.
29. Nancy Fraser, "Rethinking the Public Sphere: A Contribution to the Critique of Actually Existing Democracies," in *Habermas and the Public Sphere*, 112–113.
30. "Canadian Internet Users concerned about Release of Personal Information," Ipsos-Reid, 15 December 1999.

31. www.nua.ie/surveys (January 25, 2000).

32. Angus Reid, "Second Digital Gold Rush to be Led by Women" (March 30, 2000), www.angusreid.com/media.

33. Pippa Norris, "The Worldwide Digital Divide," (Paper for the Annual Meeting of the Political Studies Association of the UK, London, April 10–13, 2000), www.pippanorris.com

34. David J. Blair, "North American ENGOs and Resistance to Neoliberal Globalisation: From NAFTA to the MAI," (Paper presented to the International Studies Association Annual Conference, Los Angeles, March 14–18, 2000).

35. Nick Witheford (forthcoming), *The Contest for General Intellect* (Chicago: University of Chicago Press) quoted in Kellner, Douglas, "Theorizing Globalization Critically" (paper presented to the International Studies Association Annual Conference, Los Angeles, March 14–18, 2000).

36. As quoted in David J. Blair, "North American ENGOs and Resistance to Neoliberal Globalisation: From NAFTA to the MAI" (paper presented to the International Studies Association Annual Conference, Los Angeles, March 2000), 11.

37. Peter J. Smith and Elizabeth Smythe, "Globalization, Citizenship and Technology: The MAI Meets the Internet," *Canadian Foreign Policy*, 7:2 (1999): 83–107.

38. Jeremy Nelson, "Toppling the MAI: Canadian Activists Lead World in Fight for Democracy," *Canadian Dimension* (Apr.-May: 24–26, 1998): 24, as quoted in Jeffrey M. Ayres, "From the Streets to the Internet: The Cyber-Diffusion of Contention," *Annals of the American Political and Social Sciences*, 566 (November 1999): 132–143, 138.

39. Peter J. Smith and Elizabeth Smythe, "Globalization, Citizenship and Technology."

40. Report of the Standing Committee on Foreign Affairs and International Trade, *Canada and the Future of the World Trade Organization* (Ottawa: June 1999), www.parl.gc.ca

41. Robert White, Testimony before the Standing Committee on Foreign Affairs and International Trade (April 27, 1999), www.parl.gc.ca. Michelle Swenarchuk Testimony before the Standing Committee on Foreign Affairs and International Trade (April 28, 1999), www.parl.gc.ca

42. Council of Canadians, *The MAI Inquiry: Confronting Globalization and Reclaiming Democracy* (Ottawa: June 10, 1999), www.canadians.org /campaigns

43. Susan George, "Fixing or Nixing the WTO" (January 7, 2000), www.monde-diplomatue.fr/

44. All sites of four web pages or more were examined and classified. A sample only was taken of sites three pages or less. Forty search engines were used. The search was conducted in English, French, German and Spanish. The search process began in January 2000. I am confident that I captured most sites as sites, often maintain their web pages long after an event has passed.

45. www.dfait-maeci.gc.ca

46. Kroeger, "Notes for a Speech."

47. George, "Fixing or Nixing the WTO."

48. *Edmonton Journal*, Business 2, Tuesday (May 9, 2000).

49. David Held, "The Transformation of Political Community: Rethinking Democracy in the Context of Globalization," in *Democracy's Edges*, eds. Ian Shapiro and Casiano Hacker-Cordón (Cambridge: Cambridge University Press, 2000), 84–112.

50. Kymlicka, "Citizenship in an era of globalization."

51. Ronald Inglehart, "Postmodernism Erodes Respect for Authority, but Increases Support for Democracy," in *Critical Citizens*, ed. Pippa Norris (Oxford: Oxford University Press, 1999), 236–257.

52. Arendt, *The Human Condition*, 60.

53. Hon. Pierre S. Pettigrew, Minister of Trade, "On Seattle: A Collision Between Two Worlds." Speech to the Global Forum 2000, Washington, (May 15, 2000), www.dfait.maeci.gc.ca.

54. Arendt, *The Human Condition*, 198.

55. George Hoberg, Keith Banting and Richard Simeon, "North American Integration and the Scope for Domestic Choice" (paper prepared for the Annual Meeting of the Canadian Political Science Association, Sherbrooke, June 6–8, 1999), 3. See also Maureen Appel Molot, "National Governments and Social Justice: The View from North America" (paper presented at the International Studies Association Annual Conference, Los Angeles, March 14–19, 2000). Simon Reich and Luz Villasana, "Globalization, Sovereignty and Public Policy: Towards a Contingent Explanation of Governance Capabilities" (paper presented at the International Studies Association, Los Angeles, March 14–19, 2000). Geoffrey Garrett, "Global Markets and National Policies: Collision Course or Virtuous Circle," *International Organization* 52, 4 (Autumn 1998): 787–824.

56. Ekos Research Associates, "Citizenship Engagement and Globalization: Hearing the Public Voice" (presentation to IPAC National Conference, September 1, 1999), and "Rethinking Government" (December 22, 1999), www.ekos.com/press/. Frank Graves, "Rethinking Government As If People Mattered: From 'Reaganomics' to 'Humanonomics'," in *How*

Ottawa Spends, ed. Leslie A. Pal (Toronto: Oxford University Press, 1999), 37–75.

57. Thomas Homer-Dixon, *The Ingenuity Gap* (New York: Random House, 2000).

58. Arendt, *The Human Condition*.